DATE DUE

Demco, Inc. 38-293

International Crime and Punishment

International Crime and Punishment

A Guide to the Issues

James Larry Taulbee

Contemporary Military, Strategic, and Security Issues

PRAEGER SECURITY INTERNATIONAL
An Imprint of ABC-CLIO, LLC

A B C CLIO

Santa Barbara, California • Denver, Colorado • Oxford, England

Library of Congress Cataloging-in-Publication Data

Taulbee, James Larry, 1942–

    International crime and punishment : a guide to the issues / James Larry Taulbee.
      p. cm. — (Contemporary military, strategic, and security issues)
    Includes bibliographical references and index.
    ISBN 978-0-313-35588-2 (hardcover : alk. paper) — ISBN 978-0-313-35589-9
(ebook)
    1. International offenses.   2. Transnational crime.   I. Title.
    K5301.T377   2009
    345'.0235—dc22   2009016439

13   12   11   10   9   1   2   3   4   5

This book is also available on the World Wide Web as an eBook.
Visit www.abc-clio.com for details.

ABC-CLIO, LLC
130 Cremona Drive, P.O. Box 1911
Santa Barbara, California 93116-1911

This book is printed on acid-free paper ∞

Manufactured in the United States of America

To

my mother,

Nora Edna Simpson Taulbee,

and

in loving memory of my father,

Judson Taulbee

Contents

Abbreviations

AFRC	Armed Forces Revolutionary Council—Sierra Leone
ASIL	American Society of International Law
BMC	British Military Court
CCL	Allied Control Council Law
CTC	Counter Terrorism Committee of the UN Security Council
DRC	Democratic Republic of the Congo
EC	European Community (predecessor to the EU)
ECHR	European Court of Human Rights
ECOWAS	Economic Community of West Africa
EEZ	Exclusive Economic Zone
EU	European Union
GAOR	United Nations General Assembly Official Records
HRC	United Nations Human Rights Committee
ICC	International Criminal Court
ICCPR	International Covenant on Civil and Political Rights
ICG	International Crisis Group
ICJ	International Court of Justice
ICL	International Criminal Law
ICRC	International Committee of the Red Cross
ICTR	International Criminal Tribunal for Rwanda
ICTY	International Criminal Tribunal for the Former Yugoslavia
IGO	Intergovernmental international organization
IHL	International Humanitarian Law
ILC	International Law Commission
ILM	International Legal Materials
IMB	International Maritime Bureau
IMT	International Military Tribunal (Nuremberg)
IMTFE	International Military Tribunal for the Far East (Tokyo)
JNA	Yugoslav National Army
KFOR	NATO forces in Kosovo

LNTS	League of Nations Treaty Series
NATO	North Atlantic Treaty Organization
NGO	Nongovernmental international organization
NPFL	National Patriotic Front of Liberia
NSDAP	Leadership of the Nazi Party in Germany prior to and during World War II
OAS	Organization of American States
OTP	Office of the Prosecutor (ICTY, ICTY)
PA-I	Geneva Protocol Additional I
PA-II	Geneva Protocol Additional II
PCIJ	Permanent Court of International Justice
RPA	Rwandan Patriotic Army
RPF	Rwandan Patriotic Front
RUF	Revolutionary United Front—Sierra Leone
SCOR	UN Security Council Official Records
SCSL	Special Court for Sierra Leone
SOFA	Status of Force Agreement
STC	Special Tribunal for Cambodia
SUA	Suppression of Unlawful Acts treaty
UK	United Kingdom
UN	United Nations
UNAMID	African Union/United Nations Hybrid operation in Darfur
UNAMIR	United Nations Assistance Mission in Rwanda
UNPROFOR	United Nations Protection Force (Croatia)
UNTS	United Nations Treaty Series
US	United States
VRN	Yugoslav (Serbian) National Army

CHAPTER 1

Setting the Stage: Defining an International Crime

On the night of October 16, 1998, London police arrested General Augusto Pinochet Ugarte, former president of Chile. The police acted on a warrant requesting extradition issued by a Spanish judge that alleged the former dictator had committed numerous human rights crimes in Chile during his 17-year rule (1973–1990).[1] Although British *political* officials eventually permitted Pinochet to return to Chile on medical grounds in March 2000, his arrest and detention in London marked a significant turning point in contemporary legal history. While in the past exiled former heads of states had been extradited back to their own countries upon request, the Spanish warrant asserted that Spain had a valid claim to judge General Pinochet for alleged crimes against Spanish citizens in *his own* country, Chile.

The case generated shock waves throughout the world's political and legal communities. Few doubted that many of the allegations against General Pinochet rested upon valid evidence. After he led the military coup in 1973 to unseat the government of Salvadore Allende, the new leadership subsequently carried out a systematic campaign to silence or eliminate the opposition or anyone thought to support the opposition.[2] The shock to the international community came from the deviation from the time-honored principle that other sovereign states, or, rather, the governments of other sovereign states, could not pass judgment upon the actions of leaders taken *within* the borders of their own sovereign states.[3]

The Pinochet case, based upon an evolving human rights regime post–World War II, represents a defining moment in terms of the potential reach of international law in the future. Traditional international law rests upon the twin principles of sovereignty and equality. Simply stated, for purposes of international law, sovereignty formed a "hard shell" with respect to the actions of state officials. One can see this principle formally incorporated into the United Nations Charter in Article 2.7: "Nothing contained in the present Charter shall authorize the United Nations to intervene in matters which are essentially within the domestic jurisdiction of any state."[4] Traditional international law does not specify forms of government or principles that govern the relationship between a government and its citizens. To this point in time, if the government of one sovereign state felt that its nationals (citizens) had suffered an injustice in another, it would lodge a diplomatic "claim" for *denial of justice*. Such a claim would not name any one official as at fault. Under traditional international law, the liability would be that of "the state" as an abstract entity. From the standpoint of traditional *international* law, no individual would bear any liability. Note the emphasis here on international law. From the standpoint of *national* (municipal) law, individuals might bear some liability and suffer consequences from a failure to perform their duties as determined by national officials, but traditional international law rested upon the idea of *collective,* not individual, responsibility for performing duties. The Spanish warrant, citing international law, named General Pinochet as a specific individual responsible for the crimes charged and asked Great Britain to return him to Spain to stand trial as an individual for conduct that occurred solely within Chile.

One needs to pause to consider the monumental implications of the Pinochet case. It suggests that the "hard shell" protection thought to be provided by the doctrine of sovereignty now no longer applied. The idea that the rights conveyed by sovereignty translated into a duty of absolute nonintervention by one sovereign state into the domestic affairs of another had justified international inaction with respect to many egregious cases of government misconduct over the years, from that of the Khmer Rouge in Cambodia (1975–1979), to that of Idi Amin in Uganda (1971–1979), to that of government-sponsored death squads that operated in a number of Central and Latin American countries during the 1970s and 1980s. While the United Nations had set up the first international courts since Nuremberg to deal with the atrocities committed in areas of the former Yugoslavia (ICTY), in Rwanda (ICTR), and in Sierra Leone (Special Court for Sierra Leone, SCSL), the Pinochet case involved the actions of a leader during ostensible peace and the willingness of a national court to make a judgment. It thus raised some interesting questions concerning the scope of authority that national courts possessed in terms of enforcing international obligations. From the standpoint of human rights activists, the arrest of Pinochet ended what many called "the culture of impunity" that had existed for high government officials with respect to such crimes.[5] The action of the Spanish magistrate rested upon the idea of universal jurisdiction based upon the idea that some crimes are so monstrous that every nation has a duty to prosecute if the opportunity arises.

In this respect, consider the following events. During his visit to France in October 2007, a group of French activists attempted to have the former U.S. Secretary of Defense, Donald Rumsfeld, arrested for his alleged complicity in acts that violated the United Nations *Convention against Torture and Other Cruel, Inhuman or Degrading Treatment or Punishment.*[6] Rumsfeld hurriedly left France before the court hearing. Earlier, in December 2004, Canadian courts had refused to act upon a number of attempts by a Canadian peace group, Lawyers Against the War, to have President George W. Bush either arrested or declared persona non grata during his official visit because of his decision to invade Iraq.[7] In response to the NATO decision to bomb Serbia during the Kosovo crisis, the European Committee for the Defence of the Federal Republic of Yugoslavia sought to have President Bill Clinton, U.S. Secretary of State Madeleine Albright, U.S. Secretary of Defense William Cohen, NATO Commander General Wesley Clark, and NATO Secretary-General Javier Solana brought before the International Criminal Tribunal for the former Yugoslavia (ICTY) on charges of genocide, crimes against humanity, and war crimes.[8]

The ICTY did indict and bring to trial the former president of Serbia, Slobodan Milošević on charges of crimes against humanity in Kosovo, gross violations of the laws of war in Croatia, and the promotion of genocide in Bosnia.[9] In March 2003, after five years of negotiation with the Cambodian government, the Special Tribunal for Cambodia was constituted under the auspices of the United Nations. Though beset by political problems, the court issued its first indictments against members of the Khmer Rouge in July 2007.[10] The newly formed International Criminal Court (ICC) has initiated cases against two highly placed government officials from the Democratic Republic of the Congo, as well as the Minister of State for the Interior of the Sudan.[11] The ICTR has tried and convicted 16 officials on charges that include participation in crimes again humanity and genocide.[12] Several countries, mirroring Spain and Belgium, have enacted statutes that permit the use of universal jurisdiction to arrest and try anyone found within their territory who is sought for such crimes.[13]

In response to the Pinochet detention, former U.S. Secretary of State Henry Kissinger wrote a scathing indictment of the principles the Spanish magistrate used to request the arrest and extradition of General Pinochet.[14] Kissinger feared that the Pinochet precedent would be open to political abuse and would severely hamper diplomacy and policy making because officials now could face the possibility that judicial authorities in other states who disagreed with particular policies might feel compelled to intervene by issuing arrest warrants. He argued that on the one hand that "those who commit war crimes or systematically violate human rights should be held accountable."[15] On the other he stated that no one should "allow legal principles to be used as weapons to settle political scores."[16] As an example of what possibly could result, he argued: "The Pinochet precedent, if literally applied, would permit the two sides in the Arab-Israeli conflict, or those in any other passionate international controversy, to project their battles into the various national courts by pursuing adversaries with extradition requests."[17] Seemingly in a confirmation of the primary concern he voiced in the *Foreign Affairs* article, when Mr. Kissinger visited London for a conference, Peter Tatchell, a British human rights campaigner, sought to have him arrested for alleged violations of the Geneva Conventions Act of 1957, for the "killing, injuring and displacement" of millions of Vietnamese and Cambodian people during the Vietnam war.[18]

Kenneth Roth, the Executive Director of Human Rights Watch, responded to the article by citing a number of areas where the practice of the United States, as well as that of other states, belied Mr. Kissinger's major concerns.[19] Indeed, many of the hypothetical situations advanced in his article routinely have occurred with few problems.[20] Foreign states assert jurisdiction over U.S. soldiers accused of crimes on the basis of current Status of Forces Agreements (SOFAs), the United States extradites individuals, including citizens, to countries where defendants would not enjoy the constitutional guarantees associated with a trial in the United States, and Kissinger's fear of the ICC stems from a total misreading of its Statute. Additionally, Roth contended that the Pinochet case did not result in a miscarriage of justice. While no system offers perfect guarantees, sufficient safeguards exist that would inhibit the actual occurrence of many of the scenarios advanced by Kissinger. Moreover, many of Kissinger's assertions about lack of due process in other than U.S. courts have little validity. Finally, citing the longstanding U.S. rhetoric supporting human rights and the rule of law, Roth argued that "the United States should be embracing an international system of justice, even if it means that Americans, like everyone else, might sometimes be scrutinized."[21]

The debate between Roth and Kissinger highlights the tension between the assumptions that underlie traditional international law and the continually evolving human rights regime that has at its core the principle of individual accountability. A full understanding of the issues requires a brief discussion of the assumptions and processes of traditional international law as contrasted with the assumptions and practices that underlie international criminal law. The debate also illustrates a tension that exists between a perspective based upon political calculation as opposed to one based upon legal process. The reader needs to keep this distinction firmly in mind. Because they will ultimately be held responsible for the results, statesmen like Henry Kissinger are primarily interested in the nature of the potential outcomes for any initiative. Winston Churchill initially opposed the idea of trials for the Nazi leadership after World War II, noting that their "guilt was so black" that it was "beyond the scope of the judicial process."[22] On the other hand, lawyers and judges focus on process and relevant rules. This means that judges and lawyers operate under modes of fact determination entirely different from the methods employed by those in the political process. Courts require proof adduced through application of a very strict set of rules. Such proof may not always be readily available depending on the circumstances. For example, 25 years after the events in Cambodia, what problems will occur with finding credible testimony from witnesses and in securing relevant documents to support specific cases? Much to the dismay of many human rights advocates, the ICTY initially acquitted Duško (Dusan) Tadić on seven murder charges for lack of evidence. The judges then dismissed 11 of 31 charges against him on the grounds that he could not have violated the Geneva Conventions because the war in Bosnia was not an international one.[23] The next two sections take the reader through the essential elements of legal process necessary to understand how international criminal law differs from traditional international law.

International Criminal Law: A Brief Definition

The term "international crime" does not appear in any current international treaty, though the phrase "crime under international law" does.[24] The question then becomes, how can we talk about international criminal law? This may appear as a nitpicking distinction, but the observation illustrates the evolutionary and fragmented nature of the discipline. Note the emphasis on *crimes* here. It marks an important distinction that the reader must keep in mind. A comprehensive international criminal code does not exist. Hence, definitions of what should be included in the category of *international criminal law* vary. Some, Judge Antonio Cassese, for example, have argued that international criminal law includes only those *crimes* within the jurisdiction of an international court. Under this definition, the Pinochet case would not qualify. Moreover, according to Cassese, the prohibition against piracy, one of the oldest obligations that places responsibility directly on individuals, does not properly belong to the body of international criminal law because it does not meet the test of necessary elements.[25] Implementation in the sense of trial and punishment lies strictly with state authorities. The International Law Commission's (ILC) longstanding effort to develop a comprehensive criminal code produced agreement on only five international crimes: aggression, genocide, war crimes, crimes against humanity, and crimes against UN personnel.[26]

Others, like M. Cherif Bassiouni, who, because of his pioneering and unceasing advocacy, might legitimately be considered one of the modern founding fathers of international criminal law, have a broader definition that includes any crime where states or international courts have the option of prosecuting an individual on the basis of individual accountability/responsibility where they can legitimately do so.[27] For the purposes of this book, I shall use the broader definition. From a strictly technical perspective, this means the discussion will cover crimes that have transborder impact (e.g., trafficking in narcotic drugs, mercenarism, peacetime hostage taking, terrorism, child pornography and other "cyber-crimes," crimes that place the principal burden of prosecution on states such as piracy and engaging in the slave trade, as well as crimes for which states have felt the necessity to constitute international tribunals as an appropriate venue).

The Varieties of Law

Public Law and Private (Civil) Law

Understanding the relationship of international criminal law to other bodies of law requires a brief examination of the roles law presumably plays in organizing human society. The content of any legal obligation, international or domestic, always involves some specified human action/behavior either in terms of *positive requirements* or *permissions* to perform certain duties under certain circumstances *or* in terms of *prohibitions,* that is, a duty to refrain from certain actions under certain circumstances. Psychologically, when most people think of law, they tend to think in terms of prohibitions rather than in terms of permissions or positive requirements. Consider that only two of the Ten Commandments are in the form of "Thou shalt" rather than "Thou shalt *not*." Particularly when individuals think of *criminal law,* by default, they tend to think in terms of prohibitions, that is, in terms of "Thou shalt *not*" rather than "Thou shalt." They also tend to think in terms of punishment: "you do the crime, you do the time." Finally, this image of the criminal law directs us to the "cop on the corner" view of enforcement. This points up an important element of domestic criminal law. In theory, the government, as the agent of the *state,* has the primary obligation of securing enforcement in the sense of prevention and of punishment for those who violate the code. Yet the criminal code forms only one part of a broader category of regulation—*public law.* Public law consists of those laws that govern the relationship between individuals (and other entities such as corporations that have a "legal or *juristic* personality")[28] and the government. In addition to criminal law the broader category includes *administrative*[29] law and *constitutional* law.[30] The clearest examples of public law comes from laws and regulations aimed at eliminating discrimination(race, gender, disability) and those that deal with safety in the workplace (e.g., Occupational Safety and Health Administration [OSHA] standards). Violation of the obligations imposed by these laws normally entails not *criminal* penalties but rather redress of the situation in addition to fines or monetary compensation (damages) to those who suffered injury because of noncompliance.

In turn, public law constitutes only one part of modern legal codes. The bulk of all modern legal codes consists of *private* law—in the United States and Canada, this is often termed *civil* law—that regulates relationships *between individuals.*[31] Wills, contracts, property, marriage, divorce, visitation, and child custody fall into this category. Noncompliance with a legal contract or a suit involving willful damage done to one's property (i.e., a *tort* or a wrongful *civil* act)[32] or product liability normally involves a demand for compliance (enforcement), redress and/or damages, not incarceration. Settlement of many of these disputes occurs through other than judicial processes (mediation, arbitration, direct negotiation). To summarize quickly, most of the legal code in modern states consists of *noncriminal* rules where "you do the crime, you do the time" does not apply.

Here, terminology can be confusing. The term *civil law* as used here should not be confused with the Civil Code system that forms the basis of the legal system in many European states and that of the American state of Louisiana. To complicate the issue further, *private law* as used here should not be confused with *private laws* (bills) passed by the U.S. Congress. A private law (private bill) passed by Congress benefits a specific individual or group. These often involve compensation to individuals who have suffered a wrong arising out of some act (or omission or failure to act) of the government.[33]

Understanding how civil, constitutional, and administrative law differ from criminal law forms an important consideration in understanding the difference between traditional international law and international *criminal* law. Just as criminal law forms an important subset of domestic legal codes, international criminal law forms a distinct subset of international law. In domestic legal systems, civil and public law differ from criminal law in the nature of obligations, who can file a suit for noncompliance/violation, the penalties for noncompliance, and, in many countries, the standards of proof necessary to establish a breach of obligation. One additional important consideration has some bearing here, as well. In private *international* transactions that involve a legal obligation (private international law or conflict of laws) such as the sale of goods, contracts for services, or other financial transactions, when a question of noncompliance arises, the parties may have a choice of venues and courts in which to settle the dispute.[34] This seldom happens in a criminal matter. For whatever reasons, states (governments) tend to be very protective of their *criminal jurisdiction* rights. We shall return to this point later in the discussion.

With regard to enforcement, unlike the criminal law, where the primary responsibility for enforcement in the sense of arrest and prosecution for violations or noncompliance lies with the appropriate organs of state (government), the primary responsibility for initiating a complaint in civil law lies with the individual. For example, if you own rental property, civil law governs the contractual relationship between you and your tenants. If your tenants fail to pay the rent on time, *you* must initiate the appropriate procedures to collect or evict. No government (public) agency will automatically step in to assume the burden of "enforcement." Even if your tenants fail in their obligation, whether willfully or not, they will not incur criminal penalties. The "debtors prison" of Dickens does not exist in contemporary advanced industrial societies. You have a right to demand redress or restitution in the form of compensation owed for rent and damages to the property, but not "jail time."

In civil law, criminal penalties in the sense of personal physical sanctions come into play *only* if the individual has committed a criminal act such as perjury (lying under oath) or *criminal* fraud (a deliberate deception to acquire something of value without appropriate compensation or through misrepresentation of the facts, such as theft by deception, a scam, or a false insurance claim). In the Howard Hughes biography hoax perpetrated by Clifford Irving, Irving and his wife were indicted and convicted of *criminal* offenses associated with the hoax that included mail fraud, perjury, and grand larceny.[35] On the other hand, copyright infringement, representing the work of others as your own (popularly referred to as "plagiarism"), or other intellectual property theft such as patent infringement (profiting from the ideas of others) normally results in a lawsuit demanding damages (redress, restitution), not a criminal prosecution for "theft." Thus, the American Trust Company Bank, which owned the rights to *Gone with the Wind*, sued author Regine Deforges for copyright infringement, claiming that her best-selling book *The Blue Bicycle* clearly drew its story line from the earlier work.[36] The suit asked for $330,000 in damages. Similarly, the BlackBerry case involving accusations of patent infringement against Research in Motion (RIM) by NTP, Inc. stands as a good contemporary illustration.[37] NTP sued RIM, alleging that the text transmission feature of the BlackBerry wireless network required a royalty payment because it held the patent rights to any such use. RIM settled the case through *negotiation* among the parties. While negotiation does clearly exist in the American criminal justice system in the form of the plea bargain, note the difference. The negotiation centered on appropriate *compensation,* not appropriate *punishment.* RIM did "pay" for the alleged violation, but no RIM official faced any time in jail. In the Deforges case, the appeals court found no merit to the claim by American Trust after the lower court had awarded the damages asked.

Substantive and Procedural Law

As we proceed, we must also keep in mind one other important set of categories essential to an understanding of how legal systems work. We need to differentiate between *substantive* law and *procedural* law. *Substantive* law defines the offenses and the "elements" (specific acts) that constitute the defined offense. *Procedural* law specifies the rules that must be observed in applying the law in specific situations. Substantive law defines "what" in terms of obligations and breaches; procedural law specifies "how." One only need watch any TV series or movie involving courts and police to see the importance of procedural rules in the U.S. justice system. Reading someone just arrested his Miranda rights, restrictions on how police may acquire evidence (rules relating to search and seizure), the validity of certain testimony (prohibition on hearsay), and speedy trial requirements constitute important procedural rules. The procedural rules presumably guarantee the fairness of the process in making judgments about applying the substantive rules.

To make an additional point, in the U.S. legal system, the rules of *civil* procedure differ from the rules of *criminal* procedure in several important ways. These rules govern how a lawsuit may be filed, the requirements for service of process (notice), the timing and manner of discovery or disclosure, and the conduct of trials (standards of evidence and judgment). The purpose of this book does not require a systematic exposition of the technical differences between the two but just a basic understanding that the rules of criminal procedure are much more demanding. In criminal litigation in the United States, the defendant is presumed innocent. The burden of proof of guilt always lies with the state. The state must prove that the conduct of the defendant satisfied each element of the statutory definition of the crime "beyond a reasonable doubt."[38] Proof beyond a reasonable doubt means proof of such a convincing character that you would be willing to rely and act upon it without hesitation in the most important of your own affairs. It does not mean an absolute certainty. Some exceptions do exist to the rule about where the burden of proof lies. If a defendant enters a plea of insanity, he or she must provide the proof. The same holds true for defendants who claim duress or self-defense.[39]

In *civil litigation,* the burden of proof falls initially on the *plaintiff* (the person initiating the suit). A number of technical situations exist in which the burden may shift to the defendant. For example, when the plaintiff has made a *prima facie* case, the burden shifts to the defendant to refute or rebut the plaintiff's evidence. In civil litigation, the plaintiff wins if the *preponderance of the evidence* favors the plaintiff. For example, in a personal injury case, if the jury believes that there is more than a 50 percent probability that the defendant's negligent action caused the plaintiff's injury, the plaintiff wins.[40]

The O. J. Simpson cases provide an excellent illustration of the difference.[41] After a lengthy and highly publicized criminal trial, a jury found Simpson not guilty of the murder of his wife, Nicole Brown Simpson, and her friend Ronald Goldman. The Goldman and Brown families subsequently filed a *wrongful death* civil suit. A conviction in the criminal trial would have required a unanimous verdict from the jurors based upon the standard of "beyond a reasonable doubt." The verdict in the civil case required only that 9 of the 12 jurors find that the *preponderance* of the evidence supported the contention of the families that Simpson was responsible for the deaths. The jury in the civil case found Simpson liable and awarded the plaintiffs $33.5 million in compensatory and punitive damages. The second Simpson trial points up another aspect of the division between criminal and civil law. Double jeopardy does not attach if the later charge is civil rather than criminal in nature. Acquittal in a criminal case does not protect the defendant from facing a civil suit relating to the same incident.

Public International Law

Both what I have termed *traditional international law* and *international criminal law* belong to the broad category of *public* international law or the law that governs the relations between states. *Private international law,* sometimes termed conflict of laws, consists of the conventions, legal guides, and other documents and instruments that regulate private relationships across national borders, such as the sale of goods and services. This book does not deal with private international law.

Collective Responsibility versus Individual Criminal Responsibility

Traditional international law textbooks emphasize that states as collective entities, not individuals, constitute the "subjects" of international law. In the *Lotus Case* (*France v. Turkey*), the Permanent Court of International Justice (PCIJ) described the structure of traditional international law as follows:

> International law governs relations between independent sovereign States. The rules of law binding upon States therefore emanate from their own free will as expressed in conventions or by usages generally accepted as expressing principles of law. . . . Restrictions upon the independence of States cannot therefore be presumed. Now the first and foremost restriction imposed by international law upon a State is that—*barring a permissive rule to the contrary*—it may not exercise its power in any form in the territory of another State.[42]

The passage forms a concise statement of the structure and source of obligations. The basic principles flow from the idea of *sovereignty*. Sovereignty means that each state has an exclusive right to control its own territory without interference from other states. This implies a second important idea—that all states have formal equality with respect to the law. Hence, Nauru, population 9,500, has exactly the same rights and duties as China, population 1,320,000,000+. For the moment I will defer the discussion of the role of sovereignty because the question of who bears the responsibility within a state for exercising its rights or making sure obligations are carried out forms a more important concern.

If human action forms the basis of legal obligation, the question becomes, what differentiates the structure of obligations under traditional international law from that which underpins international criminal law? Simply, the structure of obligation under traditional international law rests upon the idea of *collective responsibility*; that of international criminal law relies upon the idea of *individual criminal responsibility*. To understand the difference, let us first take a detour into domestic law. In domestic law, a corporation constitutes a *legal fiction* in that the corporation, as a "collective" entity, enjoys rights and benefits that we normally associate with individuals. The corporation as a "legal person" may file lawsuits against other corporations as well as individuals, have a credit rating, negotiate contracts, apply for loans, or declare bankruptcy. Perhaps the easiest parallel involves a decision by a corporation to declare bankruptcy. The question becomes, how does the law treat the individuals in a corporation "responsible" for the bankruptcy? Clearly, the circumstances that lead to a declaration of bankruptcy involve the actions of human beings who have engaged in activities that failed to produce sufficient revenue to offset the financial indebtedness incurred. In the bankruptcy proceedings, the court considers only the financial assets of the *corporation* as a legal "person," not the individual assets of the corporate officers. Unless there is evidence of criminal wrongdoing, embezzlement, or other fraudulent transactions such as those associated with Enron,[43] the liabilities belong to the corporation as a *collective* entity, not to any individual who served in any capacity as a responsible officer.

When a violation of a legal obligation occurs in traditional international law, the responsibility to take timely and suitable action to redress the breach falls upon the abstract entity we call the *state*. In reality, this means that, because laws always involves human behavior, the responsibility falls upon the responsible agents or officials of the offending state. In effect, this usually means the *government* then in power. If these officials fail to take appropriate action, any demand for redress will again be justified in terms of the failure of the offending *state* to take action. Government officials do not bear any individual or *personal* liability under traditional international law. Such responsibility as they bear stems only from the position(s) they occupy. Hence, "punishment," if undertaken, will not be directed against the particular officials who failed to honor the obligation as individuals but against the collective entity called the state. Note that domestic law may prescribe individual liability for noncompliance or malfeasance, but that obligation does not come from any international obligation to do so. To give an absurd example, but one that makes the point, failure to make the appropriate payments for rent on a U.S. military base in a foreign country does not give that country the right to file suit to attach the personal home of the secretary of defense or secretary of the treasury to satisfy the debt. The debt belongs to the United States as a collective entity, not to any individual official.

Here one must emphasize the idea of the *state*, even though the government duly recognized by other states serves as the legal representative of the state. Moreover, the key concept is the state, even though, as we discussed earlier, all legal obligations rest eventually upon a human agent. The emphasis rests upon a simple fact of international life. The state is considered the enduring entity regardless of any change, constitutional or extraconstitutional (coup d'état or revolution) in government. A change in government does not relieve the state of its international obligations. This stands as one of the oldest principles of traditional international law. For example, consider the case of *The Sapphire*.[44] In December 1867, a private American ship, the *Sapphire*, and a French naval transport, *Euryale*, collided in the harbor of San Francisco. The *Euryale* suffered heavy damage. A suit for damages against the owners of the *Sapphire* was filed in District Court, listing Napoleon III, Emperor of the French, as owner of the *Euryale*. The court decided the case in favor of Napoleon III. The U.S. Supreme Court eventually agreed to hear the case on appeal. Before the oral arguments in the case, in February 1871, Napoleon III was deposed and a new French government (a republic) installed. The first question before the Court then became the status of the suit. Did the fact that the government of Napoleon III no longer existed mean that the suit should be dismissed? The clear answer was that the right to sue belonged to the *state* of France, not any particular government. The plaintiff in this case was not Napoleon III but the state of France. He served only as the official then empowered to act on behalf of *France*. Because the United States had recognized the successor government as controlling the sovereign power within France, the suit continued. From a pragmatic point of view, this "legal fiction" ensures the stability of the international legal regime. Consider the chaos if states could disavow their obligations every time they underwent a change in government.

The *Avena* Case

The more recent *Avena*[45] case gives a good illustration of what collective responsibility means in practice. Mexico sued the United States in the International Court of Justice (ICJ) for systematic violation of the *Optional Protocol to the Vienna Convention on Consular Relations* that defines a right of diplomatic protection. Diplomatic protection means only that a state has an interest in seeing that its nationals are treated fairly and receive any rights due to them under law. It does not infer a right to interfere actively in the judicial process. Note also that only *states* may bring cases to the ICJ. Individuals have no standing. The treaty requires that foreign nationals charged with a crime have access to a consular official from their home state. The requirement has a practical concern. Consular officials should be familiar with the local justice system and provide the information necessary to secure adequate representation and advice. If you have traveled outside the United States, think about what you do not know about the ins and outs of the justice system in other countries, even those in Western Europe. If charged with a crime, who should you contact? Do you have the right to contact anyone?

Mexico alleged that U.S. officials (local prosecutors) had failed to inform 51 Mexican nationals charged with capital murder of their right to meet with diplomatic officials from their home state (a violation of *procedural* law). The ICJ found in favor of Mexico, meaning that the *United States* now had an obligation to take action to *redress* the breach. The prosecutors and other officials involved in the cases bore no personal or individual responsibility for the failure to observe the treaty provision. They faced no sanctions other than the possibility of having to retry the cases.

Collective and Individual Responsibility: Intersections and Overlaps

In contrast, to return to our opening example, Pinochet faced a charge based directly on his actions as an individual. Pinochet, not Chile, was the responsible party, according to the warrant. Current commentators tend to stress this distinction because international tribunals have focused on individuals, not on state responsibility. Unfortunately, these two bodies of law do overlap. The relationship is considerably more complex than suggested by this simple but vital distinction. A quick survey would reveal that most of the individual offenses prohibited also constitute offenses under general (traditional) international law. In consequence, because Pinochet acted not as a private individual but as an agent of the state of Chile, his actions could potentially result in a situation where both bodies of law applied. Thus, in addition to his personal liability, Chile as a state could also bear liability *if* he and others did act in their official capacities to promote or condone the behavior. Consider that, while Milošević stood trial before the ICTY, in 1999 Croatia also brought suit against Serbia in the International Court of Justice alleging that Milošević and the Serbian government were responsible for the policy of "ethnic cleansing" during the invasion.[46] At this writing, the case has not been resolved.

Enforcement

Inevitably, the question of enforcement arises because the international context seemingly lacks all of the features that we associate with the rule of law at the domestic level. The political organization of the contemporary world is based upon sovereign states. The international context lacks a legislature that can pass rules binding on all, lacks an international police force, and lacks courts that have appropriate jurisdiction over all states. The previous discussion has covered some basics of international legal process. In it, I have suggested that the mode of enforcement that normally pops to mind, the "cop on the corner," does not adequately address the most common types of problems and issues associated with order at the international level. With this said, one of the obvious weaknesses of international law stems from its seeming ineffectiveness with respect to managing violent conflicts. Because the "cop on the corner" model does appear to fit here, much of the disillusionment with the United Nations, for example, comes from a perception that the organization has failed in its most fundamental task, that of preventing or, failing prevention, taking effective action to end conflicts.

The "cop on the corner" model represents a *vertical* scheme of enforcement that is clearly based upon our perceptions of how the criminal law works in advanced industrial democracies. Vertical systems of enforcement designate special agencies and individuals to be responsible for dealing with violations of the law. Enforcement of domestic criminal law and certain other areas of public law relies primarily on vertical systems. Earlier in this discussion, I suggested that, even in domestic law, the "cop on the corner" did not apply in full to civil law processes. Many civil law processes have a *horizontal* element in that the interested parties, rather than a separate designated agency, must initiate the action. True, at the domestic level courts exist as presumed authoritative and impartial "third party" arbiters. This provides an element often missing at the international level, but, increasingly, given the uncertainties and costs of litigation, many civil suits go to arbitration or mediation rather than trial.

Some international courts exist, but the bulk of dispute resolution between states involves horizontal processes, that is, state-to-state action. Article 33(1) of the UN Charter lists several methods of peaceful resolution available to states. Perhaps the most common method is direct negotiation through the simple exchange of diplomatic correspondence. An anomaly here comes from the fact that states may in some instances lawfully take unilateral nonforcible illegal action, a reprisal, to enforce an obligation. In response to a gross treaty violation, states may in turn terminate the treaty or engage in actions in reprisal aimed at compelling compliance.[47] Because enforcement often relies on individual state action, the enforcement of international criminal law in specific situations has been hampered by the reluctance of states to take appropriate action, as well as the recalcitrance of target states in complying with lawful directives. We discuss this further in Chapter 3.

The Evolution of International Criminal Law

International criminal law has grown out of the broader body of human rights law. As such, most categories of offenses, apart from war crimes, represent relatively new areas of concern. Earlier, I noted that no consensus exists with respect to the scope of the field. This book addresses two distinctive areas: crimes within the jurisdiction of an international court or tribunal and crimes that have potential or actual transborder effects. The two areas share a commonality—the prohibitions fall directly upon individuals and provide penal sanctions for violations. The first category includes war crimes, genocide, crimes against humanity, and aggression, sometimes described as crimes against peace. The second category draws upon international conventions that require state parties to enact appropriate domestic criminal legislation related to areas such as torture, terrorism, piracy, and drug trafficking. In both cases we shall cover the appropriate treaties, the procedural rules of jurisdiction, and the methods of cooperation among states in term of implementation. In this second category of crimes, international law provides the obligation, but the machinery of implementation depends upon domestic legislation and action by each state party.[48]

War Crimes: International Humanitarian Law

Traditional international law treats war as a legal institution. Texts published before World War II have two sections, sometimes two volumes. One set of rules governed states during times of peace; another set governed states during the "state of war." Until the 20th century, international law did not govern the transition between the two; that is, no *jus ad bellum* existed. The transition from peace to war stood as something that stood outside legal control. On the other hand, the idea of the idea of war crimes—the *jus in bello*—in the sense of appropriate behavior on the part of individuals, has some considerable resonance in western history.[49] For example, in Shakespeare's *Henry V,* the king orders the execution of Bardolph for taking items from a church prior to the battle of Agincourt, in 1415.[50] On the other hand, one should consider the slaughter of noncombatants during the Thirty Year's War (1618–1648). At Magdeburg, a center of Protestant resistance, in May 1631, imperial troops killed more than 20,000 civilians.[51] The individuals responsible had little to fear in terms of being held personally responsible. Apart from his earlier work on the law of the sea, Hugo Grotius was prompted by the excesses of this war to write his epic *De Jure Belli ac Pacis* (*On the Law of War and Peace*).[52] Many of the principles he proposed, such as that of noncombatant immunity, still provide the underpinning of contemporary international humanitarian law (law of land warfare).

Generally, in the contemporary era, a war crime is any act for which soldiers or other individuals may be punished by the enemy on capture of the offender. The category includes acts committed in violation of international law and the laws of the combatant's own country, as well as acts in violation of the laws of war undertaken *under order* and in the interest of the combatant's state of nationality. Systematic attempts to develop a modern formal *jus in bello* began in the mid-19th century. The Lieber Code, written by Dr. Francis Lieber of Columbia University and issued to Union troops during the Civil War (1863), stands as the first formal written set of orders for a national army concerning appropriate conduct.[53] The Lieber Code became the model for other national armies (Italy, Russia, France). Both the 1899 and 1907 Hague Conferences drafted conventions that sought to limit the use of certain weapons and to limit the impact of war on noncombatants. Hague IV[54] constituted the model for the more famous post–World War II Geneva Conventions.[55] The nature of conflict after World War II resulted in a second

Geneva Conference in 1974–1977 that attempted to amend and extend the rules to noninternational conflict.[56] Again in these cases, international law provides for individual criminal responsibility, not collective responsibility. The law, the *jus in bello*, makes soldiers in the field liable for their own conduct.

Genocide and Crimes against Humanity

Although we can cite many instances in history of great slaughter, events in the 20th century, in particular the Turkish campaign against the Armenians in 1915 and the policies of the Nazi leadership in Germany (and, later, in occupied Europe) aimed at systematic elimination of all Jews provided the impetus for much of the evolution of international legal regimes since World War II. The thrust of the international effort aimed at dissolving the idea that the hard shell of sovereignty could provide immunity for such intentionally brutal actions. As many have pointed out, the word "genocide" did not exist prior to 1944.[57] In that year, Raphael Lemkin, a Polish lawyer then living in Washington, D.C., published his *Axis Rule in Occupied Europe*.[58] Lemkin had struggled to find a word or words that he felt would both adequately describe the atrocities committed by the Nazi regime and evoke an immediately sense of deep moral outrage. He combined the Greek *geno* (race or tribe) with a suffix derived from the Latin *caedere* (to kill), "*cide*." Yet Lemkin intended the word to have a broader connotation than policies that promoted large-scale killing. In practice, genocide in practice may involve acts beyond the killing of people. It can include other acts of depredation such as forced abortion, sterilization, artificial infection, the working of people to death in special labor camps, and the separation of families or sexes in order to depopulate specific areas. Those who commit genocide have the purpose of destroying all institutions, culture, and language associated with the target group. Hence, genocide can occur as well through stripping a group of all elements of its cultural identity.[59]

Drafting a multilateral treaty making genocide an international crime became one of the first priorities of the newly formed United Nations. On December 9, 1948, the UN General Assembly adopted the text of the *Convention on the Prevention and Punishment of the Crime of Genocide*.[60] The Convention, originally signed by 25 states, entered into force on January 12, 1951. The United States did not ratify it until 1988. Until the Cold War ended, in the early 1990s, the treaty remained largely unused, despite the existence of some brutal regimes that committed large-scale atrocities. Events in Bosnia and Rwanda placed the convention in the spotlight when the UN Security Council authorized ad hoc tribunals, the ICTY (Yugoslavia) and the ICTR (Rwanda), to try individuals for war crimes and genocide.

Like many other terms, "crimes against humanity" is often misused in popular parlance. Newspaper accounts commonly use the idea to describe events that involve morally atrocious acts committed on a large scale, rather than in its narrower technical sense.[61] To some extent, as a category, "crimes against humanity" overlaps with genocide and common war crimes. Intent forms the fundamental distinction between crimes against humanity and genocide. Establishing a crime against humanity does not require proving an intent to destroy a group "in whole or in part," according to the definition of genocide in the 1948 convention. Crimes again humanity require only that the target group be the object of a policy that condones widespread or systematic violations of human rights such as apartheid, enslavement, deportation or forcible transfer of population, torture, rape, and forced pregnancy. We can distinguish crimes against humanity from ordinary war crimes in that they occur in times of peace as well as in wartime.[62]

The Nuremberg Charter and that of the International Military Tribunal for the Far East IIMTFE) at Tokyo represented the first time that crimes against humanity were asserted as part of positive international law. Interestingly, no specialized international convention dealing with crimes against humanity has emerged, even though the Statutes of the International Criminal Tribunal for the Former Yugoslavia (ICTY), the International Criminal Tribunal for Rwanda (ICTR), and the Rome Statute of the International Criminal Court (ICC) include the category.

Torture

Prior to the contemporary era, torture as a crime did not elicit a great deal of interest from the international community. In the era after World War II, government-sanctioned torture of prisoners became common.[63] Currently, torture constitutes an international crime both in times of war and in times of peace. One of the more interesting developments in international criminal law, perhaps because of the emergence of high-profile NGOs such as Amnesty International that mounted campaigns to raise awareness around the world, comes from the rapid emergence of torture as a crime that many now feel has become *jus cogens*.[64]

Crimes against Peace: Waging Aggressive War

Not until after World War I did states seriously undertake efforts to restrict the resort to force. The League Covenant did not contain a definition of aggression, nor did it make the resort to war "illegal." Efforts focused on making wars of aggression illegal. In 1923, a League of Nations committee produced a Draft Treaty of Mutual Assistance that attempted to define wars of aggression as an international crime as part of the collective security regime established by the Covenant.[65] It never entered into force. The 1924 Assembly of the League considered a proposed a "Protocol for the Pacific Settlement of International Disputes," commonly known as the Geneva Protocol, that defined an aggressor as any power that refused either to submit a dispute to arbitration or to accept the verdict of the arbitrating body. This Protocol offered a simple and complete solution of the problem of defining an aggressor, but it too never came into operation. In 1927, the Assembly of the League passed a resolution under which all wars of aggression were said to be prohibited and only pacific means were to be employed to settle international disputes of every kind. In 1928, the Sixth Pan-American Conference adopted a resolution asserting that a "war of aggression constitutes a crime against the human species; . . . all aggression is illicit and as such is declared prohibited."[66]

Perhaps the most famous interwar effort was the Pact of Paris, more familiarly known as the Kellogg-Briand Pact. Many analysts have derided its simple idealism and lack of impact. Still, the agreement does stand at the center of the efforts to "outlaw" *aggressive* war. Note the adjective "aggressive," because none of these proposals really prohibited every kind of war. The *General Treaty for the Renunciation of War* (Pact or Pact of Paris) was signed in Paris on August 27, 1928, by representatives of 15 states and was ratified or adhered to by 65 nations:[67]

The debate over the development of the substantive law need not detain us here. Article 6 of the Charter for the Nuremberg trials (IMT) contained the following definition of crimes against peace: "namely, planning, preparation, initiation or waging of a war of aggression, or a war in violation of international treaties, agreements or assurances, or participation in a common plan or conspiracy for the accomplishment of any of the foregoing."[68] The IMT conducted 22 trials. Nineteen of the 22 defendants were convicted. In passing here, recalling the previous contrast drawn between lawyers and judges on one hand and practical politicians on the other, note that not all those accused and tried were convicted.

The Charter of the United Nations sought to outlaw the resort to force except in self-defense. Presumably because the Charter has almost universal acceptance from contemporary states, this obligation stands as a principal of *jus cogens*. Nonetheless, since Nuremberg, no individual has stood trial for crimes against peace. Moreover, because of the continuing controversy over defining aggression, the ICC Statute does not cover aggression, leaving it for future definition. The charges against Slobodan Milošević by the ICTY focused upon crimes against humanity, not crimes against peace. Saddam Hussein stood trial before an Iraqi court. Though he had invaded Kuwait, the charges did not include any offenses connected with that operation.

Transnational (Transborder) Crimes

Globalization and technology have generated new opportunities for those who seek to make their living by taking advantage of others. Computers and the Internet have given scam artists a huge new area of opportunity. Anyone who is active on the Internet has probably received an e-mail communication that promises a great reward if he will only help the sender retrieve assets that he has moved out of the country and for some "technical" legal reasons now cannot access. While the advent of the computer has opened up a broad new area of cyber-spying for governments and the possibilities of identity theft for individuals, some very old problems, such as piracy, drug trafficking, and the slave trade persist, as well.[69] Some old practices, such as serving as a mercenary soldier in certain contexts, have now become a focus of international concern. International terrorism has also emerged as a major problem in recent years.

Piracy Piracy stands as perhaps the oldest crime specifically addressed by international law. All states have a duty to suppress piracy. This flows from both the customary law and Article 100 of the UN Convention on the Law of the Sea (III). We can speak of "universal jurisdiction" in this instance because the authority to act does not depend upon the nationality of the perpetrator. Mention piracy and images of Blackbeard, Captain Kidd, and probably Johnny Depp spring instantly to mind. Romantic images aside, piracy exists as a very real contemporary problem in several areas of the world. A Web site aimed at owners of yachts recently warned: "Unfortunately pirate attacks on yachts are becoming more frequent. Vigilance, preparation and avoidance are now required for yachts transiting high risk areas."[70] Since the early 1970s, true acts of piracy have occurred with embarrassing frequency off the western coast of Thailand, in the Gulf of Thailand, the Sulu Sea, the Java Sea, and the Celebes Sea.

Slavery In dealing with slavery, the images that come to mind for many are intimately connected to the transatlantic slave trade and southern plantations.[71] These are also images most consider as part of the past, not the present. Even though the movement to abolish slavery and the slave trade began in earnest in the early 19th century, not until 1980 did Mauritania become the last country in the world to abolish slavery officially. Slavery in some form does appear to continue in a broad belt of states extending from northwestern Africa to the eastern borders of the Arabian peninsula and possibly in isolated pockets beyond into the Asian mainland.[72] Not unexpectedly, the governments within whose territories indisputable evidence of slavery has been found deny that such an institution or practice exists. They may, in some instances, point to solemn governmental prohibitions of the practice. Despite frequent official denials, the major types of slavery (chattel slavery, debt bondage, child bondage, and prostitution) have continued to flourish. Several international conventions address the problem, but none have realistic enforcement provisions.[73]

Organized Crime and Narcotics Organized crime encompasses a wide range of illegal activities such as drug trafficking, money laundering, counterfeiting, credit card fraud, traffic in persons, illegal arms and weapons trading, criminal offenses against the environment, and even car theft. Generally speaking, organized crime can be any illegal activity that has evolved to the level of a business enterprise that has international connections. Though states have addressed some issues, such as narcotics,[74] at present no comprehensive international convention regulates these activities. Resolution 53/111 (December 9, 1998) of the UN General Assembly established an ad hoc committee open to all states for the purpose of drafting a new, comprehensive international convention against transnational organized crime. The resolution also authorized the committee to draft three additional international legal instruments (protocols) dealing with illegal transport and trafficking in migrants, illicit manufacturing of and trafficking in firearms, and trafficking in women and children. This represents an effort to update earlier conventions to reflect modern circumstances. The *Draft Convention against Transnational Organized Crime* opened for signature on December 12, 2000. It has not yet entered into force.[75]

Terrorism, Peacetime Hostage Taking, and Other Unlawful Acts Until September 11, 2001, the most devastating attack on U.S. soil, the bombing of the Alfred P. Murrah federal office building in Oklahoma City, had come from within. Until the rise of groups driven by apocalyptic religious beliefs or ethnic fervor, terrorists tended to choose targets that produced a lot of publicity, not a lot of people dead. The September 11 attacks are evidence of a disturbing trend confirmed by the bombings in Madrid in March 2004 and London in July 2005.

There are nine current Suppression of Unlawful Acts (SUA) treaties. These place the responsibility for preventing or punishing the offenses upon each state party. Three of these deal with air travel; two deal with controlling terrorism; the others focus on hostage taking, crimes against diplomatic agents, theft of nuclear materials, and the protection of oil rigs on the continental shelf.[76]

Notes

1. Anthony Faiola, "Britain Arrests Pinochet at Spain's Request; Chile Protests Detention of Ex-Dictator at London Hospital," *Washington Post,* October 18, 1998 (final edition), A1. For a lengthy discussion of the case and its implications, see Geoffrey Robertson, *Crimes against Humanity: The Struggle for Global Justice* (3rd ed.) (New York and London: New Press, 2006), 332–69 (Chapter 8).

2. See Pamela Constable and Arturo Valuenzeula, *A Nation of Enemies: Chile under Pinochet* (New York: Norton, 1993).

3. See Stephen Macedo (ed.), *Universal Jurisdiction: National Courts and the Prosecution of Serious Crimes under International Law* (Philadelphia: University of Pennsylvania Press, 2004) for an extended discussion of the principles here.

4. Charter of the United Nations, http://www.un.org/aboutun/charter/.

5. See Mahmood Monshipouri and Claude Emerson Welch, "The Search for International Human Rights and Justice: Coming to Terms with the New Global Realities," *Human Rights Quarterly* 23, no. 2 (May 2001): 370–401; Kenneth Roth, "The Case for Universal Jurisdiction," *Foreign Affairs* 80, no. 5 (September/October 2001): 150–54.

6. Of December 10, 1984; entered into force with ratification by the 20th state party, June 26, 1987. The treaty requires state parties either to prosecute any suspected torturer found on their territory, regardless of where the torture took place, or to extradite the suspect to a country that will do so. The United States ratified the Convention in 1994 but with a reservation that substituted the Eighth Amendment to the U.S. Constitution for the definition of torture included as an addendum to the Convention. For text of the treaty see http://www.hrweb.org/legal/cat.html.

7. "Lawyers Attempt to Have President Bush Declared *Persona non Grata* in Canada," http://207.44.245.159/article7349.htm; http://www.lawyersagainstthewar.org/press.html.

8. "Yugoslav Community Charges NATO and U.S. at War Crimes Tribunal," *Agence France Presse—English* (May 3, 1999), LexisNexis Academic Universe.

9. For a concise discussion of Milošević's political career, see http://news.bbc.co.uk/hi/english/static/in_depth/europe/2000/milosevic_yugoslavia/default.stm.

10. Nic Dunlop, "Cambodia's Trial by Fire," *Los Angeles Times*, August 21, 2007, A17; "Cambodia Police Arrest Khmer Rouge President," *Globe and Mail* (Canada), November 19, 2007, A16, LexisNexis Academic Universe.

11. See International Criminal Court, http://www.icc-cpi.int/home.html&l=en.

12. See Human Rights Watch, "Case Law of the International Criminal Tribunal for Rwanda: Summary of Judgments against the Accused," http://hrw.org/reports/2004/ij/ictr/1.htm.

13. See. for example, Department of Justice, Canada, "Crimes Against Humanity and War Crimes Act," http://laws.justice.gc.ca/en/C-45.9/; Interpol, "Genocide, War Crimes and Crimes against Humanity," http://laws.justice.gc.ca/en/C-45.9/; Interpol, "Genocide, War Crimes and Crimes against Humanity," http://www.interpol.int/Public/CrimesAgainst Humanity/default.asp; Sue Montgomery, "War Crimes Trial First Test of Canadian Legislation," *Montreal Gazette*, March 25, 2007; "Canada's First War Crimes Trial Gets Underway," *CBC News*, March 26, 2007, LexisNexis Academic Universe.

14. Henry A. Kissinger, "The Pitfalls of Universal Jurisdiction," *Foreign Affairs* 80:4 (July/August 2001): 86–96. For a concise *legal* critique of universal jurisdiction in contemporary practice, see Paul Chevigny, "The Limitations of Universal Jurisdiction," *Global Policy Forum* (March 2006), http://www.globalpolicy.org/opinion/2006/03universal.htm.

15. Kissinger, "The Pitfalls of Universal Jurisdiction," 91.

16. Ibid., 88.

17. Ibid., 92.

18. "Tatchell Loses Battle for Kissinger's Arrest," *BBC News*, April 24, 2002, http://news.bbc.co.uk/1/hi/uk/1948014.stm.

19. Roth, "The Case for Universal Jurisdiction," 150–54.

20. See James L. Taulbee, "A Call to Arms Declined: The United States and the International Criminal Court," *Emory International Law Review* 14 (Spring 2000): 105–56, for a discussion of these points.

21. Roth, "The Case for Universal Jurisdiction," 154.

22. Originally attributed to Anthony Eden. Cited in Mark Osiel, "Why Prosecute? Critics of Punishment for Mass Atrocity," *Human Rights Quarterly* 22, no. 1 (February 2000): 118–47; see also Martha Minow, *Between Vengeance and Forgiveness: Facing History after Genocide and Mass Violence* (Boston: Beacon Press, 1998); David A. Crocker, "Reckoning with Past Wrongs: A Normative Framework," *Ethics and International Affairs* 13 (1999): 43–64.

23. Gary Bass, *Stay the Hand of Vengeance: The Politics of War Crimes Tribunals* (Princeton: Princeton University Press, 2000), 13 ff; Michael P. Scharf, *Balkan Justice: The Story behind the First International War Crimes Trial since Nuremberg* (Durham, NC: Carolina Academic Press, 1997), 213–14, 271–88.

24. M. Cherif Bassiouni, *Introduction to International Criminal Law* (Ardsley, NY: Transnational, 2003), 166–67. Indeed, Bassiouni notes that the term "crime under international law" appears in only 34 of 281 relevant international instruments.

25. Antonio Cassese, *International Criminal Law* (Oxford: Oxford University Press, 2003), 24. Mr. Cassese served as the first president of the ICTY (1993–1997).

26. *Draft Code of Crimes against the Peace and Security of Crimes of Mankind*, May 6–July 26, 1996, *Report of the International Law Commission*, GAOR Supp. No. 10, UN doc. A/51/10.

27. Bassiouni, *Introduction to International Criminal Law*, 1.

28. An entity that has juristic personality is treated as an *artificial person* who has the capacity to enter into contracts and sue or be sued. For its application in international law, see Janne Elisabeth Nijman, *The Concept of International Legal Personality: An Inquiry into the History and Theory of International Law* (Cambridge: Cambridge University Press, 2004).

29. See Jack M. Beerman, *Administrative Law* (New York: Aspen, 2006).

30. See Philip J. Prygoski, *Constitutional Law* (12th ed.) (St. Paul, MN: Thomson West, 2007).

31. See James Gordley and Arthur Taylor von Mehren, *An Introduction to the Comparative Study of Private Law: Readings, Cases, Materials* (Cambridge: Cambridge University Press, 2006).

32. Torts involve wrongful acts other than breach of contract. While *some* torts may be crimes punishable with imprisonment, the *primary* purpose of tort law is to provide relief for the *damages* incurred and deter others from committing the same harms. See http://www.law.cornell.edu/wex/index.php/Tort#definition.

33. For a discussion, see Marc D. Yacker, *Private Bills and Federal Charters* (Washington, DC: Library of Congress, Congressional Research Service, 1979).

34. See Ruth Hayward, *Conflict of Laws* (4th ed.) (London: Cavendish, 2006).

35. See Stephen Fay, Lewis Chester, and Magnus Linklater, *Hoax: The Inside Story of the Howard Hughes-Clifford Irving Affair* (New York: Viking, 1972).

36. Newspaper accounts described this as a case of "plagiarism," but plagiarism is not a *legal* doctrine. The term as such cannot be found in any copyright or author's rights act. Lawyers may generally speak of plagiarism for cases in which the unauthorized use of a work coupled with a false attribution of authorship infringes upon the copyrights of the original author. Although both concepts may appear to the lay person as being the same, copyright infringement has a much narrower definition, and therefore acts of plagiarism may constitute copyright infringement only in very precise cases. See Francisco Javier Cabrera Blázquez, "Plagiarism: An Original Sin?" at http://www.obs.coe.int/online_publi cation/expert/plagiarism.pdf.en.

37. See "BlackBerry Lawsuit FAQ: What You Need to Know," http://www.computer world.com/newsletter/0,4902,108445,00.html?nlid=MW2.

38. See U.S. Supreme Court, *Federal Rules of Criminal Procedure: Rules of Criminal Procedure for the United States District Courts* (Eagan, MN: Thomson/West, 2002).

39. Joshua Dressler, *Understanding Criminal Law* (4th ed.) (New York: Lexis, 2006), Chap. 24.

40. See U.S. Supreme Court, *Federal Rules of Civil Procedure 3d* (Eagan, MN: Thomson/ West, 2007); see also Joshua Dressler, *Criminal Law* (Eagan, MN: West, 2005), 112–16, for a brief discussion of the difference between criminal and civil procedure.

41. For a summary and chronology of the criminal trial see http://www.law.umkc.edu/ faculty/projects/ftrials/Simpson/simpson.htm. For stories on the civil suit, see http://www. usatoday.com/news/index/nns0.htm.

42. (1927) PCIJ Rep., Series A, No. 10, 18–19. Emphasis added.

43. For a chronology and summary, see "The Fall of Enron," http://www.chron.com/ news/specials/enron/.

44. *The Sapphire*, U.S. Supreme Court, 1871, 11 Wallace 164.

45. *Case Concerning Avena and Other Mexican Nationals, 2004* ICJ Rep. 128, 43 ILM 581 (2004); http://www.icj-cij.org/icjwww/idocket/imus/imusframe.htm.

46. *Application of the Convention on the Prevention and Punishment of the Crime of Genocide* (Croatia v. Serbia and Montenegro), 1999, http://www.icj-cij.org/docket/index.php?p1=3& p2=3&code=cry&case=118&k=73.

47. For an extended discussion of these points, see David J. Bederman, *The Spirit of International Law* (Athens: University of Georgia Press, 2002), 187–93.

48. Neil Boister, "Transnational Criminal Law," *European Journal of International Law* 14 (2003): 953. For an updated bibliography, see Marilyn J. Raisch and Gail Partin, "International Criminal Law: A Selective Resource Guide," http://www.llrx.com/features/int_crim.htm.

49. For example, see Maurice Hugh Keen, *The Laws of War in the Late Middle Ages* (London: Routledge and Kegan Paul, 1965).

50. Theodor Meron, *Henry's Wars and Shakespeare's Laws: Perspectives on the Law of War in the Later Middle Ages* (Oxford: Clarendon Press, 1993), 114–16.

51. Otto von Guericke, "The Destruction of Magdeburg," in *Readings in European History* (2 vols.), ed. J. H. Robinson (Boston: Ginn, 1906), 2:211–12. Von Guericke served as the Burgomeister of Magdeburg; http://history.hanover.edu/texts/magde.html.

52. Hugo Grotius, *The Rights of War and Peace* (3 vols.), ed. Richard Tuck (Indianapolis, IN: Liberty Fund, 2005).

53. *The Lieber Code of 1863, Correspondence, Orders, Reports, and Returns of the Union Authorities from January 1 to December 31, 1863.—#7 O.r.—Series III—volume III [S# 124]* General Orders No. 100; http://www.civilwarhome.com/liebercode.htm.

54. *Convention (IV) Respecting the Laws and Customs of War on Land and Its Annex: Regulations Concerning the Laws and Customs of War on Land.* The Hague, October 18, 1907; http://www.icrc.org/ihl.nsf/FULL/195.

55. See International Committee of the Red Cross, "The Geneva Conventions: the Core of International Humanitarian Law," http://www.icrc.org/Web/Eng/siteeng0.nsf/htmlall/ge nevaconventions.

56. David P. Forsythe, "Legal Management of Internal War: The 1977 Protocol on Non-international Armed Conflicts," *American Journal of International Law* 72 (1978): 272–95; *Protocol Additional to the Geneva Conventions of 12 August 1949, and Relating to the Protection of Victims of International Armed Conflicts* (PA-I), http://www.unhchr.ch/html/menu3/b/93. htm; and *Protocol Additional to the Geneva Conventions of 12 August 1949, and Relating to the Protection of Victims of Non-International Conflicts* (PA-II) http://www.icrc.org/ihl.nsf/FULL/475?OpenDocument.

57. See Samantha Power, *"A Problem from Hell": America and the Age of Genocide* (New York: Basic Books, 2002), Chapters 1–3.

58. Raphael Lemkin, *Axis Rule in Occupied Europe* (New York: Carnegie Endowment for International Peace, 1944).

59. Power, *"A Problem from Hell,"* 43.

60. Text in *American Journal of International Law* 45 (1951 Supp.): 6; http://www. unhchr.ch/html/menu3/b/p_genoci.htm. For a discussion of the original negotiations, see Lawrence J. Leblanc, *The United States and the Genocide Convention* (Durham, NC: Duke University Press, 1991), 151–74.

61. M. Cherif Bassiouni, "Crimes against Humanity," http://www.crimesofwar.org/the book/crimes-against-humanity.html.

62. See Barry Goodman, "Crimes against Humanity during the Gulf War: A Hyperlinked Pathfinder Research Tool" (June 22, 1998), http://web.archive.org/web/20010812004424/http://diana.law.yale.edu/diana/db/war10.html.

63. See *New York Times,* August 4, 1974, E-5; and Amnesty International, *Report on Torture* (1975), as well as its *Torture in the Eighties* (1984), listing abuses in 98 countries.

64. Bassiouni, *Introduction to International Criminal Law,* 147.

65. "The Draft Treaty of Mutual Assistance," *Journal of the British Institute of International Affairs* 3, no. 2 (March 1924): 45–82.

66. See James Brown Scott, "The Sixth Pan American Conference," *American Journal of International Law* 22, no. 2 (April 1928): 351–62.

67. Text at http://www.yale.edu/lawweb/avalon/imt/kbpact.htm.

68. Text in *American Journal of International Law 39* (1945 Supp.), 257 ff. Consult *International Conference on Military Trials, London, 1945* (Department of State Publication 3080), for the texts of all proposals at the meeting. The principles contained in the 1945 Agreement were recognized as binding in international law by UN General Assembly Resolution 95 (I) (December 11, 1946); see also "Famous World Trials," http://www.law.umkc.edu/faculty/projects/ftrials/nuremberg/nuremberg.htm.

69. China Denies Pentagon Cyber-raid, *BBC News* (September 4, 2007), *http://news.bbc.co.uk/2/hi/americas/6977533.stm;* "China Rejects Renewed Accusations of Cyber Spying." *DW- World* (*Deutsche Welle*) (October 10, 2007), http://www.dw-world.de/dw/article/0,2144,2836152,00.html.

70. "Pirate Attacks, Onpassage.com; The Global Site for Cruising Yachts (November 7, 2007), http://www.onpassage.com/Emergency_Medical/Pirate_attacks.htm; "Pirate Attacks on the High Seas," CruiseBruise, http://www.cruisebruise.com/cruise_ship_pirate_attacks.html; "Cruise Ship Repels Somali Pirates," *BBC News* (November 5, 2006), http://news.bbc.co.uk/2/hi/africa/4409662.stm; "Cruise Ship Britons Attacked by Pirates," *Sunday Times* (London), November 6, 2005, http://www.timesonline.co.uk/article/0,,2087-1859626,00.html.

71. Ethan B. Kapstein, "The New Global Slave Trade," *Foreign Affairs* 85, no. 6 (2006): 103–15.

72. UNESCO, "Slave Trade Archives," http://portal.unesco.org/ci/en/ev.php-URL_ID=8780&URL_DO=DO_TOPIC&URL_SECTION=201.html; "Contemporary Slave Trade: A Symposium on Human Trafficking," http://www.humantrafficking.org/countries/eap/united_states/events/2005_09/contemporary_slave_trade.html.

73. See *Slavery Convention* (Geneva), September 25, 1926; http://www.ohchr.org/english/law/slavery.htm; also, Amnesty International—Anti-Slavery International, Council of Europe: Recommendations to Strengthen the December 2004 Draft European Convention on Action against Trafficking in Human Beings, http://web.amnesty.org/library/index/engior610012005.

74. *UN Convention against Illicit Traffic in Narcotic Drugs and Psychotropic Substances* (December 12, 1988), http://www.unodc.org/pdf/convention_1988_en.pdf.

75. Text at http://www.uncjin.org/Documents/Conventions/dcatoc/final_documents_2/index.htm.

76. *Convention for the Suppression of Unlawful Seizure of Aircraft,* done at The Hague on December 16, 1970; *Convention for the Suppression of Unlawful Acts against the Safety of Civil Aviation,* done at Montreal on September 23, 1971; *Protocol for the Suppression of Unlawful Acts of Violence at Airports Serving International Civil Aviation,* supplementary to the

Convention for the Suppression of Unlawful Acts against the Safety of Civil Aviation, done at Montreal on February 24, 1988; *Convention on the Prevention and Punishment of Crimes against Internationally Protected Persons, including Diplomatic Agents,* adopted by the General Assembly of the United Nations on December 14, 1973; *International Convention against the Taking of Hostages,* adopted by the General Assembly of the United Nations on December 17, 1979; *Convention on the Physical Protection of Nuclear Material,* done at Vienna on October 26, 1979; *Protocol for the Suppression of Unlawful Acts against the Safety of Fixed Platforms Located on the Continental Shelf,* done at Rome on March 10, 1988; *.International Convention for the Suppression of Terrorist Bombings,* adopted by the General Assembly of the United Nations on December 15, 1997; *International Convention for the Suppression of the Financing of Terrorism,* adopted by the General Assembly of the United Nations on December 9, 1999.

CHAPTER 2

Setting the Stage II: Concepts and General Principles

International criminal law forms a subset of public international law. In Chapter 1 we differentiated international criminal law (ICL) from traditional international public law by emphasizing both the nature of the obligations and the "subjects" addressed by the two branches of the law. Traditional international public law has states as its subjects; that is, normally it specifies the rights and responsibilities of one state toward another. The persons responsible for carrying out the duties and asserting the rights are the appropriate officers of the state as designated by its internal political arrangements. From the standpoint of international law, these rights and duties do not entail personal responsibility for those designated officials in the sense that a violation would entail penal sanctions. In contrast, international criminal law places responsibility directly upon the individual. Violation of an obligation has a potential penal sanction attached for the person who commits the act.

More important, unlike traditional international law, subject to certain explicit procedural requirements being met, crimes considered part of ICL *may* involve universal jurisdiction. This explains why a Spanish court, in theory, could issue a warrant for Augusto Pinochet or a French court could possibly issue a warrant for Henry Kissinger or Donald Rumsfeld (Chapter 1) for crimes committed outside normal Spanish or French jurisdiction.[1] We discuss universal jurisdiction in more detail later in this chapter. Remember also that some offenses are part of both sets of rules and hence may entail sanctions against both the state (i.e., may engage state responsibility) and specific individuals.[2]

In Chapter 1, we also made a distinction between international criminal law (genocide, crimes against humanity) and transnational (transborder) crimes such as trafficking in drugs, the slave trade, piracy, terrorism and human smuggling. This book discusses both, but most commentators now emphasize the difference between the two. Note that until the emergence of the ad hoc international courts in the 1990s, writers tended to define *international criminal law* as that part of a state's legal code that dealt with transnational crimes.[3] This reflected the simple fact that over time, as states moved to attach criminal liability to certain categories of acts, they left implementation in terms of prosecution and punishment to national courts, rather than establishing new international institutions. This new distinction has resulted in the anomaly that many crimes, such as piracy and engaging in the international slave trade, that once defined international criminal law now fall into the transnational law category.

This relatively new distinction also illustrates the rapidly evolving nature of the field. Hence textbooks and other materials written before the year 2000 may still adhere to the old definition. Some writers have also used the term "supranational law in development" to describe international criminal law.[4] This implies that international criminal law would be an overarching law above states, rather than law created by and among states. While suggestive of an ideal, the term *supranational* does not reflect either the nature of the institutions associated with international criminal law or the nature of the law they apply. None of the current international courts—ICTY (former Yugoslavia), ICTR (Rwanda), ICC, SCSL (Sierra Leone), STC (Cambodia), and ICC (International Criminal Court—qualify as "supranational" institutions. The rules these courts apply are still best described as agreement among states, not as something hierarchically superior. Moreover, their authority flows from agreements among states (statutes) that specify their scope of jurisdiction in terms of time and space. Even though, in actual practice, the distinction matters only to professionals actively engaged in the practice of international criminal law and those who aspire to practice international criminal law, the reader needs to be aware of the difference.

Thus, from a narrow technical viewpoint, an "international crime" (and hence international criminal law) now refers to violations that fall under the jurisdiction of an international court. "International crimes" presumably reflect violation of values fundamental to all members of the international community. For example, the Rome Statute of the International Criminal Court (ICC) uses the phrase "the most serious crimes of concern to the international community as a whole."[5] Confusion may occur because few of the conventions (treaties) that define international criminal offenses use the term "international crime."[6] In contrast, transnational crimes generally fall solely under the jurisdiction of national courts. For example, with respect to the prohibitions against piracy and the slave trade, international law requires that each state pass appropriate laws and take appropriate action to suppress the practices. Though clearly both piracy and the slave trade have international dimensions, no current international court has jurisdiction to try individuals for alleged acts that violate the prohibitions. Alleged offenders are tried before national courts. The same holds true for international acts of terrorism and drug trafficking. Hence, transnational law includes a focus on domestic criminal law as well as on mechanisms for interstate cooperation, such as extended jurisdiction and extradition.

Finally, protecting human rights serves as the principle purpose of international criminal law, but this observation requires a caution. Not all violations of human rights are violations of ICL. In fact, many serious violations of human rights may not fall directly under international law.[7] ICL serves as the highest, and perhaps last, resort when all other national and international mechanisms have failed. Even then, *enforcement* depends on many other contingencies.

Defining a Crime in International Law

From these last comments, the next question becomes what criteria determine a *crime* under international law, as opposed to a less serious breach. We suggest three operational tests.[8] The conduct must meet these criteria:

1. It must threaten international peace and security in a major way; that is, it harms either internationally protected individuals or fundamental interests; and,
2. It must constitute actions shockingly offensive to the "conscience of humanity;" or
3. It must constitute actions that, because of their transnational character, require a response that embodies a collective decision to prevent or suppress by the international community.

While test number three may seem open-ended, the political necessity of gaining broad international consent to any prohibition acts as a very real control on expanding the scope of ICL. Bassiouni lists 28 different categories, but general agreement exists only on the most serious crimes: piracy, slavery, war crimes, crimes against peace, crimes against humanity, genocide, and torture. This list does not constitute an exhaustive catalog of international crimes but rather is meant to highlight those considered most serious.[9]

Some Practical Problems

As a relatively new branch of law, international criminal law suffers from a very high political content that produces vague definitions and inconsistent enforcement. The experience after World War I provides a good illustration of the problems. Great Britain and the other Allied powers pressed for war crime trials after World War I, with very disappointing results.[10] The United States had little interest in the British effort to bring the Kaiser and other high officials of the Central Powers (Germany and its allies) to trial. Resisting the urge to punish those deemed responsible for the war, the arguments of the U.S. delegation in opposing trials are interesting and worth noting because they illustrates both some important political judgments, as well as some practical legal difficulties. The U.S. delegation had three main objections:

1. The uncertainty of the law to be administered—what constituted the "laws of humanity?"
2. The inclusion of heads of states in the proposed indictment;
3. The creation of the tribunal ex post facto (after the fact); that is, those being tried would not have been subject to its jurisdiction when the offenses were allegedly committed.[11]

The Japanese delegation also opposed the trials, noting:

> Our scruples become still greater when it is a question of indicting before a
> tribunal thus constituted highly placed enemies on the sole ground that they
> abstained from preventing, putting an end to, or repressing acts of violations
> of the law and customs of war.[12]

From a legal standpoint, both the U.S. and the Japanese positions reflect what
had become a basic tenet of a shared understanding of legal process, whether
domestic or international: *nullum crimen, nulla poena sine praevia lege poenali.*
Simply translated, the Latin maxim says that there can be no crime (*nullum
crimen*), and thus no penalty (*nulla poena*) without a previously existing law
specifying crime and punishment (*sine praevia lege poenali*). We find this idea in
Article 1.9 of the U.S. Constitution, which prohibits Congress from passing ex
post facto (after the fact) laws. We find this explicitly stated in the contemporary era in Article 22(1) of the Rome Statute of the International Criminal Court
(ICC): "A person shall not be criminally responsible under this Statute unless
the conduct in question constitutes at the time it takes place, a crime within the
jurisdiction of the Court."[13]

The Japanese and U.S. positions also rested upon the premise of traditional
international law that responsibility was collective, not individual. They believed
that, at the onset of World War I, no rules of international law provided for individual criminal liability for the resort to war. The proposed charges were totally ex
post facto. Nonetheless, despite the U.S. and Japanese objections, Article 227 of the
Treaty of Versailles created a court of five appointed judges to try the ex-emperor
of Germany for "a supreme offense against international morality and the sanctity
of treaties." The trial never happened because Kaiser Wilhelm found asylum in the
Netherlands. The Dutch government refused to surrender him for trial.

The Allied powers also submitted to the German governments a list of 854
names of individuals alleged to have committed prosecutable offenses. The
list included Germany's most prominent military leaders during World War I:
Moltke, Hindenburg, Ludendorff, and Tirpitz. The Allies faced a problem. Unlike that in World War II, when the Allies occupied a defeated Germany, the
surrender in World War I did not include occupation of Germany. Even as a
defeated power, the German government vigorously resisted the request. The
Allies had little desire to renew hostilities in order to secure their demands. The
list of 854 people was eventually reduced to 45, of whom 12 actually went to
trial before the German Supreme Court on charges narrowly based upon the law
of war (*jus in bello*). Only six were found guilty.[14] No individual stood trial for the
act of initiating and prosecuting the war. Indeed, Hindenberg served as president
of Germany from 1925 until his death in 1934. The verdicts and aftermath are
more thoroughly discussed in Chapter 6.

The experience of World War I does not stand in isolation. Questions of politics, law, and legitimacy in terms of enforcement continue. Many characterized

the Nuremberg and Tokyo trials after World War II as victor's justice because of the ad hoc (not permanent) and post hoc (after the fact) nature of the court and questions concerning the validity of the law the Tribunals applied.[15] Slobodan Milošević argued that the ICTY as a post hoc and ad hoc tribunal had no legitimate authority over him.[16] These objections aside, the International Military Tribunal at Nuremberg after World War II and its counterpart in Tokyo still stand as the pivotal moments in terms of defining international criminal law as a possibility under international law. Yet it took the establishment of the ad hoc tribunals for the former Yugoslavia and Rwanda in the 1990s to validate the emergence of international criminal law as more than a collection of idealistic aspirations.

Problems of Definition and Evolution

At present, international criminal law does not constitute a coherent legal code. ICL has not evolved in a logical or consistent way. Bassiouni observes that "it has developed in bits and pieces through different experiences which may or may not be linked to one another."[17] Moreover, treaties (and certainly customary law) are often vague and incomplete. They lack specificity with respect to the objective and subjective elements that determine criminality. Without going too far into technical explanations, I point out that simply making certain actions an offense under international law marks only the first step. Treaties and customary law may contain prohibitions against certain battlefield actions, such as deliberate attacks on civilians, but fail to define other essential elements necessary to turn a prohibition into an enforceable rule. They may not explain what specific acts under what specific circumstances fall under the prohibition. Furthermore, the relevant law may fail to define what consequences should follow from specific violations or to elaborate the important procedural elements necessary for prosecution.[18] Many treaties lack any provisions for enforcement at all, leaving it to states essentially to "fill in the blanks" if they choose to do so.

No international police force exists as an independent agency charged with investigating and prosecuting violations. Enforcement still depends upon the will of individual states to take action. Apart from the newly formed International Criminal Court (ICC), no other permanent international criminal tribunals exist. The ad hoc courts established under the auspices of the United Nations, the ICTY, ICTR, SCSL, and STC have limited jurisdiction in terms of time frames, territoriality, and defined crimes, as well as a limited institutional life. They cannot try alleged crimes that fall outside their constitutive charters. Even though it is a permanent court, the ICC also must operate within the terms of the Rome Statute, the treaty that defines its competence with regard to substantive law. Even more interesting, neither the authorizing resolutions for the ad hoc international courts nor the Rome Statute of the ICC contain a scale of penalties. They grant authorization to try certain crimes committed under certain circumstances but then do not deal with appropriate punishment for those who might be found guilty.

To complicate matters further, only 105 states have ratified (joined) the regime established by the ICC. Note, in contrast, that the membership of the United Nations currently stands at 202 states. This means that only slightly more than half of the UN membership have accepted the ICC as a valid institution. Moreover, three of the five permanent member of the UN Security Council—Russia, China, and the United States—have not ratified the Rome Statute establishing the ICC. Interestingly, all three have ratified the Genocide Convention, a crime included within the definition of the ICC's competence (jurisdiction). Indeed, a total of 133 states have ratified the Genocide Convention. This leads to an anomalous situation. The United States, Russia, and China may formally agree that genocide constitutes an international crime and that genocide has occurred in a specific case but then also agree that no appropriate venue, that is, a tribunal with authority and jurisdiction to try individuals so accused, may exist. Indeed, that fact alone explains the genesis of the current ad hoc tribunals.

Politics Often Rules

The evolution and elaboration of international criminal law have been very slow for many reasons. In view of our discussion, we need to examine the question of what inhibits states from undertaking action in response to obvious violations of international criminal law. A simple set of answers suffices here. Four factors condition state responses to perceived violations:

1. Assumptions about sovereignty and the prerogatives associated with it;
2. Perceptions of possible reciprocal action. Vattel's golden rule of sovereigns holds that "no one can complain when he is treated as he has treated others";
3. The expenditure of scarce resources on something not seen as a core part of national interest; and,
4. Sensitivity to charges of "victor's justice."

First, the sovereign state still forms the most important element in any effort to enforce international law. The "hard shell" idea of sovereignty, often reinforced by strong feelings of nationalism, still exerts a powerful pull. There is a fundamental tension between evolving human rights regimes that assert that all human beings have certain minimum rights and the idea that the relationship between a government and its subjects and citizens is solely a matter of domestic, not international, concern.

Second, statesmen intuitively understand the idea expressed in the old adage "What is sauce for the goose is sauce for the gander." Intervention in the internal affairs of others might invite criticism and justify, in turn, intervention by others into one's own affairs. For example, a century and a half ago, in a remarkably prescient statement directed at the avidness with which certain congressmen advocated overt support for Louis Kossuth, the leader of the Hungarian revolution, Henry Clay eloquently pointed out the quandary inherent in an active interventionist human rights policy. He noted: that, in undertaking such ventures, the United States would expose itself "to the reaction of foreign Powers, who, when they see us assuming to judge of their conduct, will undertake in their turn to judge of our conduct."[19]

In similar vein, Professor Louis Sohn, in his testimony before Congress concerning possible ratification of the International Covenant on Civil and Political Rights by the United States, said:

> I think on the one hand we always say to everybody else that our standards are higher than those of anyone else; but we will discover if we are subject to international supervision, that there are some skeletons in our closet and they will be paraded in public, and we do not like that idea.[20]

Sohn's observation certainly rang true when the accusations of Wally Bacre Ndiye, a Senegalese jurist, led to the United States' having to defend the use of the death penalty before the UN Human Rights Commission. Needless to say, many U.S. officials were outraged. Senator Jesse Helms, then Chair of the Senate Committee on Foreign Relations, wrote a heated letter to UN Ambassador Bill Richardson in which he asked:

> Bill, is this man confusing the United States with some other country, or is this an intentional insult to the US and our nation's legal system? . . . It is clear that Mr. Ndiaye's strange "investigation" is intended to be merely a platform for more outrageous accusations from U.S. critics at the United Nations.[21]

After the establishment of the ICTY, questions of personnel, funding, and arrest of those accused plagued operations. Consider also our discussion and examples in Chapter 1, particularly the response of Henry Kissinger to the idea of universal jurisdiction and the attempts to have President George W. Bush and former Secretary of Defense Donald Rumsfeld arrested. A recent commentary on international humanitarian law noted: "But the vast armature of international humanitarian law has stood largely mute, palsied in part by the fear of most national governing elites . . . that the glare of such attention might one day be turned on their own actions."[22]

Third, enforcement requires expenditures of resources, both tangible, in the form of manpower, matériel, and money, and intangible, in the sense of reputation and public support. For governments, immediate self-interest tends to override arguments based upon the good of the international community. Rhetorical support for peace, nondiscrimination, and other human rights values comes easily, but rhetoric and reality often clash when circumstances require intervention to address a major breach of "community" obligations such as the ongoing situation in Darfur (Sudan). A response in that situation would necessitate a major commitment of resources to a problem that does not directly affect the self-interest of states outside the immediate area. This explains the reluctance of states to engage in Bosnia and Rwanda in a timely fashion. Judge Antonio Casssese concludes that

"A strong reaction by States to these breaches presupposes the existence of a community interest to put a stop to them. However, the community interest in their fulfillment remains potential rather than real."[23]

Fourth, the charges of victor's justice have found resonance in that application in terms of prosecution seems to happen only to individuals from smaller, weaker states.[24] From this perspective, critics assert that Henry Kissinger, Robert McNamara, Tony Blair, Donald Rumsfeld, Madeline Albright, and others enjoy immunity from prosecution for their alleged crimes only because they were fortunate enough to be agents for very powerful countries. Advocates argue that, when major states are involved, "what is sauce for the goose" is *never* "sauce for the gander" because the rich and powerful can impose their will and judgment on the weak with little fear that others will call them to account for their own misdeeds.

Fifth, other national policies and legislation may inhibit application. Policies of amnesty may preclude international action.[25] Statutes of limitations and grants of immunity may further impede international action. These need not be absolute bars, but they do raise additional hurdles. Occasionally, international courts have considered the national legislation as invalid because it contravened rights guaranteed by international human rights law. This occurred recently (2001) in the *Barrios Altos*[26] case before the Inter-American Court of Human Rights. The court concluded that self-amnesty laws are "manifestly incompatible" with the aims and spirit of the Convention because they "lead to the defenselessness of victims and perpetuate impunity."

At this point, one may wonder, why bother? The answer lies in looking at what has been accomplished and understanding that progress depends upon evolution rather than revolution. The *Barrios Altos* decision stands as proof. Thirty years ago, most knowledgeable observers of the international scene would have rejected out of hand the idea that a Pol Pot or an Idi Amin might stand trial for their alleged crimes. Those who advocated international action to deal with the slaughter in Cambodia and Uganda were seen as idealistic dreamers. Proposals for an International Criminal Court date from 1947. Yet, what a difference 30 years makes. Slobodan Milošević, among others, was arrested and put on trial before the International Criminal Tribunal for Yugoslavia (ICTY) for crimes allegedly committed during the conflicts associated with the disintegration of the former Yugoslavia. Although many years after the fact, the United Nations has created a Special Tribunal for Cambodia to prosecute leaders of the Khmer Rouge for their participation in the mass killings that occurred under the Pol Pot regime.[27] Progress at the international level always relies upon a blend of idealism—what ought to be—tempered by pragmatism—what may be possible at the time.

Sources of International Criminal Law

From whence do *international* legal obligations spring? States do not belong to an international legislature that enacts laws for the "society of states." If no international legislature exists, the question of how one can speak of international law is a valid one. Traditional international law and international criminal law share some common sources. As a body of rules, ICL represents a hybrid. It draws both upon the evolving human rights regime at the international level and, much more than traditional international law, upon domestic (municipal) legal codes and practice. Municipal courts have played a much greater role in the evolution of international criminal law than in the development of traditional international law. The difficulty for students and practitioners stems from the simple fact that international criminal law does not embody a universal, unified, systematic legal code. Even so, international criminal law still comes primarily from the same *sources* as traditional international law. For our purposes, we begin with Article 38(1) of the Statute of the International Court of Justice, which identifies two major sources of international law and three subsidiary possibilities for determining relevant rules of law when the two major sources offer incomplete guidance. Article 38(1) authorizes the ICJ to apply:

1. *International conventions* (treaties), whether general or particular, that establish rules expressly recognized by the contesting states;
2. *International custom,* as evidence of a general practice accepted as law;
3. The general principles of law recognized by civilized nations;
4. Judicial decisions, and the
5. Teachings of the most highly qualified publicists (writers) (subject to the provisions of Article 59).[28]

The list represents a hierarchy of preference. Judges first look at treaties to see if a clear rule exists. Lawyers and judges prefer to deal with treaties because they are evidence of explicit agreement.[29] As we discussed, treaty provisions may be vague or incomplete from the standpoint of providing explicit guidance. In this case, judges examine the customary law, that is, the rules derived from state practice. Almost all states, even those subscribing to the civil code model of law (Chapter 1), recognize the existence of international customary law The problem here is that no authoritative guide to how judges should proceed in determining "state practice," the fundamental element of custom, exist. Ironically, as we shall see, the practice of civil code states has played a great role in the evolution of the customary law relevant to international criminal law. Note that another problem surfaces here.

Whether a rule derives from custom or treaty, a fundamental *procedural* rule comes into play. With one exception, *a state is bound only by those rules to which it has given its consent.* This clearly differentiates international law from domestic law. The one exception is a category of laws termed *jus cogens,* or rules so widely accepted or fundamental that no state may ignore them or attempt to contract out of them through treaties or objection. The resort to force except in self-defense, the rule that validates treaties (*pacta sunt servanda*—treaties must be observed), and rules against genocide and participation in the slave trade are generally cited as examples of *jus cogens.*

Treaties The various processes that produce multilateral treaties, such as the UN Charter, as explicit and deliberate agreements between or among states constitute the closest parallel to a legislative function at the international level. For that reason, one often sees multilateral treaties of this nature described as *law-making* treaties. For the purposes of this discussion the most important feature of treaty law comes from the simple fact that a particular treaty regime applies only to those states that have formally signed (states party) *and* ratified the agreement or later *acceded* to it.

After the final text is approved, either through a separate conference or by the General Assembly of the United Nations, a multilateral treaty is normally open for signature for a specified period of time. *Signature alone does not constitute consent.* Formal consent requires the additional stage of *ratification* after signature. If a state has not signed a treaty, it may grant consent through *accession.* Modern multilateral treaties usually have a provision that keeps the treaty "open for signature" for a specified period of time. After the specified period for signature ends, if a state has not signed, it may give its consent through accession. Accession has the same legal effect as ratification. The treaty enters into force when a specific number of ratifications or instruments of accession (normally specified in the text of the treaty) have been deposited with the appropriate office of the United Nations. For example, Article 126 of the Rome Statute of the International Criminal Court required that the court would come into being when 60 states had deposited instruments of ratification or accession.[30]

Returning to an earlier point, ICL treaties lack a uniform approach to the problems addressed. In part, this can be attributed to the disjointed and lengthy process of development. Drafters in different eras have different ideas about what is necessary and what is possible. Progress in the international milieu requires a productive interaction of idealism and pragmatism. Without idealism to set goals that transcend the demands of the immediate defined by the narrow self-interest of particular states, the essential exchanges in political interaction would remain on the most elemental level. Without a leavening dialectic with the "art of the possible"—the traditions gleaned from conservative statesmanship and experience—ideals would remain undeveloped, ethereal, and isolated from political experience. The tension between the two, reflected in the ebb and flow of decisions, ensures that the mix at any specific time will never fully satisfy advocates of either position. Yet any idea of progress must take into account both. Progress depends upon the development and application of new ideas and approaches. The practical statesman attempts to adapt these to changing circumstances by grafting them to rootstock gleaned from those practices deemed useful and successful in the past. Considering this, not surprisingly, political circumstances do seemingly generate attempts to deal with perceived threats. Aggression and genocide since World War II and narcotics and terrorism in the 1970s and 1980s serve as the most salient examples.[31]

Building on an earlier point, because diplomats and political officials, not lawyers, tend to have the responsibility of drafting and securing approval of various conventions, these almost always fall short of the ideal advocated by reformers. Even if lawyers review or do draft the text, one must never lose sight of the fact that ratification and accession involve a political process. Bassiouni points out:

> [I]n the area of regulation of armed conflict, the largest number of instruments on aggression . . . were developed during approximately the same time span. But their penal characteristics vary significantly. The main reason for this is that aggression is regarded as a crime with significantly greater political content than a war crime. . . . [A]ggression involves the responsibility of heads of state and governments and senior government officials, while war crime do not necessarily involve such personalities.[32]

This explains why no correlation exists between the nature of the subject matter and the number of relevant instruments.[33] Perceived seriousness of the crime does not necessarily mean more "legislation." Bassiouni has identified 281 conventions (treaties) covering 28 categories of criminal behavior. Seventy of these deal with war crimes, 54 with aggression. Although the treaties that set up the ICTY, the ICTR, and the ICC have included language defining genocide for the purposes of the tribunal, there is still only one general international agreement that deals with genocide.[34]

Still, given the number of treaties, the 1907 Hague Conventions, the Nuremberg Charter of the IMT, the four 1949 Geneva Conventions[35] and their additional protocols, the Genocide Convention, and the Rome Statute of the International Criminal Court are the essential documents that define the scope and content of contemporary ICL. While other treaties have sought to regulate or prohibit certain weapons (chemical, biological),[36] prohibit the use of child soldiers,[37] and eliminate the use of mercenaries,[38] these define specific crimes within the broader framework established by the core documents.

Custom Custom represents another relevant source of international law. Until shortly after the end of the 19th century, customary rules constituted the bulk of accepted general international law. Stating that an obligation rests upon custom means that no formal legal code specifies the obligations. Custom flows from what states do and from their justification for their actions (what they say). By definition, a customary rule must have two distinct elements: (1) a material element defined by *systematic practice* over time; and (2) a psychological element, the *opinio juris* or evidence that states, that is, the relevant government officials, believe the practice to be a legal obligation. Observed repeated practice by itself does not offer sufficient evidence of the existence of a rule of customary law. A customary norm represents a usage or practice that has a definite legal obligation attached to it. The psychological element, opinion juris, distinguishes a customary norm from *comity* or practices that represent good manners but that are not obligatory. To apply a rule of customary law, the court must first establish the rule, and then determine if the state has consented to the rule.

To illustrate these points, consider the opinion of the ICJ in the *Nicaragua* case:

> It is not to be expected that in the practice of States the application of the rules in question should have been perfect. . . . The Court does not consider that, for a rule to be established as customary, the corresponding practice must be in absolutely rigorous conformity with the rule. . . . [T]he Court deems it sufficient that the conduct of States should, *in general* be consistent with such rules, and that instances of state conduct inconsistent with a given rule should *generally* have been treated as breaches of that rule, not as indications of the recognition of a new rule.[39]

Needless to say, proving intent can be very difficult.[40]

Relationship between Treaties and Customary Law

To complicate the seemingly clear distinction between the two sources, some treaties have as their aim the codification of customary law.[41] These treaties seek to provide a definitive statement of obligations within certain regimes, such as that associated with diplomatic relations. The existence of a treaty that seeks to codify customary law does not totally supplant the customary regime. A state may not have signed and ratified such a treaty, but it still may be subject to the customary law the treaty seeks to codify. Still, if such a treaty has entered into force, states seeking to prove a rule may cite the treaty as one element of evidence of the rule even against states that have not accepted the treaty. The plaintiffs must then, however, also adduce proof that the nonsignatory state has consented to the customary rule in question.

General Principles of Law General principles of law recognized by civilized nations form the third source of international law. Today the expression "civilized nations" represents an artifact from an earlier era. The meaning and scope of "general principles of law" have generated extensive discussion. Most modern writers appear to regard general principles of law as a secondary source of international law, possibly helpful on occasion. When the Committee of Jurists included this source into the Statute of the Permanent Court of International Justice, in 1920, they offered several interpretations of its meaning, but the best relates to purpose. Inclusion of this provision would seem to avoid the chance that the court might fail to hand down a decision because no positive applicable rule existed. In the absence of a clear rule, the phrase *general principles* presumably would enable the court to go outside the generally accepted sources of international law and draw on relevant principles common to various domestic legal systems.[42] The exact scope of what this might include has formed the substance of continued scholarly debate, but the bulk of the opinion tends toward a very conservative interpretation—that general principles encompass only those applied by a great many states. Article 21.1(c) of the ICC Statute permits the court, when necessary, to apply:

> general principles of law derived by the Court from national laws of legal systems of the world, including as appropriate the national laws of States that would normally exercise jurisdiction over the crime, provided that those principles are not inconsistent with [the] Statute and with international law and internationally recognized norms and standards.

Importance of General Principles of Law

In the very first case heard by the ICJ, the *Corfu Channel* dispute, the court alluded to the use of circumstantial evidence as being admissible "in all systems of law."[43] To come to a meaningful decision in the *Barcelona Traction Case*,[44] which concerned the status of a privately held power company forced into bankruptcy by the Spanish government, the ICJ had to rely heavily on the domestic legal definition of a corporation as a limited liability company because nothing equivalent or parallel in the way of institutions or law existed at the international level.

With that said, general principles of law play a much greater role in international criminal law than in traditional international law. As we have noted, ICL treaties (let alone ICL customary law) leave many essential elements necessary to mount a prosecution or defense undefined. Conventions use imprecise language such as "grave breaches," "inhuman acts," "torture," and "persecution" without definitions of the specific elements that make up the crime. For example, no ICL treaty contains specific penalties for violations. Judges in the ICTY and other international tribunals have had to search national legislation for appropriate parallels. Even so, judges tend toward conservatism (in the narrow dictionary sense of the term). ICTY decisions provide some excellent illustrations. The Trial Court in the *Furundžija Case* faced the problem of defining rape as part of the more generic category of war crimes and crimes against humanity.[45] It found a set of specific elements common to definitions in most legal systems.[46]

Judicial Decisions We have already mentioned two ways in which judicial decisions may play a part as a source of international law—as *part* of the evidence to establish a customary rule in specific disputes and as *evidence* of general principles of law in application. In either instance, judges and courts *do not make* law; they interpret it. Sir Robert Jennings noted:

> This provision I understand as a necessary recognition that judges, whether national or international, are not empowered to make new laws. Of course we all know that interpretation does, and indeed should, have a creative element in adapting rules to new situations and needs. . . . Nevertheless, the principle that judges are not empowered to make new law is a basic principle of the process of adjudication.[47]

Moreover, as a reminder, the opinions of one court in one country, no matter how powerful, cannot directly modify existing rules or spawn new ones. The questions here primarily relate to the relative weight given to decisions by national courts and arbitral tribunals in contrast with those of international courts.

Publicists The writings of publicists—the works of text writers and other private commentators—represent a subsidiary source of international law. In past centuries the work of the publicist has had great importance. The writings of Grotius, Gentili, Vattel, and other notables in the history of the law has played a vital part in the growth of international law. Today, no judge willingly turns to a text to find the relevant rules, and no text writer or commentator creates international law, regardless of his or her professional eminence. Today these writings serve primarily as a means for determining varying interpretations of the law. In reading various commentators, one often runs across the phrase "the law in action versus the law in books," meant to suggest that scholars of the law may have a rather idealized version of what the law requires. At most, outstanding writers may state what the law is in their own time, may provide information on its historical development, and may speculate on and advocate future developments. To the extent that their government may adopt their suggestions and utilize them in the development of a usage or incorporate them in a law-making treaty concluded with a number of other states, the writer may be regarded as an indirect source of international law. The most striking modern example of a publicist's influence on the development of new rules of law has been the work of Rafael Lemkin, who, through his work, contributed materially to the framing of the Convention on Genocide by the United Nations. Lemkin coined the term *genocide*.[48] Nonetheless, it took concerted action by governments to create the legal regime governing the crime.

Jurisdiction

Before we discuss the principles of legality and the elements of legal regulation, we must briefly deal with jurisdiction. Jurisdiction, or an equivalent concept, forms a fundamental structural element common to all legal systems. As with many concepts, it has many different facets. In a narrow sense, and the one most often used, jurisdiction refers to the difference of specific function or scope of competence among courts and law enforcement agencies. It is the allocation of legal authority among various agencies and institutions to perform certain duties or to regulate certain categories of persons, events, and things. In international law, questions of jurisdiction form a fundamental consideration because of the assumptions that flow from the idea of sovereignty.

Perhaps the easiest illustration of this aspect of jurisdiction flows from the U.S. Constitution. The Constitution divides legal authority between the federal government and the states. The Congress of the United States has the authority to legislate with regard to certain areas; other are reserved explicitly to the legislatures of the 50 states. Jurisdiction affects the scope of institutions. We see this in the court system, where certain courts hear only cases concerning certain subject matter. So we have traffic courts, courts that hear misdemeanors, courts that hear felonies, and courts that deal only with appeals from courts lower in the hierarchy.

Jurisdiction also has a territorial component. Traffic courts operate only for offenses committed within their scope of territorial competence, whether city or county. Courts in Georgia cannot hear cases from Alabama or Florida. Similarly, laws passed by the Georgia General Assembly do not apply to citizens of Alabama or Florida unless they happen to be within the territorial limits of Georgia. Agents of law enforcement at all levels operate within specific territorial parameters in terms of international boundaries. Although sometimes informal arrangements exist, U.S. authorities may not physically cross over into Canada or Mexico to retrieve a person accused of violating U.S. law even if the violation occurred on U.S. territory.[49]

For the purposes of this book, we are interested in the jurisdiction to legislate and the jurisdiction to enforce. We also examine questions relating to the jurisdiction (competence) of international and national courts. At the international level, the authority to legislate and the authority to enforce may not be co-extensive. In certain circumstances, states have the right to pass appropriate legislation because of the nature of the crime but may not have the right to take direct enforcement measures in the sense of sending agents to arrest the perpetrator. The United States has the right to pass legislation prohibiting the counterfeiting of its currency no matter where it occurs. If the counterfeiter resides in the United Kingdom, the United States does not have the right to send its own agents to deal with the problem.

A simple principle underlies the fundamental principles of international jurisdiction—that an effective link must exist between the act or the actor and the state claiming jurisdiction. With respect to international courts, the questions involve the specific allocation of authority given to each specific court by the states party to the instrument establishing it. We cover this aspect of jurisdiction in the introduction to Chapter 3. Five principles form the basis for asserting jurisdiction at the international level. The sequence of discussion indicates a hierarchy of importance.

Territorial

Nationality (active personality)

Protective

Passive Personality

Universal

These five are not separate and exclusive. They may result in concurrent claims. Concurrent claims occur when two states assert a right to prosecute on the basis of two valid assertions of a legitimate effective connection. For example, if a French national commits a crime while in Germany, Germany has an absolute right to try and punish on the basis of territoriality. France could also assert a right based upon nationality. This would potentially become an issue only if the accused were to leave Germany after the crime and both states sought extradition or if the accused were to return to France and Germany then sought extradition.

Territorial Principle

Every country has the right to prescribe and enforce rules of behavior within its own physical boundaries. The territorial principle ranks at the top of the hierarchy because it derives directly from the twin ideas of sovereign control and equality (reciprocal recognition of sovereign prerogatives) of states in terms of rights and obligations. Aircraft and ships have nationality, but that connection may qualify as "territory" in certain circumstances (on or over the high seas, for one) and for certain purposes (e.g., marriage, birth, crimes committed on board). Some acts can generate concurrent territorial claims because elements of the crime occurred in both states. For example, if someone were to mail a letter bomb to someone in the United States from another country, both states would have a territorial claim. The country in which the missive originated would have subjective territorial jurisdiction. The country where the actual injury occurred would have objective territorial jurisdiction. The subjective territorial principle gives states the authority to prescribe laws for actions that begin within national territory but have harmful effects outside. The objective territorial principle permits states to legislate for acts that occur outside its territory but have effects within it; that is, in some circumstances, states do have a right to enact legislation that has *extraterritorial* reach.

Nationality Principle

Nationality is the second important basis for international jurisdiction.[50] Within some limits, international law permits each state to establish the criteria for acquiring nationality. States have the absolute right to change their own laws defining nationality at any time they choose so long as those changes do not violate the minimal standards accepted by the international community A sovereign state may legislate the activities of its own nationals in any way it chooses so long as its laws do not conflict with the sovereign prerogatives of another state or, increasingly, human rights law. States may enforce their own penal code against their own nationals even when the offenses have been committed abroad.

Normally individuals may acquire nationality in three ways: (1) through *jus soli* (of the soil), by being born within state territory; (2) through *jus sanguinis* (literally, through blood), by having a parent who is a national; and (3) through naturalization, by electing to take another nationality. Other possible ways are adoption and change in status of territory. For example, during the 19th and

20th centuries, when Alsace-Lorraine passed from France to Germany and back to France, the nationality of the residents changed with each transfer. Individuals may have dual nationality because these principles are not mutually exclusive.[51] United States law includes both *jus soli* and *jus sanguinis* as the basis for acquiring U.S. nationality.

Protective Principle

The protective principle comes into play when acts committed by aliens abroad endanger the security, credit, political independence, or territorial integrity of a country.[52] Jurisdiction flows from the nature of the interests injured. Fundamentally, the argument for extending jurisdiction is based upon the idea of self-defense. Most states use this principle in some form. An example would be U.S. laws that prohibit the counterfeiting of U.S. currency by individuals in other countries.

Passive Personality Principle

In contrast to the national (active personality) principle, which permits states to seek jurisdiction over nationals who commit crimes abroad, the passive personality principle permits states to claim jurisdiction over individuals (regardless of nationality) who commit crimes against their nationals abroad.[53] Until the mid-1980s, the United States did not recognize this as a valid principle. Attitudes changed because of several high-profile terrorist incidents such as the Rome airport massacre and the Achille Lauro hijacking, in which U.S. citizens were killed or injured. In 1986, the U.S. Congress enacted the *Omnibus Diplomatic Security and Terrorism* statute,[54] which specifically authorizes use of passive personality under certain limited circumstances. Even so, this principle is not widely used.

Universality Principle

This principle forms the basis of much of the evolving international criminal law regime. Yet it is still a principle that is controversial and still in development. Stephen Macedo offers a worthwhile cautionary note here: "simply because certain offenses are universally condemned does not mean that a state may exercise universal jurisdiction over them."[55] Bassiouni identifies three different possibilities in application:

1. Universal reach of national jurisdiction (piracy), though authorized by international law;
2. Extraterritorial reach of national jurisdiction (Pinochet case);
3. Universal reach of international adjudication (ICC).[56]

Much of the debate about this principle stems from the fear of abuse, not from the presumed utility of the principle. Could the powerful or the merely malicious use this principle as a political tool to go after their presumed enemies? Were the warrants sought for Rumsfeld and Kissinger based upon valid, objective legal criteria or were they efforts by those opposed to U.S. policies to obtain political leverage? Given the potential variability of national laws granting universal jurisdiction, in the absence of precise definitions and safeguards victims may "forum shop" for the venue perceived as most favorably disposed to their complaints.[57]

The current scholarly debate focuses upon the difference between a narrow definition that requires that an accused individual be within the territory of the state asserting a right to jurisdiction and a wider concept that does not require "presence." This second definition is sometimes termed "pure" universal jurisdiction because the *nature of the crime* forms the sole basis for subject matter jurisdiction. Physical presence or other requirements do not come into play. We shall deal with these issues in the discussions of case law as they actually form matters of importance for courts.

Some Other Important Preliminary Considerations

As noted earlier, as a body of law in evolution, much of international criminal law lacks "legislative" specificity. This means that courts often have to resort to domestic law (general principles) to "fill in the blanks." Despite Judge Jennings's eloquent statement about the proper role of judges, the lack of specificity means that ICL contains a very large element of judge-made law (even without a strict doctrine of precedent) because of the need for detail to meet both the substantive and procedural requirements of application in practice (principles of criminal responsibility). Moral outrage and intuitive understandings do not automatically translate into effective legal regulation in the form of rules that can be applied consistently and fairly time after time. Note that, even in domestic law, new areas of regulation often require extensive periods of evolutionary development before appropriate standards become firmly established. To cite one recent example, policing commercial transactions on the Internet is an area still very much "under construction."[58]

The problem here can be easily illustrated by reference to the "general principles" in the statutes setting up the three ad hoc UN courts: the ICTY, the ICTR, and the SCSL. All three statutes contain almost identical language defining general principles.[59] Article 7 of the ICTY on international criminal responsibility provides:

1. A person who planned, instigated, ordered, committed or otherwise aided and abetted in the planning, preparation or execution of a crime referred to in articles 2 to 5 of the present Statute, shall be individually responsible for the crime.
2. The official position of any accused person, whether as Head of State or Government or as a responsible Government official, shall not relieve such person of criminal responsibility nor mitigate punishment.
3. The fact that any of the acts referred to in articles 2 to 5 of the present Statute was committed by a subordinate does not relieve his superior of criminal responsibility if

he knew or had reason to know that the subordinate was about to commit such acts or had done so and the superior failed to take the necessary and reasonable measures to prevent such acts or to punish the perpetrators thereof.

4. The fact that an accused person acted pursuant to an order of a Government or of a superior shall not relieve him of criminal responsibility, but may be considered in mitigation of punishment if the International Tribunal determines that justice so requires.[60]

Sections 1 deals with elements of participation. Sections 2, 3, and 4 deal with issues of liability that might be advanced as justifications for action. First, note how few principles the article addresses. Second, note the lack of detail in section 1. The statutes do not contain specific answers to a great many of the potential problems that come into play when a court is trying to define the context in which a criminal act occurred; nor do they contain specific guidance for judges on how to develop such rules.[61] Among other issues, how does one specifically define what constitutes planning, instigating, ordering, committing, or aiding and abetting? For example, does writing a single e-mail or blog on the Internet that says "I believe that all Boomerangians are animals and there should be an open season on hunting them" qualify as instigating? By what standards of determination? Consider that in the *Jelesić* case, the ICTY, in attempting to establish the special intent needed to define genocide, concluded that statements made by the defendant were those of a disturbed personality, not evidence of "an affirmed resolve to destroy in whole or in part a group as such."[62]

Objective and Subjective Elements of Definition

Legislative specificity means that substantive definitions of offenses must entail both a material element (objective or *actus res*) and a mental element (subjective or *mens rea*).[63] These two elements are sometimes characterized as *guilty act* and *guilty mind*. The two principles form the essence of criminal law. A guilty mind, by itself, does not have consequences unless it results in a guilty act. You may think what you wish so long as you do not act upon the thoughts in a way that violates the law. Like former President Jimmy Carter, you may "lust in your heart," but if no overt action considered a guilty act flows from that lusting, you may lust in peace without fear of prosecution.

In terms of the material element, minimum age, mental capacity, context, and the parameters that determine whether an act falls within the prohibited categories are important considerations. For example, within domestic law, minors ordinarily have a different status from adults and different expectations of legal consequence. The same holds for those who have diminished mental capacity. The mental element, intent, determines the nature of the offense in terms of severity. While killing another human being is prohibited in every society, intent determines the severity of the offense. Was the killing premeditated, committed in the heat of the moment, accidental, an act of insanity, or justifiable self-defense?

In making the determination about severity, prosecutors look at several operational tests. The following list, based upon principles drawn from western European and American legal codes, illustrates, in very condensed form, elements important to making decision about appropriate standards to apply to conduct:

1. Willfulness—intent to produce a certain result;
2. Recklessness—awareness of unjustifiable risk;
3. Culpable negligence—lack of attention (due diligence) to generally acceptable standards of conduct;
4. Negligence (sometimes inadvertent negligence)—unawareness of the risk of a course of action.

Establishing intent is not easy even within the domestic context. Normally, courts infer intent from circumstantial evidence and on the basis of the context and the nature of the act. As one Canadian Judge Advocate has argued, given human frailty and human perfidy, actions speak much louder than words.[64]

Other elements come into play, as well. Negligence includes both overt acts and *omissions,* or a failure to act when there exists a positive duty to do so. In cases where a crime involves more than one person, all who perform the same act have equal liability. The problems come when a crime involves many different people who perform different acts that contribute to a criminal enterprise. For, example, Article 7.1 of the ICTFY states that culpability may extend beyond actual participation to planning, encouraging, organizing (instigating), and promoting (aiding and abetting). This requires relatively detailed criteria (operational standards) to differentiate among these activities for the purpose of making appropriate judgments about the degree of liability. These are examined in context of the relevant case law.

Process and Procedure: Adversarial-Accusatorial and Inquisitorial Systems

Finally, we need to consider the process through which a court arrives at a verdict.[65] This derives from some fundamental assumptions about appropriate process. Common-law states such as the United States[66] and the United Kingdom base their procedures on the adversarial-accusatorial model. Civil code states, including most of Europe,[67] as well as Japan and China, base theirs upon the inquisitorial model. Procedures of international courts meld the two approaches. For example, in civil law procedure, officers of the court system collect the evidence for both sides, the court conducts the questioning of witnesses, and cross-examination by a defending counsel rarely occurs. Trials may or may not include juries. In some cases, hearsay evidence is permitted, as are trials *in absentia.* Defendants do not necessarily have a right to testify on their own behalf. In contrast, U.S. and British procedures permit each side to gather evidence, rely upon examination and cross-examination in open court as a method of establishing the facts, and confer on defendants the right to confront their accusers (limits the use of hearsay evidence) and to offer testimony on their own behalf. The elements of these systems are discussed more fully in Chapter 3.

Notes

1. See Stephen Macedo (ed.), *Universal Jurisdiction: National Courts and the Prosecution of Serious Crimes under International Law* (Philadelphia: University of Pennsylvania Press, 2004) for a discussion of the principles and problems involved with universal jurisdiction.

2. Because of space limitations, these questions are not treated in this book. A good example of the overlap is the Lockerbie case, in which an agent of Libya was convicted for his part in the bombing of Pan Am Flight 103 in December 1988. In addition to the individual conviction, both the United States and the United Kingdom made claims for compensation from Libya. See http://www.cnn.com/LAW/trials.and.cases/case.files/0010/lockerbie/.

3. Robert Cryer, Hakan Friman, Darryl Robinson, and Elizabeth Wilmshurst, *An Introduction to International Criminal Law* (Cambridge: Cambridge University Press, 2007), 3.

4. Roelof Haverman, Olga Kavran, and Julian Nicholls (eds.), *Supranational Criminal Law: A System Sui Generis* (Antwerp: Intersentia, 2003); Roelof Haverman and Olaluwa Olusanya (eds.), *Sentencing and Sanctioning in Supranational Criminal Law* (Antwerp: Intersentia, 2006).

5. Articles 1 and 5(1), *Rome Statute of the International Criminal Court,* http://www.icc-cpi.int/about.html.

6. M. Cherif Bassiouni, *Introduction to International Criminal Law* (Ardsley, NY: Transnational, 2003), 158–61.

7. See Salvatore Zappalà, *Human Rights in International Criminal Proceedings* (Oxford: Oxford University Press, 2003).

8. Bassiouni suggests five; *Introduction to International Criminal Law,* 115.

9. See Bassiouni, *Introduction to International Criminal Law,* 136–58, for an extensive list of offenses he regards as meriting the designation "crime under international law."

10. See Gary Bass, *Stay the Hand of Vengeance: The Politics of War Crimes Tribunals* (Princeton: Princeton University Press, 2000), Chapters 3, 4.

11. "Memorandum of Reservations Presented by the Representatives of the United States to the Report of the Commission on Responsibilities," *American Journal of International Law* 14 (1920): 144ff.

12. Japanese Statement in "Report of the Commission on the Responsibility of the Authors of the War and on the Enforcement of Penalties," *American Journal of International Law* 14 (1920 supp.): 151.

13. The header for Article 22 is a shorter version of the principle: *nullum crimen sine lege.*

14. For the most comprehensive discussion of the Leipzig trials, see James F. Willis, *Prologue to Nuremberg: The Politics and Diplomacy of Punishing War Criminals of the First World War* (Westport, CT: Greenwood Press, 1982). See also Bass, *Stay the Hand of Vengeance,* Chapter 3.

15. See, for example, Richard H. Minear, *Victor's Justice: The Tokyo War Crimes Trial* (Princeton: Princeton University Press, 1971); Bass, *Stay the Hand of Vengeance,* Chapter 5.

16. For particular information about the trial, see Milosevic Trial Public Archive (Bard College) at http://hague.bard.edu/.

17. Bassiouni, *Introduction to International Criminal Law*, 23.

18. Antonio Cassese, *International Criminal Law* (Oxford: Oxford University Press, 2003), 17.

19. *Congressional Globe,* 31st Cong., 1st Sess. 116 (1850).

20. International Human Rights Treaties: Hearings before the Committee on Foreign Relations, 96th Cong. 103 (1979) (statement of Louis B. Sohn) [hereinafter Testimony 1979].

21. "Helms Protests UN Human Rights Probe in U.S.," Associated Press, October 7, 1997.

22. Lawrence Weschler, "International Humanitarian Law: An Overview," in *Crimes of War: What the Public Should Know,* ed. Roy Gutman and Davied Rieff (New York: Norton, 1999), 21.

23. Cassesse, *International Criminal Law,* 5.

24. See, for example, Richard Gwyn, "International Law Should Not Be Victors' Justice. Indicted or Convicted War Criminals Are All Citizens of Small, Poor Countries," *The Toronto Star,* July 4, 2001. Reprinted at http://www.commondreams.org/views01/0704-04.htm.

25. On the pros and cons of amnesty, see Martha Minow, *Between Vengeance and Forgiveness: Facing History after Genocide and Mass Violence* (Boston: Beacon Press, 1998), and Priscilla B. Hayner, *Unspeakable Truths: Facing the Challenge of Truth Commissions* (New York: Routledge, 2002).

26. See, for example, the *Barrios Altos* case (*Chumbipuma Aguirre et al. v. Peru),* Inter-American Court of Human Rights, March 14, 2001. For a brief summary see http://www.asil.org/ilib/ilib0410.htm#02.

27. See http://www.globalpolicy.org/intljustice/camindx.htm.

28. *Statute of the International Court of Justice,* June 26, 1945; 1055 T.S. No. 993, 3 Bevans 1179. All members of the United Nations are automatically parties to the statute.

29. For an extended discussion of custom and treaties as sources of international law, see Gerhard von Glahn and James Larry Taulbee, *Law Among Nations: An Introduction* (8th ed.) (New York: Longman, 2006), Chapter 4.

30. Text at http://www.un.org/law/icc/statute/romefra.htm.

31. For an extended discussion of this point, see James L. Taulbee, "Governing the Use of Force: Does the Charter Matter Anymore?" *Civil Wars* 4, no. 2 (2001): 1–58.

32. Bassiouni, *Introduction to International Criminal Law,* 162.

33. For a comprehensive study of ICL conventions, see M. Cherif Bassiouni, *International Criminal Law Conventions and Their Penal Provisions* (Irvington-on-Hudson, NY: Transnational, 1997).

34. *Convention on the Prevention and Punishment of the Crime of Genocide,* December 9, 1948; text at http://www.unhchr.ch/html/menu3/b/p_genoci.htm.

35. Geneva I: Wounded and Sick; Geneva II: Wounded, Sick, and Shipwrecked; Geneva III: Prisoners of War; Geneva IV: Protection of Civilian Persons.

36. E.g., *Convention on the Prohibition of the Development, Production and Stockpiling of Bacteriological and Toxic Weapons* of April 10, 1972.

37. *Optional Protocol to the Convention on the Rights of the Child on the Involvement of Children in Armed Conflicts,* opened for signature May 25, 2000, entered into force on February 12, 2002.

38. *International Convention against the Recruitment, Use, Financing and Training of Mercenaries,* December 4, 1989; http://www.unorg/documents/ga/res/44/a44r034.htm.

39. *Nicaragua v. United States* (Merits), *ICJ Reports of Judgments* 1986 at 98 (para. 186), emphasis added.

40. See Jean-Marie Henckaerts and Louise Doswald-Beck, *Customary International Humanitarian Law* (Cambridge: Cambridge University Press, 2005); Theodor Meron, *Human Rights and Humanitarian Norms as Customary Law* (Oxford: Oxford University Press, 1999).

41. For a contemporary explication see *Prosecutor v. Tadić,* ICTY (Appeals Chamber) October 2, 1995 (para. 98).

42. See Manley O. Hudson, "On Article 38," in his *The Permanent Court of International Justice, 1920–1942* (New York: Macmillan, 1943), 606–20; Rudolph B. Schlesinger, "Research on the General Principles of Law Recognized by Civilized Nations," *American Journal of International Law* 51, no. 4 (1957): 734.

43. *The Corfu Channel Case* (Great Britain v. Albania), *ICJ Reports,* 1949, p. 22; http://www.icj-cij.org/docket/index.php?p1=3&p2=3&code=cc&case=1&k=cd.

44. *Barcelona Traction, Light, and Power Co.* (Belgium v. Spain), *ICJ Reports,* 1970, pp. 3, 37; http://www.icj-cij.org/docket/index.php?p1=3&p2=3&code=bt2&case=50&k=1a.

45. *Furundžija,* ICTY, Trial Chamber II, judgment of December 10, 1998 [Case no. IT-95–17/1-T]. See also *Tadić,* ICTY Appeals Chamber II, October 1995 [Case No.: IT-94–1-AR72].

46. Interestingly, the judges could not decide if "rape" included forcible oral sex.

47. R. Y. Jennings, "The Judiciary, International, and National and the Development of International Law," *International and Comparative Law Quarterly* 45 (1996): 3.

48. See generally, "Les actes constituant un danger général (interétatique) considerés comme délites des droit des gens," *Explications additionelles au Rapport spécial présenté à la V-me Conférence pour l'Unification du Droit Pénal à Madrid* (14–20.X.1933). (Translation: "Acts Constituting a General (Transnational) Danger Considered as Crimes under International Law" [trans. James T.Fussell]) at http://www.preventgenocide.org/lemkin/;*Axis Rule in Occupied Europe: Laws of Occupation—Analysis of Goverment—Proposals for Redress* (Washington, DC: Carnegie Endowment for International Peace, 1944), Ch. 9; "Genocide as a Crime under International Law" *American Journal of International Law* 41 (1947): 145–51.

49. See Michael Hirst, *Jurisdiction and the Ambit of the Criminal Law* (New York: Oxford University Press, 2003).

50. See Ruth Donner, *The Regulation of Nationality in International Law* (2nd ed.) (Irvington-on-Hudson, NY: Transnational, 1994).

51. See Randall Hansen, *Dual Nationality, Social Rights and Federal Citizenship in the U.S. and Europe: The Reinvention of Citizenship* (New York: Berghahn Books, 2002).

52. See Iain Cameron, *The Protective Principle of International Criminal Jurisdiction.* (Aldershot, England: Dartmouth, 1994).

53. For an interesting discussion of this principle, see Michael P. Scharf and Melanie K. Corrin, "On Dangerous Ground: Passive Personality Jurisdiction and the Prohibition of Internet Gambling," *New England Journal of International and Comparative Law* 8, no. 1 (2001): 19–36.

54. 18 U.S.C. §2331 (1986).

55. Macedo (ed.), *Universal Jurisdiction,* 28.

56. M. Cherif Bassiouni, "The History of Universal Jurisdiction," in Macedo (ed.), *Universal Jurisdiction,* 63. He actually claims five, but only three are of interest here.

57. For a concise discussion of potential abuses and problems, see Cassese, *International Criminal Law,* 289–91.

58. For a very short discussion of the problems, see Amit Yoran, "Developing Liability Standards for Electronic Commerce," Riptech Security Consulting Group, http://www.isoc.org/inet99/proceedings/1h/1h_2.htm.

59. William A. Schabas, *The UN International Criminal Tribunals: The Former Yugoslavia, Rwanda and Sierra Leone* (Cambridge: Cambridge University Press, 2006), 289–90.

60. www.icls.de/dokumente/icty_statut.pdf .

61. Schabas, *UN International Criminal Tribunals,* 290–91.

62. *Prosecutor v. Jelesić,* Case No. IT-95–10, P 86 (ICTY Trial Chamber Dec. 14, 1999), paras. 102–4. http://www.un.org/icty/jelisic/trialc1/judgement/index.htm.

63. As an example of how detailed legislation in this area may be, see Washington State Legislature, Standard of Liability-Settlement, RCW 70.105D.040, http://apps.leg.wa.gov/RCW/default.aspx?cite=70.105D.040.

64. Quoted in Cassese, *International Criminal Law,* 177.

65. See, for example, Mirjan J. Damaška, *The Faces of Justice and State Authority: A Comparative Approach to the Legal Process* (New Haven: Yale University Press, 1986), 3–6.

66. See Steven J. Emanuel, *Criminal Procedure* (4th ed.) (New York: Aspen, 2005).

67. For example, see John Bell, Sophie Boyron, and Simon Whittaker, *Principles of French Law* (New York: Oxford University Press, 1998).

CHAPTER 3

Courts, Tribunals, and Other Adjudicatory Bodies

> The guilt of such individuals is so black that they fall outside and go beyond
> the scope of any judicial process.
>
> Anthony Eden (1942)

Why Courts and Trials?

Eden's oft-quoted remark highlights an important question.[1] Given the nature of the atrocities in Rwanda and Bosnia, in what sense may we speak of appropriate punishment that secures some rough justice? The sheer scale of genocidal crimes involving thousands upon thousands of killers can overwhelm almost any judicial system. The Pol Pots, Idi Amins, and Slobodan Miloševićs did not act alone. But what tribunal could hope to punish all of the guilty? Thinking in terms of retributive justice, what sentence or series of sentences could possibly balance the scale when guilt involves death and injury to thousands? We tend to think in terms of domestic criminal law systems, where the idea is that, in some measure, the law applies penalties proportionate to the crime. Occasionally, the issue of proportionality does pop up in domestic law. Trials of sadistic serial killers like John Wayne Gacy and Charles Ng often generate the feeling that no punishment could possibly "fit" the crime. Yet the crimes of the worst serial killers seem insignificant when compared to crimes against humanity and genocide. There is no such thing as *appropriate* punishment for those responsible for the horrors of Dachau and Auschwitz, the appalling level of atrocities in Rwanda and Sierra Leone, or the massacre at Srebrenica.

The question of appropriate punishment aside, the arguments for and against trials have several dimensions. Arguments for a judicial process come mainly from the Western liberal legal tradition. They focus on fairness and due process and the role that bringing at least some of those who committed the most barbarous acts to the bar may play in terms of reconciliation. Advocates argue that prosecution of the individuals responsible for specific acts avoids the attribution of collective guilt to an entire nation, provides victims with a sense that their grievances have been addressed, and establishes an impartial historical record of the crimes and events. Ideally, successful apprehension and prosecution also serve as a deterrent.[2]

Arguments against tribunals focus on practicality and on the "necessities" that flow from the diplomatic process. In Chapter 1, I noted the reasons that states prefer to avoid adjudication. Many of these reasons apply here, as well. If the panels and processes are truly impartial, states lose control of the outcomes. Politicians must be concerned with outcomes; lawyers and judges are more concerned with process. As we have noted time and again, judges and lawyers operate under modes of fact determination entirely different from the methods employed by those in the political process. Trials by their nature seem an extraordinarily awkward and unwieldy way to deal with the types of problems presented by certain types of war crimes. Trials are slow and expensive and, as the Milošević trial showed, if conducted under standards that meet modern ideas of "fairness," can give the accused a bully pulpit for his views. Courts require "proof" adduced through application of a very strict set of rules. Such proof may not always be readily available depending on the circumstances.

When the Law Lords considered Spain's petition to extradite Augusto Pinochet, they ruled that he could be extradited only for crimes committed after December 1988, the date when Britain formally implemented the Torture Convention. This left out all but the last 15 months of his 17 years in power. British authorities later ruled Pinochet too ill to stand trial. In the first trial before the ICTY, the trial chamber acquitted Duško (Dusan) Tadić on seven murder charges. The judges then dismissed 11 of 34 charges against him on the grounds that he could not have violated the Geneva Conventions because the war in Bosnia was not an international one.[3]

As the Security Council debated setting up the ICTY, many diplomats had great misgivings about the impact of possible indictments on those they saw as essential to the peace process. On July 4, 2008, the Office of the Prosecutor for the International Criminal Court submitted its first-ever application for a warrant of arrest for a head of state, accusing President Omar Bashir of the Sudan of genocide, crimes against humanity, and war crimes committed in Darfur (warrant of arrest issued March 4, 2009). Gareth Evans, president of the International Crisis Group, summarized how many see the problems:

> The judgement call that the Security Council now has to make is whether Khartoum can be most effectively pressured to stop the violence and build a new Sudan by simply letting the Court process proceed, or—after assessing the regime's initial response and continuing to monitor it thereafter—by suspending that process in the larger interest of peace.[4]

In this case, diplomats fear that if the pre-trial chamber affirms the indictment, the reaction of those in power could undermine the full deployment and operations of UNAMID (African Union/United Nations Hybrid Operation in Darfur), hinder humanitarian relief operations, and unravel the shaky North-South peace agreement. Representative of NGOs and states made similar arguments with the first indictments handed down in 2005: Bryn Higgs, Uganda Program Development Officer for Conciliation Resources, argued that the "ICC has committed a terrible blunder. To start war crimes investigations for the sake of justice at a time when northern Uganda sees the most promising signs for a negotiated settlement of the violence risks having in the end neither justice nor peace delivered."[5] The Sudan and Uganda cases illustrate perfectly the divide between judges and prosecutors on one hand and pragmatic politicians on the other. The ICC prosecutor has proceeded with his job, irrespective of the political consequences. Because of the peculiar nature of the Security Council's relationship to the ICC, it will be up to the diplomats to decide if they can live with the consequences (as they see them) of carrying this through.

This discussion has ignored a third possibility, reconciliation processes.[6] Are processes such as the "Truth and Reconciliation" process in South Africa more appropriate in some cases?[7] Archbishop Desmond Tutu, who chaired South Africa's Truth and Reconciliation Commission, summarizes the dilemma: "Ultimately it is Ugandans who have to decide what is best for them. Whatever they choose, it should not hinder reconciliation and healing and yet it should not encourage impunity and hurt the victims yet again."[8] As cogent as this may sound in humanitarian terms, it acknowledges another downside of judicial process—inflexibility. This may be particularly so as the ICC struggles to establish its credibility and legitimacy. The court has to seize cases deemed important by observers in a timely manner or be relegated to insignificance as important from its inception. The final assessment of "truth and reconciliation" projects remains considerably in the future.

The ICTR and ICTY tribunals have a sunset plan for 2010, but the ICC received its 107th accession in 2008. When the Statute entered into force with the 60th ratification, in July 2002, it became a functioning reality much quicker than many of its most ardent supporters had expected. Despite the criticisms and the continuing problems, the ICTY and the ICTR have managed to try and convict many of those most responsible for the slaughter. These two courts, as the first since Nuremberg, have solidified many aspects of international criminal law. When they began to operate, ICL represented no more than a skeleton structure. The two courts have added considerable flesh and blood to the point of constructing a recognizable body, though one that has a way to go. The process, however, has been neither easy nor cheap.

The Genesis of International Courts

In Chapter 1, I gave a brief history of attempts to establish international tribunals to try individuals for crimes. While the Leipzig and Constantinople trials after World War I represent interesting events, the major progress in development occurred after World War II. In passing, I should note one other abortive effort to construct an international court in the interwar period. In 1937, states attempted to set up an international criminal court to try terrorists.[9] Although it needed only seven instruments of ratification, the treaty never entered into force. This chapter focuses briefly on Nuremberg, Tokyo, and other immediate post–World War II tribunals, then deals with the ICTY, ICTR, ICC, and the cases before the ICJ that touch on international criminal liability. For reasons of space it deals with the SCSL and STC only in terms of structure and operations unless a case has contributed significantly to the evolution of ICL.

Nuremberg Trials

The Nuremberg trials comprised a series of trials (1945–1949) set up to prosecute prominent members of the political, military, and economic leadership of Nazi Germany. For political reasons, the Allies chose the Palace of Justice at Nuremberg, Germany, from 1945 to 1949. The first and certainly the best-known of these trials was the Trial of the Major War Criminals before the International Military Tribunal (IMT), from November 14, 1945, to October 1, 1946. The second set of trials of lesser war criminals was conducted under Control Council Law No. 10 at the U.S. Nuremberg Military Tribunals (NMT). These included the Doctors' Trial, the Judges' Trial (Ministries Case), and the British Military Court (BMC). In fact, the first set of trials occurred considerably before the IMT. For example, the "Belen" trials, which dealt with those associated with the Belsen and Auschwitz concentration camps, started in September 1945.[10]

The International Military Tribunal

As an exercise in international justice, Nuremberg illustrates most of the positives and negatives discussed earlier.[11] Many believe that war crimes trials, no matter how carefully conducted, still represent nothing more than "victor's justice." The Soviet Union participated in the Nuremberg trials even though Stalin was responsible for an estimated 4 million deaths of Soviet citizens and the Soviet Army had unquestionably committed a number of gross violations of the laws of war in Eastern Europe.[12] Questions arose about the tactics authorized by Allied air and naval commanders, as well. At bottom, many questions concerned the legal basis for the trial itself and the essential "fairness" and impartiality of the procedures adopted. For all their presumed deficiencies, the Nuremberg trials, by focusing on the alleged crimes of individuals rather than upon "holding Germany guilty" (collective responsibility), provided an important impetus for the development of the post–World War II human rights regime, as well as the rehabilitation of Germany into an ally.

The violations of the laws of war by the Axis powers and their minor allies in World War II led to demands for an effective postwar punishment of the guilty individuals. The early questions revolved around determining an appropriate method. Britain at first opposed trials because, as Anthony Eden had observed, "The guilt of such individuals is so black that they fall outside and go beyond the scope of any judicial process."[13] U.S. Secretary of the Treasury Henry Morgenthau, Jr., and U.S. Secretary of State Cordell Hull supported summary executions. Morgenthau went further by advocating the "pasturalization" of Germany. Germany should be deindustrialized, its people dispersed, and the land plowed under to form a giant pasture.[14] Secretary of War Henry L. Stimson at first embraced summary executions, then became a strong advocate for trials. Stimson believed that trials were necessary to establish beyond doubt the idea of organizational responsibility as well as the guilt of individuals responsible for the worst atrocities. Organizational responsibility meant not collective responsibility but rather that the leaders of the mainstays of the Nazi apparatus, the Gestapo and the SS, would be held responsible for the atrocities committed because of their policies and orders. Of course, Stalin had no objection to summary executions. Eventually, Stimson's advocacy of trials would prevail.

The governments of the United States, the United Kingdom, France, and the Soviet Union concluded the London Agreement for the Prosecution and Punishment of the Major War Criminals of the European Axis on August 8, 1945.[15] This instrument, also known as the London Charter, provided the details for the establishment of the International Military Tribunal (IMT). The tribunal would consist of four judges, each appointed by a party to the agreement, together with four alternates similarly chosen. The conferees chose Nuremberg as the site for symbolic reasons. It was the location for an annual mass demonstration orchestrated by the Nazi Party and the location where the anti-Semitic "Nuremberg Laws" had been proclaimed in 1935.[16]

In assessing the negotiations that led to the adoption of the agreement, one should consider the enormous difficulties involved in reconciling the different legal traditions and conceptions represented by the United States and Britain on one hand (common law) and France and the Soviet Union on the other (civil law). For example, in civil law procedure, officers of the court system assemble the evidence for both sides, the court conducts the questioning of witnesses, and cross-examination by a defending counsel rarely occurs. Hearsay evidence is permitted, as are trials *in absentia*. Defendants do not have a right to testify on their own behalf. In contrast, U.S. and British procedures rely upon examination and cross-examination in open court as a method of establishing the facts and defendants have a right to confront their accusers (there are limits on the use of hearsay evidence) and offer testimony on their own behalf. The compromise at Nuremberg involved a blend of elements from both systems. The Anglo-American method of examination and cross-examination would be used. Defendants could not only testify on their own behalf but, contrary to Anglo-American practice, be compelled to testify by the court. Because the trials would not involve juries, the Anglo-American technical rules of evidence would not apply. The court could consider any evidence it found to have probative value.[17] This included affidavits. The defendants were permitted counsel of their own choosing, or they could have counsel appointed by the IMT. The Charter provided no right of appeal.[18]

According to the London Charter, all acts covered by the agreement generated individual responsibility. Article 6 of the Charter defined the following acts as within its jurisdiction:

> (a) Crimes against Peace: Namely, planning, preparation, initiation or waging of a war of aggression, or a war in violation of international treaties, agreements or assurances, or participation in a common plan or *conspiracy* for the accomplishment of any of the foregoing (emphasis added);
> (b) War Crimes: Namely, violations of the laws or customs of war. Such violations shall include, but not be limited to, murder, ill-treatment or deportation to slave labor or from any other purpose of civilian population of or in occupied territory, murder or ill-treatment of prisoners of war or persons on the seas, killing of hostages, plunder of public or private property, wanton destruction of cities, towns or villages, or devastation not justified by military necessity;
> (c) Crimes against Humanity: Namely, murder, extermination, enslavement, deportation, and other inhumane acts committed against any civilian population, before or during the war[;][,] or persecutions on political, racial or religious grounds in execution of or in connection with any crime within the jurisdiction of the Tribunal, whether or not in violation of the domestic law of the country where perpetrated.

Article 7 of the Charter explicitly excluded the defense of sovereign immunity:

> The official position of defendants, whether as Heads of State or responsible officials in Government Departments, shall not be considered as freeing them from responsibility or mitigating punishment.

This marked a radical departure from the U.S. position concerning the trial of the Kaiser after World War I (see Chapter 1). In his opening statement the Chief Prosecutor, Supreme Court Justice Robert H. Jackson of the United States, set out the most important departure from prior practice and the rationale underlying modern international criminal law:

> Of course, the idea that a state, any more than a corporation, commits crimes, is a fiction. Crimes always are committed only by persons. While it is quite proper to employ the fiction of responsibility of a state or corporation for the purpose of imposing a collective liability, it is quite intolerable to let such a legalism become the basis of personal immunity. The Charter recognizes that one who has committed criminal acts may not take refuge in superior orders nor in the doctrine that his crimes were acts of states. These twin principles working together have heretofore resulted in immunity for practically everyone concerned in the really great crimes against peace and mankind. Those in lower ranks were protected against liability by the orders of their

superiors. The superiors were protected because their orders were called acts of state. Under the Charter, no defense based on either of these doctrines can be entertained. Modern civilization puts unlimited weapons of destruction in the hands of men. It cannot tolerate so vast an area of legal irresponsibility.[19]

The indictment had four main charges. The first count charged participation in a common plan or *conspiracy* for the accomplishment of crimes against peace. The other three charged commission of or participation in crimes against peace, war crimes, and crimes against humanity. Along with the individuals, the indictments included six criminal organizations: the Nazi[20] party leadership (NSDAP), the SS (*Schutzstaffel*—elite enforcers), the SD (*Sicherheitsdienst*—security service), and the Gestapo (*Geheime Staatspolizei*), the Reich Cabinet (*Die Reichsregierung*), the SA (*Sturmabteilung*—"Storm Troopers" or Brown Shirts), and the OKW (*Oberkommando der Wehrmacht*—High Command of the German armed forces). The SA, SD, and SS were organizations within the Nazi Party, not parts of the formal state apparatus.

The IMT conducted 22 trials over a 10-month period. Twenty-one defendants (Martin Bormann, Deputy for Nazi Party Affairs, was tried in absentia)[21] were in custody when the trials began on November 20, 1945. The defendants raised four major issues: (1) because international law applies to the acts of sovereign states only, no basis existed for punishing individuals (*nullum crimen*); (2) individuals could not be held responsible for "acts of state"; (3) the law applied was ex post facto (*nullum crimen*); and (4) the defendants were obeying the orders of their superiors, either political or military. The court handed down its judgment on September 30, 1946;[22] and sentences were pronounced on October 1, 1946. Nineteen of the 22 defendants were found guilty. Three (Schacht, Frizsche, and von Papen) were acquitted. Twelve were sentenced to death by hanging. Only 10 of the 12 defendants sentenced to death were executed. Hermann Goering committed suicide the night before his execution and Bormann, as noted, was tried and convicted in absentia.[23] The death sentences were carried out almost immediately, on October 16, 1946. The panel exonerated three of the organizations: the SA, the Reich Cabinet, and the OKW.

Assessment

Do the IMT Trials deserve the characterization "victor's justice"? The short answer is, of course, yes, but not in the pejorative way critics use the term to mean gross unfairness. The trials stand open to critique from many different perspectives. At the time, the Chief Justice of the Supreme Court, Harlan Fiske Stone, and Associate Justice William O. Douglas criticized both their colleague, Associate Justice Robert Jackson, who acted as prosecutor, and the proceedings, as did Senator Robert A. Taft, a prominent figure in the Republican Party.[24] Many senior Allied military commanders questioned the trials, let alone the convictions, of Admirals Raeder and Doenitz, and Generals Keitel and Jodl. Critics argued that the proceedings had several major flaws: arbitrary and uniformed selection of defendants, biased judges, lack of due process, ex post facto law, and one-sidedness (*tu quoque*)[25] in that the Allies did not punish similar crimes committed by their own forces.

As a prefatory note to a fuller discussion of the criticisms, I should note simply that in terms of procedural standards, the trials fell well short of the stringent requirements of modern Anglo-American trials. But the goals here did not include having perfect trials in terms of procedure. That fact alone explains the attitude of Justices Stone and Douglas. The purpose was to mete out rough justice quickly and publicly. In sum, the principal purpose was more political than legal. The question is, did the flaws undermine the result? Again the short answer is no. Sixty years after, few now argue that the trials did not result in a rough but acceptable justice.

The first set of issues related to having the Soviet Union participate when the Soviets had cooperated with Hitler in the partition of Poland and had later invaded Finland. Moreover, as noted earlier, Soviet troops had committed some serious violations of the laws of war. Finally, if the trial, according to the prosecutor Robert Jackson, aimed to set down clear lines of conduct with respect to a government's treatment of its own people, Stalin and his associates needed the lesson, as well. As a matter of self-interest, the Soviets insisted that the tribunal's jurisdiction cover only Axis war crimes and policies. In this case, power and position overrode principle.[26]

The second set of issues revolved around choosing those who would stand trial. The Allies had decided not to prosecute the Italian Fascist leadership. The Italian Fascist political elite did not escape prosecution entirely. Its members were tried later in Italian courts. Beyond that decision, while numerous members of the Nazi inner policymaking circle had committed suicide or otherwise died, several major figures (among them Adolph Eichmann) were not included in the group chosen for the high-profile trial. Obviously, the tribunal could not reasonably conduct trials for everyone accused. Most of those accused of war crimes were dealt with by military courts of the occupying powers or were returned to the scenes of their offenses and tried and punished by local courts and under local laws.[27] Those tried did represent influential groups within the Nazi ruling structure. Pragmatism played a part, as well. With the exception of Bormann, all tried were in custody.

Both the constitution of the IMT and the procedure violated some fundamental standards of due process as defined in common-law adversarial systems.[28] Critics pointed out that the judges were not impartial, the defense lacked adequate resources (including time),[29] and the rules of evidence were too lenient. Yet, judges in *criminal* cases are not required to be impartial; they are required to be fair in judging the evidence as presented and enforcing the procedural rules impartially.[30] In this case, because judges, not juries, made the decisions on the verdict, questions relating to the nature of the evidence have less validity. Unlike unschooled jurors, judges should weigh the evidence in terms of logic and consistency in a fair manner. The resource argument has no counter other than to note that, in context, it is open to question what time and additional resources would have produced in terms of evidence to counter the charges. To paraphrase an expression common in contracts, from a political standpoint, time was "of the essence." The defendants had a right to counsel, to a trial translated into German, to see all documents used by the prosecution, to call witnesses in defense, and to testify freely on their own behalf. Besides, at the time (and still in many cases), defendants in domestic trials often suffered from a significant deficiency of resources. Think of the person forced to use an overworked public defender as opposed to one who can afford to engage Johnnie Cochran or others of his stature.

Did the tribunal apply ex post facto law in violation of the *nullum crimen* principle (Chapter 2)? Crimes against humanity and crimes against peace represented two new categories of crimes. The reasoning of the judges in justifying the jurisdiction and charge of the London Charter relied upon both customary law and treaties. The difficulty with both sources stemmed from the fact that no prior treaty created individual liability for violations and no consistent practice supported the few declarations that might have suggested that certain activities might have created individual liability. Central to this argument is the fact that, while the League of Nations had developed a draft definition of aggression, that definition had never translated into more than a suggestion for states to consider. The Tribunal did consider the ex post facto problem at some length, finally evading the issue of validity by concluding that *nullum crimen* as a principle did not constitute an agreed principle of *international* law at that time. No defendant was convicted solely on either of these counts. All found guilty on these counts were also found guilty of complicity in war crimes, a well-established branch of international law.

While *politically* understandable because the Allies other than the Soviet Union had also engaged in some questionable conduct, excluding *tu quoque* as a defense left an interesting gap in terms of defining what constituted a war crime. The court never really explored in any systematic way the issue of military necessity in modern warfare. On the Allied side, for example, some tough questions surround the decisions concerning "carpet bombing" as a tactic and, more specifically, the destruction of both Dresden and Nagasaki.[31] Note that none of the indictments referenced the air war against Britain. Despite the ban on *tu quoque* arguments, the defense attorney for Admirals Doenitz and Raeder cleverly introduced a *tu quoque* argument through an assertion that unrestricted submarine warfare constituted a practice sanctioned by customary international law. As evidence of this, he cited the statement of Admiral Chester W. Nimitz, Commander in Chief of U.S. Pacific Operations, that U.S. submarines had operated under similar instructions during the war.[32] The court rejected this proposition as a matter of law, but the sentence handed down reflected the fact that it had hit a nerve. The judges found Raeder and Doenitz not guilty on that charge. We examine the boundaries of "military necessity" in more detail in Chapter 6.

Assessment

The flaws notwithstanding, the trial stands as a seminal landmark in defining international criminal law. Perhaps the most important advance stems from the definition of a "crime against humanity" as "an ordinary crime committed on a scale of barbarism unimaginable until the Holocaust."[33] Equally important, it established the precedent that those responsible for the policies and orders, not just lower-level "grunts" who may have been "just carrying out orders," bear responsibility for their actions. The mantle of "act of state," that is, the mantle of sovereignty, no longer would give an automatic free pass for actions that so flagrantly violated basic standards of humanity. That not every defendant received the death penalty and that some were found not guilty gave the tribunal some considerable credibility in terms of weighing the evidence. Questions of procedure and political expediency aside, the trials did not result in any egregious miscarriages of justice.

International Military Tribunal for the Far East (IMTFE—Tokyo)

The International Military Tribunal for the Far East (IMTFE) formed the counterpart to the IMT at Nuremberg.[34] Indeed, the Charter that set up the trials reflected the London Charter in defining its jurisdiction as war crimes, crimes against peace, and crimes against humanity, together with a separate grouping of the crime of conspiracy to commit the foregoing crimes. Even though the course of the war in the Pacific produced instances of behavior comparable to those in Europe, the IMTFE has received far less attention than its European counterpart and has had little impact. Though influenced by the London Charter, the Charter for the IMTFE did not represent the results of negotiation. It came from the *Proclamation of the Supreme Commander for the Allied Powers* (January 19, 1946) signed by General Douglas MacArthur.[35] Although the 11 belligerents that had fought against Japan had the right to nominate judges, General MacArthur had sole authority of appointment. Judges who served came from Australia, Canada, China, Great Britain, France, India, the Netherlands, New Zealand, the Philippines, the Soviet Union, and the United States. The accused faced three charges: (1) murder, (2) crimes against peace, and (3) other conventional war crimes and crimes against humanity.[36] In all, 28 individuals were indicted and tried.[37]

Even before the beginning of the trials, controversy erupted over the decision to exempt the Japanese emperor Hirohito from trial as a war criminal.[38] Other political decisions also limited the scope of jurisdiction. Prosecutors ignored a host of crimes committed again Koreans (including the "comfort women")[39] as did not charge many prominent business leaders who had been deeply involved in the war effort. The trials began in June 1946, and the judgment was handed down on November 4, 1948. The IMTFE found all of the defendants guilty—7 were sentenced to death, 16 to life imprisonment. No defendant who received a prison sentence actually served more than 10 years.[40] In 1948, in a significant decision, the U.S. Supreme Court ruled that the tribunal was not a court of the United States and that, in consequence, the Supreme Court had no jurisdiction to review or to set aside the tribunal's judgments.

The *Yamashita* Case: Command Responsibility

The *Yamashita* case stands out as one of the most controversial trials among a host of controversial trials. General Tomoyuki Yamashita and General Masaharu Homma were charged with failure to exert effective control over their troops.[41] The two cases raise the same issues of command responsibility.[42] Because of the extensive controversy associated with the final Supreme Court review of the Yamashita case, I will focus on it.[43]

After his surrender, on September 3, 1945, Yamashita was charged with unlawfully disregarding his "duty as commander to control the operations of the members of his command, permitting them to commit brutal atrocities and other high crimes" that constituted violations of the "laws of war."[44] The trial began on October 29, 1945, before a military commission set up on the authority of General Douglas MacArthur and under rules and procedures that he determined. The trial commission consisted of six army officers, five of them generals. George Guy, a member of the defense team, noted: "The Military Commission which tried General Yamashita had no 'judge learned in the law' sitting with it. True, one of the officers was designated as a 'law member' but he is not a lawyer . . . and not a member of the legal profession."[45] The defense team (six army officers) had approximately three weeks to locate witnesses, conduct research on the 123 charges, and prepare for trial.

No one denied the scope and nature of the atrocities that had occurred. In Nanking, Japanese troops had committed rape, torture, and murder on a massive scale against both civilians and POWs.[46] Some evidence suggested that many of the atrocities had been carried out on an organized and systematic basis on orders of Japanese noncoms and commissioned officers. The questions, however, revolved around the extent of Yamashita's culpability—what did he know and what could he have done, if he had known? The prosecution argued that the crimes were so widespread and egregious that Yamashita had to know.[47] The commission, on December 7, 1945, found Yamashita guilty on all charges. It sentenced him to death by hanging. His defense team filed an immediate appeal to the Philippine Supreme Court, which rejected it on the basis that the court had no jurisdiction over the U.S. Army. The defense then sent a wire to the U.S. Supreme Court requesting a stay of execution pending the submission of a writ of habeas corpus. The Court granted the stay. Oral arguments in the case occurred on January 9, 1946.

The defense argued four issues: (1) the creation of the military commission was unlawful because hostilities had ceased; (2) the charges did not contain a violation of the law of war; (3) the commission lacked authority and jurisdiction because the rules of evidence used (permitting hearsay and other "opinion" evidence) violated both U.S. military law (due process) and the Geneva Convention;[48] (4) the commission lacked authority and jurisdiction because of the failure to give advance notice of Yamashita's trial to the neutral power presenting the interests of Japan as required by Article 60 of the Geneva Convention. Chief Justice Harlan Fiske Stone delivered the majority opinion (6–2),[49] upholding the legality of the commission, the verdict, and the sentence. Associate Justices William Francis (Frank) Murphy and Wiley Rutledge delivered strong dissenting opinions.

In his dissent, Justice Murphy said: "The Fifth Amendment guarantee of due process of law applies to 'any person' who is accused of a crime by the Federal Government or any of its agencies. No exception is made as to those who are accused of war crimes or as to those who possess the status of an enemy belligerent."[50] He thought that Yamashita had been denied the right to prepare an adequate defense and had not received the benefit of the most elementary rules of evidence: "No military necessity or other emergency demanded the suspension of the safeguards of due process."[51] For our purposes, the more important argument was his view that "Had there been some element or *knowledge or direct connection* with the atrocities, the problems would be different."[52]

International Criminal Courts for Yugoslavia (ICTY) and Rwanda (ICTR)

Yugoslavia

Yugoslavia began disintegrating in 1991.[53] A country patched together after World War I, Yugoslavia had come close to disintegration during World War II, when ethnic tensions resulted in mutual slaughter by Serbs and Croats in particular. The political skills and personality of Marshal Tito (Josip Broz), who had led a partisan faction fighting against the Axis during World War II, kept the country relatively peaceful until his death, in 1981. Tito had dealt with national aspirations by creating a federation of six nominally equal republics—Croatia, Montenegro, Serbia, Slovenia, Bosnia-Herzegovina, and Macedonia. In Serbia, the two provinces of Kosovo and Vojvodina were given autonomous status. Communist rule restored stability, and good relations with the West ensured a steady stream of loans and aid. After Tito's death, his successors, by playing to their various constituencies, adopted policies that divided rather than united. In 1991, first Slovenia, then Croatia declared independence, reacting to what they perceived as an overweening Serbian ambition to dominate the federation. Slobodan Milošević, president of Bosnia, sought to ensure Serbian dominance in areas of Bosnia and Croatia that were inhabited by large Serb populations. The drive by Serbia to assert dominance and to resist secession produced a number of ugly incidents that included the shelling of Dubrovnik, the devastation of Vukovar, and the massacre at Srebenica.

The international community was extremely slow in its reaction. In October 1992, the UN Security Council voted to establish a five-member commission of experts to investigate war crimes in the former Yugoslavia. The Commission faced both financial and political problems in carrying out its task. M. Chief Bassiouni, who chaired the Commission, noted that the UN did not provide sufficient funding "to insure that the Commission would not interfere with the ongoing peace negotiations."[54] The Commission had to raise funds from other sources to fund its investigation. On the other hand, Bassiouni notes that the Commission "was given the broadest mandate of any Commission since Nuremberg."[55] It took full advantage of the mandate. The Commission submitted the longest report in Security Council history—3,500 pages and 300 hours of videotaped interviews and other evidence.

Other UN agencies joined in the investigation, as well. The Commission on Human Rights convened a first-ever special session. The statement broke new ground in referring to concern about the possibility of "genocide" in Bosnia and Herzegovina. This contrasted with the reluctance of the Security Council to use that term. The United States did press for the creation of a "Nuremberg-like" court.[56] The Commission had appointed a Special Rapporteur, who issued a report that said, "There is growing evidence that crimes have been committed."[57] On the other hand, none of the permanent members of the Security Council seemed to have any great interest in bring the issue to discussion until media reports detailing the carnage began to appear and influence public opinion. Even then, many questions remained. Diplomats working to resolve the crisis were dead set against trials because they believed the threat of prosecution would deal a severe blow to efforts to negotiate a settlement.[58] This involved an interesting irony in that many of those who possibly would be accused of committing or condoning serious crimes were seen as necessary players in resolving the conflict. Other questions related to the authority of the Security Council to establish a court of any type, given the ambiguities of its jurisdiction to deal with internal conflicts.[59]

Issues of Authority and Jurisdiction The establishment of the two courts broke new ground. The United Nations had affirmed Nuremberg and its results in an ex post resolution, but the IMT was not its creation. The answer to the question whether or not the Security Council had the power to create an ad hoc court was by no means clear. Article 29 of the UN Charter seemingly gives the SC broad powers: "The Security Council may establish such subsidiary organs as it deems necessary for the performance of its functions." Article 41 provides that:

> The Security Council may decide what measures *not involving* the use of armed force are to be employed to give effect to its decisions, and it may call upon the Members of the United Nations to apply such measures. These may include complete or partial interruption of economic relations and of rail, sea, air, postal, telegraphic, radio, and other means of communication, and the severance of diplomatic relations. (emphasis added)

Reading Article 41 as a permissive list in the sense that the included actions are meant to be suggestive rather than exhaustive would underscore the authority to establish any entities deemed necessary to the work of the Security Council. Additionally, a 1954 ICJ Advisory Opinion had upheld the right of the Security Council to establish subsidiary bodies, including tribunals.[60] The technical problem lay in the fact that the court would not wholly be an SC operation. The General Assembly would elect the judges, and the Secretary General would nominate the prosecutor. Extended negotiations finally made the arrangements palatable.

Only in February 1993 did the Security Council, by Resolution 827, establish the International Tribunal for the Prosecution of Persons Responsible for Serious Violations of International Humanitarian Law Committed in the Territory of the Former Yugoslavia since 1991 (ICTY).[61] It took a year for the court to get up and running. Judges had to be elected, a site selected, facilities acquired, and rules and procedures developed and written. Not until November was a special (chief) prosecutor named.[62] Even at that point, establishment of the court seemed a token gesture. Bass concludes, "NATO had the troops. In all of The Hague's early difficulties, the fundamental hurdle was the West's refusal to take military action against war criminals in ex-Yugoslavia."[63] While prosecutions began, not until 1998 did the political climate really support the tribunal. It took a courageous and principled political decision by the United Kingdom's prime minister, Tony Blair, to jump-start an active pursuit of those indicted.

Rwanda

On April 6, 1994, a plane carrying President Juvénal Habyarimana of Rwanda and President Cyprien Ntaryamira of Burundi was shot down by a surface to air missile as it approached Kigali (Rwanda) airport, killing all on board. Following the deaths of the two presidents, widespread killings, involving both political and ethnic dimensions, began in Kigali and spread to other parts of Rwanda.[64] Extremists from the Hutu tribe moved immediately to implement a plan that involved "cleansing" the country of the rival Tutsi tribe. Instead of taking immediate action to halt the massacre, the UN withdrew its peacekeeping force after the deaths of 10 soldiers caught up in the outbreak of violence. The killing continued through late June, not abating until an insurgent force (the Rwandan Patriotic Front, or RPF) under Paul Kagame unseated Habyarimana's successors and took power.

Unlike the fighting in Yugoslavia, the violence in Rwanda attracted attention, although the UN was slow to act in ways other than expressing concern. The Security Council condemned the violence by calling for those involved "to respect fully international humanitarian law."[65] On July 1, 1994, the UN Security Council asked the Secretary-General to appoint a commission to accumulate evidence of war crimes in Rwanda. After copious supporting material on the massacres had been secured, on November 8, 1994, the Security Council, acting on its authority under Chapter VII of the Charter, adopted the *Statute of the International Tribunal for Rwanda*.[66]

Interestingly enough, the biggest obstacles eventually came from the new Rwandan regime. By happenstance, Rwanda was serving a two-year elected term on the Security Council at the time the violence began. Initially, the new Rwandan government pressed for an international tribunal modeled on the ICTY. As negotiations wore on, it became increasingly negative toward the idea. According to UN personnel, the negativity stemmed from several factors—the realization that the tribunal could not possibly undertake the prosecution of the thousands of detainees then in Rwandan prisons, the severe limitation put on the temporal jurisdiction of the court (it could review only actions that took place in 1994), the decision not to locate the tribunal in Kigali, the lack of an independent appeals chamber (it would share an Appeals Chamber with ICTY), and the prohibition on capital punishment.[67] In the end, Rwanda voted against the Security Council resolution approving the establishment of the court. Shraga and Zacklin conclude that the reason for the negative vote stemmed from the realization by the government that the tribunal would not be responsive to the wishes of the government.[68]

Sierra Leone

Although endowed with abundant natural resources (particularly diamonds), Sierra Leone ranks as one of the poorest country in the world.[69] Since gaining independence from Great Britain, in 1961, the country has had a history of political instability. The events that led to the establishment of the SCSL began in the late 1980s. In large part, the roots of the violence stemmed from attempts to control the diamond industry.[70] The civil war in neighboring Liberia contributed, as well. Charles Taylor, leader of the National Patriotic Front of Liberia (NPFL), provided money and support to Foday Sankoh to form the Revolutionary United Front (RUF). In return, Taylor received diamonds from Sierra Leone.[71] The RUF launched its first campaign into eastern Sierra Leone from Liberia in late March 1991. In the months following, more than 100,000 refugees fled the conflict into Guinea. The government was unable to mount an effective counterattack.

The RUF's signature tactic was terror through physical mutilation. An estimated 20,000 civilians suffered amputation of arms, legs, ears, and other body parts by machetes and axes. Fighting continued in the ensuing months, with the RUF gaining control of the diamond mines. The Sierra Leone Army seemed totally ineffective. A military coup in April 1992 unseated the government, but those who staged the coup seemed no more equipped to deal with the challenge presented by the RUF than their predecessors. In desperation, the new government signed a contract with the private military firm Executive Outcomes (South Africa) to provide experienced combat troops as well as training to the army.[72] In approximately six weeks, the situation changed dramatically, with the RUF reduced to existence in border enclaves.

Under the auspices of the UN, President Kabbah and RUF leader Foday Sankoh negotiated a peace accord. The agreement made Sankoh vice president and gave other RUF members positions in the government. It called for an international peacekeeping force (UNAMISL) under the auspices of the United Nations. Almost immediately, however, the RUF began to violate the agreement, most notably by holding hundreds of UNAMSIL personnel hostage and capturing their arms and ammunition in the first half of 2000. In May 2000, the situation deteriorated to the point that British troops intervened to evacuate foreign nationals and establish order. They stabilized the situation and were the catalyst for a ceasefire and ending of the civil war. Still, not until January 2002 did the fighting end. In June 2000, President Kabbah wrote to United Nations Secretary-General Kofi Annan requesting the UN to authorize a court to deal with crimes during the conflict. In August 2000, the UN Security Council adopted Resolution 1315 requesting the Secretary-General to start negotiations with the Sierra Leonean government to create a special court. On January 16, 2002, the UN and the Government of Sierra Leone signed an agreement establishing the court.[73] The court has the authority to try those who bear the greatest responsibility for serious violations of international humanitarian law and Sierra Leonean law committed in the territory of Sierra Leone since November 30, 1996.

The International Criminal Court (ICC)

Tracing the history of efforts to construct the International Criminal Court involves following two separate tracks: the effort to draft an international criminal code and initiatives taken toward the creation of an independent international court.[74] In November 1947, the General Assembly charged the International Law Commission with two tasks: first, to formulate the principles of international law recognized in the Charter and Judgment of the Nuremberg Tribunal, and second, with careful attention to these principles, to prepare a draft code of offenses against the peace and security of mankind.[75] The creation of the court was tied to other negotiations then in progress. During the preparatory work, which produced the Genocide Convention, representatives from the United States pushed hard for the inclusion of language authorizing the creation of an international tribunal.

Delegates from the Soviet Union, among others, expressed major reservations.[76] Unlike the International Court of Justice, where jurisdiction was limited to disputes between countries, proponents of the International Criminal Court envisioned a court that would assert jurisdiction directly over individuals for certain crimes not otherwise punished in national courts.[77] Article VI of the Convention emerged as a compromise, providing for trial "by a competent tribunal of the State in the territory of which the act was committed, or by such international penal tribunal as may have jurisdiction with respect to those Contracting Parties which shall have accepted its jurisdiction."[78]

At this juncture, another issue arose. The General Assembly noted that, while the ILC's draft code listed aggression as the first offense, the General Assembly had already entrusted a special committee with the task of preparing a report on a draft definition of aggression.[79] The Assembly decided to postpone consideration of the draft code until the special committee had submitted its report.[80] That decision effectively ended active consideration of the issues for the next 25 years. Not until 1981 did the General Assembly invite the ILC to resume its work on the draft code.[81] Another 15 years passed before the Commission finally produced a second draft code.[82]

It took the events in the former Yugoslavia and Rwanda to move the issue forward in an expeditious manner.[83] In late 1992, the General Assembly requested that the ILC undertake the "elaboration of a draft statute for an international criminal court."[84] Subsequently, in 1993 and 1994, the Security Council authorized ad hoc tribunals for the former Yugoslavia and for Rwanda. The ILC moved expeditiously on the ICC assignment, issuing its report in 1994.[85] Because of continuing division over the desirability of establishing a permanent court, the Assembly first established an ad hoc committee to study the issue further and then two years later authorized a preparatory committee to prepare a statute for consideration by a conference of plenipotentiaries. Early in 1998, the preparatory commission produced a consolidated text of a statute regarding the establishment of a permanent international criminal court for adoption at a diplomatic conference held June 15–17, 1998, in Rome.[86]

At the conference, states voted to establish a permanent court by an overwhelming majority (120–7, with 21 abstentions). The Rome Statute entered into force on July 1, 2002 (60 ratifications). Of the five permanent members of the UN Security Council, Britain and France have ratified the Statute, the Russian Federation has signed it (September 2000), China has not signed, and the United States has "withdrawn" its signature. Of the other Security Council members, Germany and Italy ratified; Japan did not sign; Iran signed in December 2000; Iraq did not. Neither India nor Pakistan signed.

A Note on Other Courts

The ICTY and the ICTR established a precedent. A problem quickly emerged as many other situations evolved where advocates pressed for courts as a mechanism to deal with the issues. Cambodia and East Timor stood at the top of the list. On the other hand, Kofi Annan, the Secretary-General of the UN, resisted the pressure to set up additional ad hoc courts. His position was based upon several considerations. The post–Cold War era of cooperation among the great powers on the Security Council had passed. Wealthier nations that had borne the brunt of the considerable costs of the two operating tribunals had become averse to the creation of any institution that would increase their financial obligations. Equally important, the establishment of the International Criminal Court (ICC) provided a permanent forum that presumably would address these issues in the future. In fact, with respect to the situations in Darfur, the Democratic Republic of the

Congo (DRC), Uganda, and the Central African Republic, the ICC has issued several indictments.[87]

Statutes and Structures

The ICTY and the ICTR The Security Council established both the ICTY and the ICTR, acting under its authority granted by Chapter VII of the Charter of the United Nations. The statutes of the two tribunals share many common elements, particularly with regard to structure and procedures. In drafting the statutes, the Secretary General accepted suggestions proposed by states, individuals, and NGOs and drew upon the experience of the IMT (Nuremberg) and the IMTFE (Tokyo). To a large extent, the draft charted new legal territory. Remember that no international criminal code existed, then or now, in the sense of a single document that defines violations in detail and specifies the necessary procedural law that would guide "fair" prosecutions. The few precedents from other national courts provided minimal guidance. Because the Security Council set up the ICTY 18 months before the ICTR, the ICTY Statute had considerable impact on the ICTR, as did the Rome Statute of the ICC, then in development.

Yet, because they represent responses to quite different factual situations, the two statutes embody very different concerns. Rwanda was primarily an internal conflict, so a different body of law applied. When the UN Security Council established the ICTR, the preamble to the resolution authorizing the tribunal specifically voiced the concern that "genocide and other systematic, widespread and flagrant violations of international humanitarian law had been committed in Rwanda."[88] The Statute authorized the court to try those responsible for acts of genocide and other serious violations of international law within the territory of Rwanda, as well as Rwandan citizens who performed these acts in nearby states. As a result, almost all of the cases before the ICTR have involved charges of genocide. In contrast, very few trials before the ICTY and none before the SCSL (Sierra Leone) have done so.[89] Here I should note that the Statute of the SCSL does not included genocide as a crime within its jurisdiction because Kofi Annan, the UN Secretary-General, argued that, while the situation in Sierra Leone clearly involved crimes against humanity, it did not meet the explicit criteria for genocide as defined the Genocide Convention (see Chapter 5).[90]

Unlike the ICC, the two courts are ad hoc, meaning temporary—set up to carry out a specific task—rather than permanent. As institutions established by the Security Council (SC) under Chapter VII, their existence will terminate with a decision by the SC that international peace and security have been restored in Yugoslavia and Rwanda. Both courts have a mandate to finish by 2010.[91] This contrasts with the ICC and the ICJ, which constitute permanent institutions whose jurisdiction and authority stem from international agreements (treaties) accepted and ratified by states. Although creations of the SC, the two courts (and their prosecutors) operate as independent agencies. The SC does not control their agendas. In theory, these ad hoc courts have an advantage in that, as subsidiary organs of the SC, UN member states have an obligation to carry out any decisions that require enforcement action. In fact, as I have noted, states have consistently ignored this obligation until doing so became inconvenient. Second, because the two courts depend upon the SC to authorize monies for operations, they have suffered from chronic underfunding; states too have not paid their assessments to support the courts.[92]

Structures The ICTY and the ICTR have 16 permanent judges elected by the UN General Assembly from lists prepared by the Security Council. The ICTY also has a maximum of 12 judges *ad litem* (an ad hoc judge), while the ICTR has a maximum of 9 judges *ad litem*.[93] Because of the case loads and length of trials, in order to expedite proceedings, the Security Council has permitted a temporary expansion in the number of judges *ad litem* for both tribunals. Permanent judges are elected to four year terms and stand for reelection. Judges *ad litem* also serve four-year terms but cannot stand for reelection. No two permanent judges can be of the same nationality.[94] In composition, the courts must adequately reflect the major legal systems of the world.

Both courts are now divided into three trial chambers (originally two), each assigned three permanent judges (see Table 3.1). Trials do not involve juries. A three-judge panel presides over each trial. Each trial panel must have a minimum of two permanent judges. The two tribunals share an appeals chamber. In theory, this ensures the development of consistent practice and precedent. In fact, the case load led to an expansion of the appeals chamber in 2003. The appeals chamber consists of seven permanent judges appointed by the President of the ICTY from the permanent judges of the two courts. Two of these must be from the permanent judges of the International Criminal Tribunal for Rwanda.[95] The President of the ICTR has designated seven judges eligible for selection to the appeals chamber. The appeals chamber has its seat at The Hague in the Netherlands, but travels to Arusha when necessary.

Initially, the two courts also shared the Office of the Prosecutor (OTP). This did have the advantage of ensuring a uniform prosecutorial policy for the two tribunals, but the workload and practical problems led the SC to establish a separate Office of the Prosecutor for the ICTR in 2003. Headed by the chief prosecutor, the OTP operates independently of the Security Council, of any state or any international organization, and of the other organs of the two courts. The OTP has responsibility for investigating incidents, collecting evidence, identifying witnesses, and preparing cases for trial. The structure includes a deputy prosecutor for each tribunal. The registry, headed by the registrar, administers the everyday business of the court. The office is responsible for all communications to and from the court. Along with the president of the court, the registrar also is responsible for a number of diplomatic functions.[96]

The ICTY and the ICTR have authority to prosecute four clusters of offenses: grave breaches of the 1949 Geneva Conventions, violations of the laws or customs of war, genocide, and crimes against humanity committed on the territory of

Table 3.1   Selected International Courts at a Glance

Court	# of Judges	Selection	Term of Office	Seat
ICTY	16 permanent 12 *ad litem* (temporary increase to 16 in 2008)	Eelected by the UN General Assembly	Permanent: 4years (can be re-elected) *ad litem* 4 years (no re-election)	The Hague (Netherlands)
ICTR	16 permanent 9 *ad litem* (maximum)	Elected by the UN General Assembly	Permanent: 4 years (can be re-elected) *ad litem* 4 years (no re-election)	Arusha (Tanzania)
SCSL	11 permanent	Trial: 4 appointed by UN Secretary General; 2 by the government of Sierra Leon Appeals: 3 appointed by UN Secretary General, 2 by government of Sierra Leon	3 year terms	The Hague (Netherlands)
ICC	18 permanent	Elected by the Assembly of States Parties	9 year terms (can be re-elected; 1/3 elected every 3 years	The Hague (Netherlands}
ICJ	15 permanent	Jointly elected by the UN Security Council and the UN General Assembly	9 year terms (can be re-elected); 1/3 elected every three years	The Hague (Netherlands)

the former Yugoslavia since 1991. Unlike Nuremberg, the court has jurisdiction only over natural persons, not over organizations, political parties, administrative entities, or other legal subjects. The ICTY and national courts have concurrent jurisdiction over serious violations of international humanitarian law committed in the former Yugoslavia.[97] The ICTY can claim primacy over national courts and may take over national investigations and proceedings at any stage if it considers that doing so would prove to be "in the interest of international justice."[98] In 2007, the court referred 13 cases back to the region for trial.[99] To date, the tribunal has concluded proceedings against 106 accused out of the 161 who have been charged.[100]

As of September 1, 2007, the ICTR had concluded proceedings against 33 accused persons. In his report to the General Assembly and Security Council, the president of the court voiced three concerns. First, he emphasized that completing the tasks in the time frame proposed by the completion strategy depends upon the continued cooperation of states. Second, he noted that the tribunal will need sufficient resources to move forward. Finally, he urged states to accept the transfer of cases in order to further investigations and trials.[101]

Special Court for Sierra Leone (SCSL)

The Special Court for Sierra Leone differs from the ICTY and the ICTR in that it was created under the *joint authority* of the Government of Sierra Leone and of the United Nations to try those accused of violations of international humanitarian law (and the law of Sierra Leone) within the territory of Sierra Leone since November 30, 1996.[102] Because of the nature of its structure, which combines both international and national elements, it is often characterized as a *hybrid* court. The court consists of two trial chambers and an appeals chamber. Each trial chamber consists of three judges, two selected by the UN Secretary-General and one by the government of Sierra Leone. The appeals chamber has five judges, two nominated by the government of Sierra Leone and three by the Secretary-General of the UN. Judges serve three-year terms. While both the ICTR and the ICTY Statutes include genocide as a listed crime, the SCSL Statute does not. In the case of the SCSL, the Secretary-General explicitly noted that genocide had been excluded from the draft presented to the Security Council because no evidence existed to show that the killings, while widespread and systematic, were directed against any of the protected groups in the Convention.[103]

The prosecutor issued 13 indictments in 2003. He subsequently withdrew two of those indictments in December 2003 because the accused had died. The trials of three former leaders of the Armed Forces Revolutionary Council (AFRC) and of two members of the Civil Defense Forces (CDF) have been completed, including appeals. Trials of three former Revolutionary United Front (RUF) leaders have also been completed. Sentences were handed down on April 8, 2009. The trial of former Liberian president Charles Taylor is in the prosecution phase at The Hague.

International Criminal Court (ICC)

The International Criminal Court sits at The Hague and operates as an independent international organization.[104] In accordance with article 2 of the Rome Statute, the *Negotiated Relationship Agreement between the International Criminal Court and the United Nations* governs the relationship.[105] The Assembly of States Parties forms the management oversight and legislative body for the court. The Assembly has a permanent Secretariat and a Bureau (interim oversight) to manage the everyday operations of the court. The court consists of 18 judges elected for nine-year terms. It is divided into three functional chambers or divisions: pre-trial, trial, and appellate. The Appeals Division is composed of the president of the court and four other judges; the Trial Division consists of the second vice president and five other judges; and the Pre-Trial Division is headed by the first vice president and six other judges.[106] The other important official is the prosecutor, who heads the Office of the Prosecutor and who also is elected for a nine-year term.

Article 5 establishes the grant of subject matter jurisdiction as: "limited to the most serious crimes of concern to the international community as a whole"—genocide, crimes against humanity, war crimes, and aggression.[107] The Rome Statute, rather than referencing the relevant treaties, contains definitions of the crimes within its substantive jurisdiction listed in Article 5 within the body of the treaty. I should note that concerted attempts to include drug trafficking and "terrorism" in the list failed. More important, the *in personam* (personal) jurisdiction of the court was designed to be *complementary* to that of national courts, meaning that the ICC may try cases only where "a state is *unwilling or unable* to carry out the investigation or prosecution" (Article 17.1(a); emphasis added). Two further limitations on jurisdiction exist, as well. The court may seize cases only where the events (or portions of the events) have occurred after July 1, 2002, when the Rome Statute entered into effect. Second, double jeopardy applies. The court may not try individuals if they have already been tried in another court unless the trial was considered a sham designed to absolve the person of any guilt (Art. 20).

The court became a functioning entity in February 2003, when the Assembly of States Parties elected the 18 judges of the court. In the future, judges will have nine-year terms. The Rome Statute provides that six will be elected every three years. For the first election, to establish the necessary rotation, six judges were elected for terms of three years, six for six years, and six for nine years. The judges constitute a forum of international experts who represent the world's principal legal systems.[108] Judges must be nationals of States Parties to the Statute. The election process itself contains an interesting requirement because the Rome Statute specifies two different sets of qualifications that define eligible candidates. One list consist of candidates with established competence in criminal law and procedures and the necessary relevant experience, whether as judge, prosecutor, or advocate or in other similar capacity in criminal proceedings. The second list consists of candidates with established competence in relevant areas of international law, such as international humanitarian law and the law of human rights, and extensive experience in a professional legal capacity which is of relevance to the judicial work of the Court (Art. 36.5).

Cases may come to the ICC by recommendation of a State Party, by recommendation of the Security Council, or through the action of the chief prosecutor acting *priopio motu* (on his or her own authority).[109] Articles 11–21 of the Statute establish the bases of jurisdiction. In the case of a referral from a State Party, Article 12.2 provides that state referral must satisfy one of two conditions: the crime must have been committed on the territory of the requesting state (or within other "territorial" jurisdiction, such as aircraft or vessel registered in the state) and/or it must have been committed by a national of the requesting state. A non-State Party may refer a case if it explicitly accepts the jurisdiction of the court and agrees to cooperate fully (Art. 12.3).

The first several cases illustrate the procedure. The president of the Democratic Republic of the Congo (DRC) requested an investigation into events that occurred within the DRC after the Statute of the Court entered into force. The investigation resulted in the court issuing indictments for four individuals.[110] The UN Security Council formally referred the situation in Darfur (Sudan) to the court in 2005. A UN referral has broader scope in that it may encompass acts committed in the territory of states that are not party to the Statute and by nationals of states not party to the Statute. At this writing, the court had issued two indictments relating to Darfur.[111] Considering the nature of the situation, many human rights activists have pushed for the establishment of a special prosecutor just for Sudan. So far, the prosecutor has not acted *proprio motu*.

International Court of Justice (ICJ)

The ICJ, as a court that hears disputes between states, has a role in the criminal justice realm because issues may arise that involve issues of traditional international law. The court consists of 15 judges elected jointly for nine-year terms by the General Assembly and Security Council. Judges must represent the principal legal systems of the world. No two judges may be of the same nationality. As a reflection of the structure of the UN as well as of international politics, from its inception the court has always included judges from the United States, Russia, Britain, and France. Only states may bring cases before the court. Judges do not have to recuse themselves from litigations involving their states of nationality. Instead, if a state involved in litigation before the court does not have a sitting judge on the court, it may appoint a judge ad hoc.

Two cases illustrate the role the court may play. In the first, the issue concerns whether or not genocide as a crime may give rise to state responsibility (collective liability). Genocide as a crime clearly involves questions of individual liability, but when a government undertakes a deliberate policy that targets protected individuals, may these actions also involve *collective* liability or *state responsibility*? One such case currently seized by the court is the *Application of the Convention on the Prevention and Punishment of the Crime of Genocide* (Croatia v. Serbia),[112] where Croatia has accused the state of Serbia of sponsoring acts of genocide involving Croatian territory and citizens. Previously, Bosnia-Herzegovina had instituted suits against Serbia on the same grounds in 1993 and again in 2001.[113] The details of these cases are discussed in Chapter 5.

The second type of case arises when an issue of traditional public international law is involved. On April 11, 2000, Belgium, asserting a claim to universal jurisdiction over certain human rights violations, issued an arrest warrant for Abdulaye Yerodia Ndombasi of the Democratic Republic of the Congo (DRC). At the time, Ndombasi served in an official capacity as foreign minister of the incumbent government. The DRC immediately filed suit in the ICJ demanding annulment of the warrant. The application cited two issues:

(1) Violation of the principle that a State may not exercise [its authority] on the territory of another State and of the principle of sovereign equality among all Members of the United Nations (Article 2. 1, of the Charter); and,

(2) Violation of the diplomatic immunity of the Minister for Foreign Affairs of a sovereign State, as recognized by the jurisprudence of the Court and following from Article 41.2, of the Vienna Convention on Diplomatic Relations.[114]

In its judgment, the court found, by a vote of 13–3, that issuance of the warrant constituted violations of a legal obligation of the Kingdom of Belgium toward the Democratic Republic of the Congo. In issuing the warrant, Belgium had failed to respect both the immunity from criminal jurisdiction and the inviolability that the incumbent minister for foreign affairs of the Democratic Republic of the Congo enjoyed under international law.[115]

Problems and Prospects

As with the tribunal at Nuremberg, the ICTY and the ICTR have had to deal with the difficulties inherent in trying to draw from both the civil and the common-law traditions, as well as international human rights law.[116] Moreover, despite the Security Council mandate, the tribunals have no independent means of enforcement beyond the active cooperation of national authorities. From the beginning, the ICTY had problems in rounding up the principal planners and instigators of the events for trial. The lack of political will on the part of all involved has continually undermined efforts to arrest the individuals most responsible for the atrocities in the Balkans. A decision by Prime Minister Tony Blair in 1998 resulted in British troops acting as peacekeepers in the Balkans, actively pursuing those wanted. This resulted in a number of high-profile arrests. Under considerable diplomatic (economic) pressure, Serbia finally surrendered Slobodan Milošević in 2001 (see Chapter 5).[117] Only in July 2008 did the arrest of Radovan Karadžić, one of the most wanted, take place. His compatriot, Ratko Mladić remained at large as of late fall 2008, as did Goran Hadžić, but these are the only two of those indicted who are not in custody..

The ICTR has had a different set of problems. It has never lacked high-profile defendants because, when the RPF unseated the incumbent government, it actively pursued and arrested the ousted leaders. If anything, Rwanda has a surfeit of defendants. One report indicated that Rwandan jails had upward of 90,000 individuals imprisoned for complicity in the genocide.[118] The tribunal itself has had severe administrative problems and faced several scandals that undermined the credibility of the court. In a report, Erik Mose, the president of the ICTR (2003–2007), noted:

> The general infrastructure in Arusha was quite rudimentary in 1995. There were few tarmac roads, very unstable electricity and water supplies, and austere living conditions. Telephone and fax lines were few and unreliable. Computers and office equipment were not readily available in Arusha and had

to be imported from abroad, resulting in delays. As of September 1995, the Tribunal had no courtrooms, offices, prison, legal officers or secretaries. The Registry started its activities in hotel rooms. The Tribunal could only move into a small section of its headquarters in the AICC [Arusha International Conference Center] in November 1995, one year after the Security Council decided to set up the ICTR.[119]

Additionally, a report released by the United Nations Office of Internal Oversight Services in March 2002 identified several serious acts of corruption. These involved "fee splitting" between defendants and defense lawyers, other actions that clearly constitute malpractice, dismissals for professional incompetence, employment of a defense investigator who had participated in the genocide, and kickbacks to a staff member from lawyers who wished to obtain expeditious payment for their services.[120]

Scandals aside, questions of cost form an area of major concern. Adhering to the ideal of fair trials has a hefty price tag. Consider the costs of maintaining the basic structure (overhead), including salaries for judges, prosecutors, and support staff and the upkeep of facilities, apart from the cost of trials. To use the ICTY as an example, apart from the 16 permanent and 12 *ad litem* judges, the bulk of the fixed costs come from salaries and maintenance of a staff of 1,200. In a statement to the UN General Assembly in 2004, Judge Theodor Meron, president of the ICTY, directly addressed the funding problems. He argued that the lack of funds threatened to undermine the body's work at a crucial time because the tribunal had to reduce staff by more than 100—about 10 percent of its strength.[121]

Add to the ongoing fixed costs those of conducting actual trials.[122] Trials may last two years. Some defense costs may be reduced because since 2003 defense lawyers have been paid on a lump sum basis. The savings here, however, may be offset by the increased number of high-level defendants, which has produced more complex trials.[123] One must consider, in addition to fees for defense attorneys, other administrative costs related to operating in an international environment. For example, fairness demands that all have easy access to the relevant documents. Again to quote Erik Mose:

> The documents are all subject to disclosure and must be translated for legal teams and the accused. Translation may be required of thousands of pages into at least one official language of the Tribunal. The number of witnesses is often considerable, and interpretation of all testimony is required in three languages. Witnesses have often to be extracted from a difficult environment, afforded considerable protection before and after testimony and sometimes relocated. The staff and counsel involved in cases come from different cultures and traditions, and effective communication requires new skills and extra efforts. Defence Counsel have to leave their other casework for considerable periods to spend time working at the ICTR in Arusha, usually away from their practices.[124]

At the moment, the ICTR has largely overcome these problems and has gained considerable momentum toward completing its mandate by the agreed sunset date of 2010.

Assessing the Impact

In sum, what have the courts accomplished? Obviously, we have to weigh the negatives against the accomplishments. Nonetheless, as a reminder of the ongoing controversies here, remember that, for many individuals, the weights assigned to the various elements in the balance sheet and thus the worth of the overall projects will vary according to deeply held prior assumptions (philosophical beliefs) about the merits of undertaking the project in the first place. The questions then revolve around more than appropriate measures of weights; they involve selecting the appropriate elements to include in the balance sheet as part of any evaluation. The positions reflect many different dimensions. Some have been addressed earlier in this chapter, some in earlier chapters. I will here recap those voiced most often.

Adherents of *political realism* reject the effort out of hand as no more than an expensive cosmetic window dressing that may produce some short-term results but that have no meaningful long-term impact. Many who oppose U.S. participation in the ICC go beyond this position to assert that institutions such as the ICC actually have a long-term negative impact.[125] A second variant of this position asserts that inflexible judicial solutions undercut diplomatic peacemaking efforts or that, as Henry Kissinger has argued (Chapter 1), by substituting the perspectives of judges for those involved in the political process, they complicate the diplomatic process unnecessarily, if not undermine it altogether. Other critics focus on the reality that the mechanisms of legal process inevitably mean that only a few will be punished, undercutting the very idea of justice. Still others emphasize that reconciliation, not retribution, provides the necessary process for healing the schisms opened and exacerbated by situations such as that in Rwanda.[126]

Philosophical objections aside, what have the courts accomplished? The ad hoc courts represent first steps. They faced enormous difficulties in that they literally had to develop and evolve both procedural standards and substantive definitions from scratch. On the positive side, the courts have succeeded in that task. They also have managed to prosecute a number of high-profile defendants, including ex-heads of state. Cost-effectiveness aside, punishing some perpetrators still sends a message because other potential offenders may live in fear that they will be prosecuted next. In that sense, the courts have both established a relatively coherent body of practice and made inroads into the "culture of impunity." The trials have had another, perhaps unintended consequence. They have produced important oral and documentary evidence crucial to a full understanding of the events in the former Yugoslavia, Rwanda, and Sierra Leone. Without the trials, much of the full horror of the events revealed through investigation and testimony quite possibly would not have become part of any permanent record. Governments, participants, and even victims often suffer from selective amnesia, albeit for different reasons. To a great extent, history as we know it comes from the records of victors, not losers.

In looking back, two fundamental questions emerge: at what cost, and to what effect? Even the staunchest of advocates acknowledge that, to have an ongoing impact, the process needs much improvement. Robertson concludes that the future depends upon whether or not the ICC and other international courts "can overcome their crippling failure to work expeditiously and effectively—and especially, cost effectively."[127] Consider not only the length and cost of individual trials but the length of time the entire process has taken. Granted, during the early years, part of the reason for this is that judges, conservative by training and experience, proceeded very cautiously because they had no firm guidelines. Everyone involved knew that each early case charted new ground. Thus, all participants proceeded cautiously and carefully. Future cases in other courts may proceed more expeditiously because they may draw upon this "cautious and careful" approach. If they cannot, this will become a serious impediment to the dreams of abolishing the "culture of impunity."

The Milošević trial, in terms of length, cost, and the seeming inability of those responsible for making decisions to move it along expeditiously, gave critics much to criticize. It illustrates all of the problems attendant on developing a completely new legal regime at the international level. The trial made real, and in prime time, all of the potential pitfalls of international legal procedure as a tool of retributive justice. In the first international trial of a head of state, the court, among other decisions, chose to err on the side of granting the defense considerable latitude in presenting its case rather than give the impression of unfairness by imposing strict procedural limits.[128] The ICC needs to take this trial as the paradigm case of what must be improved if it is to establish credibility and legitimacy.

Do these cases exert enough of a "compliance pull" to act as deterrents to future perpetrators? Sadly, the answer here must be, for the moment, no. The troubled genesis of the courts and the sporadic and often reluctant support given by many states in terms of putting their "blood and treasure" in support of the principles they mouth in public raise questions of how far-reaching the collective processes will be in terms of deterrence. Though deterrence is often advanced as a rationale for international justice, here we should note that it does not offer the best standard for evaluation, even at the domestic level. We tend to overestimate the impact of deterrence as a factor in winning compliance with domestic law. Burglaries, car theft, and murder continue as major problems for domestic police. The fact that some who commit these acts have received punishment does not necessarily deter others from committing the same offense, sometimes over and over. Considering the sporadic application and the ponderous pace of international justice, one should not expect that these trials will exert a deterrent effect in the short run. On the other hand, the precedents that have been established liability for certain acts does mark progress. The international climate with respect to the validity of international criminal law has undergone a sea change over the past 15 years. The problem will be to maintain the momentum established by the tribunals.

To reiterate some points in a paraphrase, the wheels of international justice, when they have rolled, have rolled slowly, ponderously, and at great expense. Over the next five years, the ability of the ICC to bring those indicted to trial in a timely manner, and conduct trials in an expeditious fashion will tell us much about the future. At the same time, keep in mind that the ICC also faces considerable start-up costs in terms of establishing its own "institutional culture" and procedures. While not as great as those associated with the ad hoc courts because the ICC can draw on the experience of the ad hoc courts, as well as their substantive and procedural precedents, the court will still face the necessity of carving out its own niche, that is, establishing its own credibility. The progress in executing the indictment against President Omar al-Bashir for acts of genocide in Darfur will provide an immediate test for the court, as well as for the seriousness of the international community in moving forward.[129]

A Final Note: The United States and the ICC

The policy of the United States with respect to the ICC can be summed up simply: the United States will back the court only if it guarantees that no U.S. citizen will ever face prosecution before it.[130] Note that the fear of an independent court does not rest upon unwarranted concerns. Recall the discussions in Chapter 2 of the attempts to secure warrants of arrest for President George W. Bush, President Bill Clinton (for the bombing of Serbia), former Secretary of State Henry Kissinger, and former Secretary of Defense Donald Rumsfeld for violations of international humanitarian law. The concerns of the United States have genuine foundations. In terms of outliers, China and Russia, two other permanent members of the UN Security Council, have joined the United States in not ratifying the Statute. Thus, three of the five permanent members remain outside the ICC regime; France and Great Britain have joined. On the other hand, the ICC is now a reality, with more states acceding to the regime each year.

It is difficult to see what active opposition to the ICC has gained the United States in the years since the Rome Conference. Opposition has severely damaged its leadership with regard to issues and actions relating to war crimes and crimes against humanity, while adding to its reputation as a crybaby and bully. How can you promote a regime if you then wish to claim a "special exemption"? Leadership by dictation may have worked in the Cold War, but others now have powerful voices and the capacity to project their own visions of world order. Rather than seeing the Rome Conference as the latest instance of multilateral diplomacy gone awry, the United States should treat it as a positive lesson for future reference. Rather than engaging in an extended discussion here, I ask whether the United States would have more influence on what the ICC does if it were a State Party to the treaty (an insider) rather than an outsider, no matter how powerful.

Notes

Epigraph quoted in Gary Bass, *Stay the Hand of Vengeance: The Politics of War Crimes Tribunals* (Princeton: Princeton University Press, 2000).

1. For a concise treatment of these issues, see Bass, *Stay the Hand of Vengeance: The Politics of War Crimes Tribunals* (Princeton: Princeton University Press, 2000); Geoffrey Robertson, *Crimes against Humanity: The Struggle for Global Justice* (3rd ed.) (New York: New Press, 2006), 244–50, 401–6.

2. See *Making Justice Work,* Report of the Century Foundation/Twentieth Century Fund Task Force on Apprehending Indicted War Criminals (1998), 27–29. See also Bass, *Stay the Hand of Vengeance,* 1, 28–33. Bass argues that liberal states "commonly see their enemies not as mere foes, but as war criminals deserving punishment" (35).

3. Bass, *Stay the Hand of Vengeance,* 13 ff; Michael P. Scharf, *Balkan Justice: The Story Behind the First International War Crimes Trial since Nuremberg* (Durham, NC: Carolina Academic Press, 1997), 213–14, 271–88.

4. International Crisis Group, "New ICC Prosecution: Opportunities and Risks for Peace in Sudan," http://www.crisisgroup.org/home/index.cfm?id=5571&l=1&m=1.

5. Josefine Volqvartz, "ICC under Fire over Uganda Probe," CNN (February 23, 2005), http://globalpolicy.igc.org/intljustice/icc/2005/0223iccfire.htm.

6. See Martha Minow, *Between Vengeance and Forgiveness: Facing History after Genocide and Mass Violence* (Boston: Beacon Press, 1998), for an excellent treatment of the issues here.

7. See Truth and Reconciliation Commission, http://www.doj.gov.za/trc/; for the report see http://www.info.gov.za/otherdocs/2003/trc/.

8. Quoted in Volqvartz, "ICC under Fire over Uganda Probe."

9. Manley O. Hudson, "The Proposed International Criminal Court," *American Journal of International Law* 32 (1938): 549–54. The Convention had an interesting ratification procedure. Actually, two conventions had been negotiated: the *Convention for the Prevention and Punishment of Terrorism* and the *Convention for the Creation of an International Criminal Court.* In order to ratify the criminal court convention, states had to first ratify the terrorism convention. Even though the statute required only seven ratifications to enter into force, it never received the necessary approval. League of Nations Document, C.547(I).M.384(I).1937.V.

10. *The Belsen Trial* (Trial of Josef Kramer and 44 Others), Case No. 10, British Military Court, Luneburg, 1 September 17–November 17, 1945. For a concise summary of the proceeding, see http://www.ess.uwc.ac.uk/WCC/belsen1.htm.

11. For the relevant primary documents here, see The Avalon Project at Yale Law School, http://www.yale.edu/lawweb/avalon/imt/proc/judcont.htm.

12. In 1940, Stalin ordered the execution of somewhere between 21,000 and 25,000 Polish POWs. Although it did not cause the most deaths, the most noted massacre in the west was the Katyn Forest massacre. For a brief discussion, see http://www.cnn.com/SPECIALS/cold.war/episodes/01/spotlight/index.html.

13. Quoted in Bass, *Stay the Hand of Vengeance.*

14. Morgenthau's plan was endorsed by both Roosevelt and Churchill at the Quebec Conference (September 1944). Telford Taylor, *The Anatomy of the Nuremberg Trials*

(Boston: Little, Brown, 1992), 29, 31. An incident in June 1944 gave the U.S. antitrial advocates additional ammunition. The 12th SS Panzer Division killed 64 Allied POWs. In another incident during the Battle of the Bulge (December 1944), the 1st SS Panzer Regiment captured and killed 72 American soldiers. See "The 1st SS Panzer Division's Dash Westward, and Operation Greif," http://www.army.mil/cmh-pg/books/wwii/7-8/7-8_11.htm.

15. Text in *American Journal of International Law 39,* 257 (1945 Supp.). Consult *International Conference on Military Trials, London, 1945* (Department of State Publication 3080), for the texts of all proposals at the meeting. The principles contained in the 1945 Agreement were recognized as binding in international law by UN General Assembly Resolution 95 (I) (December 11, 1946).

16. Taylor, *The Anatomy of Nuremberg,* 61.

17. Taylor, *The Anatomy of Nuremberg,* 61–64.

18. Several other issues arose, as well. The United States insisted upon including a charge of conspiracy. This would permit prosecutors to prosecute organizations (i.e., the Nazi Party, the Gestapo) for *conspiracy* to commit various war crimes and atrocities. A guilty verdict would brand the group as criminal; then any member of these organizations could be convicted merely upon proof that he had been a member of the group because he was thereby part of a larger criminal enterprise. Unfortunately, while a favorite of U.S. prosecutors, the idea has no foundation in continental law. The other three powers finally agreed but limited its application to the single charge of initiating aggressive war.

19. The Avalon Project at Yale Law School, *Trial of the Major War Criminals before the International Military Tribunal: Proceedings,* 22 Volumes (The Red Set), Volume 1, http://www.yale.edu/lawweb/avalon/imt/proc/11-21-45.htm.

20. National Socialist German Workers Party, *Nationalsozialistische Deutsche Arbeiterpartei*. See, "A Teacher's Guide to the Holocaust," http://fcit.usf.edu/HOLOCAUST/TIMELINE/nazirise.HTM.

21. The more curious question is why they did not indict Heinrich Mueller, the head of the Gestapo, *in absentia,* or, for that matter, Adolph Eichmann, who was Mueller's subordinate but who was directly responsible for running the death camps.

22. Text of judgment and the sentences reprinted in *American Journal of International Law* 41 (1947): 172–332. See also Taylor, *The Anatomy of Nuremberg,*; Georg Schwarzenberger, "The Judgment of Nuremberg," *Tulane Law Review* 21 (1947): 329; Quincy Wright, "The Law of the Nuremberg Trial," *American Journal of International Law* 41 (1947): 37.

23. The tribunal refused to accept accounts that claimed Bormann had died prior to the end of the war.

24. See John F. Kennedy, *Profiles in Courage* (New York: Harper and Row, 1964), 189–90. Taft was one of President Franklin Delano Roosevelt's (and, later, President Harry S. Truman's) sharpest critics.

25. *Tu quoque* may be translated "I did it, but you did it also."

26. For a brief summary see Robertson, *Crimes against Humanity,* 246–49.

27. See Maximillian Koessler, "American War Crimes Trials in Europe," *Georgetown Law Journal* 39, no. 1 (1950): 18–112; William B. Cowles, "Trials of War Criminals (Non-Nuremberg)," *American Journal of International Law* 42, no. 2 (1948): 299–319. By late November 1948, a total of 7,109 defendants had been arrested for war crimes, including the major cases at Nuremberg and Tokyo. The trials that took place resulted in 3,686 convictions and 924 acquittals. Of those convicted, 1,019 received death sentences, and 33 defendants committed suicide. Prison sentences were received by 2,667, and 2,499 cases

were still pending. By the end of 1958, the Western Allies had convicted 5,025 Germans of war crimes, 806 being sentenced to death (486 were actually executed), and the Soviet Union had convicted around 10,000, many of whom were sentenced to 25 years in jail and others, to death. In the years since 1948, many other culprits have been discovered by their own governments (mostly in France and West Germany) and have been tried for war crimes.

28. Robertson argues that "the only serious departures from Anglo-American trial procedures were standard features of Continental systems." *Crimes against Humanity,* 250.

29. You will see this referred to as "equality of arms."

30. This is a representative argument: "Attractive as this argument may sound in theory, it ignores the fact that it runs counter to the administration of law in every country. If it were true then no spy could be given a legal trial, because his case is always heard by judges representing the enemy country. Yet no one has ever argued that in such cases it was necessary to call on neutral judges. The prisoner has the right to demand that his judges shall be fair, but not that they shall be neutral. As Lord Writ has pointed out, the same principle is applicable to ordinary criminal law because 'a burglar cannot complain that he is being tried by a jury of honest citizens.'" Arthur Lehman Goodhart, "The Legality of the Nuremberg Trials," *Juridical Review* (1946), reprinted in Guénaël Mettraux (ed.), *Perspectives on the Nuremberg Trial* (Oxford: Oxford University Press, 2008), 29.

31. The raid occurred February 13–15, 1945, about three months before German surrendered on May 8. Although the Allies considered Dresden a military target, many regarded the city as a cultural landmark that had little industry and few other facilities of military importance. Hence the destruction and the number of civilian casualties (13 square miles of the central city destroyed, with casualties maximally estimated at 40,000 dead) seemed excessive. Similarly, many have questioned the "necessity" of dropping a *second* atomic bomb, this time on Nagasaki.

32. Robert Cryer, Hakan Friman, Darryl Robinson, and Elizabeth Wilmshurst, *An Introduction to International Criminal Law* (Cambridge: Cambridge University Press, 2007), 95–96; Robertson, *Crimes against Humanity,* 248.

33. Robertson, *Crimes against Humanity,* 252.

34. The best analysis of the Tokyo trials still is Richard Minear, *Victor's Justice: The Tokyo War Crimes Trial* (Princeton: Princeton University Press, 1971).

35. Text of Charter at www.icwc.de/fileadmin/media/IMTFEC.pdf.

36. John C. Watkins, Jr. and John Paul Weber (eds.), *War Crimes and War Crime Trials: From Leipzig to the ICC and Beyond: Cases, Materials and Comments* (Durham, NC: Carolina Academic Press, 2005), 286.

37. During the trials, two defendants died and one was unable to stand trial because of mental incompetence. For a critical treatment, see Minear, *Victor's Justice.* For an interesting dissent attacking the basis for the charges against the defendants, see the opinion of Judge R. M. Pal (India), in *The United States of America et al. against Sadeo Araki, et al.,* reprinted in Watkins and Weber, *War Crimes,* 337–43. Judge Pal argues, "The acts alleged are, in my opinion, all acts of state and whatever these accused are alleged to have done, the did that in working the machinery of the government, the duty and responsibility of working the same having fallen on them in due course of events" (338).

38. For a discussion, see Kerry Creque O'Neill, "A New Customary Law of Head of State Immunity: Hirohito and Pinochet," *Stanford Journal of International Law* 38 (2002): 289–317. O'Neill argues: "[T]he Hirohito question and the Pinochet case, with regard to their impact on the development of a customary international law concerning prosecutions

of former heads of state, are more similar than they are different. Upon an examination of the motivations for the two decisions, it appears that in both cases extralegal concerns drove the legal outcomes" (290).

39. For a relatively dispassionate and accurate account, see "Human Slavery: Japanese Sex Slavery before, during and after World War II," Religious Tolerance, http://www.reli gioustolerance.org/sla_japa.htm.

40. Watkins and Weber, *War Crimes,* 287.

41. General Homma had commanded the forces that had forced General Douglas MacArthur from the Philippines in 1942. See Richard L. Lael, *The Yamashita Precedent: War Crimes and Command Responsibility* (Wilmington, DE: Scholarly Resources, 1982), 26; see also A. Frank Reel, *The Case of General Yamashita* (Chicago: University of Chicago Press, 1949). Reel served as part of General Yamashita's defense team.

42. It also raised the issue of the validity of military commissions. At this point, I am more concerned with the substantive finding than with the evaluation of the procedural issues.

43. *In Re Yamashita* 327 U.S. 1 (1946).

44. George F. Guy, "The Defense of Yamashita," *Wyoming Law Journal* 4 (1950): 156. Guy served as part of General Yamashita's defense team.

45. Guy, "Defense of Yamashita," 161–62.

46. See Timothy Brooks (ed.), *Documents on the Rape of Nanking* (Ann Arbor: University of Michigan Press, 1999).

47. Lael, *Yamashita Precedent,* 83.

48. Note that the references here are to the 1929 Geneva Convention (*Convention between the United States of America and Other Powers, Relating to Prisoners of War; July 27, 1929*).

49. Associate Justice Robert Jackson was the prosecutor at Nuremberg.

50. *Yamashita,* note 43, 26.

51. *Yamashita,* note 43, 27–28.

52. *Yamashita,* note 43, 39; For an excellent discussion of Murphy's views on the Yamashita case, see, J. Woodford Howard, *Mr. Justice Murphy: A Political Biography* (Princeton: Princeton University Press, 1968), especially 367–71, 375. Direct knowledge became an important consideration in the Krstić trial, *Prosecutor v. Krstić,* ICTY, Appeals Chamber, Judgment of April 19, 2004 [IT-98–33-A] (see Chapter 6). In the appeal of the Krstić conviction for genocide, the ICTY Chamber found that the General lacked the intent to commit genocide but had knowledge that others intended to do so.

53. For a lengthy examination of the politics and timeline involved in establishing the tribunals, see Willam A. Schabas, *The UN International Criminal Tribunals: The Former Yugoslavia, Rwanda and Sierra Leone* (Cambridge: Cambridge University Press, 2006), 3–46; and Daphna Shraga and Ralph Zacklin, "The International Criminal Court for the Former Yugoslavia," *European Journal of International Law* 5, no. 1 (1994): 1–22.

54. M. Cherif Bassiouni, "Combating Impunity for International Crimes," *Colorado Law Review* 71, no. 2 (2000): 417–18.

55. Bassiouni, "Combating Impunity," 417.

56. This stands as an interesting anomaly, given the reluctance of both the Bush and Clinton administrations to use word "genocide." See Samantha Power, "Bystanders to Genocide," Atlantic.com, http://www.theatlantic.com/doc/200109/power-genocide/2; and Samantha Power, *A Problem from Hell": America and the Age of Genocide* (New York: Basic Books, 2002), Chapter 9.

57. Quoted in Schabas, *UN Tribunals,* 18.

58. Michael Scharf noted: "Frm the beginning, the Security Council's motives in creating the tribunal were questionable. During the negotiations to establish the court . . . it became clear that several of the Security Council's permanent members considered the tribunal a potential impediment to a negotiated peace settlement." Michael Scharf, "Indicted for War Crimes. Then What?" *Washington Post,* October 3, 1999, B01. Note that both China and Russia had reason to be wary—China because of Tiananmen Square and Russian because of Chechnya.

59. Note that this is a separable issue from that in the Tadić trial, where the question became whether certain aspects of international humanitarian law apply to internal conflicts. This has to do with the interpretation of what affects *international* peace and security to the extent that Article 2.7 (domestic jurisdiction clause) does not rule out action by the SC.

60. *Effects of Awards of Compensation Made by the United Nations Administrative Tribunals,* ICJ Reports (1954), http://www.icj-cij.org/docket/index.php?p1=3&p2=4&code=unac&case=21&k=d2.

61. United Nations, *Secretary-General's Report on Aspects of Establishing an IT, 32 ILM* 1163, 1192 (1993); International Tribunal, "Rules of Procedure and Evidence," 33 *ILM* 484 (1994); see also James C. O'Brien, "The International Tribunal for Violations of International Humanitarian Law in the Former Yugoslavia," *American Journal of International Law* 87, no. 4 (1993): 639–58; Diane F. Orentlicher, "Yugoslavia War Crimes Tribunal," *American Society of International Law Newsletter* (June-August 1993), *ASIL Focus* no. 1.

62. Theodor Meron, "War Crimes in Yugoslavia and the Development of International Law," *American Journal of International Law* 88, no. 1 (1994): 78–88. At this time, Meron, who would later serve as president of the court, wrote, "[D]espite its desirability, it is probable that the tribunal will not be very effective." Theodor Meron, "The Case for War Crimes Trials in Yugoslavia," *Foreign Affairs* 72, no. 3 (1993): 122.

63. Bass, *Stay the Hand of Vengeance,* 224. See also Gerard Prunier, *The Rwanda Crisis* (New York: Columbia University Press, 1997).

64. The 1994 events had been preceded by a series of massacres that began with the overthrow of the Tutsi king in 1959. Significant violence directed at the Tutsis occurred in 1959, 1963, 1966, 1973, 1991, 1992, and 1993. Daphna Shraga and Ralph Zacklin, "The International Criminal Court for Rwanda," *European Journal of International Law* 7, no. 4 (1996): 502.

65. UN SCOR, S/RES/912 (21 April 1994).

66. UN SCOR, S/RES/955 (8 November 1994). Text of the Statute at http://www.un.org/ictr/statute.html. The original text was appended to the resolution.

67. Shraga and Zacklin, "The International Criminal Court for Rwanda," 504; Schabas, "UN Tribunals," 29.

68. Shraga and Zacklin, "The International Criminal Court for Rwanda," 504.

69. The following discussion draws primarily on Lansana Gberie, *A Dirty War in West Africa: The RUF And the Destruction of Sierra Leone* (Bloomington: Indiana University Press, 2005).

70. The 2006 film *Blood Diamonds,* starring Leonardo DiCaprio, took its plot line from the events in Sierra Leone.

71. In December 2000, the UN General Assembly unanimously adopted a resolution on the role of diamonds used to fund conflicts, particularly in Africa. UN GAOR A/RES/55/56 (December 1, 2000). The General Assembly recognized that "conflict" (blood) diamonds formed a crucial element in the ongoing wars in parts of Africa.

72. For concise discussions of the role of Executive Outcomes, see James Larry Taulbee, "Mercenaries, Private Armies and Contemporary Policy Options" *International Politics* 37, no. 4 (December 2000): 433–55; James Larry Taulbee, "The Privatization of Security: Modern Conflict, Globalization and Weak States," *Civil Wars* 5, no. 2 (September 2002): 1–24.

73. UN SCOR S/RES/1315 (January 16, 2002).

74. For a concise history, see James L Taulbee, "A Call to Arms Declined: The United States and the International Criminal Court," *Emory International Law Review* 14 (Spring 2000): 105–56.

75. G.A. Res. 177(II), U.N. Doc. A/519 (1947).

76. For a discussion of the original negotiations, see Lawrence J. Leblanc, *The United States and the Genocide Convention* (Durham, NC: Duke University Press, 1991), 151–74. Ironically, the concerns of theSoviet Union (e.g., diminution of sovereign prerogatives) expressed during the negotiations mirrored many of the concerns expressed by members of the U.S. Senate during the first, and subsequent, debates over possible ratification.

77. Creation of a permanent court that would hear cases of international criminal law has been widely discussed by scholars for more than a century and has been seriously debated since the conclusion of World War I.

78. Convention on the Prevention and Punishment of the Crime of Genocide, December 9, 1948, 78 U.N.T.S. 277.

79. On the basis of the recommendations of the Special Committee, the General Assembly finally adopted the Definition of Aggression by consensus in 1974. G.A. Res. 3314, U.N. GAOR, 29th Sess., Supp. 31, U.N. Doc. A/9631 (1974).

80. G.A. Res. 897(IX), U.N. GAOR, 9th Sess., Supp. No. 21, U.N. Doc A/2890 (1954).

81. U.N. GAOR, 36th Sess., U.N. Doc. A/Res/36/106 (1981).

82. Report of the International Law Commission on the Work of Its Forty-Eighth Session, U.N. GAOR, 51st Sess., Supp. No. 10, at 14, U.N. Doc. A/51/10 (1996).

83. See *International Criminal Responsibility of Individual and Entities Engaged in Illicit Trafficking in Narcotic Drugs across National Frontiers and Other Transnational Criminal Activities: Establishment of an International Criminal Court with Jurisdiction over Such Crimes,* G.A. Res. 44/39, U.N. GAOR, 44th Sess., Supp. No. 49 at 311, U.N. Doc. A/444/49 (1989).

84. U.N. GAOR, 47th Sess., U.N. Doc. A/Res/50/46 (1992).

85. The ILC draft statute and commentaries are found in the Report of the International Law Commission on the Work of Its Forty-Sixth Session, U.N. GAOR, 49th Sess., Supp. No. 10, at 43, U.N. Doc. A/49/10 (1994).

86. Rome Statute of the International Criminal Court, July 17, 1998, 37 I.L.M. 999 The vote was 120–7, with 21 abstentions; http://www.icc-cpi.int/home.html.

87. For a summary, see International Criminal Court Cases, http://www.icc-cpi.int/cases.html.

88. UN SCOR, S/RES/953 (1994), Preamble, para. 3. See also Sharaga and Zacklin, "The International Criminal Court for Rwanda," 501–18.

89. See Chapter 6 for a full discussion.

90. See Article 2, Statute of the Special Court for Sierra Leone, and Schabas, *The UN International Criminal Tribunals,* 162.

91. UN SCOR S/RES/1503 (August 28, 2003); UN SCOR S/RES/1504 (September 4, 2003). See also *Completion Strategy of the International Criminal Tribunal for Rwanda,* May 2005 (S/2005/336), which contains estimates relating to the workload.

92. Erik Mose, President of the ICTR (2003–2007) noted in an address to the UN General Assembly (November 15, 2004), "It is a paradox that indispensable financial contributions are not paid when the Tribunal is doing its utmost to complete its task. We cannot maintain the speed if the brakes are on. A slowing down of the judicial process may also mean that Member States have to pay their contributions for longer periods of time. As stated in our Annual Report, the Tribunal strongly recommends that it continues to receive sufficient resources to enable it to comply with the deadlines set by the Security Council"; http://69.94.11.53/ENGLISH/speeches/mose151104.htm.

93. A judge who participates only in a particular case or a limited set of cases (same as a judge ad hoc). *Ad litem* literally means "for the legal action." Judges *ad litem* were not part of the original structure but were added later, in 2001, because of heavy case loads and long trial length.

94. If a judge has dual nationality, the state where he or she exercises civil and political rights will determine nationality in terms of eligibility for election.

95. Originally, the ICTR had only two judges assigned to the appeals chamber. This changed with Security Council Resolution 1329 in 2000. UN SCOR S/RES/1329 (November 30, 2000). This resolution also authorized the addition of *ad litem* judges. See also UN SCOR S/RES/1512 (October 27, 2003), which expanded the number of *ad litem* judges.

96. ICTY at a Glance, http://www.un.org/icty/glance-e/index.htm.

97. On April 7, 2006, the appeals chamber upheld the decision to refer the Mejakić et al. case, involving four accused, to Bosnia and Herzegovina for trial. The appeals chamber dismissed eight of the grounds in the Joint Defense Appeal and allowed one in part; http://www.un.org/icty/latest-e/index.htm.

98. ICTY at a Glance.

99. Report of the International Tribunal for the Prosecution of Persons Responsible for Serious Violations of International Humanitarian Law Committed in the Territory of the Former Yugoslavia since 1991, UN GAOR-SCOR, Doc. A/62/172–S/2007/469 (August 1, 2007).

100. Summary, Report of ICTY 2007.

101. Report of the International Criminal Tribunal for the Prosecution of Persons Responsible for Genocide and Other Serious Violations of International Humanitarian Law Committed in the Territory of Rwanda and Rwandan Citizens Responsible for Genocide and Other Such Violations Committed in the Territory of Neighbouring States between 1 January and 31 December 1994, UN GAOR/SCOR, Doc. A/62/284–S/2007/502 (August 21, 2007).

102. About the Special Court, http://www.sc-sl.org/about.html.

103. Schabas, *The UN International Criminal Tribunals,* 162.

104. Article 4 of the Statute states: "The Court shall have international legal personality."

105. Text at http://www.icc-cpi.int/library/asp/ICC-ASP-3-Res1_English.pdf.

106. See http://www.icc-cpi.int/organs/chambers.html.

107. Article 5(2) has a caveat: "The Court shall exercise jurisdiction over the crime of aggression once a provision is adopted in accordance with articles 121 and 123 defining the crime and setting out the conditions under which the Court shall exercise jurisdiction with respect to this crime. Such a provision shall be consistent with the relevant provisions of the Charter of the United Nations." Considering the history of international efforts to define aggression, the provisions for amending the statute (7/8ths of the Assembly of

States Parties) raise serious doubts about future incorporation of this crime into the court's mandate.

108. Seven are from the Western European (and others), 4 from the Latin American Caribbean Group, 2 from the Asian Group, 3 from the African Group, and 2 from the Group of Eastern Europe. Seven are female, and 11 are male judges.

109. For a list of current cases, see http://www.icc-cpi.int/cases.html.

110. Their names are Thomas Lubanga Dyilo, Bosco Ntaganda, Germain Katanga, and Mathieu Ngudjolo Chui.

111. The indicted are Ahmad Harun and Ali Kushayb.

112. For full details, see Pending Cases, *Application of the Convention on the Prevention and Punishment of the Crime of Genocide (Croatia v. Serbia)*; http://www.icj-cij.org/docket/index.php?p1=3&p2=1&code=cry&case=118&k=73.

113. *Application of the Convention on the Prevention and Punishment of the Crime of Genocide (Bosnia and Herzegovina v. Serbia and Montenegro)* (1993); Judgment of July 11, 1996; Application for Revision of the Judgment of July 11, 1996 in the *Case concerning Application of the Convention on the Prevention and Punishment of the Crime of Genocide (Bosnia and Herzegovina v. Yugoslavia)*, Judgment of February 26, 2007.

114. *Application Instituting Proceedings (17 October 2000), Arrest Warrant of 11 April 2000 (Democratic Republic of the Congo v. Belgium)*.

115. *Arrest Warrant of 11 April 2000 (Democratic Republic of the Congo v. Belgium)* (Merits), Judgment of February 14, 2002.

116. See Faiza Patel King and Anne-Marie LaRosa, "The Jurisprudence of the Yugoslavia Tribunal: 1994–1996," *European Journal of International Law* 8, no. 1 (1997): 123–80.

117. See Payam Akhavan, "Justice, Power and the Realities of Interdependence: Lessons from the Milošević and Hussein Trials," *Cornell Journal of International Law* 38 (2005): 973–82. For another assessment, see Julie Kim, *Balkan Cooperation on War Crimes Issues: 2005 Update,* Congressional Research Service #RS22097 (March 28, 2005).

118. "Rwanda Starts Prisoner Releases," BBC. Rwanda's authorities have begun releasing more than 36,000 genocide suspects from its overcrowded jails; http://news.bbc.co.uk/1/hi/world/africa/4726969.stm.

119. Erik Møse, "Main Achievements of the ICTR," *Journal of International Criminal Justice* 3, no. 4 (2005): 920–43.

120. Report of the Secretary-General on the activities of the Office of Internal Oversight Services, *Follow-up Investigation into Possible Fee-splitting Arrangements Between Defence Counsel and Indigent Detainees at the International Tribunal for Rwanda and the International Tribunal for the Former Yugoslavia,* UN GAOR, Doc. A//56/836 (February 26, 2002). Note that the ICTY has had scandals, as well. Note the title of the report. See also Dina Temple-Raston, *Justice on the Grass: Three Rwandan Journalists, Their Trial for War Crimes, and a Nation's Quest for Redemption* (New York: Free Press, 2005), 122–24.

121. "Former Yugoslavia: President of War Crimes Tribunal Says Funding Problems Serious," http://www.globalpolicy.org/intljustice/tribunals/yugo/2004/1116funding.htm.

122. Sylvia de Bertodano, "What Price Defence? Resourcing the Defence at the ICTY," *Journal of International Criminal Justice* 2 (2004): 503–8.

123. De Bertodano, "What Price Defence," 504–5.

124. Møse, "Main Achievements of the ICTR," 928.

125. For example, "The very idea of an international criminal court may well be a dangerously utopian one to begin with. As various critics of the ICC have pointed out, courts derive whatever democratic legitimacy they may enjoy from being embedded in

more comprehensive systems of government in which their powers are checked by democratically accountable institutions." John Rosenthal, "A Lawless Global Court: How the International Criminal Court Undermines the UN System," *Policy Review* 123 (February-March 2004); http://www.hoover.org/publications/policyreview/3439981.html.

126. See, for example, Martha Minow, *Between Vengeance and Forgiveness: Facing History after Genocide and Mass Violence* (Boston: Beacon Press, 1998), and William A. Schabas and Shane Darcy (eds.), *Truth Commissions and Courts: The Tension between Criminal Justice and the Search for Truth* (Dodrecht, Netherlands: Kluwer, 2004), for a good discussion of the issues here.

127. Robertson, *Crimes against Humanity,* 620.

128. For a comprehensive critique by a participant, see Gideon Boas, *The Milošević Trial: Lessons for the Conduct of Complex International Criminal Proceedings* (Cambridge: Cambridge University Press, 2007).

129. "Sudan promised to turn Darfur into a graveyard yesterday as it reacted with fury to charges laid by an international prosecutor accusing President al-Bashir of genocide, crimes against humanity and war crimes. The threat was made by an official in Darfur after Luis Moreno-Ocampo, the chief prosecutor of the International Criminal Court (ICC), called for the arrest of Omar al-Bashir for his Government's ruthless campaign of violence in the war-torn region." "Sudanese president Omar al-Bashir charged with genocide," London Times Online (July 15, 2008), http://www.timesonline.co.uk/tol/news/world/africa/article4330605.ece.

130. See James L. Taulbee, "A Call to Arms Declined: The United States and the International Criminal Court," *Emory International Law Review* 14 (Spring 2000): 105–56 for a lengthy discussion and evaluation of U.S. objections.

CHAPTER 4

Crimes against Humanity

If a man is killed in Paris, it is murder; if the throats of fifty thousand people are cut in the east, it is a question.

Victor Hugo

This anguished observation highlights the problems of marshaling the international community to deal with the issues raised by deliberate large-scale killing. The incident most often used to illustrate the truth of this proposition occurred in Berlin on March 14, 1921. A 24-year-old Armenian émigré shot and killed Mehmet Talaat,[1] the former Turkish head of state. As minister of the interior in 1915, Talaat bore much of the responsibility for the forcible deportation of Armenians from Turkey's eastern provinces to Syria. Most historians blame him for the barbarity of the operation, which resulted in the deaths of hundreds of thousands of people. The Turkish government had previously been implicated in the Hamidian massacres (1894–1897)[2] in Armenia and Turkey and in another massacre in 1909. These two earlier incidents had resulted in the deaths of an estimated 200,000 Armenians, but the international community had not reacted in ways that might discourage future policies directed to the same end.

When the Ottoman government began to purse a similar policy in 1915, France, Great Britain, and Russia had issued a joint declaration condemning the systematic killing of Armenians by the Turkish government.[3] The declaration accused Turkish officials of "crimes against humanity and civilization" and spoke of personal accountability:

> In view of these new crimes of Turkey against humanity and civilisation, the Allied governments announce publicly to the Sublime Porte[4] that they will hold personally responsible [for] these crimes all members of the Ottoman Government and those of their agents who are implicated in such massacres.[5]

At the end of the war, Talaat and others had sought asylum in Germany, their ally during the conflict. Germany had resisted demands by the British and the French to hand Talaat over to the Allied powers for prosecution. Ironically, the British formed the driving force behind the desire to have trials to punish those accused of forcibly deporting and killing Greeks and Armenians resident in the Ottoman state during World War I. They would be less willing to purse this course after World War II. As an aside, after a prolonged and sensational trial, a German jury acquitted Talaat's assassin, Soghomon Tehlirian.

The problem here, as we have discussed previously, comes from the simple fact that statements such as the joint declaration may mark evidence of great concern, but they do not make new law in and of themselves. Prior to this assertion, one cannot find any consistent practice that might support the statement as a declaration of existing law. In this regard we should note that the original Russian statement referred to "crimes against *Christianity* and civilization" (emphasis added), not humanity and civilization.[6]

The British had pressed the new Turkish government to take action against those responsible for the massacre. The pressure resulted in a number of arrests. Many of those detained were high-ranking members of the government. Among the detainees was Said Halim Pasha, who had served as Grand Vizier (head of government) from 1913 through 1917. The government arrested a total of 107 suspects.[7] The arrests generated large-scale unrest within Turkey. The government quickly began prosecution using a special court-martial. The first trials resulted in convictions for Kemal Bey, the provincial lieutenant governor of Yozgart, and Major Tevfik Bey, commander of the police in the same district. Tevfik received a sentence of 15 years at hard labor. Bey received the death penalty, which the government immediately carried out. The sentences and execution added to the unrest.

The Turkish government did start trials for the more prominent of the others accused, including Said Halim Pasha. Bass notes that not until the Nuremberg and Tokyo trials after World War II would such high-ranking officials face a court demand for accountability for their actions.[8] These trials quickly bogged down because of domestic political interference and events within Turkey. Britain then seized custody of most of those accused still within Turkish prisons and transported them to Malta with the idea of trying them in British courts. Nationalist sentiment ran high in Turkey. Many Turks felt that those on trial had not committed any offense beyond safeguarding the security of the state. The government further undermined the legitimacy of the prosecutions when it used the opportunity to arrest opposition leaders on various pretexts that had little to do with the Armenian massacre. Among prisoners still in Turkish custody, escapes were common; others were freed. The court-martial did proceed, but in "safe mode." True, the court convicted Talaat and Enver and sentenced them to death, but Turkey did not have custody of them. Both were living safely in Germany. Many of those in custody in Turkey were acquitted.

All criminal proceedings halted when civil war broke out. Eventually, the Nationalist faction led by Mustafa Kemal (later Kemal Attaturk) succeeded in overthrowing the incumbent Ottoman government. In the course of action, the Nationalists took 29 British soldiers as prisoners. These became the pawns in a negotiation that led to a trade—the Turks in British custody for the British soldiers held by Kemal. No matter the passion for "justice" for the Armenians, the fate of British soldiers and subjects in the here and now prevailed. Short-term pragmatic concerns based upon the desire to protect British nationals took precedence over "justice" for the Armenians. Under the Treaty of Lausanne (Switzerland), signed in 1923, the British agreed to the trade and also to desist from any further attempts to prosecute those accused.

Evolution of a Norm

In terms of mass killing, crimes against humanity may be as old as humanity itself.[9] Yet, only since World War II has a legal regime evolved that defines the included offenses as criminal under international law. From a modern standpoint, however one wishes to characterize various actions, "might" may not have necessarily made right in the sense of moral (or legal) justification, but might certainly provided the victor or the stronger the opportunity for great slaughter. If we look at the historical record, we find that humanitarian concerns have not been very evident over the centuries. From a pragmatic view, in many places and times, the land conquered had value; the people who had occupied it did not, except perhaps as slaves to be sold or used. Indeed, large-scale killing in antiquity is not difficult to find. The Old Testament alone records a number of instances. In the Book of Joshua, God commands the total destruction of Jericho, Ai, and five other cities. God also commands the total destruction of the Amalekites and punishes King Saul for his failure to carry out the task exactly as ordered (I Samuel 15:1–16:1). Alexander the Great systematically crucified 2,000 young men who had fought for Tyre after totally sacking the city. Rome's final solution to the fears generated by Carthage was the total destruction of the city.[10]

Context: Thresholds (Objective Requirements) and Crimes

As a category, the definition of crimes against humanity has until recently lacked precision.[11] Note that a legal definition for ICL must have several essential elements. First, it must stipulate a *context*. Second, it must enumerate the *offenses* included when committed within that context. Third, it may identify specific categories of victims. Fourth, it must specify a *threshold,* or specific conditions that separate the crimes identified from other offenses.

I use the term "threshold" deliberately because the analogy to a threshold in a doorway perfectly captures the idea. To pass a threshold, to go through a door, for example, means that one goes from one defined area to another. The category "crimes against humanity" has two separate thresholds. The first specifies the elements essential to establish the context necessary to qualify an offense as a crime that falls into the category. The second threshold defines the criteria or tests necessary to establish *specific individual acts* within the context as crimes against humanity, rather than ordinary crimes. These form two separate considerations and problems for prosecutors. Just because a rape or murder or other felonious act took place within a specific context does not necessary mean that the crime constitutes a crime against humanity. It could be a random act, not directly associated with the broader context.[12] In the case of crimes against humanity, the first threshold establishes the jurisdiction of the court.

To use an example from domestic law, many U.S. states have enacted laws prohibiting "hate crimes" and have established more severe penalties for those convicted of committing these offenses than for those convicted of similar crimes without the element of hate. The domestic statutes establish explicit criteria, the *threshold,* that prosecutors must satisfy in terms of evidence in order to try to convict someone of committing a hate crime, as opposed to an ordinary crime.[13] If a hoodlum beats up a randomly selected victim or if someone attacks and injures a friend or acquaintance in a fit of rage, the acts merit prosecution but do not qualify as hate crimes because the factual elements of the crimes do not establish the necessary requirements. On the other hand, under most state laws, if a hoodlum chooses a random victim or someone attacks and injures a neighbor because of that person's race or religion, the acts possibly meet the threshold requirements to be tried as hate crimes.

While instructive, in one important sense this domestic analogy does not quite capture the international process. In domestic law, prosecutors must *first* establish the elements of the crime, that is, adduce proof that the accused individual did commit the alleged crime. Then they must show that the actions pass the threshold defining hate crimes. At the international level, because prosecutors must first establish jurisdiction, they must show that the alleged crime occurred within the situation defined by the contextual threshold before they can move to prove that the specific individual should be held accountable for the crime.

Only with the trials before the various ad hoc courts (ICTY, ICTR, SCSL) have more precise formulations emerged. Unlike genocide and the acts that comprise war crimes, which have widely accepted definitions drawn from conventions, the term "crimes against humanity" appears in a number of different instruments that offer varying definitions. Much of the incoherence stems from the genesis of the category.[14] Because the category of crimes against humanity originated as an attempt to plug gaps in the existing law governing war crimes, until the Rome Statute of the ICC the elements delimiting the context and the crimes included within the jurisdiction of the various ad hoc courts that have tried cases have been situation-specific rather than inclusive.

The first attempt at a concise definition occurs in the Charter setting up the Nuremberg trials (IMT).[15] Article 6 (c) of the London Charter defined crimes against humanity as:

> Namely, murder, extermination, enslavement, deportation, and other inhumane acts committed against any civilian population, before or during the war;[,]

> or persecutions on political, racial or religious grounds in execution of or in connection with any crime within the jurisdiction of the Tribunal, whether or not in violation of the domestic law of the country where perpetrated.

At the outset, we should note a longstanding debate over the significance of Nuremberg—did the Charter create new law, or did it merely give a more precise formulation to a rather inchoate customary law?[16] This is a fundamental question because, as discussed in Chapter 2, the principle of nonretroactivity presumably precludes trials based upon "new law," that is, norms not extant at the time of the alleged acts. Clearly, no formal convention established individual liability for other than war crimes; nor can one find systematic practice supporting the evolution of customary rules. The question, simply put, became this: did the need to enforce accountability for such mass atrocities recognized as unquestionably criminal by almost everyone trump the need for strict legality?[17]

Within its judgments, the IMT evaded the question of retroactivity. Only 2 of 16 defendants (Streicher and von Schirach) charged with crimes against humanity were found guilty solely of crimes against humanity. In the judgments in both cases, the tribunal blurred the distinction between war crimes and crimes against humanity by suggesting that crimes against humanity within the context of the war formed a class of war crimes. Moreover, the tribunal did not accept any evidence of crimes committed before hostilities began.[18] This effectively limited the context to only those acts committed during the period of war. Hence, Scharf notes: "While the public perception is that the Nuremberg trial provided a comprehensive account of the Holocaust, in fact that was the one thing the Nuremberg Tribunal was legally precluded from doing."[19]

While most commentaries tend to focus upon Nuremberg, prosecutions took place in many other settings and venues. The core ideas in Article 6(c) can be found in all of the various instruments authorizing trials, but we find interesting variations in terms of specific elements. Note that this does not represent nitpicking. The variations have a very real impact on what a specific court can and cannot prosecute as a "crime against humanity." This does not mean that particular action does not qualify as a "crime." It does mean that if an act does not fit all the elements necessary to the definition of a "crime against humanity" as specified in the treaty or other instrument setting up the tribunal, it will fall outside the jurisdiction of that court.

Two good examples come from the ICTY. The tribunal's first trial was *Prosecutor v. Tadić* (May 7 to November 28, 1996).[20] The judges had three main issues: (1) did the war in Bosnia meet the test of "an international armed conflict"; (2) did widespread and systematic abuse against Serbs occur; and (3) did Tadić personally engage in criminal acts against non-Serbs (and to what extent)? Note here the sequence of the issues addressed. Affirmative answers to the first two were needed in order to proceed to the third. The first issue divided the court (2–1, Judge McDonald dissenting), resulting in "not guilty" verdicts on several counts on the basis that individuals within the sector did not have "protected status."[21]

The defendant did not really contest the second, and sufficient testimony from witnesses confirmed a number of charges related to the third. The sentencing judgment was rendered on July 14, 1997.[22] A second good example comes from the ICTY Statute that limits the jurisdiction of the court to acts within an armed conflict. For most cases, this did not present a significant limitation (see Judge McDonald's dissent in the Tadić case), but the requirement did mean that the court lacked jurisdiction for any crime against humanity that occurred between the Dayton Peace Agreement (December 14, 1995)[23] and the outbreak of hostilities in Kosovo in late 1999, even though the acts met the definitions according to customary international law.[24]

The different definitions in the various instruments that set up war crime tribunals after World War II also prove instructive here. The definition from the Charter that set up the IMTFE (Tokyo), Article 5(e), omitted "religious" from the definition, as well as "any civilian population." Thus, unlike the IMT, the jurisdiction of the Far Eastern Tribunal potentially included large-scale killing of military personnel in an unlawful war.[25] The legislation, Allied Control Council Law No. 10 (CCL 10), that governed trials conducted by the Allies in their zones of occupations in Germany added imprisonment, torture, and rape to the list of offenses included.[26] It also omitted the requirement that crimes against humanity be connected to the war by omitting the phrase "before or during the war" included in Article 6(c) of the IMT Charter.[27]

Between the prosecutions related to World War II and the events of the 1990s in Rwanda, Bosnia, and Sierra Leone, only a handful of cases in various domestic courts involved allegations involving crimes against humanity.[28] In these, the contextual element surfaced as a major divide between courts that followed the IMT provisions that required a connection to wartime acts and acts against civilian populations and those that adopted the broader CCL 10 standard that did not.

Between World War II and the events of the 1990s, the Apartheid Convention (1973)[29] and the *Inter-American Convention on Forced Disappearance*[30] suggested two additional offenses, but the defining moments in refining the category came with the Security Council creation of the ICTY (Yugoslavia) and the ICTR (Rwanda) and the entry into force of the Rome Statute of the International Criminal Court.[31] In developing the Statutes for the ICTR and the ICTY, the Security Council drew upon CCL 10, but Article 5 of the ICTY Statute expanded the essential *contextual* element to any armed conflict, whether international or *internal* in character, but still limited the scope to civilian population. Article 3 of the ICTR Statute added two additional elements: widespread or systematic attacks and discriminatory grounds (national, political, ethnic, racial, or religious). It does *not* require armed conflict as a condition. Article 7 of the ICC Statute[32] combines most of the contextual elements of the two ad hoc tribunals and expands the list of offenses to include forced transfer of population, sexual slavery, enforced prostitution, forced pregnancy, enforced sterilization, sexual violence, enforced disappearance, and apartheid. On the other hand, the ICC Statute does not include "discrimination" as a contextual element. Courts other than the Rwanda tribunal have resisted treating "discrimination" as a necessary element.[33] Nor can one find widespread, systematic support for its inclusion among other authorities.

Finally, we should note that all contemporary lists of crimes include the category "other inhumane acts." While this may seem a vague formulation, it serves as a residual category to address the contingency that any list of offenses, no matter how carefully and thoroughly compiled, may not capture all of the possibilities. In terms of practical application, the category does not stand alone. The parameters of any crime that a prosecutor feels may fall with this category must still conform to the standards used to define the elements of other crimes against humanity as well as those found in other major human rights instruments.[34]

Crimes against Humanity: Continuing Issues and Clarifications

Because of the paucity of practice until recent prosecutions by the ad hoc tribunals, questions continue. Most involve technical debates that *may* have some relevance to actual cases in *some* instances. Others concern fundamental questions of scope because they form threshold (objective) conditions that separate crimes against humanity from ordinary crimes. Here an interesting problem again comes from our prior discussion in Chapter 2: to what extent is the ICC Statute, as a treaty, declaratory of customary law?[35] Curiously, the issues here revolve around both the inclusion of new elements and the possible omission of some of the older ones. For example, while the designation "crimes against humanity" originated to fill a gap in international humanitarian (war crimes) law, the *objective* contextual threshold has evolved beyond requiring armed conflict as a precondition. We noted the difference between the ICTR Statute and the ICTY Statute (Article 5), with one requiring "armed conflict" while the other does not. Early on, the ICTY adopted the stance that Article 5 formed only a jurisdictional requirement inserted by the Security Council, not a principle of customary international law.[36]

A second issue concerns the target population. Relying upon the case law after World War II, Cassese eloquently maintains that the stipulation "against a civilian population" narrows the context supported by customary law.[37] Others have concluded that the standard requires only a *predominantly* civilian population.[38] Still a third opinion suggests that the distinction serves to separate attacks on military forces, legitimate under international humanitarian law, from unlawful attacks on civilians.[39] The tendency of courts has been to construe this requirement in broad fashion in order to enforce the underlying principles defining crimes against humanity.[40] Courts have held that the phrase "directed against" means that civilians must form the primary target of any attack, not just be present as incidental victims. Hence, in the *Blaskić* case, the ICTY appeals chamber found "that the presence within a population of members of resistance groups, or former combatants, who have laid down their arms, does not alter its civilian characteristic."[41]

A third question concerns the relationship between war crimes (international humanitarian law) and crimes against humanity, because the category "crimes against humanity" did evolve from gaps in international humanitarian law. Simply explained, while war crimes are individual acts that occur in connection with an armed conflict, crimes against humanity involve a *widespread or systematic attack against any civilian population,* even in the absence of an international or internal conflict. The "widespread or systematic attack" element formed an implicit requirement in earlier prosecutions, although it took the first cases before the ICTY for judges to seize the issues and develop explicit tests and criteria to define the threshold.[42] While crimes against humanity may occur within an armed conflict, the idea of "attack" and "armed conflict" are logically independent and distinct. Unlike the requirements of the laws of war, an "attack" that sets the context for crimes against humanity within an armed conflict embodies more than the conduct of hostilities—it specifically relates to the deliberate mistreatment of people who are not taking an active part in the conflict.[43]

A fourth issue emerged during the drafting of the ICC Statute concerning whether or not a government policy element is needed as a contextual element. Of course, the genesis of crimes against humanity stemmed from the perceived necessity to punish a government for extreme abuse of its own nationals. Section 7 of the ICC Elements of Crimes states that "It is understood that 'policy to commit such attack' requires that the State or organization actively promote or encourage such an attack against a civilian population." On the other hand, the decisions of the ICTY, tribunals have interpreted the customary law to mean that it did not require a policy element.[44] Still, Article 10 of the Rome Statute, referring to the articles defining the jurisdiction of the court, also provides that "Nothing in this Part shall be interpreted as limiting or prejudicing in any way existing or developing rules of international law for purposes other than this Statute." This seems to leave open the possibility that customary law in terms of practice other than that of the ICC could support a wider set of circumstances.

Issues in Application: Explicitly Defining the Threshold—Objective Elements (*Actus Reus*)

The phrase "widespread and systematic attack against any civilian population" contains many terms that need precise definition before judges can apply them to a given event. Even in "refining" the requirement, the layman may think that terms such as "substantial" or "significant" as measures remain ambiguous, but the events within a specific context determine how judges use these yardsticks to calculate. To illustrate without engaging in an extended technical analysis, consider the following issues in terms of developing standards applicable to establishing a threshold. Courts must, within the mandate of their constitutive Statutes, explicitly:

Determine what actions constitute an attack

Determine what constitutes a civilian population

Define widespread and systematic

First, note that, as a threshold element, an "attack" is not itself a crime against humanity. Rather, it forms the necessary circumstances (context) within which specific crimes may be characterized as crimes against humanity rather than as ordinary offenses. Second, as used here, the term "attack" has a broader connotation than physical violence. It need not involve the direct use of armed force. "Attack" can also denote a broad course of conduct involving severe mistreatment. As an example, a policy of *apartheid* qualifies as an attack.[45] Article 7 (Crimes against Humanity) of the ICC Elements of Crimes defines "attack" as follows:

> "Attack directed against a civilian population" in these context elements is understood to mean a course of conduct involving the multiple commission of acts referred to in article 7, paragraph 1, of the Statute against any civilian population, pursuant to or in furtherance of a State or organizational policy to commit such attack. The acts need not constitute a military attack.[46]

Some connection must exist between the broader "attack" and the actions of an accused individual, but, the individual acts by an accused do not have to be performed by large number of others. In other words, an individual may commit an act of sexual violence as part of the "attack," but whether that act can be characterized as a crime against humanity does not depend upon how many others have committed acts of sexual violence that may be considered connected to the attack; nor does it necessarily imply than an individual needs to perform more than a single act if other conditions are met. The trial chamber in *Tadić* reasoned that "Clearly a single act by a perpetrator taken in the context of a systematic or widespread attack against a civilian population entails individual criminal responsibility and an individual need not commit numerous offenses to be liable."[47]

Absent a connection to the wider context, an act of rape may simply be an act of rape, a common crime not connected to anything but the circumstances of the moment. The serial rapist, barring a connection to a more widespread series of events resulting in the abuse of a particular group, does not commit a crime against humanity even if he targets a specific female population. We explore this further in the discussion of the terms "widespread or systematic."

The second consideration involves the definition of "any civilian population." This, along with "widespread or systematic," defines the scope (or breadth) of the attack. It also ratifies the innovation of Nuremberg in that it means that government officials may be prosecuted for mistreating their own citizens. Before Nuremberg, the scope of international humanitarian law did not cover attacks by a government on its own population. The term "any" means that the target population can have a generic character. Ethnicity, nationality, religion, or other parameters do not matter. A prosecutor does not have to prove that every victim was a member of a targeted group, only that the person was a civilian and became a target as part of the campaign against a targeted group. Second, a "population" consists of a sizable group of individuals who have some distinctive characteristics that mark them as targets. A small group such as political opponents of a regime or a crowd assembled for a demonstration does not qualify unless the acts taken against the group form part of a broader series of related actions. In this sense, the concept of populations "operates as a minimum standard for determining which group of people may be said to be targeted by an attack."[48]

The final contextual requirement, "widespread or systematic," defines scope. Even though the Statutes of the ICTR and SCSL include this standard, that of the ICTY does not stipulate it as a condition. Nonetheless, from the first, both ICTY trial and appeals chambers adopted it as a measure in their judgments, arguing that it formed a requirement from the customary law. Note that the test is disjunctive, meaning that a situation needs to meet only one, not both tests; presumably it can be either widespread or systematic.[49] Even so, to establish that an attack meets the threshold requirements in terms of scope (numbers) seemingly implies using elements of both. Imagining "widespread" on the scale necessary to trigger this marker seems from both a logical and a practical standpoint to incorporate some elementary form of organization or planning.

Note that international law does not specify minimum numerical requirements. The actual determination requires a calculation relevant to the other necessary contextual elements. This has resulted in a number of different definitions, but, stripped to its essence, widespread "refers to the scale of the acts perpetrated and the number of victims."[50] Authorities often quote the ICTR trial chamber in *Akayesu:* "'widespread' may be defined as massive, frequent, large-scale action, carried out collectively with considerable seriousness and directed against a multiplicity of victims."[51]

Logically, this does raise two separate sets of circumstance: widespread attack may be *either* "the cumulative effect of a series of inhumane acts or the singular effect of an inhumane act of extraordinary magnitude."[52] The term "systematic" has elicited a number of different suggested tests, as well. All embody some idea of organization that exhibits a deliberate pattern or method. This helps establish the nonrandom character of the actions in question or the nonaccidental repetition of similar criminal conduct on a regular basis.[53]

These three requirements set the threshold very high. Political opponents of repressive regimes often seek to have events classified as crimes against humanity in efforts to marshal support and pressure from others for their cause. In the absence of very large numbers or other factors that might generate attention and the will to take action from states with the resources to do so, the unfortunate fact is that state-sponsored torture, terror, and murder persist in many parts of the world. For example, do the actions of the military government in Myanmar (Burma) against Aung San Suu Kyi and her followers in the National League for Democracy (NLD) qualify as crimes against humanity? The attack on an NLD convoy near Depayin village in May 2003 targeted about 300 people and left an estimated

70 dead and scores of injured and wounded. The attack was not the first, and evidence exists to support a claim of systematic targeting. Nonetheless, while, at a minimum, the incidents constitute severe violations of law, they probably do not meet the standards in terms of scope to be considered crimes against humanity.[54] This judgment is not intended to minimize the gravity of the offenses committed. Rather, it serves a reminder of an earlier point—that the crimes discussed here are considered the *most* serious. It also serves as a sad commentary on the current status of enforcement of basic human rights law. Crimes of lesser stature may still go unpunished.

Defining the Threshold—Subjective Element (*Mens Rea*)

The subjective element (*mens rea,* or guilty mind) form the essential connection between the individual actions of an accused and the broader context. Article 30 of the ICC Statute provides the following guidelines for the mental element of all crimes:

1. Unless otherwise provided, a person shall be criminally responsible and liable for punishment for a crime within the jurisdiction of the Court only if the material elements are committed with *intent and knowledge.* (emphasis added)
2. For the purposes of this article, a person has intent where:
    (a) In relation to conduct, that person means to engage in the conduct;
    (b) In relation to a consequence, that person means to cause that consequence or is aware that it will occur in the ordinary course of events.
3. For the purposes of this article, "knowledge" means awareness that a circumstance exists or a consequence will occur in the ordinary course of events. "Know" and "knowingly" shall be construed accordingly.

Paragraphs 3 and 4 of the General Introduction of the Elements of Crimes provide further clarification and guidance:

> (3) Existence of intent and knowledge can be inferred from relevant facts and circumstances.
>
> (4) With respect to mental elements associated with elements involving value judgement, such as those using the terms "inhumane" or "severe," it is not necessary that the perpetrator personally completed a particular value judgement, unless otherwise indicated.[55]

The ICTY Trial Chamber in *Blaskić* said: "It follows that the *mens rea* specific to a crime against humanity does not require that the agent be identified with the ideology, policy or plan in whose name masse crimes were perpetrated nor even that he supported it."[56] Simply put, to prove that an offense is a crime against humanity, the prosecutor has to produce evidence in support of three fundamental contentions: (1) that the accused performed the action; (2) that the act objectively fell within the parameters of the broader attack; and (3) that the accused had some knowledge (or reason to know) of the broader context.[37] The third consideration stands as a separable problem apart from the mental elements necessary to prove commission of an individual crime. In this sense, the requirement does not equate to "intent" or "motive" as normally understood. As with "hate crimes," it forms the subjective threshold that elevates an otherwise ordinary crime to more serious status, but the prosecutor does *not* have to show the accused had bias or animus toward the victims. Schabas argues in this respect that some of the earlier ICTY judgments that suggested that the *mens rea* requirements excluded acts carried out for purely personal motives are incorrect.[58] Proof that the accused has some knowledge of the context is sufficient to establish guilt.

Elements of Specific Crimes

Table 4.1 lists the offenses currently associated with crimes against humanity. In the following list I have chosen to summarize major issues rather than analyze the technical elements of each separate crime in depth.

Table 4.1   Crimes against Humanity

Must be committed as part of a widespread *or* systematic attack on a civilian population.

Murder

Extermination

Deportation/Forcible Transfer

Imprisonment

Torture

Sexual Violence

   rape

   sexual slavery

   forced pregnancy

   enforced prostitution

   enforced sterilization

   other acts of sexual violence of "comparable gravity"

Persecution

Enforced Disappearance

Apartheid

Other Inhumane Acts

Source: Rome Statute of the International Criminal Court, Article 7.

- *Murder:* Acts of intentional killing whether premeditated or not[59]
- *Extermination*: Mass or large-scale killing. What distinguishes this from simple murder is "killing within a context of mass killing." "[T]here must be evidence that a particular population was targeted and that its members were killed or otherwise subjected to conditions of life calculated to bring about the destruction of a numerically significant part of the population."[60] The difference between extermination and genocide stems from the fact that genocide requires special intent to destroy a specific group.
- *Enslavement:* The capture, acquisition, sale, exchange, transport, or disposal of persons with intent to reduce them to slavery or to sell or exchange them.[61] Forced marriage, child exploitation, and forced labor may fall into this category, as well.
- *Deportation or forcible transfer:* Deportation generally involves sending individuals across an international border, while forcible transfer refers to internal displacement. The acts here do not necessarily have to involve physical force.
- *Imprisonment:* Arbitrary deprivation of physical liberty without due process of law.
- *Torture:* Intentional infliction of severe physical or mental pain or suffering upon a victim by a government agent or someone acting as a surrogate for such an agent.
- *Sexual violence:* "[A]ll serious abuses of a sexual nature inflicted upon the physical and moral integrity of a person by means of coercion, threat of force or intimidation in a way that is degrading and humiliating for the victim's dignity."[62]
- *Persecution:* The intentional and severe deprivation of fundamental human rights on illegal discriminatory grounds. While this offense formed an element of the IMT Charter, it lacked precise definition until the ICTR and the ICTY tackled the issues. Four points are relevant here. First, a particular intent to target a person or group must be proven. Knowledge alone is not sufficient. Second, persecution requires a connection to other crimes.[63] Third, it necessitates "discriminatory grounds." Last, the acts must be of a gravity comparable to that inherent in other crimes against humanity.[64]
- *Enforced disappearance:* "[T]he arrest, detention or abduction of persons by, or with the authorization, support or acquiescence of, a State or a political organization, followed by a refusal to acknowledge that deprivation of freedom or to give information on the fate or whereabouts of those persons, with the intention of removing them from the protection of the law for a prolonged period of time."[65]
- *Apartheid:* "'The crime of apartheid' means inhumane acts of a character similar to those referred to in paragraph 1, committed in the context of an institutionalized regime of systematic oppression and domination by one racial group over any other racial group or groups and committed with the intention of maintaining that regime."[66]

Some Thoughts on Perspective

Defining these crimes in the abstract does not give an adequate idea of scale, nor necessarily does citing chapter and verse with respect to numbers. The "law of large numbers" operates here. Individuals can easily relate to the dead and injured in a major auto crash on an Atlanta freeway or to the victims of a serial killer. But, at a certain level, numbers fail to have an emotional impact unless extended media coverage provides graphic visual images to prod us to engage our imagination in ways that we might resist otherwise and, without repeated prodding, continue to resist. Truly, can one visualize multiple thousands or millions? Realistically, most people cannot grasp the extent of these crimes without a considerable amount of direct graphic evidence because they find them so totally beyond their experience and expectations of ordinary human behavior.

Bosnia: A Brief Summary

The end of the Cold War in the late 1980s and early 1990s sparked great hope for an era of peace. Instead, what ensued was an era of violence. The string of atrocities that first gained the world's attention occurred in the Balkans. Media tended to emphasize the religious divide between Christians and Muslims, but the gulf between Roman Catholics (Croats) and Eastern Orthodox (Serbs) has generated conflict, as well. The divides themselves did not cause the conflicts. They provided the opportunity for ambitious individuals to exploit them by stirring up extreme prejudice in service of their own political agendas. In the contemporary cases, the use of mass media, particularly radio and television, to promote and incite ethnic hatred played an enormous role.[67] While many have spoken of longstanding hatreds, events in Yugoslavia just prior to and during, World War II have the most relevance to the events of the 1990s. During World War II, the Croat Ustashas,[68] a group originally founded to achieve Croatian independence, formed a puppet government in the German-occupied sector of Yugoslavia (contemporary Croatia and Bosnia-Herzegovina). The Croats regarded the ethnic Serbian population as a threat to national integrity. In a 1941 speech, Viktor Gutich, the governor of western Bosnia, urged that Croatia be "thoroughly cleansed of all Serbian dirt."[69] The Croats established a death camp at Jasenovac that mirrored Dachau and Auschwitz in its efficiency. By the end of the war, an estimated 500,000 to 700,000 Serbs had been killed and another 1 million forcibly driven out of the country. The Ustashas were defeated and ousted by Yugoslav partisans led by Marshal Josip Broz (who took the name Tito as his alias during the resistance).[70] At the end of the war, the Serbs returned the favor by slaughtering an estimated 100,000 Croats.

Tito established a unified Yugoslavia that consisted of six federal republics, Bosnia-Herzegovina, Croatia, Macedonia, Montenegro, Serbia, and Slovenia, and two "autonomous regions," Kosovo and Vojvodina, within the Republic of Serbia. He managed the ethnic tensions within and among the various republics through force of his personality and repressive tactics. With his death, in 1980, the tensions once again rose to the surface, fanned by the resurgence of a Serbian nationalism seemingly bent on dominating the other republics.[71] The aggressive posture and tactics adopted by Slobodan Milošević, when he assumed the presidency of Serbia, in 1989, led to the decision by Croatia and Slovenia to secede from the federation and to declare their independence in June 1991. Both refused to give any guarantees concerning treatment of the Serbs living within their territories. Milošević ordered the invasion of Slovenia by the JNA (Yugoslav National Army), but Slovenia successfully repelled the effort.

Milošević then turned his attention to Croatia. There the JNA, assisted by local Serb partisans, quickly occupied almost one-third of Croatian territory. After some months of fighting, the two sides agreed to the deployment of a UN peacekeeping force (UNPROFOR) to supervise the withdrawal of JNA troops and the disarmament within Croatia.[72] In January 1992, the European Community (now the European Union) recognized Croatia as an independent state. In Bosnia-Herzegovina, Radovan Karadžić, the leader of the Bosnian Serbs, threatened that attempts to establish an independent state would "make the Muslim people disappear . . . if there is a war."[73] On April 6, 1992, the European Community recognized the newly independent nation of Bosnia-Herzegovina. On the same day, Karadžić declared the formation of Republika Sprška (the Serbian Republic of Bosnia-Herzegovina). Soon after, the Bosnian Serbs, with the assistance of the JNA, attacked both the Croatian and Muslim populations (in the northeast and the south). As predicted by Karadžić, the Muslim population failed to put together a concerted resistance effort. In less than a month, it was reduced to having control over little more than small enclaves within Bosnia. Srebenica and Sarajevo became synonyms for systematic, unprovoked attacks on civilian populations.

The invasion produced a huge exodus from Bosnia. One observer noted that, within a month of Bosnia's declaration of independence, more than 400,000 people had fled; by the end of July, the number of displaced persons had reached 2.5 million.[74] The evidence suggests that the Serbs routinely used rape as a tactic, not only against Muslim women but against Croat women, as well. Estimates of the number of women raped range from 30,000 to 50,000. Bell-Fialkoff notes that in Yugoslavia, thousands of women, many of them minors, were interned in rape camps.[75] One of the first reporters granted access to concentration camps established by the Serbs wrote: "The Serbian conquerors of northern Bosnia have established two concentration camps in which more than a thousand civilians have been executed or starved and thousands more are being held until they die."[76]

The First Defendant: Duško Tadić

The *Duško Tadić* case, as the first before the ICTY, had enormous significance because the court clarified a number of issues needed to give substance to the scant customary law and to the barebones Charters authorizing various tribunals.[77] Most of Tadić's crimes clearly were offenses covered by international humanitarian law. The question quickly became whether they could be considered crimes against humanity. Other questions surrounded the decision to begin with such a bit player, Ideally, the court would have preferred to start with someone who had occupied a position of some authority, but pragmatism ruled. The tribunal was in place. Germany had Tadić in custody. Public opinion, human rights activists, and the media demanded action.

The initial indictment charged Tadić with 34 counts of breaches of the Geneva Conventions, violations of the laws and customs of war, and crimes against humanity (murder, rape, and torture).[78] As Scharf notes, Richard Goldstone, the prosecutor, did not seek an indictment on the charge of genocide, even though Germany has issued the original arrest warrant on that charge.[79] This reflected a pragmatic decision. As noted before (and as covered in the last part of this chapter), genocide requires adducing proof of a specific intent. As we shall discuss, generating sufficient evidence to prove this for low-level defendants can be a daunting endeavor. Goldstone would have had to prove that Tadić specifically intended to further the Serb policy of ethnic cleansing. Apart from his status as a foot soldier in the hierarchy of culpability who had clearly and willingly participated in the ethnic cleansing of his village, Tadić was not officially employed by any agency in any capacity, nor did he have any claim to "authorship" of the ideas on which he acted. He was a consumer turned activist in a vicious way, not an originator or producer.

Prosecution of Tadić had risks and benefits. As the first international prosecution since Nuremberg to be based on crimes against humanity, the case would become a precedent for better or worse. The question, however, became how significant the precedent would be if the court tried only persons involved at Tadić's level? Nonetheless, the stakes for the tribunal were high in terms of both political credibility and financial outlay. The high monetary costs alone for this single trial, $20 million dollars,[80] highlighted finance as a continuing problem. What benefit did the international community receive for the money expended? The tribunal could stage trials for only a small minority of those who actually took part in the campaign of atrocities. If the trials involved only foot soldiers, what impact would they have on deterring future mass killings? What impact would a few trials of low-level participants have on the reconciliation and healing process?

Moreover, from this perspective, the continuing questions related not so much to the operations of the tribunal but to the level of support beyond lip service given by the NATO powers and the members of the Security Council. Up to the time of the Tadić verdict, the United States, the United Kingdom, and other powers involved in the area clearly lacked the political will to go after and arrest the big fish even though the court had issued indictments against them. In this sense, it was not the political credibility of the tribunal that was in question but the political will and credibility of its sponsors. The court could have real relevance only to the extent that it received the necessary political backing from the international community. Only with the election of Tony Blair and the Labour Party in the United Kingdom in May 1997 did the pendulum swing toward active pursuit of major players.[81] Bosnian Serb generals Tihemar Blaskić, Radislav Kristić, and Zdravko Tolimir, along with former Bosnian Serb president (Republika Sprška) Biljana Plavšić, among other high-ranking officials, have been captured or surrendered for trial.

Other questions surfaced with respect to procedure. Because witnesses feared retaliation, the court permitted anonymous and hearsay testimony. Finding, transporting, and housing witnesses posed a major challenge. Even so, many witnesses refused to testify, fearing retaliation. The length of trials ran up costs. The two most-wanted fugitives, former Sprška President Radovan Karadžić and former Army Chief of Staff General Ratko Mladić, continued to elude arrest.[82] Karadžić was finally captured in July 2008. Note again that when Goldstone issued these indictments, he received a great deal of criticism from the diplomatic community because they feared the prosecutions would hinder the peace process.

In his application to the German government for custody of Tadić, Goldstone summarized the essence of the crimes:

> He was involved in the forced removals of Muslims from the villages of the Prijedor region and the looting and destruction of Muslim houses. . . . He was involved in assaults of prisoners at the camps and at the military barracks. . . . Among the most widely witnessed events that Tadić was involved was the murder of Emir Karabasic, Jasmin Hrnjic, and Enver Alic. These three prisoners were brutally beaten and tortured by Tadić and others, using metal rods, truncheons, and knives, to the point of unconsciousness. Tadić then forced a fourth prisoner to drink motor oil from the garage and then bite off the testicles of the unconscious prisoners. The prisoners died as a result of their torture.[83]

The tribunal's first task revolved around giving precise definition to the threshold requirements that separated crimes against humanity from ordinary violations of the laws of warfare. Specifically, Tadić stood trial for the murder of 13 individuals and participating in the torture of 19 others. But, while the definitions and tests developed by the tribunal for establishing what constituted crimes against humanity became guidelines for future prosecutions, Tadić's conviction set a threshold standard in a more direct way. Given his status as a low-level participant rather than a planner, the opinions in the various decisions and judgments established the lower parameters for conduct that would satisfy the threshold tests for meeting the "widespread or systematic attack on a civilian population" standard. Note that the court did find Tadić innocent on a large number of counts (he was convicted only on 11 of the 34 counts of the original indictment), some for technical reasons, some for lack of evidence (witnesses refused to testify). The trial should send a cautionary message about the difficulties of successful international prosecution that follow standards of fairness and impartiality.

On the other hand, as a testament to the trial chamber, the final judgment "stands as a "measured and impartial finding of historical fact . . . as the most authoritative analysis so far of evidence about the factors which brought such a barbaric war to the Balkans."[84] In this case, the tribunal focused upon developing evidence that met the test of "objective fact" insofar as observers can determine such, rather than a version that supported the charges with an eye toward convictions. Despite a major embarrassment and cost, it also set benchmarks for the application of important standards of international humanitarian law.[85] First steps can often result in missteps. On balance, given that the judges had to do an enormous amount of research with little precedent on which to base these judgment, Tadić received a fair trial. From the standpoint of "ultimate" responsibility, as a small fish, Tadić has importance only in the sense that no one who participated in or supported "ethnic cleansing" should have escaped responsibility.[86] The ultimate reality is that international courts can try only a few.

The Milošević Trial

The Milošević trial was the first ever trial of former head of state by an international criminal tribunal.[87] As such, it confronted problems that no other trial had had to deal with. In one sense, starting with smaller fish let the tribunal work out some of the kinks and snags before taking on more high-profile cases. Nonetheless, taking on the big fish proved a very difficult task. Geoffrey Robertson notes that the proceedings were dubbed the "trial of the century," but the trial turned out to be a very severe test of the international justice system. Robertson argues that, by Milošević's death, in 2006, the case had just barely earned passing marks as a test run.[88] Had the tribunal had this as its first case, the result could have dealt a crippling blow to the idea of international prosecution for such crimes.

In May 1999, the ICTY issued the first indictment against Milošević, then president of the Federal Republic of Yugoslavia.[89] Eventually, the prosecutor would issue a total of three indictments. The first had four separate counts:

Count 1: Deportation (a crime against humanity)

Count 2: Murder (a crime against humanity)

Count 3: Murder (a violation of the customs of war)

Count 4: Persecution (a crime against humanity)

The indictment alleged that Milošević and his allies had directed a campaign of ethnic cleansing in which 600,000 to 800,000 Albanian Kosovars were expelled from their homes and deported or internally displaced.[90] Several points apply here. First, note that the charges did not include genocide or complicity in genocide. Second, the charges flowed from two different theories of liability: command responsibility (the responsibility of a superior for actions committed by his subordinates) and personal responsibility for committing, planning, instigating, ordering, or aiding and abetting war crimes and crimes against humanity. As the civilian commander of the Yugoslav military and police forces, Milošević had an affirmative legal obligation to prevent his forces from committing, encouraging, or enabling others to commit atrocities in Kosovo. Third, these charges stemmed not from the earlier support of the Bosnian operation but rather from later events in Kosovo. Fourth, the indictment alleged not that Milošević had personally committed the crimes listed but rather that by dint of position he directed a criminal enterprise that engaged in these acts. For the moment I will defer commentary on the issues connected with command responsibility. I will address these issue in Chapter 6 because they have more direct relevance in that context. Indictments alleging similar offenses with regard to Croatia (indictment issued October 2001) and Bosnia (November 2001) came later.

After the initial indictment, the government of Yugoslavia refused to hand Milošević over to The Hague for trial.[91] Almost two years elapsed before pressure for reform within Serbia and from the international community led Serb leaders to make gestures of potential cooperation. Many powerful domestic political forces, including the army (VJN), opposed transferring Milošević to The Hague and have continued to oppose other transfers, perhaps because the top leaders saw their own fate tied to that of Milošević. Indeed a number of indictments of top army commanders followed.[92] Many Serbs regarded Bosnian Serb leaders Radovan Karadžić and Ratko Mladić as heroes.[93] The pressure from outside mounted. The United States and the EU had clearly indicated that the quid pro quo for future economic assistance was Serbian cooperation with The Hague tribunal. The United States in particular had clearly predicated its participation in a scheduled donors conference scheduled for late June 2001 on the surrender of Milošević. The timing of the transfer caused considerable unrest in Serbia. It occurred on a day important in Serbian history—St. Vitus Day, June 28—the date of the Battle of Kosovo, in 1389, and of the assassination of Archduke Franz Ferdinand, in 1914.[94] Under similar circumstances, an aid package from the United States and the prospect of negotiations to join the EU moved Prime Minister Kostunica, a bitter critic of the ICTY, to slowly hand over 16 suspects in 2005.[95]

As one of the most complex criminal trials in history, the Milošević trial highlighted the weaknesses of the adversarial system (Chapter 2) as a method of trial for war crimes on such a scale. It lasted four years and one month, ending with the death of the defendant many months before its expected conclusion. From the outset of the trial, Milošević challenged the authority of the court. The trial exhibited all of the circus elements that critics of international prosecutions see as undermining the credibility of international prosecutions Most observers noted that Milošević had no interest in acquittal. The procedural rules provided him with a soapbox to attack the credibility of the court and to proclaim his own status as a victim of unwarranted persecution and prosecution. This permitted him to play the role of heroic victim struggling against unfair odds. Trained as a lawyer, he ostensibly conducted his own defense, even though he did not lack for volunteers to form a defense team. In fact, during the long preparation, he secretly consulted with a team of lawyers. Given his health issues and intransigence in following rules, the trial chamber finally imposed counsel in September 2004. This led to another series of practical and procedural issues. Witnesses he called in his defense refused to testify unless he questioned them.[96] In a surprising decision, the appeals chamber reversed the trial court's decision to impose counsel as a violation of Milošević's rights.[97] This decision highlights the problems in the sense that it seemed to reward recalcitrance in the name of fairness.

Boas concisely summarizes the issues connected with the Milošević trial: "Courts and tribunals applying international criminal law have an obligation to ensure that a trial is fair, and they have an obligation to ensure that it is expeditious."[98] Finding the appropriate balance between the two elements in such a complex proceeding is very difficult. Any determination of fairness relies upon a very complex interaction of rights, interests, and obligations. The balance among these has often changed significantly over the years. Changes in the balance may have significant sociological, economic, and political consequences.

Just as a note in passing, consider the U.S. Supreme Court decisions in *Brown v. Board of Education, Miranda,* or *Roe v. Wade.*[99] Domestic criminal courts may rely upon several centuries of practice; international criminal litigation has less than two decades of development.

In part, the problems stem from expectations. As we pointed out, in such high-profile cases, the legitimacy of the tribunal may be on trial as much as the defendant. The expense and the spotlight lead to insistence upon "getting it right" without sufficient precedent to guide decisions. For lack of a better explanation, proceeding by "trial and error" produces a trial with errors. Judgments of "fairness" come from an assessment of how egregious the errors are perceived to be. This goes beyond technical disputation among learned observers because political practitioners, not the legal community, form a large part of the intended audience with respect to impact.

Notes

Quoted in Vahankn N. Dadrian, "Genocide as a Problem of National and International Law: The World War I Armenian Case and Its Contemporary Legal Ramifications," *Yale Journal of International Law* 14, no. 2 (1989): 223.

1. In Turkish Mehmed Talât Paşa, one of the three "pashas" (leaders of the "young Turks") who emerged as leaders after the 1909 "revolution." In the text, I have chosen to use older spellings, Talaat and Pasha. The other two were Ismail Enver and Ahmed Djemal. The following draws upon Dadrian, "Genocide as a Problem of National and International Law: The World War I Armenian Case and Its Contemporary Legal Ramifications," 221–328, and Gary Bass, *Stay the Hand of Vengeance* (Princeton: Princeton University Press, 2000), 106–46. Little has been written about the trials, though much has been written about the events leading up to them.

2. Named for Abdul-Hamid II (Abd al-Hamid II), Sultan of Turkey (deposed 1909).

3. See Bass, *Stay the Hand of Vengeance*, Chapter 4; Samantha Power, *A Problem from Hell* (New York: Basic Books, 2002), Chapter 1, and Ben Kiernan, *Blood and Soil: A World History of Genocide and Extermination from Sparta to Darfur* (New Haven: Yale University Press, 2007), Chapter 10.

4. The official name of the government of the Ottoman Empire. It comes from a French translation of the name of the gate ("Gate of the Eminent") through which one had to pass to gain access to the block of buildings in the Tokapi Palace in Constantinople (Istanbul) that housed the principal departments of government.

5. Quoted in Antonio Cassese, *International Criminal Law* (Oxford: Oxford University Press, 2003), 66.

6. Cassese, *International Criminal Law*, 66.

7. Bass, *Stay the Hand of Vengeance*, 122–23.

8. Bass, *Stay the Hand of Vengeance*, 126.

9. See Frank Chalk and Kurt Jonassohn, *The History and Sociology of Genocide: Analyses and Case Studies* (New Haven: Yale University Press,1990); Kiernan, *Blood and Soil*.

10. For an account, see, Polybius, *The Histories* (trans. Evelyn S. Schuburgh) (Bloomington: Indiana University Press, 1962), Books 36–39.

11. Note that domestic legislation often has a problem with vague definitions, as well. The Georgia Supreme Court recently struck down the Georgia hate crime law. It allowed increased penalties for crimes when a victim was chosen because of "bias or prejudice." The legislation left those two words largely undefined. The court said that that standard could be applied to any prejudice, "no matter how obscure, whimsical or unrelated to the victim." Ariel Hart, "Georgia Court Strikes Down Law on Hate," *New York Times,* October 26, 2004, http://leighhouse.typepad.com/blog/files/georgia_court_strikes_down_law_on_hate.pdf.

12. If one lives in a major metropolitan area in the United States, murders and rapes form part of the everyday context. No prosecutor feels the need to claim that the individual acts relate to a broader context in order to enhance the seriousness of the individual acts. In this case, thresholds still define the seriousness of the particular offense, that is, whether the charge should be first-degree murder or manslaughter or whether the rape involved a serious beating or other "aggravated" acts.

13. See Alison M. Smith, "Constitutional Limits on Hate Crime Legislation" *CRS Reports for Congress* (Congressional Research Service) RS 22812 (February 20, 2008), http://assets.opencrs.com/rpts/RS22812_20080220.pdf; and "Introduction: Hate Crime Laws," Anti-Defamation League, http://www.adl.org/99hatecrime/intro.asp.

14. See Beth van Schaack, "The Definition of Crimes against Humanity: Resolving the Incoherence," *Columbia Journal of Transnational Law* 37 (1999): 787ff.

15. London Agreement for the Prosecution and Punishment of the Major War Criminals of the European Axis (August 8, 1945). Text in *American Journal of International Law* 39 at 257 (1945 Supp.). Consult also *International Conference on Military Trials, London, 1945* (Department of State Publication 3080), for the texts of all proposals at the meeting. The principles contained in the 1945 Agreement were recognized as binding in international law by UN General Assembly Resolution 95 (I) (December 11, 1946).

16. For an extended discussion of this point, see M. Cherif Bassiouni, *Crimes against Humanity in International Criminal Law* (2nd rev. ed.) (The Hague: Martinus Nijhof, 1999), 123–76.

17. See Egon Schwelb, "Crimes against Humanity," *British Yearbook of International Law* 23 (1946): 178 ff. For a more concise argument on this point see Cassese, *International Criminal Law,* 71–73.

18. Van Schaack, "Definitions of Crimes," 803–7.

19. Michael P. Scharf, *Balkan Justice* (Durham, NC: Carolina Academic Press, 1997), 9.

20. ICTY Case No. IT-94–1-T; http://www.un.org/icty/tadic/trialc2/judgement/tad-sj970714e.pdf.

21. See Article 2 of the statute creating the court. http://www.un.org/icty/legaldoc-e/index.htm

22. See http://www.un.org/icty/tadic/trialc2/judgement/tad-sj970714e.pdf.

23. Text at http://www.ohr.int/dpa/default.asp?content_id=379.

24. William A. Schabas, *The UN International Criminal Tribunals: The Former Yugoslavia, Rwanda and Sierra Leone* (Cambridge: Cambridge University Press, 2006), 189.

25. Bassiouni, *Introduction to International Criminal Law,* 420–21.

26. For a short discussion of the trials here, see John C. Watkins, Jr., and John Paul Weber, *War Crimes and War Crime Trials: From Leipzig to the ICC and Beyond: Cases, Materials and Comments* (Durham, NC: Carolina Academic Press, 2005), 191–96.

27. Bassiouni, *Introduction to International Criminal Law,* 421.

28. The cases were in France, the Netherlands, Israel, Canada, and Australia. See Robert Cryer, Hakan Friman, Darryl Robinson, and Elizabeth Wilmshurst, *An Introduction to International Criminal Law* (Cambridge: Cambridge University Press, 2007), 194–98.

29. *International Convention on the Suppression and Punishment of Apartheid*, Adopted and opened for signature and ratification by General Assembly resolution 3068 (XXVIII) of November 30, 1973. It entered into force, July 18, 1976; text at http://www.unhchr.ch/html/menu3/b/11.htm.

30. Belem Do Para, Brazil, September 6, 1994; entered into force, March 28, 1996; text at, http://www.oas.org/juridico/English/sigs/a-60.html.

31. *Statute of the International Tribunal for the Former Yugoslavia*, adopted May 25, 1993, by UN General Assembly Resolution 827; as amended May 13, 1998, by UN General Assembly Resolution 1166; as amended November 30, 2000, by UN General Assembly Resolution 1329; http://www.icls.de/dokumente/icty_statut.pdf; *Statute of the International Criminal Tribunal for Rwanda*, S/RES/955 (1994), November 8, 1994; http://69.94.11.53/ENGLISH/basicdocs/statute/2007.pdf.

32. *Rome Statute of the International Criminal Court*, July 17, 1998, UN Doc. A/CONF.183/9; text at http://www.un.org/law/icc/statute/romefra.htm.

33. The ICTY Trial Court in the *Tadić* case did initially embraced the standard. *Prosecutor v. Tadić*, ICTY, Trial Chamber II, Judgment of May 7, 1997 [Case No. IT-94-1], para. 652. The ICTY appeals chamber later explicitly rejected discrimination as a criterion, noting that it applied only to cases before the ICTR. *Prosecutor v. Tadić*, ICTY, Appeals Chamber, Judgment of July 15, 1999 [Case No. IT-94-1-A], paras. 282–305.

34. See the statement by the ICTY trial court in *Prosecutor v. Kupreškić, et al.*, ICTY, Trial Chamber II, Judgment of January 14, 2000 [Case No. IT-95-16-T], paras. 711–12.

35. For a concise treatment of this issue in a broader context, see Theodor Meron, "Revival of Customary Humanitarian Law," *American Journal of International Law* 99, no. 4 (2005): 817–34.

36. For an extended discussion, see Guénaël Mettraux, "Crimes against Humanity in the Jurisprudence of the International Criminal Tribunals for the Former Yugoslavia and for Rwanda," *Harvard International Law Journal* 43, no. 1 (2002): 263–68; and *Prosecutor v. Tadić*, ICTY, Decision on the Defense Motion for Interlocutory Appeal on Jurisdiction, October 2, 1995 [Case No. IT-95-16], para. 141.

37. For a summary of the argument, see Cassesse, *International Criminal Law*, 72–74; also specifically on the ICC, 91–94.

38. Mettraux, "Crimes against Humanity," 252–59. *Prosecutor v. Tadić*, ICTY, Judgment of May 7, 1997 [Case No. IT-94-1], para. 638.

39. Cryer et al., *International Criminal Law and Procedure*, 193–94; Mettraux, "Crimes against Humanity, 245–50.

40. See the statement in *Prosecutor v. Kupreškić*, et al., ICTY, Trial Chamber II, Judgment of January 14, 2000) [Case No. IT-95-16-T], para. 568; and *Prosecutor v. Blaskić*, ICTY, Trial Chamber, Judgment of March 3, 2000 [Case No. IT-95-T], para. 214.

41. *Prosecutor v. Blaskić*, ICTY, Appeals Chamber, Judgment of July 29, 2004 [Case No. IT-95-14-A], para. 113.

42. *Prosecutor v. Tadić*, ICTY, Trial Chamber II, Judgment of May 7, 1997 [Case No. IT-94-1-T], para. 644; *Prosecutor v. Akayesu*, ICTR, Trial Chamber, I Judgment of September 2, 1998 [Case No. ICTR-96-4), para. 580. See also Schabas, *The U N International Criminal Tribunals*, 191–96.

43. Mettraux, "Crimes Against Humanity," 245–46.

44. In particular see *Prosecutor v. Kunarac et al.*, ICTY, Appeals Chamber, Judgment of June 12, 2002 [Case No. IT-96–14/2-A], para. 101.

45. *Prosecutor v. Vasiljević*, ICTY, Trial Chamber I, Judgment of November 29, 2002 [Case No. IT-97–32-T], paras. 29, 30.

46. See http://www.icc-cpi.int/library/about/officialjournal/Element_of_Crimes_English.pdf.

47. *Prosecutor v. Tadić*, ICTY, Trial Chamber II, Judgment of May 7, 1997 [Case No. IT-94–1], para. 656.

48. Mettraux, "Crimes against Humanity," 255.

49. As a note in passing, the French text in the ICTR does use "et" (and) rather than "ou" (or), which presumably means that a situation has to meet both conditions, but the English text is normally taken as the more authoritative in terms of applicable standards.

50. Schabas, *The UN International Criminal Tribunals*, 192.

51. *Prosecutor v. Akayesu*, ICTR, Trial Chamber, Judgment of September 2, 1998 [Case No. ICTR-96–4), para. 580.

52. *Prosecutor v. Kordić, et. al.*, ICTY, Judgment of February 27, 2001 [Case No. IT-95–14/2], para. 179.

53. *Prosecutor v. Kunarac, et al.*, ICTY, Appeals Chamber, Judgment of June 12, 2002 [Case No. IT-96–14/2-A], paras. 94 and 429.

54. For an argument that supports an opposing view, see Michael C. Davis and C. Raj Kumar, "An Opinion on the Depayin Massacre as a Crime against Humanity," http://www.article2.org/mainfile.php/0206/113/.

55. See http://www.icc-cpi.int/library/about/officialjournal/Elements_of_Crimes_English.pdf.

56. *Prosecutor v. Blaskić* ICTY, Trial Chamber I, Judgment of March 3, 2000 [Case No. IT-95–14-T], para. 257.

57. *Prosecutor v. Tadić*, Appeals Chamber, Judgment of August 15, 1999 [Case No. IT-94–1-A], para. 271.

58. Schabas, *The UN International Criminal Tribunals*, 195–96.

59. Some variation in practice has emerged here because of a variance in definition between the English text and the French text of the ICTR and the ICTY. The French text uses the term *assassinat* rather than *meurtre*. Under French law, *assassinat* requires proof of premeditation. The ICC Statute uses *meurte*. For a lengthy discussion see, Kriangsak Kittichaisaree, *International Criminal Law* (Oxford: Oxford University Press, 2001), 102–4.

60. *Prosecutor v. Kristić*, ICTY, Trial Chamber I, Judgment of August 2, 2001 (Case No. IT-98–33-T), para. 503.

61. *Slavery Convention*, August 25, 1926, 60 LNTS 253, 212 UNTS 17. See text at http://www1.umn.edu/humanrts/instree/f1sc.htm.

62. *Prosecutor v. Furundžija*, Trial Chamber II, Judgment of December 10, 1998 [Case no. IT-95–17/1-T], para. 186.

63. ICC Statute, Article 7.1(h).

64. *Prosecutor v. Kupreskić*, ICTY, Trial Chamber II, Judgment of January 14, 2000 [Case No. IT-95–16-T], para. 619.

65. ICC Statute, Article 7.2(I).

66. ICC Statute, Article 7.2(h). For a list of specific acts that make up this category, see *International Convention on the Suppression and Punishment of Apartheid*, General Assembly resolution 3068 (XXVIII) of November 30, 1973. Entered into force, July 18, 1976; 1015 UNTS 243.

67. For example, see the "Radio Machete case": *Prosecutor v. Ferdinand Nahimana, Jean-Bosco Barayagwiza & Hassan Ngeze*, ICTR, Trial Chamber I, Judgment and Sentence of December 3, 2003 [Case No. ICTR-99–52-T].

68. Croatian Revolutionary Group: the name means "urprising" or "to stand up, arise."

69. Andrew Bell-Fialkoff, "A Brief History of Ethnic Cleansing," *Foreign Affairs* 72, no. 3 (Summer 1993): 116.

70. Though normally referred to as Marshal Tito in the popular press and elsewhere, Tito was the alias Josip Broz adopted during his active participation in the activities of the Communist Party during the 1930s.

71. See Laura Silber and Allan Little, *Yugoslavia: Death of a Nation* (New York: Penguin, 1997); Misha Glenny, *The Balkans: Nationalism, War and the Great Powers, 1804–1999* (New York: Viking, 2000).

72. UN SCOR, Resolution 743 of 21 February 1992.

73. Silber and Little, *Yugoslavia*, 215.

74. Bell-Fialkoff, "A Brief History," 118.

75. Bell-Fialkoff, "A Brief History," 120.

76. Roy Gutman, quoted in Scharf, *Balkan Justice*, 30.

77. See Scharf, *Balkan Justice*, 94–101, and Robertson, *Crimes against Humanity*, 394–99.

78. Text at http://www.un.org/icty/indictment/english/tad-ii950213e.htm; also in Scharf, "Appendix C," *Balkan Justice,* 257–269.

79. Scharf, *Balkan Justice*, 101.

80. Scharf, *Balkan Justice*, 224.

81. Robertson, *Crimes Against Humanity: The Struggle for Global Justice* (3rd ed.) (New York: New Press, 2006), 406.

82. For Karadžić, two counts of genocide (Article 4 of the Statute—genocide, complicity in genocide); five counts of crimes against humanity (Article 5 of the Statute—extermination, murder, persecutions on political, racial, and religious grounds, persecutions, inhumane acts [forcible transfer]); three counts of violations of the laws or customs of war (Article 3 of the Statute—murder, unlawfully inflicting terror upon civilians, taking hostages); and one count of grave breaches of the Geneva Conventions (Article 2 of the Statute—willful killing).

83. Quoted in Scharf, *Balkan Justice*, 99.

84. Robertson, *Crimes against Humanity*, 397.

85. One of the prosecution's main witnesses swore that he had seen Tadić kill his own father. The defense produced the father in court for a rather dramatic reunion. Luckily, this occurred before the verdict, rather than after. Nonetheless, it proved a very damaging event for the prosecution.

86. See ICG Balkans Report No. 103, *War Criminals in Bosnia's Republika Srpška: Who Are the People in Your Neighbourhood*, November 2000.

87. For a balanced critical assessment of the trial, see, Gideon Boas, *The* Milošević *Trial: Lessons for the Conduct of Complex International Criminal Proceedings* (Cambridge: Cambridge University Press, 2007).

88. Robertson, *Crimes against Humanity*, 410; see also his prefatory comments in Boas, *The Milošević Trial*, xi–xvii.

89. Also indicted were Milan Milutinović (President of Serbia), Dragoljub Ojdanić (Chief of Staff of the Yugoslav army), Nikola Šainović (Deputy Prime Minister), and Vlajko Stojiljković (Minister of Internal Affairs) with responsibility for deporting 740,000 Kosovo Albanians and for the murder of 340 others.

90. *Prosecutor v. Milošević*, ICTY, Prosecution's Pre-Trial Brief of November 26, 2001, para. 3.

91. Although there appeared to be near-unanimous agreement among Serbia's politicians that Milošević should be put on trial, most felt that this should be done at home and that he should be tried for his crimes against his own people. International Crisis Group, Balkans Briefing, *Milošević in the Hague: What It Means for Yugoslavia and the Region*, Belgrade/Brussels, July 6, 2001, 6.

92. See, for example, *Prosecutor v. Pavković, et al.* ICTY, Initial Indictment of October 2, 2003 [Case No. IT-03–70].

93. ICG Balkans Briefing, *Milošević*, 6–8.

94. Also on this day in 1989, Slobodan Milošević addressed approximately 1 million Serbs at Gazimestan in Kosovo to commemorate the 600th anniversary of the Kosovo Battle. That speech contained the first open threat of violent conflict by a Socialist Yugoslav leader: "Six centuries later, again, we are in battles and quarrels. They are not armed battles, although such things cannot be excluded." ICG Balkans Briefing, *Milošević*, 6.

95. Julie Kim, *Balkan Cooperation on War Crimes Issues: 2005 Update*, CRS Report for Congress No. RS22097 (March 28, 2005).

96. Boas, *The Milošević Trial*, 242–43.

97. *Prosecutor v. Milošević*, ICTY, Reasons for Decision on Assignment of Defence Counsel, September 22, 2004 [Case No. IT-02–54-T].

98. Boas, *The Milošević Trial*, 271.

99. *Brown v. Board of Education of Topeka*, U.S. Supreme Court 347 U.S. 483 (1954); *Miranda v. Arizona*, U.S. Supreme Court, 384 U.S. 436 (1966); *Roe v. Wade*, U.S. Supreme Court, 410 U.S. 113 (1973).

CHAPTER 5

Genocide

The relatively low impact of the genocidal killing of one million Armenians on modern public consciousness raises serious questions about the ability of the international community to prevent or punish genocide.

Vahankn N. Dadrian

In Chapter 2, I characterized genocide as the "international crime among crimes," the one considered most heinous among all others. In an Advisory Opinion, the ICJ defined genocide as "a crime under international law involving a denial of the right of existence of entire human groups, a denial which shocks the conscience of mankind and results in great losses to humanity, and which is contrary to moral law and to the spirit and aims of the United Nations."[1] The Armenian genocide and the events of World War II led to the creation of the Genocide Convention (1948).[2] Yet, the hope embodied in this document rapidly faded. The cry "never again" unfortunately gave way to the reality of "again and again." One analyst noted that "Five decades of non-enforcement have left the Genocide Convention's core terms shrouded in considerable ambiguity, making it that much easier for recalcitrant politicians to equivocate."[3] Antonio Cassese, who served as a judge on the ICTY, states that "at the *enforcement* level the Convention has long proved a failure."[4] The quotation by Dadrian that heads this chapter summarizes the frustration of many with respect to enforcement of the provisions of the Convention. Though visualized in the Convention, no *international* court with jurisdiction to try *individuals* accused of genocide existed until the UN Security Council authorized the ad hoc tribunals for Yugoslavia and Rwanda. As the authorization for the first permanent international court, the ICC Statute includes genocide as a crime within its jurisdictions. Still, not until a half-century after the original draft of the Convention opened for signature and ratification did a trial and conviction of an individual for crimes comprising genocide occur. In 1998, the ICTR found Jean-Paul Akayesu guilty of genocide and direct and public incitement to commit genocide.[5] Bosnia brought the first case alleging *collective responsibility* for genocide by Serbia to the ICJ in 1993.[6] Note here that the victim state initiated the suit. No third party had stepped forward in defense of the norms embodied in the Convention. No action was taken against the Pol Pot regime in Cambodia or against Saddam Hussein for his genocidal campaign against the Kurds.[7]

The record raises many questions that go beyond the scope of this book. The psychological aspects of genocide alone would require a book. What factors account for the willingness of ordinary people to participate in such atrocities? How could anyone ever become so cruel and sadistic? Why would anyone even attempt to justify or deny a genocide? What motivates ordinary people to commit extraordinary crimes?[8] The answers here seem to require much more than the simple and often advanced explanations of racial hatred and "brainwashing."

A Crime without a Name

Henry Morgenthau, the American ambassador to Turkey (1913–1916) during the first Wilson administration, watched the unfolding policy of the systematic slaughter of Armenians with great concern. He termed it "race murder" because no existing English word captured the full horror of the events he observed.[9] Others referred to the policy as the "crime without a name." Even though the United States would not officially take a position, Morgenthau felt morally compelled to express his personal feeling about what he saw as unacceptable. The answer he received from Mehmet Talaat, the Turkish head of state, reveals much about the following discussion of these crimes: "Why are you so interested in the Armenians anyway? . . . You are a Jew, these people are Christians. . . . What have you to complain of? Why can't you let us do with these Christians as we please?"[10] From a contemporary perspective informed by concern for human rights, this statement evokes outrage. Yet, it represents a common theme across the years. Indeed, Milošević made similar arguments in his defense.

To give some perspective on the development of ICL over time, we must note that the Charter of the IMT (Nuremberg) included "crimes against humanity" but did not identify genocide as a separate crime. At the time of drafting, the term had not yet entered the modern lexicon of identifiable words, let alone defining a separable and identifiable "crime." Genocide is "an act committed with the intent to destroy, in whole or in part, a national, ethnical, racial, or religious group."[11] The word was deliberately coined by Dr. Raphaël Lemkin in his *Axis Rule in Occupied Europe*.[12] The practices of the German government before and especially during World War II in relation to the attempt to eliminate entire groups of its own citizens and, later, citizens of occupied states led to the question of whether such acts of destruction could be regarded solely as domestic acts or whether they constituted a class of crimes against humanity. Genocide in practice goes beyond the killing of people. It includes other acts of depredation such as forced abortion, sterilization, artificial infection, the working of people to death in special labor camps, and the separation of families or of the sexes in order to depopulate specific areas.

The Genocide Convention

After World War II, the UN General Assembly moved quickly to address these issues. On December 13, 1946, the General Assembly unanimously adopted Resolution 96 (I), in which it condemned genocide as a crime under international law. The Assembly also requested the Economic and Social Council to begin studies toward a draft convention on genocide. The Security Council, in turn, asked the Secretary-General to prepare a first draft and to circulate it among the members for comment. In 1948, the Economic and Social Council (ECOSOC) appointed an ad hoc committee consisting of seven members to revise the original draft. Upon completion, ECOSOC, after a general debate, decided, on August 26, 1948, to send the draft to the General Assembly for study and action. After further study in Paris by the Legal Committee of the General Assembly, action followed in the parent body. On December 9, 1948, the General Assembly adopted the Convention on the Prevention and Punishment of the Crime of Genocide.[13]

The convention affirms the criminality of genocide in time of peace as well as in time of war (Art.1). Article 2 defines the offense:

> In the present Convention, genocide means any of the following acts committed with intent to destroy, in whole or in part, a national, ethnical, racial or religious group, as such:

a. Killing members of the group;
b. Causing serious bodily or mental harm to members of the group;
c. Deliberately inflicting on the group conditions of life calculated to bring about its physical destruction in whole or in part;
d. Imposing measures intended to prevent births within the group;
e. Forcibly transferring children of the group to another group.

Persons committing any of the acts listed in Article 3 are subject to punishment, whether they are constitutionally responsible rulers, public officials, or private individuals (Art. 4). The parties to the convention undertook the obligation to enact the necessary domestic legislation to give effect to the convention and, in particular, to provide effective penalties for persons guilty of the forbidden acts (Art. 5). Persons charged with any of the enumerated acts are to be tried by a competent tribunal of the state in which the act was committed or by such international penal tribunal as may have jurisdiction with respect to those contacting parties that have accepted its jurisdiction (Art. 5). This now includes the International Criminal Court if conditions for exercise of its jurisdictional reach are met.

States party to the Convention have the obligation to pass appropriate and effective domestic legislation making genocide a crime. They also agree to making genocide an extraditable offense exempt from claims to "political motivation/asylum" (Art. VII). Article VIII of the Convention permits any State Party to request "the competent organs of the United Nations to take such action under the Charter of the United Nations as they consider appropriate for the prevention and suppression of acts of genocide or any of the other acts enumerated in article III." Note that this provision authorized the Security Council to set up the ICTY, ICTR, SCSL, and the Special Tribunal for Cambodia. The Convention places a primary duty to prosecute on the state where the genocide occurs, but it does foresee the possibility of other courts having jurisdiction, as well.[14]

In passing, we should note what the definition in the Convention does not cover. It does not cover "all groups" of people, however one may define a group. With the exception of religious groups, where membership clearly is voluntary, the Convention definitions apply to groups constituted by involuntary membership through birth.[15] This means that, with the exception of religion, the groups that an individual may join through voluntary choice do not qualify. It does not provide either an extended definition of the categories or criteria that one might use to construct an operational definition. It does *not* encompass political, cultural, or economic genocide. Because of definitional difficulties, these three concepts were deliberately omitted. As Cassese notes, intending to kill all of the communists in a country may constitute a horrific crime, but it does not qualify as genocide.[16] Hence, the definition covers "ethnic cleansing" in Bosnia but would not apply to Stalin's systematic elimination of dissidents or to his extermination of an economic class (the *kulaks,* or independent farmers). On the other hand, given the widespread and systematic nature of the attacks, he might have been charged with crimes against humanity. The original charges against Pinochet brought by the Spanish Magistrate included genocide, but British Magistrates found that Pinochet's actions did not fit the definition. Of the three omissions, that of cultural genocide, normally defined as the destruction of the language and culture of a group, has drawn the most attention and concern.

The Genocide Convention came into force on January 12, 1951, with the deposit of the 25th instrument of ratification. In June 2008, the Convention had 141 State Parties. The legislative history of U.S. ratification, while not exemplary, is rather interesting. By the end of 1985, the Convention had been pending in the U.S. Senate (intermittently because of lapses in presidential submissions during the John Foster Dulles era) for almost 36 years. In September 1984, President Reagan urged the Senate to give its consent quickly to the ratification of the Convention, but senatorial opposition again buried the consent in committee. The Senate gave its consent to the ratification of the convention on February 19, 1986, by a vote of 83–11, but it took two more years to gain congressional passage of legislation needed to implement the treaty by making genocide punishable under federal laws and setting penalties for violators. The House then passed the implementing legislation in April 1988, and the Senate did so on October 15, 1988. The Senate version of the bill was officially called "The Proxmire Act" in honor of Senator William Proxmire (D, Wisconsin), who with unmatched dedication had delivered more than 3,300 speeches in favor of ratification. Beginning on January 11, 1967, Senator Proxmire had repeated his call for action every day the Senate was in session.

The Stockholm Declaration on Genocide Prevention

Talk and declarations of intent are cheap.[17] Effective intervention is not. The reluctance to engage in a timely fashion remains the Achilles heel of effective prevention. Still, states easily support the principles of prevention. Fifty-five countries, including the United States, the United Kingdom, Canada, France, Germany, Japan, and Russia, signed the Stockholm Declaration on Genocide Prevention in January 2004, just as the situation in Darfur came to world attention. The signatory states pledged to cooperate in developing early-detection mechanisms and committed to support research into methods of prevention and to explore, "seriously and actively, the options presented at the Forum for action against genocidal threats, mass murders, deadly conflicts, ethnic cleansing as well as genocidal ideologies and incitement to genocide." As a declaration, the document has no legal force, even though many human rights advocates hailed it as the most significant step forward since the signing of the Genocide Convention, in 1948. The issue, however, remains one of political will, not resources. One should not be totally cynical here, however. Over time, support of commitments that many originally considered as "mouth honor," that is, saying the appropriate words in public to indicate commitment without the concomitant political will to carry out the obligations, has come back to haunt governments.

The Politics of Genocide

As noted, many instances of genocide have occurred after the drafting and entry into force of the treaty. Recent examples of genocide not directly connected with international war are the intermittent (1959–1973 and 1988) massacres that took place in Burundi during intertribal fighting between the Tutsi and Hutu groups; the wholesale killing of Cambodians at the hands of their own government during the reign of Pol Pot; the reported mass killings of members of the Muslim minority in Chad in 1979;[18] and Saddam Hussein's campaign against the Kurds in 1988. At present, the situation in Darfur (Sudan) has caught the attention of the international community.[19] To throw in a cautionary note here, not all instances of mass killing may meet the technical (and rather narrow) definition of genocide. We discuss the problem of appropriate characterization with respect to Darfur later in this chapter. Advocates often use the word "genocide" because they wish to emphasize the serious nature of a situation. Because of its genesis and its close association with the events of the Holocaust, the word almost automatically evokes horrific images. In contrast, the phrase "crimes against humanity," which can be equally horrendous, lacks the built-in emotional connection.

New impetus for the prevention and prosecution of genocide was given by the internecine strife in parts of the former Yugoslavia. In December 1992, to express its concern over events in Yugoslavia, the UN General Assembly adopted the Resolution and Declaration on the Rights of Persons Belonging to

National or Ethnic, Religious, and Linguistic Minorities (December 18, 1992).[20] Bosnia-Herzegovina instituted proceedings (March 20, 1993) in the International Court of Justice against the Federal Republic of Yugoslavia (Serbia and Montenegro). The court ordered provisional measures concerning application of the Genocide Convention on two occasions.[21] Resolution 827 of the United Nations Security Council (May 25, 1993) established the ICTY. The court has jurisdiction over three categories of crime committed within the territory of the former Yugoslavia between 1991 and the Dayton Agreement in 1995: genocide, crimes against humanity, and violations of the laws or customs of war. It can try only individuals, not organizations or governments. The maximum sentence it can impose is life imprisonment.

A large-scale killing of a population began in the African state of Rwanda in April 1994, with casualties among the Tutsi element estimated at 600,000 to 800,000. The United Nations appointed a special investigator for human rights, who soon called for trials for those accused of the massacres. He asserted that the crimes were "well-orchestrated" and blamed the then Rwandan government.[22] UN Security Council Resolution 955 (November 8, 1994) created the ICTR. The court was authorized to try both those responsible for acts of genocide and other serious violations of international law within the territory of Rwanda and Rwandan citizens who performed these acts in nearby states. The court's jurisdiction was further defined in terms of time frame. The acts had to have occurred between January 1 and December 31, 1994.[23]

Crimes against Humanity and Genocide

The defendants at Nuremberg, if prosecuted today, would be charged with genocide. As we noted earlier, the Genocide Convention makes it clear that genocide may occur in peacetime as well as in times of conflict, whether international or intrastate.[24] Genocide does form a category within the broader ambit of crimes against humanity. While the requirements for genocide somewhat resemble those necessary to establish "persecution" as a crime against humanity, acts related to genocide require a *specific intent* to produce a *specific result*. Persecution applies to civilian populations in general; genocide requires "an *intent* to destroy, in whole or in part, a national, ethnical, racial or religious group, as such" (emphasis added). Persecution depends upon objective circumstantial thresholds that do not require a specific intent to *destroy or eliminate* a group; genocide does Moreover, genocide does not have any threshold requirements with regard to scale or gravity (see Chapter 4).

This leads naturally to the question of scope. For example, can a solitary individual commit an act of genocide if no discernible pattern of behavior among others exists? The trial chamber in *Jelisić* suggested the possibility of a lone wolf, but neither other tribunals nor respected academicians find the supposition supportable.[25] In another case, an ICTY trial chamber set out reasons to discount such speculations. All too often, advocates use the word "genocide" to gain attention and to add emphasis to their allegations of misconduct. The prosecutor for the ICTY noted that to reserve the character of genocide as the ultimate crime:

> [I]n the interests of international justice, genocide should not be diluted or belittled by too broad an interpretation. . . . [I]t should be reserved only for acts of exceptional gravity and magnitude which shock the conscience of humankind.[26]

The victim in the crime of genocide is the *group*, not the individual members. A major difficulty stems from the fact that persons accused of genocide must be found guilty on the basis of their own individual acts, but these acts must be clearly linked to a larger pattern of systematic collective conduct that meets the rather narrow definition of genocide. As I noted in the discussion of crimes against humanity (Chapter 4), not every crime committed during a widespread and systematic attack on a population necessarily constitutes a crime against humanity. Moreover, as befitting its status as the ultimate crime, the requirements to prove that an individual act constitutes genocide are far more stringent than those to establish a crime against humanity. The prosecutor must establish that the individual who committed the act acted with intent "to destroy, in whole or in part, a national, ethnical, racial or religious group, as such" within a much broader pattern of conduct that has the same purpose.

The Rome Statute of the ICC addresses this question by adding a contextual requirement. Article 6 of the Elements of Crimes states: "The term 'in the context of' would include the initial acts in an *emerging pattern*" (emphasis added). This seems a reasonable addition, but note that only the ICC is bound to apply this requirement. Still, it is hard to conceptualize the ideas of extermination or elimination without some idea of scale (gravity) and pattern. One or two individual incidents, despite avowed intent, might be "hate" crimes but not genocide. So, the August 1999 attack by Buford O. Furrow, a member of the white supremacist group Aryan Nations, on a Jewish day-care facility in Los Angeles may qualify in terms of intent but, as an isolated event, does not merit prosecution as genocide.[27] Similarly, the same applies to the April 1999 "London nail bomber," David Copeland, who during a 12-day bombing campaign aimed at London's black, Asian, and gay communities killed three and injured 129.[28] Moreover, with respect to Copeland's targets, while the Asian and black communities fall under the definition, the gay community does not.

Some Definitions

Only four groups receive protection from the Genocide Convention (and the ICC Statute). Throughout the course of this treatise I have continuously focused on the need for precise definitions. As noted, the Convention does not contain extended definitions for the terms used.

1. *Ethnical group* members share a common language and culture. Note that the group may be self-identified or identified through definition by others outside of the group. The others advancing a definition may be the accused perpetrators of genocide.[29]
2. *Racial group* members share hereditary physical traits. Often these coincide with a particular geographic area. These stand apart from religious, linguistic, national, or cultural factors.[30]
3. *National group* members share a common *legal* bond based upon common citizenship.[31] Note here that this reduces the term "national" to its narrow legal denotation.
4. *Religious groups* may be self-identified or defined by third parties.

As social constructs, groups may or may not have precisely defined boundaries that give them an "objective" existence. Upon reasoned reflection, we may conclude that the four groups do not form distinct categories but instead have considerable overlap. For example, in the *Akayesu* case, the ICTR trial chamber, despite the obvious evidence of widespread slaughter, had great difficulty in determining whether the Tutsi formed a protected group under the terms of the Genocide Convention and the Statute that created the court.[32] To the lay person, the answer may seem obvious, but the trial chamber sought to apply the categories as inclusive and separate rather than complementary and overlapping. Hence, its definition of an ethnic group as one "whose members share a common language and culture" did not provide sufficient grounds to separate Tutsi from Hutu.[33] At the time of the massacre, both tribes spoke the same language, and the cultural differences were minor. The judges finally relied upon the fact that by law all Rwandans had to carry an identification card that specified Hutu, Tutsi, or Twa[34] to establish the necessary connection. The trial chamber may have created the difficulty for itself by a misreading of the preparatory notes (*travaux préparatoires*) associated with the Genocide Convention. The judges sought to define a "stable and permanent group." This wording does not appear in the Convention.

While the *Akayesu* trial chamber may have created some difficulties for itself, the crisis in Darfur illustrates the problems of determining a group in a manner that falls within the definitions of the Convention. The media and others have used the word "genocide" to describe the ongoing situation. Again, few outside the government of Sudan dispute the evidence of large-scale, indiscriminate killing. The problem with this characterization is that the victims of the attacks do not make up ethnic, racial, or religious groups distinct from those mounting the attacks. Gerard Prunier accurately describes it as "the ambiguous genocide."[35] The groups share religion and language, although increasingly the divide has been characterized as between "Arabs" who support the government and "Africans" who do not. The UN Commission established to investigate concluded:

> The various tribes that have been the object of attacks and killings (chiefly the Fur, Massalit and Zaghawa tribes) do not appear to make up ethnic groups distinct from the ethnic group to which persons or militias that attack them belong. They speak the same language (Arabic) and embrace the

same religion (Muslim). In addition, also due to the high measure of inter-marriage, they can hardly be distinguished in their outward physical appearance from the members of tribes that allegedly attacked them. Furthermore, inter-marriage and coexistence in both social and economic terms, have over the years tended to blur the distinction between the groups. Apparently, the sedentary and nomadic character of the groups constitutes one of the main distinctions between them. It is also notable that members of the African tribes speak their own dialect in addition to Arabic, while members of Arab tribes only speak Arabic.[36]

The interesting fact here comes from the impact of the perceptions of other governments and the media, which have insistently defined the conflict as between Arabs and Africans:

> Those tribes in Darfur who support rebels have increasingly come to be identified as "African" and those supporting the government as the "Arabs." A good example to illustrate this is that of the Gimmer, a pro-government African tribe and how it is seen by the African tribes opposed to the government as having been "Arabized." Clearly, not all "African" tribes support the rebels and not all "Arab" tribes support the Government. Some "Arab" tribes appear to be either neutral or even support the rebels. . . . The Arab-African divide has also been fanned by the growing insistence on such divide in some circles and in the media. All this has contributed to the consolidation of the contrast and gradually created a marked polarisation in the perception and self-perception of the groups concerned. *At least those most affected by the conditions explained above, including those directly affected by the conflict, have come to perceive themselves as either "African" or "Arab."*[37]

These comments do not mean that crimes have not been committed, only that the characterization of genocide does not necessarily provide the best *legal* characterization of the situation.

In his commentaries, William Schabas has made two important points with respect to the problems of definition. First, he has pointed out that other international instruments have not expanded the list but rather treated the four categories as jointly defining protected groups.[38] For example, Article 1.1 of the *International Convention on the Elimination of All Forms of Racial Discrimination* defines *racial discrimination* as "any distinction, exclusion, restriction or preference based on race, colour, descent, or national or ethnic origin which has the purpose or effect of nullifying or impairing the recognition, enjoyment or exercise, on an equal footing, of human rights and fundamental freedoms in the political, economic, social, cultural or any other field of public life."[39] Second, this approach does not require that a group fit exactly into one or another category, however they might be defined.

On the basis of my discussion, further questions stem from the issue of who determines the characteristics and boundaries that define a group. May one rely solely upon self-identification, or is the criterion outside perceptions of the factors that define group identity, no matter how subjective? By what criteria and authority may third parties (courts or others) determine that a particular individual belongs to a specific group? To what extent can the criteria used by the accused perpetrators, whether or not objectively valid, define the group under attack? Many of these questions cannot be answered in the abstract but seem to require a judicious blend of "objective" requirements and "subjective" perceptions. To proceed solely on the subjective perceptions of perpetrators could result in the designation of a totally imaginary group that has no objective referents. To proceed solely on objective grounds risks having a real group that does not have sharply defined characteristics fall outside the definition. This means that determining whether a group falls within the "protected" groups requires "a case-by-case analysis" "by reference to the objective particulars of a given social or historical context, and by the subjective perceptions of the perpetrators."[40]

Establishing Individual Criminal Liability

Like crimes against humanity, genocide involves large numbers of victims and crimes committed by many perpetrators. Courts must find some way to connect actions by an individual to the broader context. To reiterate the point, not every offense and not every listed offense committed within the time frame and area of the alleged genocide necessarily qualifies as an act considered part of the broader pattern. Establishing individual responsibility has its pitfalls, given the problem of witness credibility, access to documents, distance, elapsed time, and lack of specific forensic evidence. The courts have used several theories of liability—command responsibility, conspiracy, joint criminal enterprise, incitement/instigating, and aiding and abetting—to make the connections.[41] Theories of liability will be discussed further in Chapter 7.

Courts and Cases

Almost all of the cases before the ICTR have involved charges of genocide. In contrast, very few trials before the ICTY and none before the SCSL (Sierra Leone) have done so. In large part, this flows from the difference in the Statutes, which reflected a difference in legislative concerns. While both the ICTR and the ICTY Statutes include genocide as a listed crime, the SCSL Statute does not. When the UN Security Council established the ICTR, the preamble to the resolution authorizing the tribunal specifically voiced the concern that "genocide and other systematic, widespread and flagrant violations of international humanitarian law had been committed in Rwanda."[42] In the case of the SCSL, the Secretary-General explicitly noted that genocide had been excluded from the draft presented to the Security Council because no evidence existed to show that the killings, while widespread and systematic, were directed against any of the protected groups listed in the Convention.[43]

Prohibited Acts: *Actus Reus*

Just as the Convention limits the type of groups covered, it also limits the acts that qualify. Not every offense committed with the requisite intent results in a charge of genocide. The Genocide Convention (and the ICC Statute) includes five categories of acts. Article 4 of the ICTY and Article 2 of the ICTR simply reproduce the relevant parts of the Convention (see Table 5.1). One must keep in mind that genocide constitutes the most heinous international crime. Accordingly, standards of evidence and proof must reflect the gravity of the crime. This observation simply emphasizes the difference between the casual use of the word to describe incidents and the formal criteria necessary to establish "genocide" as the "crime of crimes" committed by an individual, rather than a war crime, a crime against humanity, or an ordinary crime.

Those who drafted the Convention clearly intended to go beyond simple killing or complicity in killing. In assessing Nazi policy in Germany, we conclude that deliberate killing formed the most obvious aspect of the Holocaust experience, but the focus on killing and the concentration camps tended to overshadow other policies that would have long-term consequences. Note that Table 5.1 includes both *prohibited* and *punishable* acts. In addition to genocide, the punishable list

Table 5.1   Genocide

Prohibited Acts (*Actus Reus*)

Killing

Causing Serious Bodily Harm (enslavement, starvation deportation, persecution)

Deliberate Infliction of Conditions of Life Aimed at Physical Destruction
in Whole or in Part (deprivation of resources necessary
to survival forced migration)

Measures to Prevent Procreation

    forced sterilization

    forced abortion

    sexual mutilation

    prohibition of marriage

Forcible Transfer/Removal of Children

Punishable Acts

Genocide

Conspiracy to commit genocide

Direct and public incitement to commit genocide

Attempt to commit genocide

Complicity in genocide

Source: Article 2, Genocide Convention.

includes, in addition to direct participation in the acts defined as genocide, conspiracy and incitement to commit genocide, "attempted" genocide, and complicity in genocide.

The list of prohibited acts does not differ much from that which defines crimes against humanity, nor do the operational definitions differ significantly. In addition to this list, the general elements of criminal responsibility listed in the Statutes apply, as well. So, planning, instigating, ordering, and aiding and abetting apply here, as well.[44] For that reason, the discussion that deals with the operational definitions of specific acts with regard to specific individual acts will serve for this section, as well. Their use with respect to genocide is covered in this chapter in the discussion of specific cases.

The same cannot be said of "punishable" acts. The Statutes of the ICTY and the ICTR directly incorporate Article III of the Genocide Convention. This includes the *inchoate* (incomplete) offenses of conspiracy, incitement, and attempt. While the Statutes of the ICTR and the ICTY have a general provision that deals with *complicity* that applies to all crimes, the specification of these elements sets genocide apart from the other crimes in the Statutes. The term "inchoate" means that the actions constituting the offense occurred prior to, and in preparation for, the acts. An inchoate offense constitutes a crime within itself, meaning that an individual may be convicted of the offense of conspiracy, incitement, or attempt even if the crime of genocide never happens. So, if two or more individuals make plans to rob a liquor store, they have committed the offense of conspiracy even if they never carry out the robbery. Note here that mere negotiations to form a plan do not suffice. Successful prosecution will depend upon evidence of an agreement. As a note in passing, no tribunal has issued an indictment for an attempt to commit genocide, and no individual has been charged with attempted genocide.

Complicity, on the other hand, requires that the events have occurred. Complicity in conspiracy is redundant; complicity to incite or attempt would be conspiracy. In terms of trials for genocide, this charge has not played a great role, in part because the more general provision in the Statutes permit, indictment for "aiding and abetting." Where indictments have charged individuals with complicity, those convicted have had a more direct involvement in commission of acts. No individual has been convicted of complicity alone.

In terms of material elements defining genocide, the ICC Statute adds a contextual factor not found in the Genocide Convention, although, given the collective nature of the crime, it seems to form a logical requirement. With respect to each prohibited act, the conduct must take "place in the context of a manifest pattern of similar conduct directed against that group or was conduct that could itself effect such destruction."[45] Note also that the test has two disjunctive elements. The first makes clear that genocide requires acts that define a clear, well-defined pattern, not just sporadic and isolated occurrences. The second addresses the possibility that the conduct might employ particularly powerful methods, such as the use of weapons of mass destruction. Saddam Hussein's attack on the Kurds in 1988 (the Anfal "ethnic cleansing" campaign), which involved poison gas, illustrates this possibility.[46] Along these same lines, although courts have not insisted that one must prove an orchestrated plan, they have noted that a genocidal campaign might be difficult to carry out without one.[47]

The Mental Element: *Mens Rea*

As noted earlier, the targets of the acts matter, but establishing the mental element (*mens rea*) presents a more important threshold requirement. To be deliberately repetitious, in dealing the genocide, we must keep in mind the idea that this constitutes the most serious crime one can commit. We must also keep in mind that Jean Paul Akayesu (Rwanda) was the first person accused of genocide to stand trial before an international tribunal. Thus, the ICTR broke new ground. This placed a great burden on the court because the judges and prosecutors had no prior case law to guide them. At best, determining the content of customary law involves a laborious process: finding relevant materials, reconciling differences in practice among states, determining whether a particular rule has binding status, and ascertaining whether the rule gives rise to individual liability as required by international criminal law. Where no prior practice exists, judges have to tread very delicately between a conservatism that undermines the purpose of the tribunal and an innovative activism that reflects an idealism based upon what the law "ought to be."

The ICC's provisions on the mental element of crimes (Art. 30) state that the prohibited acts must be committed with "intent and knowledge." Because the definition of genocide specifically requires intent, judgments of guilt have tended to conflate intent and knowledge in presuming that the defendant knew that destruction of the group would occur in the ordinary course of events.[48] Sorting out the convoluted reasoning of various tribunals would require an expedition into technical explication quite beyond that needed for the present discussion. Here, however, we must distinguish intent must from motive. Intent involves the willful commission of an act or engaging in conduct meant to cause a certain consequence. Motive involves the purpose (the "why") of the act. Though tribunals have occasionally used the language of "motive," the definition of genocide speaks only of intent. *Why* a person engages in the conduct or particular course of action has no bearing on guilt or innocence, although public statements about attitudes toward a particular group may form part of the evidence to establish intent.

The intent of the accused must be "to destroy" the protected group "in whole or in part." Earlier we alluded to the question of scope in determining what "whole" or "in part" means. It depends, first of all, upon, as noted, how one defines the "group." Then, what standards are to be used? Does quantity matter in the sense of a threshold number or percentage? Or can one use a qualitative standard that focuses on the importance to the group of those killed? While the ordinary person may think of genocide in terms of the Holocaust, the definition goes far beyond defining the crimes in simple numbers. Clearly, the Holocaust serves as the defining incident, but it is only one case. Numbers do matter, but sometimes the numbers can relate to "who" rather than "how many." For example, systematically killing all men of military age and forcibly removing the women (Bosnia) could have the consequence of eliminating a targeted group.

Rather than looking for an abstract answer, judges have tried to develop standards that adequately take the context into account. Two terms have emerged as guides: "substantial," which indicates a quantitative dimension, and "significant," which indicates a "qualitative" dimension (and can also indicate a quantitative dimension)."[49] To the question of whether the massacre of the Muslim community of Srebenica qualifies as genocide even though the numbers were relative small, the trial chamber in the *Krstić* case reasoned:

> [T]he intent to destroy a group, even if only in part, means seeking to destroy a distinct part of the group as opposed to an accumulation of isolated individuals within it. Although the perpetrators of genocide need not seek to destroy the entire group . . . they must view the part of the group they wish to destroy as a distinct entity which must be eliminated as such.[50]

In this case, the Bosnian Serbs deliberately targeted men of military age, resulting in the deaths of 7,000 8,000 people. The appeal chamber's decision sets out an interesting standard in interpreting what "in part" means. It first found that the action met the "specific intent" requirement in that its purpose was the destruction of Bosnian Muslims in Srebenica. Killing the men (and the subsequent forcible removal of the women) would have long-term consequences for the potential survival of the community. The court then used a cumulative (additive) connection in finding that this action qualified as genocide because it formed part of a larger campaign against all Bosnian Muslims.

Nonetheless, tribunals have set the bar here very high. To the consternation of prosecutors and human rights advocates, judges have kept the bar high. The reasoning of the panel in the dismissing the charges in the *Jelisić* case (ICTY) indicates that convicting low-level players, the Tadićs and Jelisićs, will be very difficult because of the problem of establishing special intent for participants at this level. Prosecutors would have to establish that low-level participants had knowledge of the broader context in which the individual actions occurred or, if a plan existed, of the plan. At this point, the urge to ensure the widest possible accountability for heinous crimes conflicts with the reality of strict judicial requirements of evidence and procedure.

Rwanda in Brief

Because the Statute of the ICTR focuses on genocide, a brief summary of events seems appropriate as an introduction to discussion of particular cases.[51] The Rwandan Patriotic Front (RPF) was founded, in 1987, by Tutsi refugees in Uganda. The first Tutsi refugees had fled to Uganda to escape ethnic purges that occurred in Rwanda in 1959. These resulted from the "social revolution" of 1959, which overthrew the Tutsi-led monarchy.[52] Initially, 50,000 to 70,000 Tutsi fled, but the refugee population had swelled to about 200,000 by 1990. The stated purpose of the RPF was to facilitate repatriation of Tutsi to Rwanda. President Juvenal Habyarimana of Rwanda had taken a hard line against the return. On October 1, 1990, the Rwandan Patriotic Army (RPA), the armed wing of the RPF, invaded northern Rwanda. At first, Habyarimana did not see the rebels as a serious threat, but that changed when the RPA rapidly advanced and threatened the capital, Kigali. After that initial success, troops from France and Zaire, called in to aid the Habyarimana regime, forced the RPA to retreat in some disarray. The RPA then, in classic Mao fashion, retreated to the "hills," regrouped under Paul Kagame, and began a guerrilla campaign to unseat the government. The war reached a stalemate, and the two sides entered into peace negotiations in July 1992 that lasted a year and resulted in the signing of the Arusha Accords in early August 1993.The agreement would have created a government in which Hutu and Tutsi would share power. A United Nations peacekeeping force (UNAMIR) was to oversee the implementation.[53]

The difficulty arose from the decision of the president and his close colleagues to use the RPF/RPA activities as a means of bolstering support for the regime. They began portraying Tutsi inside Rwanda as RPF collaborators. For three and a half years, they worked to redefine the population into "Rwandans," meaning those who backed the president, and the *ibyitso,* or "accomplices of the enemy," meaning the Tutsi minority and those Hutu opposed to him. The campaign to create hatred and fear of the Tutsi played upon memories of past domination by the minority. Singling out most Tutsi was easy. Since the 1930s, a law had required that all Rwandans register and carry an identity card that had an ethnic designation on it.[54]

In order to stay in power, Habyarimana, in 1990, had bowed to internal pressure to end his party's (National Revolutionary Movement for Development) monopoly on power. He announced plans to transform the Rwanda government into a multiparty democracy. Rival parties sprouted quickly to contend for popular support. Several of them created youth wings ready to fight to defend partisan interests. By early 1992, Habyarimana had begun providing military training to the youth of his party, who were thus transformed into the paramilitary militia known as the *Interahamwe* (those who stand/attack together). Under the guise of a "civilian self-defense" program, soldiers and political leaders distributed firearms and other weapons to the paramilitary militias and other supporters of Habyarimana. Because of potential costs, they advocated arming most of the young men with machetes. Businessmen close to Habyarimana imported enough machetes to arm every third adult Hutu male.[55]

Several bloody incidents involving the *Interahamwe* prior to the massive killing in April 1994 went unpunished. In particular, Hutu extremists had rejected the Arusha agreement. They set out to terrorize Tutsi and those Hutu politicians who supported the peace process. In 1993, several thousand Rwandans were killed, and some 9,000 were detained. This established a climate in which violence for political ends seemed legitimate.[56] Despite a large amount of advance preparation, the actual slaughter did not begin as a widespread, orchestrated killing spree that relentlessly moved to its ugly conclusion. Rather, it evolved and spread over time as participants recruited others through threats and incentives. The early organizers included military and administrative officials, as well as politicians, businessmen, and others with no official posts. Carrying out the plan required control of the state apparatus. This meant more than putting in place persons sympathetic to the plan as leaders. They had to secure the collaboration and cooperation of other officials throughout the system. Human Rights Watch noted:

> By appropriating the well-established hierarchies of the military, administrative and political systems, leaders of the genocide were able to exterminate Tutsi with astonishing speed and thoroughness. Soldiers, National Police (*gendarmes*), former soldiers, and communal police played a larger part in the slaughter than is generally realized. In addition to leading the first killings in the capital and in other urban centers, soldiers and National Police directed all the major massacres throughout the country. Although usually few in number at sites of massive killing, their tactical knowledge and their use of the weapons of war, including grenades, machine guns, and even mortars, contributed significantly to the death tolls in these massacres. It was only after the military had launched attacks with devastating effect on masses of unarmed Tutsi that civilian assailants, armed with such weapons as machetes, hammers, and clubs, finished the slaughter. In addition, the military encouraged and, when faced with reluctance to act, compelled both ordinary citizens and local administrators to participate in attacks, even travelling the back roads and stopping at small marketplaces to deliver the message.[57]

On April 6, a plane carrying Habyarimana and the president of Burundi, Cyprien Ntaryamira, was destroyed by a rocket as it approached Kigali airport. Observers agree that this event provided the spark for the following massacre. The Hutu coalition immediately blamed the RPF and asserted that Kagame had given the order. Kagame (RPF) blamed the extremist elements in Habyarimana's own party. An inquiry conducted by the French accused Kagame. No conclusive evidence has ever appeared that affixes responsibility for the rocket attack.[58] Rather than actively intervening, the UN withdrew the peacekeeping force after 10 of its members were killed. The killing stopped only when the RPF, under the leadership of Kagame, successfully routed government troops and took control of the country, ironically enough on July 4, 1994. At this writing, Kagame is serving a seven-year term as president of Rwanda. The next election should be in 2010.

The Prosecutor of the Tribunal against Jean Paul Akayesu

As noted earlier, this trial is the first in history of a person accused of genocide.[59]

Allegations of Fact The Republic of Rwanda is divided into 11 prefectures.[60] These 11 prefectures are further divided into communes. Jean Paul Akayesu served as mayor of the Taba commune (prefecture of Gitarama, territory of Rwanda) between January 1, 1994, and December 31, 1994. As mayor, he had the duty to maintain public order within his commune, subject to the authority of the prefect. He had exclusive control over the communal police, as well as any other police officers put at the disposition of the commune. He was responsible for the enforcement of laws and regulations and for the administration of justice, also subject only to the authority of the prefect.

Between April 7, 1994, and the end of June 1994, hundreds of civilians (here-inafter "displaced civilians") sought refuge at the communal headquarters. The majority of the displaced civilians were Tutsi. During this time, female displaced civilians were regularly taken by armed local militia and/or communal police and subjected to sexual violence and/or beaten on or near the bureau communal premises. Displaced civilians were also murdered frequently on or near the bureau communal premises. These acts of sexual violence were generally accompanied by explicit threats of death or bodily harm. The female displaced civilians lived in constant fear, and their physical and psychological health deteriorated as a result of the sexual violence, beatings, and killings.

The indictment alleged that Akayesu knew that the acts of sexual violence, beatings, and murders were being committed and was at times present during their commission. Further, it was charged that he facilitated the commission of the sexual violence, beatings, and murders by allowing the sexual violence and beatings and murders to occur on or near the bureau communal premises. By virtue of his presence during the commission of the sexual violence, beatings, and murders and by his failure to prevent the sexual violence, beatings, and murders, he encouraged these activities. In addition to these general charges, the indict-ment detailed a number of specific incidents.

Charges and Defense The indictment charged Akayesu with 15 offenses that included genocide, complicity in genocide, direct incitement to commit geno-cide, and various crimes against humanity (as defined in the Statute of the court). During the trial, the defense argued that Akayesu was a "scapegoat" who found himself accused only because he was a Hutu and a mayor at the time of the mas-sacres. In his closing argument, the defense attorney claimed that witnesses had colluded in a "syndicate of informers" that would denounce particular individuals for political reasons or in order to take over their property.[61] In this connection, he quoted Rene Degni-Segui, the Special Rapporteur of the Commission on Human Rights on Rwanda, who recounted a story of a demonstrably innocent Rwandan who had been denounced by 15 witnesses as a participant in the genocide.[62]

Verdict The chamber found him guilty on 9 of the 15 counts named in the indictment. These included genocide (murder) and crimes against humanity (rape, torture, and extermination). He received a sentence of life in prison.

> The Chamber holds that, as a blanket allegation to undermine the credibility
> of prosecution witnesses, this allegation can carry no weight, for two reasons.
> First, an attack on credibility which is not particularised with respect to indi-
> vidual witnesses is no attack at all on those witnesses' credibility; it is merely
> a generalised and unsubstantiated suspicion. Doubt can only arise where the
> criteria for doubt are fulfilled. . . . It is to be noted that during the trial the
> Defence did not put, nor even suggest, to a single prosecution witness that
> he or she was lying because he or she had been drawn into a syndicate of
> informers and instructed as to how to testify against the accused, or that the
> witness was lying because he or she wished to take the accused's property.

In addition, for the first time, the chamber also determined that rape and sexual
violence can constitute genocide in the same way as any other act of serious
bodily or mental harm, if such acts were committed with the intent to destroy a
particular group targeted as such.

The Radio Machete Trial: Ferdinand Nahimana, Jean-Bosco Barayagwiza, and Hassan Ngeze

The next case we discuss, dubbed "The Media Case" or, often, the "Radio
Machete" trial, gained a great deal of attention because it raised interesting issues
of freedom of speech.[63] Many countries have decided that there is a point at which
hate speech should be stopped. Article 19 of the ICCPR states that "Everyone
shall have the right to hold opinions without interference," but, it also states
that the exercise of the rights "carries with it special duties and responsibilities."
Restrictions may be lawfully placed on speech to protect "the rights or reputa-
tions of others" and for "the protection of national security of public order or of
public health or morals."[64] Still, what is the difference between intent to promote
hate that is protected under freedom of speech and intent to promote hate that
amounts to conspiracy to commit genocide?

In Rwanda, people get most of their information from radio broadcasts. Until
1993, Rwanda had only one national station, the government-owned Radio
Rwanda. Then the government gave a license to Ferdinand Nahimana and Jean-
Bosco Barayagwiza to start RTLM (Radio-Télévision Libre des Mille Collines).
It denied licenses to other applicants who might have offered competing view-
points.[65] RTLM introduced talk radio to Rwanda. The station was the country's first
and only privately owned alternative to government programming. Its "popularity
had as much to do with its lack of competition as with the programming choices
its directors made. . . . In a country where secrets were legion and half-truths told,
it seemed that Radio Milles Collines was . . . willing to tell its listeners what was
really happening."[66]

The three men named in the indictment were charged with being responsible
for the venomous broadcasts of what Rwandans called "Radio Hate."[67] Ferdinand
Nahimana and Jean-Bosco Barayagwiza founded RTLM; Hassan Ngeze served as
the editor of *Kangura* magazine, which ran vicious anti-Tutsi propaganda pieces

that commentators often read or discussed on the air.[68] One witness in the trial said that RTLM "spread petrol throughout the country little by little, so that one day it would be able to set fire to the whole country."[69] In the 80-page indictment, the prosecutor charged the three with inciting fellow Hutus to commit genocide. These men became the first journalists accused of such serious crimes since 1946, when the Nazi editor Julius Streicher was sentenced to hang at Nuremberg for calling for the murder of Jews. The following case except focuses on the role of RTLM in the events of 1994.

Allegations of Fact The indictment alleged that the programming on RTLM promoted ethnic stereotyping in a manner that promoted contempt and hatred for the Tutsi population. RTLM broadcasts called on listeners to seek out and take up arms against the enemy identified as the RPF, the *Inkotanyi* (nickname given to the RPF), the *Inyenzi* ("cockroaches"), and their accomplices. RTLM broadcasts equated all of these with the Tutsi ethnic group. After April 6, 1994, the virulence and the intensity of RTLM broadcasts propagating ethnic hatred and calling for violence increased. These broadcasts called explicitly for the extermination of the Tutsi ethnic group.

Nahimana was described as the founder and director of the company. Barayagwiza was his second in command. They represented RTLM externally in official capacities. Internally, they controlled the financial operations of the company and held supervisory responsibility for all activities of RTLM, taking remedial action when they considered it necessary to do so. Nahimana also played an active role in determining the content of RTLM broadcasts, writing editorials and giving journalists texts to read. On several RTLM broadcasts, Ngeze called for the extermination of the Tutsi and political opponents of the Hutu. He defended the extremist Hutu ideology that called for extermination of the Tutsi.

Charges The three accused were charged in separate indictments but tried jointly. All were charged on counts of genocide, conspiracy to commit genocide, direct and public incitement to commit genocide, complicity in genocide, and crimes against humanity (persecution and extermination). In addition, Ngeze was charged with crimes against humanity (murder). All were charged with individual criminal responsibility under Article 6(1) of the Statute for these crimes. Nahimana was additionally charged with superior responsibility under Article 6(3) in respect of direct and public incitement to commit genocide and the crime against humanity of persecution. Barayagwiza and Ngeze were charged with superior responsibility under Article 6(3) in respect of all the counts except conspiracy to commit genocide.

Defense Jean-Bosco Barayagwiza elected not to attend his trial. He stated that he did not have confidence that he would be afforded a fair trial in light of the appeals chamber's reversal of its decision ordering his release before the trial. All three claimed that a political motivation, not a desire for justice, lay behind their indictment. The defense raised the free speech standards of the United States. It also argued the need to promote vigilance with respect to an armed and dangerous enemy. They argued that the Tutsi had organized themselves into groups intent upon seizing power in Rwanda. The situation demanded strong action to protect the state.[70]

Verdict   The tribunal convicted all three of genocide and conspiracy to commit genocide, direct and public incitement to commit genocide, and persecution and extermination as crimes against humanity. It convicted Nahimana and Ngeze on five of seven charges and Barayagwiza on five of99 charges. Nahimana and Ngeze received life sentences. Because of what the judges considered violations of his rights, Barayagwiza received a sentence of 35 years less time already served (8 years).

Appeals Chamber Judgment   The three accused lodged an appeal against the trial judgment on various grounds of errors of fact and law. The appeal was heard in January 2007, and the verdict was rendered on November 28, 2007.[71] In its judgment, the appeals chamber reversed several parts of the trial judgment. It acquitted all three of conspiracy to commit genocide and of all genocide charges relating to their involvement with RTLM and *Kangura*.

The reasoning of the chamber dealt with several important elements. First, Nahimana and Ngeze had argued that the trial chamber had erred in that it included acts against opponents of the Hutu who could not be part of the Tutsi protected group. The chamber found that the perception of the offenders as to identity was a valid factor in determining whether or not particular individuals belonged to a group but, in this instance they held that no evidence existed to show that the accused had such perceptions.[72] Second, the appeals chamber reversed Nahamina's conviction for genocide because, though he was the founder of RTLM, he had not played an active role after April 6, 1994.[73] Moreover, no evidence existed that he had ordered any on-air personality to incite the murder of Tutsis.[74] Barayagwiza, originally convicted for "superior responsibility," also had his conviction reversed on the grounds that the evidence was insufficient to establish that he had effective control over journalists and others after April 6.[75]

Perhaps the most important part of the decision related to the charge of "direct and public incitement" to commit genocide. The trial chamber had taken a rather broad and somewhat confused position on the relationship among "hate speech," freedom of speech, and incitement to genocide. The decision had generated some considerable commentary.[76] For example, Diane Orentlicher had argued that the trial chamber had broadened the standard considerably beyond what the Convention (and the court's Statute) required:

> Speech made punishable by the convention is limited to words that advocate the commission of genocide by the speaker's intended audience. However

pernicious, propaganda that instead seeks to induce racial, religious, or national hatred is beyond the reach of the convention's provision on "direct and public incitement to commit genocide."[77]

The appeals chamber discussed the difference between instigation as an inchoate crime and direct and public incitement at some length. It did not agree that the trial chamber had blurred the distinction between hate speech and public direct incitement. It agreed with the trial chamber that cultural context and the nuances of the local language could be analyzed with an eye toward what the audience might have read into certain words and phrases.[78] Nahimana's original conviction for "instigation" was overturned because the available evidence did not establish sufficient personal involvement. His conviction for "superior responsibility" was upheld. With respect to Ngeze, the chamber decided that some articles published in 1994 did constitute direct and public incitement to commit genocide and affirmed that conviction.

The ICTY and Genocide

The ICTY has charged only a few individuals with genocide. The first, Goran Jelisić, was a low-level participant who had the nickname of the "Serbian Adolf." He pled guilty to 15 counts of crimes against humanity and 16 counts of violations of the laws or customs of war relating to murders, beatings, and the plunder of private property in the municipality of Brčko in the northeastern part of Bosnia and Herzegovina in May 1992. He fought the charge that he was an accomplice to genocide. The trial chamber acquitted him on the charge. The chamber found that, given the evidence, genocide had not occurred in Brčko. It is impossible to be an accomplice to a crime (that is, to aid and abet) that others have not committed.[79] The appeals chamber found that the trial chamber had made an incorrect assessment of the evidence on the genocide count, but it did not reverse the acquittal. Jelisić received a 40-year sentence.[80]

Radislav Krstić was chief of staff of the Drina Corps of the Army of Republika Sprška (VRS) and then its commander during the time of the Bosnian Serb takeover of the United Nations "safe haven" of Srebrenica in July 1995. He was convicted of genocide, violations of the laws or customs of war, and crimes against humanity. On appeal, the chamber upheld the trial chamber, finding that genocide had occurred in Srebenica. It also found that the main staff of the VRS clearly had the specific intent to destroy a significant part of the Bosnian Muslim population. It, however, reduced the charge of committing genocide to aiding and abetting on the basis that Krstić lacked the specific intent necessary to be a direct perpetrator. The court used the theory of "joint criminal enterprise" to link Krstić to the crimes. This permitted the use of circumstantial evidence to establish the connection. In reducing the charge, the panel reasoned that the standard for direct participation was much higher—it required "unequivocal proof" of intent.[81]

The ICJ and Genocide

The ICJ decides cases brought between states.[82] Potentially, under customary law, a state could have a collective responsibility for genocide. The question of whether accession to, or ratification of, the 1948 Genocide Convention also may yield a basis for collective responsibility formed one of the more interesting questions surrounding the case. Bosnia sought to hold Serbia liable, rather than individual Serbs. If successful, Bosnia could have collected a huge sum in reparations. An interesting irony here—if Yugoslavia had stayed one state, the case would not have been possible. Bosnia would not have had standing because it would have lacked the requisite status as a sovereign state.

The decision illustrates both the possibilities and the frustrations of litigation to settle such disputes. The court found that the Genocide Convention did create state responsibility in addition to the requirement that States Parties take steps to prevent individuals from committing the prohibited and punishable acts and to punish them if they do. With some dissenting opinions, the court held that a State may be found in violation of the treaty when it commits genocide. In addition, it found that a State can be complicit in genocide, as well. It found that genocide had occurred in Bosnia, affirming the ICTY's findings in *Krstić*.[83]

At this point, the decision took an interesting twist. The court ruled that Serbia was guilty of failing to prevent the massacre of 8,000 Bosnian Muslims at Srebrenica in 1995 but that it was not directly guilty of acts of genocide during the war between Serbia and Bosnia. The decision took the form of several votes. On the key issue, the court decided by a vote of 13–2 that Serbia had not committed genocide, through its organs or persons whose acts engaged its responsibility under customary international law. In another vote, however, the court found by a vote of 12–3 that Serbia had violated its obligation to prevent genocide. In reasoning parallel to that in the *Krstić* and *Jelisić* cases, the court held that Bosnia did not provide sufficient evidence to establish "special intent" on the part of Serbian officials. The court excoriated Serbia for the omission in not acting with due diligence to prevent the massacres, but it did not find a connection sufficient to justify the charge of genocide. The question that cannot be answered is this: if Milošević had lived and his trial had gone to conclusion, would the ICJ have delayed its decision until his trial had come to a conclusion? An equally interesting conjecture is: does the decision in this case, with 15 judges examining the evidence presented by Bosnia, suggest that Milošević could have received a verdict of not guilty?

Notes

Vahankn N. Dadrian, "Genocide as a Problem of National and International Law: The World War I Armenian Case and Its Contemporary Legal Ramifications," *Yale Journal of International Law* 14, no. 2 (1989): 225.

1. Advisory Opinion, *Reservations to the Convention on the Preservation and Punishment of the Crime of Genocide*, May 28, 1951, *ICJ Reports 1951*, 23. Text at http://www.icj-cij.org/docket/index.php?p1=3&p2=4&k=90&case=12&code=ppcg&p3=4.

2. *Convention on the Prevention and Punishment of the Crime of Genocide,* December 9, 1948; text at http://www.unhchr.ch/html/menu3/b/p_genoci.htm.

3. Diane F. Orentlicher, "Genocide," in Roy Gutman and David Rieff (eds.), *Crimes of War: What the Public Should Know* (New York: Norton, 1999), 153.

4. Antonio Cassese, *International Criminal Law* (Oxford: Oxford University Press, 2003), 97. Emphasis in the original.

5. *Prosecutor v. Akayesu,* ICTR, Trial Chamber, Judgment of September 2, 1998 [ICTR-96–4].

6. Application of the Convention on the Prevention and Punishment of the Crime of Genocide (Bosnia and Herzegovina v. Serbia and Montenegro) (1993); Judgment of July 11, 1996. Application for Revision of the Judgment of July 11, 1996, in the *Case concerning Application of the Convention on the Prevention and Punishment of the Crime of Genocide (Bosnia and Herzegovina v. Yugoslavia)*, Judgment of February 26, 2007.

7. Human Rights Watch, *Genocide in Iraq: The Anfal Campaign against the Kurds* (New York: Human Rights Watch, 1993); http://www.hrw.org/reports/1993/iraqanfal/.

8. For some insight into these issues, see Philip Zimbardo, *The Lucifer Effect: Understanding How Good People Turn Evil* (New York: Random House, 2007).

9. Samantha Power, *"A Problem from Hell": America and the Age of Genocide* (New York: Basic Books, 2002), 5–13.

10. *Ambassador Morgenthau's Story,* http://www.homepage-link.to/turkey/morgenthau.html.

11. *Convention on the Prevention and Punishment of the Crime of Genocide,* Article 2.

12. Raphaël Lemkin, *Axis Rule in Occupied Europe* (New York: Carnegie Endowment for International Peace, 1944), 79; Raphaël Lemkin, "Genocide as a Crime under International Law," *American Journal of International Law* 41, no. 1 (1947): 145. The word "ethnocide" has also become a common synonym for cultural genocide. William Schabas, *Genocide in International Law: The Crime of Crimes* (Cambridge: Cambridge University Press, 2000), 25, n. 71.

13. Text in *American Journal of International Law* 45 (1951 Supp.), 6. For a discussion of the original negotiations, see Lawrence J. Leblanc, *The United States and the Genocide Convention* (Durham, NC: Duke University Press, 1991), 151–74. Ironically, the concerns of the Soviet Union (e.g., diminution of sovereign prerogatives) expressed during the negotiations mirrored many of the concerns expressed by members of the U.S. Senate during the first, and subsequent, debates over possible ratification. See also Josef. L. Kunz, "The United Nations Convention on Genocide," *American Journal of International Law* 43, no. 4 (1949): 738–46.

14. Geoffrey Robertson, *Crimes against Humanity: The Struggle for Global Justice* (3rd ed.) (New York: New Press, 2006), 263–43.

15. *Prosecutor v. Akayesu,* para. 511. Note that the trial chamber in this case did hold that the Convention applied to any stable and permanent group. The statement has had very limited impact because others have chosen to interpret the Convention conservatively and literally.

16. Antonio Cassese, *International Criminal Law* (Oxford: Oxford University Press, 2003), 96–97. See also Beth Van Schaack, "The Crime of Political Genocide: Repairing the Genocide Convention's Blind Spot," *Yale Law Journal* 106 (1996–1997): 2259–92.

17. *The Stockholm Declaration on Genocide Prevention* (January 28, 2004); http://www.preventgenocide.org/prevent/conferences/StockholmDeclaration28Jan2004.htm.

18. See William Shawcross, *Deliver Us from Evil: Peacekeepers, Warlords and a World of Endless Conflict* (New York: Simon and Schuster, 2000); Power, *A Problem from Hell.*

19. Gerard Prunier, *Darfur: The Ambiguous Genocide* (3rd ed.) (Ithaca, NY: Cornell University Press, 2008).

20. G.A. Resolution 47/135 of December 19, 1992. Text in *International Legal Materials* 32 (1993): 911; and at http://www.unhchr.ch/html/menu3/b/d_minori.htm.

21. Order of September 12, 1993, in *International Legal Materials* 32 (1993): 1599. See also Anthony D'Amato, "Peace v. Accountability in Bosnia," *American Journal of International Law* 88 (1994): 500, and J. J. Paust's criticism of same, in *idem* (1994), 715.

22. See Lucia Mouat, "UN Tackles Genocide in Europe and Africa," *The Christian Science Monitor,* July 1, 1994, at 7.

23. See, Paul J. Magnarella, "The Background and Causes of the Genocide in Rwanda," *Journal of International Criminal Justice* 3, no. 4 (2005): 801; Jean Mukimbiri, "The Seven Stages of the Rwandan Genocide," *Journal of International Criminal Justice* 3, no. 4 (2005): 823–36; Linda Melvern, "The Security Council in the Face of Genocide," *Journal of International Criminal Justice* 3 (2005): 847–60; Erik Møse, "Main Achievements of the ICTR," *Journal of International Criminal Justice* 3 (2005):, 920–43; Payam Akhavan, "The Crime of Genocide in the ICTR Jurisprudence," *Journal of International Criminal Justice* 3, no. 4 (2005): 989–1006.

24. Article 1, *Convention on the Prevention and Punishment of the Crime of Genocide*, December 9, 1948; text at http://www.unhchr.ch/html/menu3/b/p_genoci.htm.

25. *Prosecutor v. Jelisić* Trial Chamber I, Judgment of December 14, 1999 [IT-95-10, P 86], para. 400. For a discussion see Schabas, *Genocide,* 207–9; and William Schabas, "Darfur and the 'Odious Scourge': The Commission of Inquiry's Findings on Genocide," *Leiden Journal of International Law* 18, no. 4 (2005): 877.

26. *Prosecutor v. Karadžić and Mladić,* ICTY, Transcript of Hearing [Cases No. IT-95–5 and IT 95–18].

27. "L.A. Shooting Suspect Charged with Hate Crimes," CNN, August 12, 1999; http://www.cnn.com/US/9908/12/california.shooting.03/.

28. BBC, "Nailbomber Set Out to Terrorize," June 8, 2000; http://news.bbc.co.uk/1/hi/uk/782876.stm.

29. *Prosecutor v. Akayesu,* para. 513. See also *Prosecutor v. Kayishema and Ruzindana,* ICTR, Judgment of May 21, 1999 [[ICTR-95-1-T], para. 98.

30. *Prosecutor v. Akayesu,* para. 514.

31. *Prosecutor v. Akayesu,* para. 512.

32. For a critique, see Schabas, *Genocide,* 109–14.

33. *Prosecutor v. Akayesu,* para. 512–15.

34. Also Batwa. The Twa are perhaps the best known of a number of pygmy groups that range across equatorial Africa.

35. Gerard Prunier, *Darfur: The Ambiguous Genocide* (3rd ed.) (Ithaca, NY: Cornell University Press, 2008); Schabas, "Darfur and the 'Odious Scourge,'" 871–85.

36. International Commission of Inquiry on Darfur, Report to the Secretary-General, UN Doc. S/2005/60 (January 25, 2005), para. 508.

37. International Commission of Inquiry on Darfur, Report to the Secretary-General, UN Doc. S/2005/60, para. 510. Emphasis added.

38. Schabas, *Genocide,* 109–14.

39. Adopted and opened for signature and ratification by General Assembly Resolution 2106 (XX) of December 21, 1965 (entry into force, January 4, 1969); http://www.unhchr.ch/html/menu3/b/d_icerd.htm.

40. Robert Cryer et al., *An Introduction to International Criminal Law* (Cambridge: Cambridge University Press, 2007), 173.

41. "Aiding and abetting" often are regarded as less serious because the charge implies "secondary" participation because it does not require direct commission of prohibited acts. Accordingly, the requirements for establishing "aiding and abetting" are somewhat less stringent. Establishing guilt does require that the prosecution show that the acts or omissions (failure to perform a duty such as policing) contributed substantially to the crime. *Prosecutor v. Blaskić,* ICTY, Appeals Chamber, July 29, 2004 [Case No. IT-95–14-A], paras. 47, 48.

42. UN UN SCOR, S/RES/953 (1994), Preamble, para. 3.

43. William A. Schabas, *The UN International Criminal Tribunals: The Former Yugoslavia, Rwanda and Sierra Leone* (Cambridge: Cambridge University Press, 2006), 162.

44. ICTY Statute, Article 7.

45. ICC, *Elements of Crimes,* Section 6. Emphasis added.

46. BBC News, "Charges Facing Saddam Hussein," July 1, 2004; http://news.bbc.co.uk/1/hi/world/middle_east/3320293.stm

47. See e.g., *Prosecutor v. Jelesić,* Judgement para. 48; *Prosecutor v. Kayishema and Ruzindana,* Judgement, para. 94.

48. In the appeal of the Krstić conviction for genocide, the ICTY Chamber found that the General lacked the intent to commit genocide but had knowledge that others intended to do so. The judges reversed the conviction but found him guilty of "aiding and abetting." *Prosecutor v. Krstić,* ICTY, Appeals Chamber, Judgment of April 19, 2004 [IT-98–33-A], paras. 134, 140. This seems a bit of legal sophistry somewhat at odds with general assumptions about complicity in the common law—if you knowingly aid and abet, you have intent to commit the crime.

49. Schabas, *The UN International Criminal Tribunals,* 169.

50. *Prosecutor v. Krstić,* ICTY, Trial Chamber I, Judgment of August 2, 2001 [IT-98–33-T], para. 590.

51. See Gerard Prunier, *The Rwanda Crisis* (New York: Columbia University Press, 1997); Scott Straus, *The Order of Genocide: Race, Power, and War in Rwanda* (Ithaca, NY: Cornell University Press, 2008); Dina Temple-Raston, *Justice on the Grass: Three Rwandan Journalists, Their Trial for War Crimes, and a Nation's Quest for Redemption* (New York: Free Press, 2005), 1–46; Ben Kiernan, *Blood and Soil: A World History of Genocide and Extermination from Sparta to Darfur* (New Haven: Yale University Press, 2007); Human Rights Watch, *The Genocide: The Strategy of Ethnic Division* (1999); http://www.hrw.org/reports/1999/rwanda/Geno1-3-02.htm#P21_7273.

52. Rwanda and Burundi became independent in 1962.

53. Robertson, *Crimes against Humanity,* 80.

54. Temple-Raston, *Justice on the Grass,* 19.

55. Human Rights Watch, *The Genocide.*

56. Human Rights Watch: *The Genocide;* Samantha Power, "Bystanders to Genocide," The Atlantic.com, http://www.theatlantic.com/doc/200109/power-genocide/2.

57. Human Rights Watch, *The Genocide.*

58. BBC News, "Kagame Accused over Plane Attack" (March 10, 2004), http://news.bbc.co.uk/1/hi/world/africa/3497688.stm. Without trying to sort out the competing claims, the political motivation here stands out. The French military controlled the Kigali airport at the time of the incident. The French also had provided very strong military and political aid to the incumbent government.

59. *Prosecutor v. Akayesu,* Indictment [Case no: ICTR-96–4-I]; http://69.94.11.53/ENGLISH/cases/Akayesu/indictment/actamond.htm.

60. Drawn from, *Prosecutor v. Akayesu,* Indictment [Case no: ICTR-96–4-I]; http://69.94.11.53/ENGLISH/cases/Akayesu/indictment/actamond.htm.

61. James C. McKinley, Jr., "U.N. Tribunal, in First Such Trial Verdict, Convicts Rwandan Ex-Mayor of Genocide," *New York Times,* September 3, 1998.

62. *Report on the Situation of Human Rights in Rwanda* submitted by Rene Degni-Segui, Special Rapporteur of the Commission on Human Rights, under paragraph 20 of resolution S-3/1 of May 25, 1994, UN Doc. A/49/508/Add.1, S/1994/1157/Add.1(November 14, 1994).

63. ICTR, Trial Chamber I [ICTR-99–52-T] (2003).

64. See also Article 10(2) of the *European Convention on Human Rights.* For an interesting exchange on these issues, see Human Rights Brief, "Point/Counterpoint," http://www.wcl.american.edu/hrbrief/03/2point.cfm. See also Radio Free Europe, "Europe: Case of Swedish Pastor Convicted of Hate Speech Tests Limits of Freedom," http://www.rferl.org/featuresarticle/2005/01/d0e0334d-17b7-4d39-82c7-a012302d48f6.html.

65. Temple-Raston,"Radio Hate"; Temple-Raston, *Justice on the Grass.*

66. Temple-Raston, *Justice on the Grass,* 2–3.

67. Temple-Raston, "Radio Hate".

68. For brief profiles of the three, see ICTR, "The Media Trial," http://69.94.11.53/default.htm.

69. *Prosecutor v. Ferdinand Nahimana, Jean-Bosco Barayagwiza and Hassan Ngeze,* ICTR, Trial Chamber I, Judgment and Sentence of December 3, 2003 [ICTR-99–52-T], para. 23.

70. Temple-Raston, *Justice on the Grass,* 113.

71. *Nahamina et al. v. Prosecutor.,* ICTR, Appeals Chamber, Judgment of November 28, 2007 [ICTR 99–52-A]. See also *Nahamina et al.,* ICTR, Appeals Chamber, Summary of Judgment, http://69.94.11.53/default.htm.

72. *Nahamina et al. v. Prosecutor.,* ICTR, Appeals Chamber, Judgment of November 28, 2007 [ICTR 99–52-A], para. 496.

73. *Nahamina et al. v. Prosecutor.,* ICTR, Appeals Chamber, para. 589.

74. *Nahamina et al. v. Prosecutor.,* ICTR, Appeals Chamber, para. 596.

75. *Nahamina et al. v. Prosecutor.,* ICTR, Appeals Chamber, para. 635.

76. For example, see, Diane F. Orentlicher, "Symposium: International Criminal Tribunals in the 21st Century: Criminalizing Hate Speech in the Crucible of Trial: *Prosecutor v. Nahimana,*" *American Unviversity International Law Review* 21 (2006), 557–96; H. Ron Davidson, "The International Criminal Tribunal for Rwanda's Decision in *The Prosecutor v. Ferdinand Nahimana et al.:* The Past, Present, and Future of International Incitement Law," *Leiden Journal of International Law* 17 (2004): 505–19.

77. Orentlicher, "Symposium," 569.

78. *Nahamina et al. v. Prosecutor,* ICTR, Appeals Chamber, paras. 695, 696.

79. William A. Schabas, "The *Jelisić* Case and the *Mens Rea* of the Crime of Genocide," *Leiden Journal of International Law* 14 (2001): 127.

80. *Prosecutor v. Jelisić,* ICTY, Appeals Chamber, Judgment of July 5, 2001 [IT-95–10-A].

81. *Prosecutor v. Krstić,* ICTY, Appeals Chamber, Judgement of April 19, 2004 [IT-98–33-A], para. 126.

82. Application for Revision of the Judgment of July 11, 1996, in the *Case concerning Application of the Convention on the Prevention and Punishment of the Crime of Genocide (Bosnia and Herzegovina v. Yugoslavia),* Judgment of February 26, 2007. The decision comprises 351 pages.

83. ICJ Bosnia 2007, 278–97.

CHAPTER 6

War Crimes: International Humanitarian Law

Silent enim leges inter arma [in war the laws are silent].

Cicero

The quote that heads this chapter seemingly has considerable face validity. Considering some of the savage acts over the course of history, the idea that the resort to arms might be constrained in some way by the force of law must elicit skepticism. The Old Testament of the Bible relates numerous instances of total destruction in the sense of killing every living being, including children.[1] As an example and warning to others who opposed him, Alexander the Great crucified 2,000 young men after the fall of Tyre, putting the crosses along the main road to the city. Rome completely destroyed Carthage. In another classic quote, when criticized by the citizens of Messina for violating a treaty the city had with Rome, Pompey the Great is reported to have said, "Won't you stop citing laws to us who have our swords by our sides?"[2] Seventeen hundred years later, the massacre of 20,000 to 30,000 persons at Magdeburg in 1631 exemplified the carnage that occurred during the 30 Years' War. The atrocities committed by both sides in this conflict spurred Grotius, generally considered the "father" of modern international law, to write his most famous treatise, *De jure belli ac pacis* (On the law of war and peace).[3] In prior chapters, we have discussed many of the events of the 20th and early 21st centuries that have caused moral outrage and concern.[4]

The *Jus ad Bellum* and the *Jus in Bello*

At this point, we need to distinguish between two different concepts. Historically, the law on the use of force has been divided into two distinct categories: the *jus ad bellum*, which presumably governed the *resort to war,* and the *jus in bello,* the law governing individual conduct within war. Much of the prior discussion has focused upon the *jus in bello* for good reason. For much of human history, war and violence have formed a natural fact of life. In terms of the *jus ad bellum,* might did make right. "Victor's justice" prevailed in the sense that the vanquished had no say or recourse. Rome's destruction of Carthage had little justification in terms of security threat, but victors write history.[5] Rome, as a victor, did not face accusations that its victory was tainted because it violated the rules. For much of human history, war has not been an NCAA sport with appropriate investigations and penalties for violations of rules. The idea of making war more humane does at times appear to be an oxymoron.

Despite the obvious tensions inherent in the idea of imposing limits on struggles that can involve fundamental questions of life and death or, at the minimum, questions of quality of life, slavery, or extreme oppression for example, we find that many civilizations from around the globe have evolved standards that apply to conflicts with others.[6] From a modern standpoint, these may seem insignificant, irrelevant, remarkably permissive, or merely observation of meaningless ritual. Beyond a mention of existence, these do not form part of our concern. While Grotius and others laid the foundations, the primary roots of contemporary international humanitarian law emerged only in the wake of the Crimean War (1854–1856).

The *Jus ad Bellum*

Even though the secular just war tradition emerged during the latter part of the 16th century, marking an important transition in the evolution of modern international law, it produced no meaningful restraints on the resort to war. In reading the classic commentaries, one should not presume that they had any effect on the policies of the time. In large part, they merely acknowledged that war as an institution formed an integral part of the fabric of international politics. The 16th- and early-17th-century writers considered the precursors to Grotius, who focused on clarifying the circumstances covered by the *jus ad bellum,* with an eye toward strengthening and expanding the *jus in bello.* The classics in the law give priority in space and attention to hostile relations among nations, a practice justified by the "normality" of such relations, compared with the relative abnormality of peace among the states of Europe. Controlling the resort to force became an issue only in the aftermath of World War I and a priority only after World War II.

The first part of this chapter addresses questions relating to the *jus ad bellum,* slightly redefined to mean the right to resort to *force.* The second part covers the basics of the *jus in bellum* and examines modern war crimes trials. In particular, the discussion emphasizes the importance of defining contexts. From the earlier discussion, one should quickly understand that the phrase "use of force" contains a minefield. Consider how many different descriptions of conflicts appear in the contemporary literature discussing various situations in which force has been used. In addition to war, one finds civil war, internal armed conflict, international armed conflict, humanitarian intervention, hostilities, police action, and hostilities, to name just a few.

The Classic Definition of War

Prior to World War II, the world of the international lawyer was much simpler. The resort to *war* was not illegal, though we do see attempts in the interwar period to limit the recourse to force. The idea of self-help and self-preservation formed the cornerstone, the essential underpinnings, of state sovereignty. Until the 20th century, states had few ties that produced transactions links of sufficient importance and magnitude to constitute opportunities for exploitation in the form of effective threats of disruption, suspension, or negation. Apart from persuasion, subsidy, and bribery, armed coercion or the threat of armed coercion often formed the only means of influence available. The twin principles of necessity and proportionality presumably governed both force short of war (reprisal and retaliation) and conduct within war (*jus in bello*), but the resort to war remained embedded within a relatively open-ended definition of necessity.[7] States could and did use force to gain political advantage.[8] In this political climate, Lassa Oppenheim's classic definition captures the essential features: war is a contention, through the use of armed force, between states, undertaken for the purpose of overpowering one another.[9]

In examining textbooks written prior to the creation of the UN Charter, one always finds two distinct sections (sometimes two distinct volumes): the law of peace and the law of war.[10] One set of laws governed states during peaceful relations; another set of laws governed states during war. International law said nothing about the transition from peace to war. The law did not prohibit war; rather, it viewed the institution as a normal function of sovereign states. The rights claimed did not have to have legal or moral merit. Failing to gain its objective by peaceful means, a state had a right to pursue its aims by recourse to force. The possibilities included the extinction of independence through conquest or the loss of sovereign territory. This required only a formal declaration of war, setting up a "state of war" in which the formal laws of war applied. From a legal point of view, a state of war did not have to mean open clashes between armed forces. It meant only that relations between the two states, and between the two states and third-party states, were now controlled by the laws of war. A declaration of war had the interesting result that third-party states had then to declare themselves either belligerents and allies, that is, as actively supporting one warring side or the other, or neutrals, supporting neither. The two positions, belligerent ally or neutral, determined which set of rather complex rules would govern behavior between the warring states and the third-party state.

Pre-Charter Attempts to Regulate the Use of Force

The arrival of the mass army and the continuing discoveries of more efficient weapons led, in the late 19th century, to the first serious attempts to limit war as a legally accepted method of enforcing legal rights and changing the rules of law. The two Hague Conferences of 1899 and 1907 represented early efforts to mitigate the impact of war.[11] Neither of these conferences seriously addressed the idea of limiting the right of states to resort to war. Rather, they concentrated upon the idea of making war more humane by elaborating the *jus in bello*.[12] The conferees had planned another meeting in 1914. Ironically, it was canceled because of war.

The Covenant of the League of Nations provided in its preamble an acceptance by the contracting parties of an obligation not to resort to war. Nonetheless, the Covenant did not totally outlaw war. Member states could still go to war under certain conditions (Art. 12; Art. 13; Art. 15(7); Art. 17). The downside of the Covenant lay in the fact that the League had no effective way to impose collective sanctions on violators. In theory, Article 16 of the Covenant did provide for the imposition of sanctions against a member of the League of Nations that had resorted to war in violation of its obligations under the Covenant. The organization managed to invoke the provisions of Article 16 in only one of five instances in which such a violation did take place.—against the Italian invasion of Ethiopia in 1935. These proved ineffective. In its final act before its demise, the organization did expel the Soviet Union from membership for its invasion of Finland.

Efforts to Outlaw Aggressive War

For our purposes, the effort to outlaw aggressive war has more interest. As early as 1923, the Treaty of Mutual Assistance—which never came into force—attempted to identify wars of aggression as an international crime. The equally abortive Geneva Protocol of 1924 similarly labeled aggressive war a crime (in its preamble) and in its Article 2 imposed an obligation on all parties to the agreement to refrain from war except in the specific circumstances listed in the treaty. The Assembly of the League passed a resolution in 1927 that sought to prohibit all wars of aggression. States should utilize only pacific means to settle international disputes of every kind. In 1928, the Sixth Pan-American Conference adopted a resolution asserting that a "war of aggression constitutes a crime against the human species . . . all aggression is illicit and as such is declared prohibited."

Kellogg-Briand Pact (Pact of Paris, 1928)

Much has been written about the Kellogg-Briand Pact, deriding its idealism and lack of impact. Still, the agreement does stand at the center of the efforts to outlaw *aggressive* war. Note the adjective "aggressive," because none of these proposals really purported to prohibit every kind of war. In August 1928, 15 states signed the General Treaty for the Renunciation of War (Kellogg-Briand Pact or Pact of Paris) in Paris. Eventually, 65 states ratified or accepted the treaty.[13]

To reiterate earlier points about other agreements, the pact did not abolish the institution of war as such. It still permitted resort to war in legally permissible self-defense and as an instrument of collective action to restrain an aggressor. As with the Covenant, the treaty also did not abolish resort to war between a party to the agreement and a country not party to the agreement. The treaty, furthermore, did not prohibit the resort to war against a country that had violated the treaty's provisions. The Pact of Paris failed to provide a means of enforcing compliance and, even more important, did not define the measures and methods through which relations between states might be changed without resorting to force.[14]

The reason to spend some time in examination here has to do with the debate over the validity of several charges made at the Nuremberg war crimes trials.[15] Arguably, aggressive war had become a crime, but statesmen and lawyers alike still postulated an essential connection between the availability of force as a sanction and the preservation of state interests. Despite the trappings of a treaty, the instrument had little effect on state practice. Many of the states that had signed it denied its validity through their own practice. Armed conflicts in the ensuing decade were both more numerous and more serious than they had been between 1919 and 1928.[16] As another prominent contemporary international lawyer has recently noted, "A process of decision making constitutes a normative system only when those affected believe that in general they have an obligation to obey its results."[17]

Beyond the question of consistent practice lies the simple fact that no instrument created individual personal liability for violation of any of its provisions. True, a number of the Allies had sought to hold Kaiser Wilhelm personally responsible for initiating World War I. Not only did the trial not happen, but two major states advanced strong and compelling objections to the attempt on both legal and pragmatic grounds. Significantly, no state subsequently advanced the idea that individual liability should be part of any of the myriad proposals directed at controlling resort to war. More significant, questions regarding individual liability did not form even a minor topic of discussion among the legal literati of the interwar period.

The United Nations

The experience of World War II and the approaching abolition of the League of Nations combined to bring out a renewed attempt to circumscribe resort to force by the provisions incorporated in the Charter of the United Nations. Article 2 of that document contains the key obligations. While writers tend to focus on Article 2.4, Article 2.3 is no less important:

2(3). All Members shall settle their international disputes by peaceful means in such a manner that international peace and security, and justice, are not endangered.

2(4). All Members shall refrain in their international relations from the *threat or use of force* against the territorial integrity or political independence of any state, or in any other manner inconsistent with the Purposes of the United Nations. (emphasis added)

The Charter went beyond the provisions of the Pact of Paris in that the members of the United Nations renounced not only their right to go to war—except in instances of individual or collective self-defense (Articles 51 and 52)—but also their right unilaterally to resort to the threat or the use of force. One should note that the only reference to war in the Charter occurs in its preamble ("determined to save succeeding generations from the scourge of war"). Elsewhere, "threat or use of force" and "threat to the peace, breach of the peace, or act of aggression" are used in reference to situations in which the new organization, through the Security Council, could take action under specified conditions.

From the beginning, the organization struggled. Apart from the Cold War divisions that undermined the agreement necessary for the Security Council to function, the types of violence that constituted breaches or threats to the peace did not fit the models foreseen by the authors of the Charter. Charter operations presupposed that armed conflicts would be between two territorial states conducted by regular army forces that would be clearly identified through distinctive uniforms and insignia.[18] So, the Charter definitions do not cover the modern development of what some have called a *status mixtus,* or intermediacy that attempts to create a legal category of limited recourse to force between peace and war. Although advocated in different guises, the concept has not yet become a part of accepted international law, despite its advocacy by several well-known jurists.[19] In view of the fact that a large number of modern armed conflicts have taken place without an official declaration of a state of war, I will use the term "armed conflict," when I deemed it desirable, in the discussion to follow.

Over the past 50 years, incidents that fit the Charter assumptions have been the exception, rather than the rule. The range of conflicts in which states have resorted to force extends from responses to terrorism and/or transboundary guerrilla raids to "cod wars" over fishing rights (Iceland and the United Kingdom) to overt invasions (Iraq and Iran, Vietnam and Cambodia) that do fit the classic definitions of war. Certainly, the framers of the Charter did not foresee the range of internal conflicts that has had important international impacts. Finally, nuclear weapons changed the prudential calculus associated with large-scale conventional war. The political dynamics of self-determination and economic justice displaced interstate war as a principal concern. Nonstate actors began to play major roles, sometimes as initiators of low intensity transborder military activity against states. Weak states fell prey to internal wars fueled by societal cleavages of various types. The UN, so fundamentally tied to a statist foundation, had to face demands that it support and promote policies that transcend state claims to absolute primacy, such as human rights and, preeminently, self-determination.

Aggression: Another Controversy over Definitions

One of the more interesting features of the evolution of international law in the 20th century stems from the massive amount of effort spent in trying to define aggression. For many, defining aggression became important because, as the idea developed through the 1920s and 1930s, self-defense, as a legitimate use of force, was seen as a response to aggression, or the illegitimate or illegal use of force. Curiously, in the period between the two world wars, a divergence of opinion emerged among jurists and statesmen over whether it was a good idea to develop a precise legal definition of aggression. The League had spent much time in trying to develop a definition of aggression. The efforts of the League and others reflects a "legislative" perspective in that those engaged sought to develop definitions and standards to guide future practice through consultation, debate, and parliamentary diplomacy. On the other hand, others felt that a definition should evolve out of state responses on a case-by-case basis. They believed that the complexity of circumstances required that a definition emerge from actions in actual situations and the resulting judgments of the collective organs of the international community. This would permit a full appreciation of the facts in any particular situation that might arise. Those holding this view argued that a rigid definition might be abused by an unscrupulous state to fit in with its aggressive design. An opinion widely held in Britain rejected the attempts to define aggression because it would be "a trap for the innocent and a signpost for the guilty."[20] Frank B. Kellogg (of Kellogg-Briand fame) himself noted:

> It seems to me that any attempt to define the word "aggression," and by exceptions and qualifications to stipulate when nations are justified in going to war with one another, would greatly weaken the effect of any treaty such as that under consideration and virtually destroy its positive value as a "guaranty of peace."[21]

The United Nations spent a great deal of time on the issue, as well.[22] Unlike the League, the General Assembly did approve a vague definition in Resolution 3314 (XXIX) by consensus (without a vote).[23] The Resolution states that "A war of aggression is a crime against international peace" (Article 5.2). The Declaration of Friendly Relations and Cooperation among States has a similar provision.[24] It should be kept in mind that General Assembly resolutions do *not* create obligatory rules of international law; beyond that, these provisions beg the question of what constitutes a war of aggression. The 1996 ILC draft Code of Crimes against the Peace and Security of Mankind does provide that "An individual, who as leader or organiser, actively participates in or orders the planning, preparation or waging of aggression committed by a State shall be responsible for a crime of aggression" (Article 16). Note that this again presumes a prior definition of what acts constitute aggression. Moreover, the draft Code has not entered into a form open for debate and adoption.

Of equal interest here is the change in styles of justification over the past 40 years. As a legal term, aggression has somewhat fallen out of use. Recent texts in international law have spent little or no time in examining this debate.[25] The issue, however, continues; the Statute of the ICC contains language that would permit the court to add "aggression" to its jurisdiction when a precise set of criteria defining the crime has been developed. The difficulty here lies in the fact that when and if such a set of defining criteria is created, its adoption will present a formidable challenge. Any alteration in the Statute requires a 7/8ths majority of States Parties. Significant divisions still exist with regard to approach and scope.

Beyond Aggression: Defining Armed Conflict

Since World War II, the legal significance of the term "war" has all but disappeared. Those who write about conflicts may still use the term to describe serious conflicts, and statesmen may use the term to describe a seriousness of effort. At present, the United States has asserted that it is engaged in a war on terrorism, but this has little *international legal* significance. States no longer declare war in the legal sense. The Geneva Conventions and the two Protocols Additional apply to "armed conflicts."[26] The commentaries on Common Article 2 of the four conventions notes: "There is no need for a formal declaration of war, or for recognition of the existence of a state of war, as preliminaries to the application of the Convention. The occurrence of *de facto* hostilities is sufficient." The commentary notes that the insertion of the phrase "armed conflict" was deliberate because:

> A State which uses arms to commit a hostile act against another State can always maintain that it is not making war, but merely engaging in a police action, or acting in legitimate self-defence. The expression "armed conflict" makes such arguments less easy. Any difference arising between two States and leading to the intervention of members of the armed forces is an armed conflict within the meaning of Article 2, even if one of the Parties denies the existence of a state of war. It makes no difference how long the conflict lasts, or how much slaughter takes place.[27]

This statement still leaves open a number of questions because sporadic border raids or other occasional "hostilities" that involve the armed forces of two states appear to fall short of an armed conflict because an armed conflict seems to imply a level of intensity and some duration beyond an occasional raid or clash.[28] Consider, as well, the relationship between the ICC and the Security Council. If aggression ever becomes part of the ICC jurisdiction, could the Court make an independent finding of aggression if the Security Council fails to do so? Pragmatically and politically, would it dare to do so? Other issues arise with respect to the scope of application of the Geneva Conventions, but I will defer these until later in the chapter.

Aggressive War as an International Crime

The Nuremberg and Tokyo tribunals relied upon the Pact of Paris (the Kellogg-Briand Pact) to establish the waging of aggressive war as a crime. As I have pointed out, using the treaty in this fashion is problematic because it did not purport to create individual liability. Two judges on the Tokyo panel, Pal and Roling, wrote pointed dissenting opinions based upon the idea that the trials had violated the *nullum crimen* criterion. Two points are germane here. First, neither tribunal convicted any defendant solely on the basis of the principle. Second, regardless of the questionable provenance of the idea at Nuremberg and Tokyo, the trials did firmly establish the principle for future tribunals, even though no court has attempted to charge individuals with this crime since the trials immediately after World War II. Unlike war crimes that occur within the conflict, aggression relates to the initiation of a war (*jus ad bellum*). As such, it also involves issues of *state responsibility* (collective responsibility). A finding of aggression also then becomes a prerequisite for defining other classes of crimes. Aggression differs from all other international crimes because, unlike genocide, crimes against humanity, or ordinary war crimes, only those in positions of leadership who have influence and authority over policy planning and initiation can be accused of it. In sum, aggression is a crime committed by high-level policymakers. It requires participation at the highest level of decision making, not just complicity in carrying out the decision once made.

Interestingly, the various courts since World War II have interpreted the charge very narrowly. In the *Von Leeb et al.* case (the High Command Case) tried under CCL10, the court addressed the cases of 14 individuals (13 generals and 1 admiral) who held high-ranking positions in the German military. Field Marshal von Leeb ranked just below Field Marshal von Runstedt in terms of seniority of service among the top officers in the German military. The court acquitted all of the defendants on this charge because they did not participate as "planners and initiators" at the highest level.[29]

Because of the lack of practice since Nuremberg and its aftermath, the debates here tend to be interesting only to academic international lawyers disputing issues that have not been part of any litigation. The customary law still relies on the practice of the Nuremberg, Tokyo and other post–World War II tribunals. The debate does involve important questions. Space (and purpose) precludes a comprehensive analysis of the issues here, but let me note that the debate involves questions relating to unilateral "humanitarian intervention" (think Rwanda, as well as the U.S. decision to invade Iraq).

War Crimes (*Jus in Bello*)

From Westphalia to the present, "war law" (*jus in bello*) has focused upon mitigating the impact of war upon civilians. The International Committee of the Red Cross (ICRC) provides a concise summary of purpose:

> International humanitarian law is a set of rules which seek, for humanitarian reasons, *to limit the effects of armed conflict.* It protects persons who are not or are no longer participating in the hostilities and restricts the means and methods of warfare. International humanitarian law is also known as the law of war or the law of armed conflict.[30]

International humanitarian law (IHL) covers two areas: (1) the protection of those who do not take part or who are no longer taking part in fighting, and (2) restrictions on the *means* of warfare (in particular, weapons) and the *methods* of warfare, such as military tactics.[31]

Three principles have determined the growth of the "laws of war." One is the principle that a belligerent is justified in applying any amount and any kind of force considered necessary to achieve the goal of a conflict—the defeat of the enemy. The second principle holds that, because of humanitarian considerations, any violence not necessary for the achievement of that goal should be prohibited; and the third holds that a certain amount of chivalry, a spirit of fairness, should prevail in the conduct of hostilities—that certain practices involving fraud and deceit should be avoided.[32] In sum, IHL does not address why a conflict exists. Its primary focus is on alleviating or minimizing the human suffering brought on by war.

World War I and World War II

Although I mentioned the efforts of the two Hague Conferences earlier, almost no one anticipated the nature and impact of World War I. The last major conflict between two European adversaries, the Franco-Prussian War, had occurred in 1870–1871. Military planners and statesmen had believed that technology would make war short, thus limiting casualties on the battlefield and the impact of war on noncombatants. World War I proved both assumptions tragically wrong. The advent of the submarine, machine gun, and longer-range, more powerful cannon, coupled with the evolution of the airplane and the submarine, produced circumstances that the delegates to the 1907 Hague Conference did not foresee. The devastation and the human carnage did spark additional attempts to write new rules, and states made repeated attempts to revise the rules (Madrid, Monaco, and Liège), but the effort produced only the ban on chemical and bacteriological weapons[33] and the *Geneva Convention between the United States of America and Other Powers, Relating to Prisoners of War* (July 27, 1929).[34] This last is the "Geneva Convention" often referred to in films about World War II.

The aftermath of World War II brought a concerted effort to update the rules. The United Nations and the International Committee of the Red Cross (ICRC) spearheaded the drive to develop international humanitarian law. The Geneva Diplomatic Conference of 1949 drafted four conventions:

> **Geneva I:** Amelioration of the Condition of the Wounded and Sick in Armed Forces in the Field;
>
> **Geneva II:** Amelioration of the Condition of Wounded, Sick and Shipwrecked Members of Armed Forces at Sea;
>
> **Geneva III:** Treatment of Prisoners of War; and
>
> **Geneva IV:** Protection of Civilian Persons in Time of War.

Because of the nature of conflicts that emerged after World War II, the International Committee of the Red Cross organized two sessions of a Conference of Government Experts (1971 and 1972) in Geneva to draft additional concrete rules that would be applicable to armed conflicts. These took the form of additional protocols (or amendments) to the 1949 Geneva conventions. A Diplomatic Conference on Reaffirmation and Development of International Humanitarian Law Applicable in Armed Conflicts met in Geneva from 1974 to 1977. This conference produced two additional conventions, intended to supplement the existing conventions,, rather than to replace them: Protocol Additional to the Geneva Conventions of August 12, 1949, and Relating to the Protection of Victims of International Armed Conflicts (PA-I), and Protocol Additional to the Geneva Conventions of August 12, 1949, and Relating to the Protection of Victims of Non-International Conflicts (PA- II). Both treaties extended many of the rules developed in the 1949 Geneva Conventions and added some new regulations. The two treaties are referred to in this text as PA-I and PA-II. Both entered into force on December 7, 1978.[35] The most radical change was the extension of rules to cover noninternational conflicts.[36]

What Is a War Crime?

Needless to say, war or armed conflict suspends ordinary rules of conduct. Individuals may not be punished for lawful acts of war. Hence, killing within the appropriate context is not a crime. Generally, a war crime is any act for which soldiers or other individuals may be punished by the enemy on capture of the offender. The category includes acts committed in violation of international law and the laws of the combatant's own country, as well as acts in violation of the laws of war undertaken *by order* and in the interest of the combatant's state of nationality.

One important category of war crimes comprises "grave breaches" of the Geneva Conventions. Convention IV defines a grave breach as:

> wilful killing, torture or inhuman treatment, including biological experiments, wilfully causing great suffering or serious injury to body or health, unlawful deportation or transfer . . . taking of hostages and extensive destruction and appropriation of property, not justified by military necessity and carried out unlawfully and wantonly.[37]

The ICC Statute incorporated the grave-breaches provision (Art. 8.2(a)). Of the ad hoc tribunals, only the ICTY explicitly references the Geneva Conventions (Art. 2). In part, this reflects a belief that the grave-breaches regime may apply only to international armed conflicts, not internal or noninternational conflicts.[38]

Thresholds and Contexts

Four important observations apply here. First, for IHL to apply, one must first determine that an armed conflict exists.[39] Do hostilities between states require a certain level of intensity and protracted time frame before IHL applies, or does it apply to any resort to force between states? Opinion remains divided on this issue. No clear guidelines with respect to defining specific threshold conditions for *international* armed conflict have emerged from the practice of the ad hoc tribunals. Prosecutors have treated the issue as an evidentiary one specific to each individual case.[40]

Second, to what extent do the rules applicable to international armed conflict apply to internal armed conflict? Here we see an interesting evolution. While Geneva PA-II significantly extended the regulations applicable to internal armed conflict, many questioned whether the law of war crimes applied. The early 1990s witnessed an upsurge in internal conflicts. As discussed in earlier chapters, these often had severe consequences for surrounding states. In drafting the ICTR Statute, the Security Council had to deal expressly with the question of war crimes and internal armed conflict. It did so by directly incorporating Common Article 3 of the Geneva conventions and most of the provisions of PA-II directly into the Statute.[41] Shortly after, the ICTY Appeals Chamber in the *Tadić* case took the issue head on, suggesting that a number of rules and principles (including common Article 3) applied to internal conflicts.[42] The Rome Statute of the ICC explicitly identified and incorporated some core rules, indicating some convergence between the two regimes.

Third, the question of distinguishing an internal conflict where the rules would apply from a riot or other relatively minor disorders remains an open question. Authorities agree that duration (conflict is of a protracted nature), intensity, and level of organization are the essential criteria.[43] Many other technical questions not germane to this discussion remain. For our purposes, taking note of the question and potential problems inherent in it will suffice.

Fourth, not all crimes committed during an armed conflict are war crimes. The criminal conduct must be not only within the context but associated with the conflict.[44] Ordinary crimes remain ordinary crimes to be prosecuted by local authorities if they do not meet the twin test. A rape or murder committed by a civilian against another civilian within the geographic and temporal area of a conflict does not necessarily constitute a war crime. To assess the nature of the crime, one must take into account the status of the perpetrator, the status of the victim, and the purpose of the act.[45]

Crimes and Sanctions

Current ideas about the nature of war crimes represent striking departures from traditional legal attitudes toward the subject. For many years, offenses against the laws of war constituted crimes against the municipal law of belligerents, not violations of international law.[46] The defenses of "act-of-state" and superiors' orders conditioned prosecutions for war crimes because they served as appropriate defense responses to allegations of misconduct. The *municipal* character of penal offenses against the laws of war was based also on the orthodox belief that international law put obligations directly on individuals as subjects. Only one of the pre–World War

I conventions that dealt with war crimes contained language providing for any type of sanction to be applied to states or to individuals for violations of the rules governing warfare. These presumed appropriate municipal legislation. Article 3 of the Fourth Hague Convention of 1907 forms the sole exception. It called for payment of compensation by a belligerent state found guilty of violating the treaty.

After World War II, some treaties, such as the 1949 Geneva Conventions, directly provided for sanctions for violations. Customary law also forms a source of sanctions. The lack of consistency and coherence can lead to confusion because not every violation of the rules contained within IHL constitutes a war crime. As a body of law, IHL contains large numbers of technical and administrative regulations. For example, many articles in Geneva III pertain to food, sanitary facilities, clothing, and general living conditions. Insisting that minor violations of these technical and administrative provisions give rise to criminal liability makes little sense. It would be similar to asserting that minor violations of speed limits or traffic regulations should carry major penal sanctions in the form of jail time. The point here is that, for violations to be considered crimes rather than instances of noncompliance, they must involve a certain degree of seriousness in terms of consequences flowing from noncompliance. As stressed in Chapters 4 and 5, contextual factors play an important role. Depriving POWs of soap and toilet paper form minor violations of the regulations concerning the handling of POWs; the abusive treatment of Senator John McCain and his fellow POWs in North Vietnam constitutes crimes. The term "grave breach" has come to signify what constitutes a violation.

The appeals chamber early in the *Tadić* case used the twin tests of "basic values" and "consequences for the victim."[47] This decision became the defining precedent for all cases following. The *Tadić* decision also dealt with one other evolutionary change. The chamber held that many elements of the law, both customary and treaty derived, applied to internal conflicts (civil wars) of a large scale and protracted nature, as well as to those that have an international character.

Cassese identifies five categories of war crimes:

1. Crimes committed again persons who are either not taking part or no longer taking part in hostilities—impermissible actions toward enemy civilians or POWs.
2. Crimes again enemy combatants or civilians through resort to impermissible tactics of warfare—attacks against civilians meant to create terror; attacks directed at the sick and wounded; intentional starvation; torture; indiscriminate bombings; and the taking of hostages.
3. Crimes against enemy combatants or civilians through resort to impermissible means of warfare—poison gas, dum-dum bullets.
4. Crimes against specially protected individuals or objects: medical personnel, hospitals, ICRC (or Red Crescent) personnel.
5. Crimes involving the improper use of flags, ensigns, or other emblems—abuse of a flag of truce or of the ICRC (or Red Crescent), that is, using them as a ruse or trap.[48]

To reiterate an earlier point, the conventions apply not only to cases of declared war but also to all other armed conflicts that may arise between two or more of the contracting parties, even if the existence of a state of war is not recognized by any of them.

We must keep in mind another point made earlier that is essential to understanding the complexities of "who can lawfully be killed." Lawful combatants may willfully kill other lawful combatants. They may not kill or otherwise mistreat noncombatants or use unlawful means in accomplishing their missions. Civilians may die as an incidental consequence of lawfully conducted military operations (the unfortunate term "collateral damage"), but this does not create liability for those involved. While the principle of noncombatant immunity stands at the heart of IHL, the additional requirements of purpose and intent serve to circumscribe it. For civilian and noncombatant casualties to engage personal liability, a prosecutor would have to prove that the civilians were deliberately targeted and not just at the wrong place at the wrong time. One of the essential elements in defining a crime is the "status" of individuals at the time of their act(s): were they lawful (privileged) combatants?

Evolution   Perhaps the most significant addition to the list of war crimes has occurred with the recognition of all forms of sexual violence as war crimes. In one sense, this does not represent an evolution. The progress stems from the willingness to prosecute rather than ignore such actions. For example, Article 27 of Geneva IV stipulates that women should be protected, but it does not then define "rape" as a "grave breach" in the manner of other crimes. The Statutes of the ad hoc tribunals did not explicitly list any sexual crimes, though the courts did eventually address the issue. The ICC Statute includes a list of sexual crimes: rape, sexual slavery, and enforced prostitution, among others.[49]

A Note on Prohibited Weapons   Prohibitions on weapons flow from two different rationales. The first bans weapons, such as antipersonnel mines, that are inherently indiscriminate with regard to victims. The second bans weapons that cause excessive pain, unnecessary suffering (hollow-point or expanding bullets). The extent of the prohibitions remains a controversial topic.[50] The Nuremberg Charter did not include any reference to prohibited weapons, even though the concept was firmly established in both customary and conventional law.[51] The ICTY Statute does refer to "poisonous weapons or other weapons calculated to cause unnecessary suffering."[52] The Statutes of the ICTR and the SCSL contain no mention of prohibited weapons. The ICC Statute incorporates a considerably attenuated list.[53] It does not expressly prohibit chemical and biological weapons.[54] Notably, the prosecutors for the ICTY have not charged any defendants with a crime under this article of the Statute.

Privileged Combatants

One other provision plays a central role—the definition of a lawful or "privileged" combatant.[55] First developed in Article 1 of the Fourth Hague Convention of 1907, the definition has not varied a great deal since. The 1949 Geneva Conventions distinguish among lawful combatants, noncombatants, and unlawful (usually termed "unprivileged") combatants. Note that the conditions specifying what is lawful apply not only to armies but to militias, volunteer corps, or other units that meet certain conditions. They must be:

1. Commanded by a person responsible for his/her subordinates;
2. Having a fixed distinctive emblem recognizable at a distance;
3. Carrying arms openly; and,
4. Conducting their operations in accordance with the laws and customs of war.

Under IHL, lawful combatants should have certain "privileges." If captured, lawful combatants have *prisoner-of-war* (POW) status. POW status requires that prisoners receive humane treatment, defined as entitling them to the same maintenance as troops of the same rank of the captor state. This provision has caused some controversy because it sets a standard that for some countries would result in POWs having a higher standard of maintenance than that enjoyed by the majority of the country's citizens. POWs cannot be used as forced labor. They should be confined only to the extent that their detention is guaranteed and must not be punished except for acts committed by them *after* their capture unless they have committed an unlawful act prior to capture. Protected or privileged combatants can be tried only for specific violations of the laws of war. They have immunity from prosecution for lawful acts of war.

An unsuccessful attempt to escape may result only in disciplinary punishment; on the other hand, force may be used against prisoners to prevent an escape, and it is considered lawful to shoot at, and kill, an escaping prisoner. The movie *The Great Escape* drew upon a real incident in World War II.[56] Seventy-six prisoners held at Stalag Luft III escaped through tunnels painstakingly dug over several months. Seventy-three were recaptured. In direct violation of the rules, Hitler ordered the execution of 50 of the recaptured to set an example. The Nuremberg charges against Field Marshal Wilhelm Keitel included this incident because the execution order was issued over his signature.

If, on the other hand, an escaping prisoner commits criminal offenses not directly connected with his escape, he may be punished for those acts. The following case illustrates this principle. In *Rex v. Brosig*,[57] a German prisoner of war, moved to Canada for detention, escaped by hiding in a prisoner-of-war mailbag. The bag eventually found its way to the mail car of a Canadian train. Brosig cut his way out of the bag and opened another mailbag containing parcels. From these he took some cigarettes, some chewing gum, and a bottle of perfume. He smoked some of the cigarettes and used some of the gum and also some of the perfume. When he was captured, the magistrate charged him with theft from the mails. The magistrate court that tried the initial case dismissed the charge. The Crown appealed to the Court of Appeal. The issue was whether an escaping prisoner of war could be charged with the theft of goods stolen in the course of his escape and used by him. The court found that the looting of the mailbag was not an act necessary to Brosig's escape. It served no military purpose and represented an offense against civil authority for the personal advantage of the prisoner of war.

Any World War II film involving captured soldiers has the obligatory scene where, under interrogation, a soldier gives only his name, rank, and registration number. Under both the earlier (1929) and the post–World War II conventions, a POW is required to give that information but no more. Moreover, no physical or mental torture, nor any other form of coercion, may be inflicted on prisoners of war to secure from them information of any kind whatsoever (Art. 17.4). Article 19.1 states that "Prisoners of war shall be evacuated, as soon as possible after their capture, to camps situated in an area far enough from the combat zone for them to be out of danger." In particular, Article 23.1 states that "No prisoner of war may at any time be sent to, or detained in, areas where he may be exposed to the fire of the combat zone, *nor may his presence be used to render certain points or areas immune from military operations.*"[58]

Allegations of mistreatment of Iraqi POWs by British and American troops surfaced in May 2003.[59] In late July, the U.S. Army filed charges against four members of the military police accused of hitting Iraqi prisoners and breaking their bones at Camp Bucca, in southern Iraq. Eight marines, including the commanding officer, were charged in the death of Nagam Sadoon Hatab at Camp Whitehorse. An investigation into alleged abuses at Abu Ghraib prison outside Baghdad began in January 2004. A full-scale scandal flared in April 2004 when photographs of U.S. personnel abusing prisoners were published. Seventeen soldiers, including officers, were removed from duty. The Army charged 10 soldiers with "maltreatment, aggravated assault, battery, and dereliction of duty." Four were convicted by court martial Six others reached plea deals, with all except one receiving prison sentences. All received dishonorable discharges. The Army demoted the commanding officer at the prison from brigadier general to colonel.[60]

Unprivileged Combatants

The terms "unprivileged" and "unlawful" do not appear in any treaty or document. The treaties and documents relevant to IHL deal only with privileged and lawful combatants. The absence of formal definitions of the rights of the unprivileged has led to an interesting debate. The variety of terms used to characterize and describe illegal participants—unlawful combatants, unprivileged belligerents, terrorists, enemy combatants, insurgents—gives evidence of their uncertain status:[61] Unlike privileged combatants, captured unlawful combatants can be tried and punished under municipal law for their unprivileged belligerency, even if their hostile acts complied with the laws of war. The contemporary debate concerns the conditions under which they may be held, as well as their rights with respect to interrogation and trial for alleged crimes. More recent commentary has supported the idea that, while unprivileged status may deprive combatants of the benefits of POW status, it cannot deprive them of a right to humane treatment.[62]

The uncertainty in terms of defined rights has real political consequences. The possibility of extending combatant status to "terrorists" formed one reason given by the United States for refusing to ratify Geneva PA I. President Ronald Reagan stated that the perceived legitimization of "wars of national liberation" and the granting of combatant status to irregular forces that do not satisfy the traditional criteria for legitimate participation "would endanger civilians among whom terrorists and other irregulars attempt to conceal themselves."[63]

Much of the recent discourse has centered on the prisoners captured in Afghanistan, characterized as "enemy combatants," and held by the United States at Guantanamo Bay. Allegedly, these individuals fought for the Taliban and/or were associated with Al Qaeda. Until recently, they have been held without charge and without access to attorneys or courts.[64] Then-Secretary of Defense Donald Rumsfeld stated that the United States would treat the detainees humanely as a matter of policy but denied that there was any *legal* obligation to do so.[65] The U.S. Attorney in the *Hamdi* case, Paul J. McNulty, stated that "it is well-settled that the military has the authority to capture and detain individuals whom it has determined are enemy combatants" and that such combatants "have no right of access to counsel to challenge their detention."[66] The case involved Yasser Esam Hamdi, a 21-year-old detainee captured on the battlefield in Afghanistan. The government had characterized Hamdi, who was born in Louisiana but reared in Saudi Arabia, as an "enemy combatant," rather than a POW. The government claimed that the designation as an enemy (or unlawful) combatant presumably deprived Hamdi of the protection of the Geneva Conventions and U.S. courts of any claim to jurisdiction.[67]

While space does not permit a thorough discussion of the problems here, I must note that U.S. courts have yet to deal with the international law issues. To this point, the relevant issues have turned on the procedural complexities of U.S. domestic law.[68] Until the U.S. Supreme Court decisions in *Rasul v. Bush*[69] and *Hamdi v. Rumsfeld*[70] in June 2004, while lawyers debated the international legal ramifications of the Bush administration's position, U.S. courts focused on the scope of their competence to deal with many of the relevant issues. The areas of concern involved (1) the effective territorial reach of the U.S. Constitution—whether federal courts have jurisdiction with respect to Guantanamo Bay (particularly the capacity to hear habeas corpus petitions);[71] (2) an interesting (but ongoing) separation of powers issue—whether the president has the *sole* authority (without judicial review) to define the status of detainees taken in various operations against the Taliban and Al Qaeda; and, (3) questions relating to the status (nonself-executing or self-executing) of the Geneva Conventions.[72] U.S. courts have yet to rule on the substantive questions of how to determine "enemy combatant" status or who has the right to do so.

Two defendants have come before military commissions under the 2006 Military Commissions Act.[73] Early in 2007, the Australian citizen David Hicks, a Taliban supporter, pled guilty to a charge of "material support for terrorism." After his conviction, the United States returned him to Australia to serve out a nine-month sentence, now completed.[74] The second case involved Salim Ahmed

Hamdan, accused of being Osama bin Laden's driver. Because military commissions do not have to adhere to the very strict procedural requirements of a "constitutional trial" as defined by U.S. criminal law and practice, the trial before a military commission generated a great deal of criticism related to its "fairness."[75] Critics have focused on the looser rules of evidence and what they perceive as practices that handicap the defense teams and keep them from having "an equality of arms" with the prosecution. Even so, a six-member panel of military officers acquitted Hamdan of the charge of "conspiring to attack civilians" but found him guilty of providing material support to terrorism. The prosecution had demanded a 30-year sentence; the panel gave him 5-1/2 years.[76]

Termination of Captivity The Hamdan trial raises another issue—length of detention. The Geneva Conventions visualize a situation of traditional war of state against state, not an open-ended conflict. Article 118 states: "Prisoners of war shall be released and repatriated without delay after the cessation of active hostilities." Given the indeterminate nature of contemporary conflicts, this raises some interesting questions with respect to the Guantanamo detainees. In the past, problems have occurred with repatriation because detainees did not wish to return to their home countries or because of other continuing political differences between the former belligerents.[77] The issue with respect to the Guantanamo detainees centers on the open-ended nature of the alleged hostilities. The Bush administration noted that even if Hamdan served out his sentence, he would not be released because he still would be regarded as an enemy combatant. At this writing, the issue remains unresolved.

Other Considerations: Necessity and the Principle of Proportionality

Earlier I referred to the principle of proportionality as defining many areas of the law regulating the use force.[78] With respect to the *jus in bello,* this simply means that, in any operation, the damage to civilians should not exceed the estimated military advantage of the attack.[79] The principle of proportionality forms the offset for claims of military necessity because, realistically, in modern conflicts, it is not realistic to expect to avoid civilian casualties altogether. The principle also clearly demonstrates the extreme tension between military objectives and humanitarian considerations that runs throughout IHL. The application in practice has three elements:

1. An estimate of the extent of injury to civilians and damage to civilian property;
2. An estimate of the "concrete and direct overall military advantage" gained from the operation; and,
3. An estimate of the relative weight of element 2 with respect to the considerations generated by element 1.[80]

Obviously, this involves very rough calculations made under great stress and urgency (the "fog of war"). The simple formulation in the abstract depends upon variables difficult to assess under ideal conditions, let alone in contexts where information may be sketchy at best and calculations with respect to "military advantage" may depend upon estimated future outcomes within a broader strategy. Finally, the equation requires comparing apples and oranges in that no common unit of measure exists with respect to the elements that constitute the two calculations.[81]

Stefan Oeter focuses upon some other related critical issues here.[82] Sometimes singled out under the idea of "the principle of distinction," these relate to the actual selection of targets. Presumably, "purely civilian" targets should be off limits, but how should one treat commercial enterprises that make a contribution to military action? The International Committee of the Red Cross (ICRC) has compiled a list, but, as discussed earlier, the problems begin when one moves from the abstract to decisions in the field. The law seemingly requires that some distinction be made between important and unimportant targets, yet, with regard to telecommunications and transport, does that distinction make sense? As the belligerent destroys essential links, logic tells us that the less important links will rise to the level of the essential. Actually, with modern telecommunications, a rational strategy (as in the Gulf War) might dictate the destruction of as much of the capability as quickly as possible. The fact is that, in modern industrial societies, many facilities, such as electric grids and production installations, may have dual use as military support and as suppliers of essential civilian services. A distinction based upon "fundamental importance" provides no reasonable restraint. On the other side, excluding or severely limiting these targets opens opportunities to funnel "military support" into "civilian firms" through subcontracting and decentralization.[83] Note the dilemma. It cannot be resolved in the abstract. Add to this the fact that judgments may be made with hindsight by individuals who may or may not have military experience.

The issues have come front and center in Iraq and Afghanistan. Press reports often focus on civilian casualties associated with operations from a perspective that conveys the impression that such casualties could have been avoided with more careful planning and execution. Without meaning to sound callous or insensitive, I suggest that the unfortunate part of any war is the toll taken on civilians, but under the conditions of contemporary internal wars and insurgencies legitimate military objectives are often closely (and deliberately) located in proximity to concentrations of civilians. Because of the ambiguities, Oeter argues that decisions makers ought to be allowed "a considerable margin of appreciation."[84] In the cases handled by the ad hoc tribunals, these issues have not been systematically explored because the prosecutors have focused upon the easier charge to prove—attacks on prohibited targets.[85]

Notes

Cicero, *Pro T. Annio Milone Oratio*, IV.11, *The Latin Library;* http://www.thelatinlibrary.com/cicero/milo.shtml. English translation at The Perseus Digital Library, Gregory Crane (ed.), http://www.perseus.tufts.edu/cgi-bin/ptext?doc=Perseus:text:1999.02.0020& query=text%3DMil.%3Atext%3DMil.%3Achapter%3D4%3Asection%3D11.

1. For example, see the account of the destruction of the city of Ai, *Joshua* 8:14–29.

2. "Pompey" in Plutarch, *Plutarch's Lives* (trans. John Dryden) (New York: Random House, n.d,), para. 10 (745).

3. Grotius, *The Law of War and Peace = De jure belli ac pacis* (trans. L. R. Loomis) (Roslyn, NY: W. J. Black, 1949); Grotius, *Hugonis Grotii De jure belli ac pacis libri tres: in quibus jus naturae & gentium, item juris publici præ cipua explicantur: cum annotatis auctoris, ex postrema ejus ante obitum cura multo nunc auctior; accesserunt & annotata in Epistolam Pauli ad Philemonem* (trans. F. W. Kelsey) (Buffalo, NY: Hein, 1995, reissue of 1925 Oxford University Press ed.).

4. There are many general histories of warfare. See for example, Philip Bobbitt, *The Shield of Achilles: War, Peace and the Course of History* (New York: Knopf, 2002)

5. Brian Caven, *The Punic Wars* (New York: St. Martin's, 1980); Adrian Goldsworthy, *The Punic Wars* (London: Cassell, 2000).

6. For example: K. S. Pritchett, *The Greek State at War* (5 vols.) (Berkeley and Los Angeles: University of California Press, 1977–1991); Alan Watson, *International Law in Archaic Rome: War and Religion* (Baltimore: Johns Hopkins University Press, 1993); Maurice Keen, *The Laws of War in the Late Middle Ages* (London: Routledge and Kegan Paul, 1965); Majid Khadduri, *War and Peace in the Law of Islam* (Baltimore: Johns Hopkins University Press, 1955).

7. Curiously, while war was not governed by law, presumably the law did regulate the resort to force short of war (reprisal, retaliation). As Brownlie points out, during the 19th century, as mass armies, increasing interdependence, and public opinion made war more expensive and difficult to justify both politically and pragmatically, states increasingly resorted to limited uses of force rather than all-out war. In the customary law, reprisal and retaliation were forms of self-help, ostensibly governed by the twin principles of necessity and proportionality. Ian Brownlie, *International Law and the Use of Force by States* (Oxford: Clarendon Press, 1963), 27–28. See also Derek Bowett, "Reprisals Involving the Recourse to Armed Force," *American Journal of International Law* 66, no. 1 (1972): 1; and Robert W. Tucker (Comment), "Reprisals and Self-Defense: The Customary Law," *American Journal of International Law* 66, no. 3 (1972): 586–96; James L. Taulbee and John Anderson, "Reprisal *Redux*," *Case Western Reserve Journal of International Law* 16 (1984): 309–37. In the customary law, self-defense and reprisal were forms of self-help governed by time frame (necessity), purpose (principle of proportionality), and appropriate targets. Prior to the 1920s, the literature on the customary law differentiated between retaliation and reprisal.

8. See Emerich de Vattel, *Le droit des gens ou principes de la loi naturelle: appliqués à la conduite et aux affaires des nations and des souverains* (Vol. 1) (reproduction of books I and II of the 1758 edition) (1916; Buffalo, NY: Hein, 2005), 531–41; J. H. W. Verzijl, *International Law in Historical Perspective,* Vol. 8 (Leiden: A.W. Sijthof, 1968), 39–40; Lassa Oppenheim, *International Law: A Treatise* (5th ed.) (2 vols.) (ed. Hersh Lauterpacht) (London and New York: Longmans Green, 1935–1937); James. L. Brierly, *The Law of Nations: An Introduction to the International Law of Peace* (Oxford: Clarendon Press, 1928).

9. Oppenheim, *International Law,* 2:201. There appear to be as many definitions as there are writers on the subject. See the collection of many different ones in Clyde Eagleton, "The Attempt to Define War," *International Conciliation* no. 291 (June 1933): 237.

10. For example, see the first edition of Oppenheim, *International Law* (London: Longmans Green, 1905).

11. Arthur Eyffinger, *The 1899 Hague Peace Conference: "The Parliament of Man, the Federation of the World"* (The Hague: Martinus Nijhoff, 1999).

12. See for example, the Preamble to the 1907 Hague Conventions. *Laws and Customs of War on Land (Hague IV)*, October 18, 1907; http://www.yale.edu/lawweb/avalon/lawof war/hague04.htm#iart1.

13. Text at http://www.yale.edu/lawweb/avalon/imt/kbpact.htm. The key provisions:

> Art. 1. The High Contracting Parties solemnly declare in the names of their respective peoples that they condemn recourse to war for the solution of international controversies, and renounce it as an instrument of national policy in their relations with one another.
>
> Art. 2. The High Contracting Parties agree that the settlement or solution of all disputes or conflicts of whatever nature or of whatever origin they may be, which may arise among them, shall never be sought except by pacific means.

These two articles make up the sum of the obligations in the treaty. Article 3 deals with the question of entry into force.

14. Quincy Wright, "The Meaning of the Pact of Paris," *American Journal of International Law* 27, no. 1 (1933): 39–61; and especially Edward M. Borchard (Comment), "The Multilateral Treaty for the Renunciation of War," *American Journal of International Law* 23, no. 1 (1929): 116–20.

15. "War for the solution of international controversies includes a war of aggression, and such a war is therefore outlawed by the Pact." *Trial of the Major War Criminals before the International Tribunal, Nuremberg, 14 November 1945–1 October 1946*, 1 (1947): 220, (Blue Series), Library of Congress, Military Legal Resources (42 volumes) at http://www.loc.gov/rr/frd/Military_Law/NT_major-war-criminals.html.

16. See Brownlie, *International Law and the Use of Force by States*, 249–50; Anthony Arend and Robert J. Beck, *International Law and the Use of Force: Beyond the UN Charter Paradigm* (London: Routledge, 1993), 23–25. The author does not share this view of the status of the customary law, Kellogg-Briand and Nuremberg pronouncements notwithstanding. I would argue that the vague language in Kellogg-Briand and the retrospective judgment at Nuremberg placed no meaningful restraints on states in terms of developments in the customary law. I fail to see the basis for certainty that Brownlie accords to practice in the 1930s.

17. Tom Farer, "Editorial Comment: Beyond the Charter Frame: Unilateralism or Condominium," *American Journal of International Law* 96, no. 2 (2002): 361.

18. For the attempt to update the *jus in bello* to reflect the varieties of post–World War II conflict, see *Protocol Additional to the Geneva Conventions of 12 August 1949, and Relating to the Protection of Victims of International Armed Conflicts* (Protocol I), and *Protocol Additional to the Geneva Conventions of 12 August 1949, and Relating to the Protection of Victims of Non-International Armed Conflicts* (Protocol II), *International Legal Materials* 16 (1977): 1391–1449.

19. Georg Schwarzenberger, "Jus Pacis ac Belli?" *American Journal of International Law* 37 (1943): 460; Philip C. Jessup, "Should International Law Recognize an Intermediate Status between Peace and War?" *American Journal of International Law* 48, no. 1 (1954): 98–103. See also Myres McDougal and Florentine Feliciano, "The Initiation of Coercion: A Multi-Temporal Analysis," *American Journal of International Law* 52, no. 2 (1958): 241–59.

20. Edward Borchard, "The Renunciation of War," (1928), http://www.yale.edu/law web/avalon/kbpact/kbbor.htm.

21. Quoted in Borchard, "The Renunciation of War." For a modern critique of the efforts to define aggression, see Julius Stone, *Aggression and World Order* ((Berkeley: University of California Press, 1958). Kellogg was U.S. Secretary of State at the time.

22. For a sample of the debate here see, "Question of Defining Aggression," Summary of the Record of the 93rd Meeting (May 31, 1951), *Yearbook of the ILC,* at 89. UN Doc. A/CN.4/ SR93; http://untreaty.un.org/ilc/documentation/english/a_cn4_sr93.pdf.

23. Text, with explanatory comments by the Special Committee, in *American Journal of International Law* 69, no. 1 (1975): 480. See Julius Stone, "Hopes and Loopholes in the 1974 Definition of Aggression," *American Journal of International Law* 71, no. 2 (1977) 224; and Benjamin Ferencz, "The United Nations Definition of Aggression: Sieve or Substance?" *World Issues* 2 (April-May 1977): 26–28.

24. GAOR, Res. 2625 (XXV) of November 1970.

25. See, for example, Mary Ellen O'Connell, *International Law and the Use of Force: Cases and Materials* (New York: Foundation Press, 2005), and Michael Byers, *War Law: International Law and Armed Conflict* (London: Atlantic, 2005), both of which discuss the "use of force" but give little attention to aggression.

26. Common Article 2 of the four original conventions uses the phrase "all cases of declared war or of any other *armed conflict.*" Note also *Protocol Additional to the Geneva Conventions of 12 August 1949, and Relating to the Protection of Victims of International Armed Conflicts* (Protocol I), and *Protocol Additional to the Geneva Conventions of 12 August 1949, and Relating to the Protection of Victims of Non-International Armed Conflicts* (Protocol II), *International Legal Materials* 16 (1977): 1391–1449.

27. International Committee of the Red Cross, Commentary, *International Humanitarian Law: Treaties and Documents,* Chapter 1, para. 1; http://www.helpicrc.org/ihl.nsf/ COM/370-580005?OpenDocument.

28. For a discussion of these issues with respect to differentiating between self defense and reprisal, see, Taulbee and Anderson, "Reprisal *Redux,*" 316.

29. *The United States of America vs. Wilhelm von Leeb et al.* (Case No. 12), http://www. archives.gov/research/captured-german-records/microfilm/m898.pdf.

30. ICRC, http://www.icrc.org/web/eng/siteeng0.nsf/html/humanitarian-law-factsheet.

31. See Dieter Fleck (ed.), *The Handbook of Humanitarian Law in Armed Conflicts* (Oxford: Oxford University Press, 1999).

32. Oppenheim, *International Law* (5th ed.) Volume 2: 227. Stefan Oeter, "Methods and Means of Combat," in Fleck (ed.), *Handbook of International Humanitarian Law,* 441–79.

33. *Protocol for the Prohibition of the Use in War of Asphyxiating, Poisonous or Other Gases, and of Bacteriological Methods of Warfare* (June 17, 1925); text at http://fas-www.harvard. edu/~hsp/1925.html.

34. Text at http://www.yale.edu/lawweb/avalon/lawofwar/geneva02.htm (The Avalon Project at Yale University).

35. Texts of the 1907 Hague Conventions (and annexes) are in the *American Journal of International Law* 2, no. 1 (1908): 90, 117, 153, 167; and at The Avalon Project, Yale University Law School, http://avalon.law.yale.edu/subject_menus/lawwar.asp. The text of most important treaties dealing with war (up to 1982) are in Adam Roberts and Richard Guelff (eds.), *Documents on the Laws of War* (2nd ed.) (Oxford: Clarendon Press, 1989). See also Keith Suter, *An International Law of Guerrilla Warfare: The Global Politics of Lawmaking* (London: Francis Pinter, 1984), for an account of the negotiations surrounding PA I and PA II.

36. For a well-documented analysis of PA II, see David P. Forsythe, "Legal Management Internal War: The 1977 Protocol on Noninternational Armed Conflicts," *American Journal of International Law* 72, no. 2 (1978): 272. Because almost all countries that participated in the formulation of PA-II were opposed to incorporating any sort of enforcement mechanism in the instrument, the determination of its applicability still rests, in essence, with the governments and other agencies (including rebel movements) involved in any given noninternational armed conflict.

37. Article 147, *Geneva Convention IV.*

38. *Prosecutor v. Tadić,* Appeals Chamber, Judgment of July 15, 1999 [IT-94-1-A], para. 83–84.

39. Christopher Greenwood, "Scope of Application of Humanitarian Law," in Fleck (ed.), *Handbook of International Humanitarian Law,* 39–64.

40. William A. Schabas, *The UN International Criminal Tribunals: The Former Yugoslavia, Rwanda and Sierra Leone* (Cambridge: Cambridge University Press, 2006), 242, 246.

41. Schabas, *The UN International Criminal Tribunals,* 233–34. Note that the jurisdictional questions involve some relatively complex technical issues. Schabas points out that, despite the Secretary-General's statement that the ICTR's jurisdiction was more expansive than that of the ICTY, in point of fact, the subject matter jurisdiction is more restricted (236).

42. *Prosecutor v. Tadić,* ICTY Appeals Chamber (Interlocutory Appeal), Judgment of October 2, 1995, paras. 126–29.

43. *Prosecutor v. Tadić,* ICTY Appeals Chamber (Interlocutory Appeal), Judgment of October 2, 1995, para. 70.

44. ICC Elements of Crimes, Article 8.2(a).

45. Schabas, *The UN International Criminal Tribunals* 236–39; Robert Cryer, Hakan Friman, Darryl Robinson, and Elizabeth Wilmshurst, *International Criminal Law and Procedure* (Cambridge: Cambridge University Press, 2007), 238–41.

46. George Manner, "The Legal Nature and Punishment of Criminal Acts of Violence Contrary to the Laws of War," *American Journal of International Law* 37, no. 3 (1943): 407, 414–15.

47. *Prosecutor v. Tadić,* ICTY Appeals Chamber (Interlocutory Appeal), Judgment of October 2, 1995, para. 94.

48. Antonio Cassese, *International Criminal Law* (Oxford: Oxford University Press, 2003), 55–57.

49. ICC Elements of Crimes, Article 8.2(b).

50. In an advisory opinion requested by the World Health Organization on the legality of the threat or use of nuclear weapons, the ICJ thoroughly discussed the customary and conventional law. *Legality of the Threat of Use of Nuclear Weapons* (Advisory Opinion) (1996), ICJ Reports 226; and http://www.icj-cij.org/docket/index.php?p1=3&p2=4&code=unan&case=95&k=e1.

51. See the 1899 and 1907 Hague Conventions, and the *Protocol for the Prohibition of the Use in War of Asphyxiating, Poisonous or Other Gases, and of Bacteriological Methods of Warfare,* June 17, 1925.

52. ICC Elements of Crimes, Article 3(a).

53. Article 8.2(b), paras xvii–xx. Note, however, that their use could still be considered a war crime if the evidentiary context establishes that the use contravened other provisions of the Statute.

54. See Herman von Hebel and Daryl Robinson, "Crimes with the Jurisdiction of the Court," in Roy S. Lee (ed.), *The International Criminal Court: The Making of the Rome Statute*

(The Hague: Kluwer Law, 1999), 113–16, for a discussion of the politics with regard to this section.

55. See Knut Ipsen, "Combatants and Non-Combatants," in Fleck (ed.), *Handbook of International Humanitarian Law in Conflict,* 105–207.

56. While this incident was not unique and did not involve the largest number of escapees on record, because of the fate of those recaptured and the film, it is probably the best known. The TV series *Hogan's Heroes* probably drew upon this incident for its premise. The movie drew on the personal account of a prisoner who remained in the camp. See Paul Brickhill, *The Great Escape* (New York: Norton, 1950).

57. Ontario Court of Appeal, March 1, 1945, 2 D. L. R. 232.

58. Emphasis added. On the acceptance of the Potsdam Declaration by the Japanese government, some 600,000 Japanese soldiers surrendered to Soviet forces in Manchuria, Sakhalin, and the Kurile Islands. Most of the captives were deported to northern Soviet regions to perform reconstruction work. Some 68,000 of the prisoners died before repatriation. See the interesting case of war claims by former prisoners in *Kamibayashi et al. v. Japan,* Tokyo District Court, April 18, 1989, in *International Legal Materials 29* (1990): 391.

59. Marc Lacey, "Aftereffects: Human Rights; Iraqi Detainees Claim Abuse by British and U.S. Troops," *New York Times,* May 17, 2003, 11. Three of the four accepted nonjudicial punishment in lieu of a court martial. Punishment included an administrative discharge and forfeiture of two months' pay. Two accepted a reduction in rank. Charges were dropped against the fourth.

60. David S. Cloud, "Private Gets 3 Years for Iraq Prison Abuse," *New York Times,* September 28, 2005, 20.

61. Kenneth Watkins, "Warriors without Rights? Combatants, Unprivileged Belligerents, and the Struggle over Legitimacy," Program on Humanitarian Policy and Conflict Research, Harvard University Occasional Paper Series, No. 2 (Winter 2005), 5–6; http://www.hpcr.org/pdfs/OccasionalPaper2.pdf.

62. Derek Jinks, "The Declining Status of POW Status," *Harvard International Law Journal* 45 (2004): 368–70.

63. "Letter of Transmittal, Agora: The U.S. Decision Not to Ratify Protocol I to the Geneva Conventions on the Protection of War Victims," *American Journal of International Law* 81, no. 4 (1987): 911.

64. Philip Shenon, "Appeals Court Keeps an American Detainee and His Lawyer Apart," *New York Times,* July 13, 2002, 8.

65. Fact Sheet, White House Press Office, "Status of Detainees at Guantanamo," (February 7, 2002); http://www.whitehouse.gov/news/releases/2002/02/20020207–13.html.

66. Katharine Q. Seelye, "Traces of Terror: The Courts; U.S. Defends Limits on American in Custody," *New York Times,* June 20, 2002, 20; see Thomas Franck, "Criminals, Combatants or What? An Examination of the Role of Law in Responding to the Threat of Terror," *American Journal of International Law* 98, no. 4 (2004), 1686.

67. See, in contrast, the case of John Walker Lindh, captured at the same time as Hamdi. After considerable debate, the government decided to try him in a civilian court. Wayne Washington, "Fighting Terror/American Taliban; Lindh Makes Deal, Enters Guilty Pleas Agrees to Aid Government, Faces 20-Year Sentence," *Boston Globe,* July 16, 2002, A1.

68. For a comprehensive study of military commissions, see Louis Fisher, *Military Tribunals and Presidential Power: American Revolution to the War on Terrorism* (Lawrence: University of Kansas Press, 2005).

69. 124 S. Ct. 2686 (2004).

70. 124 S. Ct. 2633 (2004).

71. The founders thought this important enough to include in the Constitution. For the definitive treatment, see Randy Hertz and James S. Liebman, *Federal Habeas Corpus Practice and Procedure* (5th ed.) (2 vols.), (Newark, NJ: LexisNexis, Matthew Bender, 2005).

72. If a treaty is considered "self-executing," the courts may interpret and apply it as written. If it is considered "nonself-executing," then it requires enabling legislation by the Congress. The United States has treated most human rights treaties as nonself-executing.

73. Public Law 109-366 (October 17, 2006).

74. See http://www.defenselink.mil/news/Mar2007/US%20v%20David%20Hicks%20ROT%20(Redacted).pdf.

75. Human Rights Watch, "US: Hamdan Trial Exposes Flaws in Military Commissions" (August 6, 2008); http://www.hrw.org/english/docs/2008/08/05/usint19540.htm.

76. Jerry Markon, "Goal of the Hamdan Trial: Credibility Prosecutors Seek Decisive Conviction of Former Driver, "*Washington Post,* July 27, 2008, A02; Tim Reid, "Analysis: Bin Laden Driver Salim Hamdan Trial a Disaster for George Bush," Times Online, August 8, 2008; http://www.timesonline.co.uk/tol/news/world/us_and_americas/article4482417.ece.

77. See Pittman B. Potter, "Repatriation of Korean Prisoners of War," *American Journal of International Law* 47, no. 4 (1953): 651; Howard S. Levie, "Legal Aspects of the Continued Detention of the Pakistani Prisoners of War by India," *American Journal of International Law* 67, no. 4 (1973): 512.

78. Yoram Dinstein, *The Conduct of Hostilities under the Law of International Armed Coflict* (Cambridge: Cambridge University Press, 2004), 119–28.

79. From a philosophical viewpoint, the standard actually has two components—one of value, one of effect. These are very different, but, because of the problems in separating "value" from "effect," most writers simply focus on effect.

80. Article 8.2(b)(iv) of the ICC Statute.

81. Cryer et al., *An Introduction to International Criminal Lawe,* 251. For an extended discussion of the problem with respect to a practical problem, see W. J. Fenrick, "Targeting and Proportionality during the NATO Bombing Campaign against Yugoslavia," *European Journal of International Law* 12, no. 3 (2001): 499.

82. Oeter, "Methods and Means of Combat," in Fleck (ed.), *Handbook of International Humanitarian Law,* 160–61; Dinstein, *Conduct of Hostilities,* 82–110.

83. Oeter, "Methods and Means of Combat," in Fleck (ed.), *Handbook of International Humanitarian Law,* 161.

84. Oeter, "Methods and Means of Combat," in Fleck (ed.), *Handbook of International Humanitarian Law,* 161.

85. *Prosecutor v. Strugar,* Trial Chamber II, Judgment of January 31, 2005 [IT-01–42]; *Prosecutor v. Kordić and Čerkez,* Trial Chamber III, Judgment of February 26, 2001 [IT-95–14/2].

CHAPTER 7

Prosecution and Defense in International Courts

Make crime pay; become a lawyer.

Will Rogers

Collective Enterprise, Individual Culpability

To this point, I have discussed crimes while referring to rulings of courts, articles of conventions, and other authorities to illustrate the evolution of the substantive law. In this chapter, I focus on the elements of developing indictments, permissible defense arguments, and other important procedural concerns, such as the rights of the accused. As prosecutors draw indictments and marshal evidence for trial, they face a challenging task when presented with the three classes of crimes discussed in Chapter 4–6. They must establish an essential connection between the behavior of an individual and the broader context that defines the crimes. As I have noted in a number of instances, a crime that occurs during a war or genocidal massacre may be just an ordinary crime, having nothing to do with other events. This distinguishes these crimes from the transboundary crimes discussed in Chapter 8. Conviction of someone accused of engaging in the narcotics or slave trade does not depend upon proving that the individual acted with knowledge of, and in support of, a broader pattern of criminal conduct or within the context of an international or internal war. Just as murder is murder whether it qualifies as a crime against humanity or not, piracy is piracy whenever or wherever it occurs.

To complicate the task, the Statutes of the ad hoc international tribunals did not contain explicit guidance with respect to scope and definitions of the principles of liability but presumably expected the panels to draw on customary international law.[1] To draw on earlier points, this represented a reach in many respects because of the *nullum crimen* (ex post facto) principle. To obtain a conviction, prosecutors have to prove that the forms of criminal participation that underlie the charges actually have a firm basis in prior practice in *international* law. Moreover, the prosecution then has to prove that all of the elements defining a particular crime have been satisfied. The ICC Statute in its Elements of Crimes does list and define forms of liability with respect to each of the offenses within its jurisdiction.

Keep in mind also one other important difference. Domestic law enforcement tends to focus upon those who actually carry out the acts, though prosecutors do use some forms of joint liability (e.g., conspiracy). In international criminal law, while those who commit specific acts fall within its ambit, the principle focus is on those at a high level who plan, organize, or order the events that define the broader context because of the presumption that they bear a far greater burden of guilt that the low-level person who commits a specific act in carrying out the broader plan. This perspective emphasizes the group nature of the crimes. Some members of the group may participate in the sense of overt criminal acts, but the activities of others in terms of planning, instigating, or ordering form an essential component in facilitating the activities of the actual perpetrators. In one sense, this flips a traditional distinction between primary and secondary participation that exists in domestic criminal law. Normally, the person who commits the act is regarded as the primary perpetrator, while those who plan, instigate, or abet in planning or instigation are regarded as secondary perpetrators.[2]

Context makes a difference. Consider that one can make a strong case that the planners and organizers who facilitated the Rwandan genocide or the Holocaust should bear a far heavier burden of responsibility than lower-level individuals who committed various offenses, because the planners and organizers are responsible for the totality, not just a few death or injuries. Although limited by the language in the Statute, the appeals chamber in *Tadić* said that "such responsibility for serious violations of international humanitarian law is not limited merely to those who actually carry out the *actus reus* of the enumerated crimes but appears to extend also to other offenders. . . . Whoever contributes to the commission of crimes by the group of persons or some members of the group, in execution of a common criminal purpose may be held to be criminally liable."[3] While, as noted earlier in Chapter 4, *Tadić* represented the target of opportunity to jump start the process, Mettraux argues that "Over the years . . . the Tribunals have turned their attention almost exclusively towards high-level perpetrators."[4] In 2004, the focus made it into the Rules and Procedures of Evidence of the ICTY. Judges may now refuse to confirm indictments of lesser participants.[5] One suspects that this decision reflects a pragmatic concern over both cost and time.

Chapter 2 outlined some general principles of personal liability in domestic law, as well as two principles that define liability in the abstract, *actus reus* (guilty act) and *mens rea* (guilty mind). Each of the principles discussed has both a substantive and a mental element. Article 30 of the ICC Statute provides: "Unless otherwise provided, a person shall be criminally responsible and liable for punishment for a crime within the jurisdiction of the Court only if the material elements are committed with intent and knowledge."[6] In fact, the legitimate exercise of jurisdiction by a tribunal over an individual (*ratione personae*) depends upon four conditions:

1. It must be provided for in the Statute in some manner;
2. It must have existed under customary international law at the relevant time;
3. The form of liability must have been perceivable at the time to anyone engaging in the conduct; and
4. The person charged must have reasonably been able to foresee that the conduct could result in criminal liability if apprehended.[7]

The jurisdiction of the ad hoc tribunals and the ICC is restricted to natural persons. Unlike Nuremberg, political parties or other collective associations cannot be prosecuted under the Statutes of any of the tribunals. This has an important consequence because it means that an individual cannot be prosecuted simply for membership in a "criminal organization or enterprise." Prosecution requires proof of overt acts.

Some other critical distinctions come into play here. *Mens rea* refers to *intent,* not to *motive*. Intent and motive are two very different elements of a crime. Generally, intent is an implicit rather than an explicit consideration, because the assumption is that intent flows from the act—if you did the crime, you intended to do the crime. The General Introduction to the Elements of Crimes in the Rome Statute, paragraph 3, states: "Existence of intent and knowledge can be inferred from relevant facts and circumstances." At trial, a defendant must produce exculpatory evidence and argument—for example, insanity, intoxication, self-defense, or accident—to refute that presumption. On the other hand, motive involves *why* a person did the crime. Despite all the agonizing over motive in TV and movie dramas, intent, rather than motive, is a major factor in establishing liability. While not totally irrelevant to establishing guilt or innocence, motive is a factor in determining the severity of the crime—did the consequences result from premeditation, from action "in the heat of the moment," from reckless behavior, or from inadvertent or unforeseen circumstances? With that said, there are *two* areas of ICL where motive does come into play. The provisions defining both genocidal acts and persecution as defined under Crimes against Humanity, though specifying intent, can be read as requiring proof of motive.[8]

The various statutes and conventions utilize the following principles to define liability: commission, planning, instigating, ordering, aiding and abetting, joint criminal enterprise, superior/command responsibility, and complicity. These do not represent self-contained categories and may overlap in many cases. When they do overlap, the prosecutor and the court must decide which of the competing principles best describes the nature of the act. Cassese notes another important consideration. In actual case law at the international level, these principles serve primarily a descriptive, classificatory purpose. They define the modality, that is, *the type,* of participation, not the degree of culpability.[9] Hence, although intuitively one might try to assign a hierarchy in terms of degree of guilt (e.g., command responsibility ranking above aiding and abetting or complicity), the charges carry little weight in and of themselves with respect to penalties if found guilty. The degree of participation stands apart from the charge itself. One final observation applies here with respect to penalties. Because ICL does not draw upon a unified code, no uniform scale of penalties exists. I discuss penalties later in this chapter.

The Statutes of the ICTY and the ICTR also differ from that of the ICC in terms of defining "criminal responsibility" (liability). They do not recognize inchoate crimes (see discussion in this chapter). With the exception of genocide, the ad hoc tribunals require that the accused actually have carried out (completed) the acts in question. The ICC Statute permits prosecution for an "attempt" to commit any crime over which the tribunal has jurisdiction. The ICC Statute also has some slightly different language with respect to defining criminal participation. It speaks of "solicitation" and "inducement,"[10] whereas the Statutes for the ICTY and ICTR use "instigation."[11] The terms seem to refer to the same set of acts, both theoretically and practically. Indeed, in terms of formal definitions, "instigation" means "solicitation." Instigation involves motivating another individual to commit a crime.[12]

Commission and Perpetration

In determining individual liability, territory rather than nationality generally comes into play. By its Statute, in addition to territorial jurisdiction, the ICTR does have the right to try offenses committed on the territory of adjacent states if committed by Rwandan nationals. The court has never made a charge under this provision, perhaps because of the complex circumstances involved. Many participants may not have been citizens, having been born and raised as refugees. The ICC (Art. 12) has jurisdiction over nationals of States parties and over crimes committed upon the territory of States parties regardless of nationality. The other Statutes make no reference to nationality as a basis for jurisdiction. For the ICTY, the essential consideration is that the offenses have some *territorial* connection with the former Yugoslavia. Mettraux notes that this includes "foreign mercenaries, NATO personnel, KFOR soldiers, or paramilitary groups of any ethnic affiliation."[13]

The Statutes also have one other important provision in defining participation. Official position does not grant immunity from prosecution. Article 7.2 of the ICTY (Art. 6.2 of the ICTR; Art. 27 of the ICC), states that "the official position of any accused person, whether as Head of State or Government or as a responsible Government official shall not relieve such person of criminal responsibility nor mitigate punishment." Simply, official position cannot provide immunity for conduct. In these cases, unlike before, rank *doth not* have its privileges. Position does not protect a person from liability.[14] Going back to the fundamental rationale for international prosecution, this forms the most important extension of jurisdiction because it clearly aims at the "culture of impunity." In *Kunarac et al.,* the trial chamber held that there is

no privilege under international criminal law which would shield State representatives or agents from the reach of individual criminal responsibility. On
the contrary, their acting in official capacity could constitute an aggravated
circumstance when it comes to sentencing, because he or she illegitimately
used and abused a power which was conferred upon him or her for different
legitimate purposes.[15]

A caution here is in order. First, readers might review the points about jurisdiction
made earlier in this chapter. This provision applies to *international* tribunals
that have jurisdiction defined by Statute. Such jurisdiction is limited either by
territorial focus and time frame (ad hoc tribunals) or by the necessity of consent
to the treaty establishing the court (ICC). At the moment, the limited nature of
the "exception" does not establish a presumption of a customary law that *national*
courts may utilize. The *Yerodia* case discussed in Chapter 5 (*Democratic Republic of
the Congo v. Belgium*),[16] which upheld immunity for an official currently serving in
an official capacity, still holds. Of course, that immunity attaches to the position,
not to the individual, meaning that after the person leaves, immunity no longer
applies unless the conduct in question did qualify as acts of state.

Establishing Personal Liability

Article 25.3(a) of the ICC defines direct participation as having occurred when
a person "[c]ommits such a crime, whether as an individual, jointly with another
or through another person regardless of whether that other person is criminally
responsible." In principle, all persons who participate in the commission of a
crime bear liability for their acts. In *Tadić,* the ICTY appeals chamber defined
commission as "the physical perpetration of a crime by the offender himself, or
the culpable omission of an act that was mandated by a rule of criminal law."[17]
A culpable omission results from a failure to act when one had a duty to act.[18]
In terms of direct participation, ordering and soliciting/inducing the crime stand
as forms of direct participation. A person instigates a crime if his conduct stands
as a clear contributing factor to the actions of the person who committed the
physical act.[19]

Seemingly simple and to the point, this formulation still leaves open many
questions. Not all the permutations and combinations of possibilities need concern us. Suffice it to say that commission may involve more than one perpetrator,
and the relationship among these can raise interesting technical questions with
regard to how an individual may be charged. Did all the participants perform the
same act, or did they perform different acts that contributed to the end result?
What defines "joint commission" as distinguished from "aiding and abetting" or
"complicity"?

Consider the following hypothetical situation.[20] The accusation involves the
act of torture of an individual. Under order from superiors, someone may order
or direct the actual form of torture. A medical doctor may be in attendance to

make sure the measures used do not cause death. Apart from the interrogator(s), another person observes to gather the information desired. Other individuals provide food for the inquisitors and medicine for the victim. Do all of these activities carry the same *degree* of liability? The answer here goes back to my note about degrees of participation. All who take part in a common criminal activity and who share the requisite knowledge and intent share criminal liability because each contributes to the crime (and the results), but not all will receive the same sentence upon conviction because some actions had more impact than others in context. Those who provided food and medicine certainly contributed in the sense of support for those who actually ordered or carried out the torture. The question will always concern the extent that their activities contributed to the offense as defined by final result. Planning, complicity, instigation, and aiding and abetting all involve questions of degree.

To assess degree of participation, judges look at *mens rea*. In Chapter 2, I discussed several categories of liability drawn from the common-law tradition: premeditation, simple intention, recklessness, and negligence. Civil code systems use different terms that approximate these.[21] While the categories do not directly correspond, the differences have mattered only occasionally as judges from different systems have sought to reconcile definitions. With the exception of genocide cases, which form a special exception in every instance, judgments have normally required only proof of intentional action (as distinguished from accident), not premeditation.[22] This has not solved all problems because adducing degrees between "deliberate intent" and "negligent" can still prove a formidable task because rarely does direct evidence exist.[23] The Trial Chamber in *Blaskić* reconciled the difference by concluding: "The *mens rea* constituting all the violations of Article 2 of the Statute includes both guilty intent and recklessness which may be likened to serious criminal negligence."[24]

Inchoate Offenses

Inchoate crimes,[25] sometimes described as incomplete or preparatory crimes, involve acts that demonstrate an inclination to commit a criminal offense. In other words, even if the criminal acts did not actually occur, a person who engages in actions that might have resulted in the crime can still be held liable. In domestic law, inchoate crimes include planning, attempt, conspiracy, and solicitation/instigation. At the international level, some controversy exists concerning whether or not planning can be included in this category. The premise behind inchoate offenses derives from the idea that prevention forms a legitimate part of the criminal justice enterprise. The following are general observations about inchoate crimes.

First, with the exception of conspiracy, a person cannot be charged with an inchoate offense and the actual crime. For example, one cannot be charged with attempted murder and murder.[26] Prosecutors must choose one or the other. Conspiracy differs in that one can be charged with drug trafficking and conspiracy to smuggle drugs, for example. Second, inchoate offenses generally carry lesser penalties, although the sentence for an inchoate crime may be equal to the penalties for the actually crime. For example, the penalties for solicitation of prostitution may be equal to the penalties for prostitution itself, but penalties for attempted murder are considerably less than those for actually committing murder. Third, conviction for an inchoate crime requires that the prosecutor prove that an individual had a specific intent (*mens rea*) to commit or contribute to the actual crime. Fourth, inchoate crimes must involve some overt action toward completion of the crime. Just thinking about committing a crime does not constitute a criminal offense. You can fantasize about robbing a bank to alleviate financial problems or murdering your spouse, even to the point of drawing up elaborate plans in the privacy of your own home, so long as you take no overt action to put the plan into effect.

Attempt forms the offense closest to the actual commission of the crime itself, while solicitation stands the most removed. Attempt involves trying to commit a crime but failing to complete the intended actions. Threats and challenges may also qualify as attempt. Solicitation consists of asking another party to commit a crime. Even if the solicited party does not commit the crime, the asking party can be charged with solicitation. For example, a person who seeks out someone to murder his spouse may be charged with solicitation even if the person asked did not accept the mission.

Conspiracy involves an agreement to perform together an illegal, wrongful, or subversive act. As noted, this crime can be charged in addition to the crime itself; an individual can be charged with murder or attempted murder and conspiracy to commit murder. In order to establish a conspiracy offense, the prosecutor does not have to prove that all of the people named in the indictment were members of the scheme or that the members had planned together all of the details of the scheme. The making of the agreement itself forms the essence of the charge. Proof of conspiracy requires three elements: (1) evidence of an agreement between two or more individuals to undertake an unlawful action; (2) evidence that each person willfully became a member of the conspiracy; and (3) evidence that at least one of the members knowingly committed an overt act in execution of the plan.[27] Conspiracy is a favorite prosecutorial weapon because, given the standards of proof, it is relatively easy to obtain a conviction.

Conspiracy as an Inchoate Crime and ICL   Charges at Nuremberg included conspiracy to commit crimes against peace. Prosecutors did not apply the charge to either war crimes or crimes against humanity. The charge actually had little effect on the Nuremberg trials because the "conspiracies" later resulted in later crimes. The Tokyo trials, although the charge was again limited to crimes against peace, took a very broad view, characterizing the events as "an all inclusive seventeen-year conspiracy involving all the accused."[28] Contemporary tribunals have ignored both. Prosecutors have not used conspiracy with respect to war crimes or crimes against humanity.

Genocide, as always, stands as an exception. Both the ICTR (Art. 2.3(b)) and the ICTR (Art. 4.3(b)) Statutes include conspiracy. The definitions make it clear that conspiracy to commit genocide can be regarded as an inchoate crime. In *Musema,* the ICTY defined conspiracy to commit genocide as an "agreement between two or more people."[29] However, what makes this charge difficult to prove as an inchoate crime is establishing the requisite *mens rea,* the special intent to "destroy, in whole or in part, a national, ethnic, racial or religious group as such."[30] (See Chapter 5)

Joint Criminal Enterprise and Co-Perpetration (Common Intent)

The Statutes of the ICTY and the ICTR do not explicitly refer to "joint criminal enterprise." Judges have inferred its applicability from Article 7.1 of the ICTY Statute, which provides that "A person who planned, instigated, ordered, committed or otherwise aided and abetted in the planning, preparation or execution of a crime referred to in articles 2 to 5 of the present Statute shall be individually responsible for the crime." Article 25.3(a) of the ICC Statute refers to commission "jointly with another." How best to characterize the idea of "joint participation" has been a question that has generated considerable controversy. In some cases, individuals might share equal responsibility. Contrast the following example with that of torture used in the previous section. A paramilitary group attacks a village, rounds up all of the men, marches them outside the village, then systematically executes them and buries them in a mass grave. In this case, all may share equal liability unless individuals can show circumstances that would mitigate, not eliminate, their culpability in the overall enterprise. The application and elaboration of this form of liability has largely come through the work of the judges of the ICTY.

The appeals chambers for the ad hoc tribunals have resisted developing the idea of co-perpetration, relying instead upon "joint criminal enterprise." This preference gives rise to some interesting disputes because, as noted, none of the Statutes mention joint criminal enterprise as a form of liability. The utility of the idea of joint criminal enterprise is that all of those included may be guilty of the crime regardless of the specific part played by each in the actual commission of the crime. It has its controversial elements. Nonetheless, the appeals chambers have developed two levels of joint participation:

1. All participants share the same intent and purpose and act upon that intent;
2. Crimes committed by individuals as part of the joint criminal enterprise contribute to the overall "intent and purpose" in that they contribute to a pattern of "ill-treatment."[31]

The two share a common *mens rea.* A "joint criminal enterprise requires (1) a number of individuals; (2) the existence of a common plan or purpose that involves commission of a crime under the Statute; and (3) participation of the accused in the common effort in the sense of committing a crime defined in the Statute. Schabas notes that joint criminal enterprise "has seemed particularly helpful in prosecuting leaders for a broad range of acts committed by participants with whom there is, in practice, not real 'agreement' to commit a crime."[32] The prosecutor for the ICTY has used joint criminal enterprise as a basis for indicting senior military and political leaders.[33] The prosecutor for the Sierra Leone court (SCSL) has also used it as the principal basis for assessing criminal responsibility.[34]

The distinction between the two forms of participation defined by joint criminal enterprise lies in the *mens rea,* the mental element. In this case, we can speak of levels. The first level requires that an individual or a group of individuals have shared intent to commit the particular offense. The second level involves a "personal knowledge of the system of ill-treatment" and the commission of overt acts with the "intent to further this ill-treatment."[35] The participation can be direct or indirect and does not require any threshold level with respect to the significance of the contribution to the plan.

Though it dates back to Nuremberg, this principle remains a source of controversy. The nature of the debates focus upon the imprecise use of the concept across cases. Mettraux cites three problems: (1) the risk that liability might be inferred from simple association with other members of the group; (2) the fact that the definition of "joint criminal enterprise" in the indictments often is "no more than a general description of events that form the background to the charges"; and (3) the sheer number of alleged "joint criminal enterprises," many of which may have overlapping membership but which are described inconsistently in different indictments issued at different times.[36] To this, Danner and Martinez add a fourth: the excessively broad nature of many of the indictments in terms of defining purpose could give rise to almost an unlimited liability for all participants in certain contexts.[37] At present, indictment for joint criminal enterprise does not require meeting a threshold requirement. The fundamental worry stems from the current elasticity of the idea. At the bottom, you have Tadić, accused of killing five people. At the other end, if one extrapolates the reasoning in the "extended version," almost every single Hutu in Rwanda would bear some criminal responsibility for what happened. Nonetheless, it remains a staple in the repertoire of prosecutors.

Command (Superior) Responsibility

This principle, even though it has a long history, does not form a part of any domestic legal code as a method of assessing liability for ordinary criminal offenses.[38] It is specific to international law, particularly to the conduct of military operations. Prior to Nuremberg and Tokyo, it did not extend to the civilian sector. The prosecutors at Nuremberg did not use the principle to any great extent, but those for the Tokyo trials used it extensively. The trial of General Yamashita after World War II was the first in modern history to be based upon the principle. More than 60 years later, it remains a source of extreme controversy, from the standpoint of both procedural flaws and the expansive nature of the substantive standard used.[39] Essentially, the Yamashita tribunal held that a military commander could be held responsible for the acts of subordinates even if he had no knowledge of those acts and questionable capacity to take effective action to suppress them.

The three Statutes for the ad hoc courts (ICTY, ICTR, SCSL) contain the same language defining the principle. The fact that any act within the jurisdiction of the tribunals "was committed by a subordinate does not relieve his superior of criminal responsibility if he knew or had reason to know that the subordinate was about to commit such acts or had done so and the superior had failed to take the necessary and reasonable measures to prevent such acts or to punish the perpetrators thereof."[40] Article 28 of the Rome Statute (ICC) has a much more detailed definition, but the elements remain the same: it requires a superior-subordinate relationship, knowledge, and failure to act on that knowledge to prevent the action or punish the perpetrator.[41] It applies to both civilian and military "commanders." Note that the indictment against Slobodan Milošević included a charge of command responsibility.[42]

Perhaps the best way to understand the scope of this principle is to contrast it with "ordering." Both require a superior-subordinate relationship, but the liability in command responsibility lies in the failure to act, that is, in not taking action to prevent or punish (a "commission of omission") when one has a duty to do so. The superior does not share the criminal liability of the perpetrator. No causal connection exists. The superior did not take any overt action in support of the crime. The liability attaches solely to the actions or, more accurately, the lack of action on the part of the superior. In one respect, it resembles "complicity" (aiding or abetting or joint criminal enterprise), but command responsibility does not require that the superior have had constructive knowledge of the offense committed by the subordinate (aiding and abetting) prior to its occurrence, nor does it require or imply the existence of a common plan. Moreover, the superior-subordinate relationship does not form part of complicity liability.

The issues here come from the definition of what constitutes a superior-subordinate relationship. The "superior" does not have to occupy a position of formal authority in sense of appointment or election. Control may be de facto (in fact), rather than de jure (in law). Within the context of a specific situation, the question revolves around whether the superior could reasonably have exercised "effective control" over those considered subordinates.[43] Effective control implies the power to prevent and the authority to punish, meaning that a de facto superior must be able to exercise control over subordinates similar in effect to that of a de jure superior.[44] Evidence that an individual had "substantial influence" over subordinates is not sufficient.[45] Prosecutors must demonstrate that the actions required in terms of prevention or punishment were within the "material possibility" of the superior.[46]

Schabas concludes that, as a principle of liability, command responsibility has not proven an effective tool. Indeed, he argues that trying to prove liability under the standards has resulted in a waste of time and resources with little to show in return. He identifies only one case, that of General Strugar,[47] in which the conviction rested primarily upon the application of command responsibility. He notes that this case forms "the most traditional of paradigms: a military commander in an international armed conflict, whose liability arises with respect to methods of warfare."[48]

Planning

One who plans or designs a crime is criminally responsible.[49] A person may be convicted of planning without any overt participation in the actual perpetration of the crime, but the participation must have been substantial enough in the sense of "formulating" a plan or endorsing "a plan prepared by another."[50] Planning overlaps with the idea of "conspiracy." The difference lies in that, while one can plan alone, conspiracy requires at least two participants. Important here is the *mens rea*. The accused has to have the intent (which can be inferred from actions) to carry out the plan. Though there seems to be some variance of opinion, Schabas argues that, at the international level, planning does not constitute an inchoate offense. Conviction for planning a crime must involve proof that the crime itself actually took place.[51] Others seem less sure, but the practice to date seems to support his conclusion. The arguments in opposition focus on the necessity of being able to prevent crimes. So Cassese argues:

> The rationale is international criminal law aims not only to punish persons found guilty of crimes, but also to prevent persons from engaging in serious criminal conduct. Consequently, in cases of doubt criminal rules must be interpreted as being also designed as far as possible to prevent offences.[52]

Perhaps the fact that so far no one has been convicted solely of planning by the tribunals indicates this may be more a statement of ideals than of actual practice. The decisions of the courts seem to reflect pragmatic considerations in terms of how far the international community might go with respect to prosecution. Bringing to bar those directly involved in the commission of egregious crimes has proven difficult enough. One must wonder what the deterrent effect of a virtually nonenforceable standard might be.

Ordering

"Ordering" means that a person in a position of authority uses his position to get another person to commit an offense.[53] While closely related to "instigating," ordering requires a superior-subordinate relationship. The relationship does not have to be a legal one; the only question is whether the person giving the order had the authority to do so.[54] The transmission of the order can be established by circumstantial evidence. The order does not have to be given directly to the person who carries it out. It may pass through any number of intermediaries. Nor does liability rest solely with the author of the order. A person who passes it down through the chain of command can be liable, as well.[55] The offender must be aware that the execution of the order may result in a crime.[56] A person normally will not be convicted of both ordering and committing the crime. Conviction for the actual commission will suffice. Ordering is not an inchoate offense. For an individual to bear liability for "ordering," the crime has to have occurred or been attempted.[57]

Instigating, Inducing, and Inciting

Instigating means urging, encouraging, or prompting another to commit a crime.[58] Although akin to solicitation, instigation is not an inchoate offense except in the case of genocide. Proving a case of incitement to genocide does not require evidence that anyone attempted or committed a genocidal act. Instigation may take many forms. The instigation must be a cause of the act but does not necessary have to be the only cause.[59] The accused must be aware of the substantial possibility that a crime will result from the instigation.[60] The ICTR "Media" trial (also known as the Radio Machete trial) involved the editor of the newspaper *Kangura* and two principals in the radio station RTLM. The three were accused of incitement to genocide through editorials and broadcasts. The court found that incitement "implies a desire on the part of the perpetrator to create by his actions a particular state of mind necessary to commit such a crime in the minds of the person(s) he is so engaging."[61]

Many questions arise here. The trial chamber in "The Media Case" defined the *mens rea* in terms of "an intent to *directly* prompt or provoke another to commit genocide" (emphasis added). Perhaps the most challenging issue is trying to define "direct." This is not a simple task. The trial chamber in *Akayesu* stated that audience and context, as well as linguistic and cultural factors, had to be taken into account.[62] Here genocide again stands apart. Prosecutors must prove that persons charged with instigating or inciting genocide must themselves have the specific intent to commit genocide.[63]

Aiding and Abetting

This form of liability is noncontroversial. It involves secondary responsibility, sometimes characterized as being an "accessory." The accused does not commit the act but in some way facilitates it through direct assistance (aiding) or sympathetic support (abetting).[64] The difference between the two has little practical significance because prosecutors have consistently linked the two together. No indictment at the international level has charged just one or the other. As a form of "accessory" liability, aiding and abetting occurs when an individual has carried out an act that materially assists in the commission of the crime or gives the perpetrator encouragement or moral support.[65] For an individual to be convicted of aiding and abetting, the crime has to have been carried out. One can aid or abet at any stage of a crime—planning, preparation, or execution. Television and movie script writers seem to love the term "accessory before and after the fact" as terms that police and district attorneys use as a matter of course in trying to convince recalcitrant witnesses to cooperate.

In the practice of the ICTY and the ICTR, aiding and abetting do have a threshold requirement. The contribution of the accused must have had a "substantial effect" in facilitating the commission of the crime.[66] It does not have to be an essential element but must be considered in context depending upon "the effect of the assistance and on the knowledge of the accused."[67] The definition in the ICC Statute (Art. 25.3(c)) does not have an explicit threshold requirement. From a practical point of view, this omission probably has little significance, given that the precedent is now well established as part of international jurisprudence. Consider, also, that, in order to establish the legitimacy of the charge, cases before the ICC involve "big fish," not "minnows." It is doubtful that, in such cases, the question of trying to assess a threshold for "substantial contribution" would be of major concern.

Aiding and abetting also presume that the individual has knowledge of what the perpetrator meant to do (*mens rea*) and, with that knowledge, made a decision to provide assistance.[68] Individuals may also be charged with failing to act (omissions) if they were present and failed to carry out a duty expected of them because of their position or responsibility. For example, if members of the police observe acts clearly in violation of the law and take no action, they have failed to perform an expected duty (an omission). Ordinarily, aiding and abetting are considered a less serious offense than direct perpetration, but a conviction for aiding and abetting does not depend on the apprehension, trial, and conviction of the perpetrator of the original act. The liability of the accomplice stands apart from that of the perpetrator.

The *actus reus* in question differs from that for instigation or solicitation in that the activities that "assisted" in the commission of the crime need not have a causal connection in terms of motivating the action by the perpetrator. The ideas also have considerable overlap with joint criminal enterprise. The difference is that an aider or an abettor merely has to have knowledge. A participant in a joint criminal enterprise has to share the common purpose, the intent, of the principal offender.[69] The potential overlap comes because courts have not set minimum (threshold) requirements that fix conclusively what "sharing purpose" and "participation" mean in defining a joint criminal enterprise. Indeed, the *Kvočka* appeals panel noted that "the significance of the accused's contributions will be relevant to demonstrating that the accused shared the intent to pursue the common purpose."[70] Yet, joint criminal enterprise seems to fall into the primary category of direct commission, rather than the secondary one of accomplice liability.

Defense: Grounds for Excluding Criminal Responsibility

ICL texts spend a great deal of time on the elements of crimes and the principles of liability, focusing on prosecution. Most texts devote little or no attention to questions relating to factors that may be raised in defense. Simply put, a defense attempts to answer an allegation of wrongdoing. Psychologically, even in domestic trials, one can sense a general lack of sympathy for defendants charged with heinous offenses. Eser notes that the aversion may stem from the idea that "[b]y providing perpetrators of brutal crimes against humanity . . . with defences for their offenses, we have effectively lent them a hand in finding grounds for excluding punishability."[71] Nonetheless, the right to a defense represents a fundamental principle of criminal law at any level.[72]

Logically, defense strategies reduce to three categories: "justifications," "excuses," and "failure of proof." All seek to demonstrate why criminal liability should not attach to the conduct in question. Justifications and excuses relate to the requirements of the substantive law. Failures of proof stem from the prosecution's inability to meet the requirements of procedural law in marshaling enough evidence to establish the case. Looking back, the O. J. Simpson case turned on the failure of the prosecutors to establish guilt "beyond a reasonable doubt." Justifications give reasons why the conduct in question fell within acceptable legal standards and thus did not constitute an offense. For example, actions that fall within the parameters of self-defense (necessary and proportional to the threat) justify conduct, such as killing another, that otherwise might be considered an offense. An excuse seeks to find reasons why, given a particular set of circumstances, the accused should not bear blame (insanity, abuse, drunkenness). The distinction between justifications and excuses is very difficult to make in the abstract, even though they do make a difference in application. Justifications exonerate a defendant entirely. While defense based upon excuses *may* have the same result, more often they become factors in assessing the degree of culpability in terms of assessing appropriate sentences.

Of the ad hoc tribunals, the three Statutes address grounds for defense only with the intent to prohibit certain defense assertions in justification.[73] Article 31 of the Rome Statute of the ICC does include a section on "Grounds for Excluding Criminal Responsibility." Even though it constitutes the first systematic elaboration of potential defenses in ICL, as such it does not purport to be a comprehensive listing. Article 31.3 notes that "the Court may consider a ground for excluding criminal responsibility other than those referred to in paragraph 1." Nonetheless, the listing forms a good set of guidelines for defense lawyers. Articles 32 and 33 also are germane in that they deal with situations of mistakes in fact and in law. Though the Rome Statute stands as the apex of the hierarchy here, the customary law, past trial practice, and other general principles of law may also furnish other grounds and strategies.

Official-Position and Head-of-State Immunity and Statutes of Limitations

Two defenses are not permissible at the international level: statutes of limitations and claims to immunities of various kinds. *The Convention on the Non-Applicability of Statutory Limitations to War Crimes and Crimes against Humanity* entered into force in November 1970.[74] It simply specifies that no country can establish time limits for prosecution for the offenses designated. Article 29 of the ICC Statute stipulates that no crime within the jurisdiction of the court will be subject to any time limit with regard to prosecution.

As we have noted earlier, prior to Nuremberg, official position proved a defense against prosecution. The London Charter of the IMT explicitly ruled out official position as a permissible defense argument. The Statutes of the ad hoc UN tribunals and the Rome Statute of the ICC also do not permit defendants to use official position as a bar to prosecution. Article 27.1 of the ICC Statute provides:

> This Statute shall apply equally to all persons without any distinction based on official capacity. In particular official capacity as a Head of State or government or a government official shall in no case exempt a person from criminal responsibility under this Statute, nor shall it, in and of itself, constitute a ground for reduction of sentence.

Article 27.2 also stipulates that immunities or other "special procedural rules" that may attach to a position may not be raised as a bar to prosecution. Note that this presumably applies to currently serving heads of state and officials, as well as those not longer in office such as Pinochet, who may have some special status under domestic law.

Superior Orders

Paralleling the defense of immunity, the defense of superior orders has a considerable pedigree.[75] It focuses attention on the fundamental tension between evolving international law and military discipline and other chains of authority or command. Note that for ICL, the defense of superior orders clearly has been used by both civilian and military personnel. In the first edition of his classic text in 1905, Lassa Oppenheim, one of the most cited authorities on international law in the first half of the 20th century, wrote that "If members of the armed forces commit violations by order of their Government, they are not war criminals and cannot be punished by the enemy."[76] However, by the revised and updated sixth edition in 1940, his protégé and editor, Sir Hersh Lauterpacht, wrote:

> The fact that a rule of warfare has been violated in pursuance of an order of the belligerent Government or of an individual belligerent commander does not deprive the act in question of its character as a war crime. . . . [M]embers of the armed forces are bound to obey lawful orders only.[77]

The Nuremberg Charter (Art. 8) expressly noted that superior orders did not excuse conduct but could be considered in mitigation of punishment.[78] The Geneva Conventions have no provisions concerning superior orders. While the Statutes of the ad hoc tribunals essentially repeat the Nuremberg language, the Rome Statute (Art. 33) uses a "manifestly illegal" test.

Remember first that the person who gave the order still bears the primary responsibility for his or her own conduct in issuing the order. ICC Article 33 stipulates that raising the defense of superior orders requires that defendants satisfy a three-part test: (1) the subordinate must have had a legal obligation to obey the superior; (2) the person did not know the order was unlawful; and (3) the order was not manifestly unlawful. Article 33.2 states categorically that "For the purposes of this article orders to commit genocide or crimes against humanity are manifestly unlawful."

In satisfying the first test, some questions could arise regarding irregular troops or insurgents. Can the test be read as simply requiring a superior-subordinate relationship; that is, would any superior-subordinate relationship that meets the authority and control tests (command responsibility) meet the requirement? Given the clarity of the requirement, the answer would seem to be no. The relationship has to be a legal one. This would rule out the defense for insurgents, irregulars, or other groups that lack hierarchical command structures mandated by law.

Considering the second element, keep in mind that a plea of ignorance of the law does *not* necessarily shelter a subordinate from liability. The ignorance can be willful (don't ask, don't tell). The issue revolves around the circumstances under which fault (culpability) can still attach to "ignorance" when considered within the context of decision. Here, the problem stems from reasonable expectations about the level of knowledge required to determine the illegality of an order. Hence, the second and third elements must be considered together, because reason dictates that different standards should apply to people in different situations. Thus, higher expectations concerning knowledge of their legal responsibilities and acceptable action within those parameters should apply to highly trained military lawyers or senior officers and officials, while a lower standard might apply to raw recruits, those just out of basic training, or low-level functionaries.

Even so, any pleas of ignorance must be reasonable and credible. The questions again involve specifying a threshold test that would define "manifestly" in addition to the two explicit exclusions in Article 32.2. The controversies go well beyond the scope of the book. For our purposes, the statement of the Supreme Court of Israel in the *Eichmann* case will suffice:

> [t]he distinguishing mark of a "manifestly unlawful order" should fly like a black flag above the order given; . . . [n]ot formal unlawfulness, hidden or half-hidden, nor unlawfulness discernible only to the eyes of legal experts, but a flagrant and manifest breach of the law.[79]

Culture and "common knowledge" may also enter into the calculation.[80] Still, if the order was manifestly illegal, ignorance does not matter. Liability attaches.

Duress and Necessity

Often the plea of duress and necessity is combined with that of superior orders. Common law traditionally separates duress and necessity.[81] Duress, sometimes characterized as *compulsion,* flows from the actions of other people. Necessity stems from circumstances other than direct threats from others.[82] Note that these justifications in defense occur when an innocent life has been taken. One should keep these two definitions in mind even though the ICC Statute (Art. 31.1) conflates them. Some differences between civil code and common law apply with respect to how courts treat the two in assessing culpability. The issue boils down to a fundamental ethical problem: the criteria to determine, under dire conditions that threaten innocent lives, who decides who should live and who should die?[83] Is there a real necessity to save one's own life if it means taking another innocent life?

Both systems use proportionality tests but make different assumptions about the scope of the defense. Duress or necessity does not provide a full justification in common-law systems that involve murder. It may serve to mitigate punishment, but it does not justify the act. In most civil law systems, duress and necessity do provide a complete defense, but the court focuses more on the elements of choice.[84] Janssen states that "In most of these systems, the distinction between compulsion and necessity is made more sharply, leading to an *excuse* and a *justification,* respectively, and concentrating more on the accused's perception than on who or what caused the urges to commit the offense."[85] Did the person make a choice in the belief that it embodied the lesser of two evils?

At the international level, under what circumstances may a defendant plead duress or necessity? The activities that generate liability under international criminal law require group participation. Within the contexts, individuals may be subjected to extreme pressure to participate. None of the Statutes of the ad hoc courts mention duress or necessity. Nonetheless in *Erdemović* the ICTY had to address the issue directly.[86] Dražen Erdemović had been a member of the Serb army. In July 1995, Erdemović, along with the rest of his unit, was sent to a farm outside Pilica, where he was ordered to execute unarmed Muslim men from Srebenica who had surrendered to the Bosnian Serb army. When Erdemović refused to participate, his commanding officer told him that he would be shot along with the others if he did not comply. Reluctantly, Erdemović took part in the killings, personally murdering, by his own estimate, 70 people.

The trial chamber, using criteria originally developed in the *Krupp* case (CCL10),[87] ruled that duress does not form a complete defense but may be taken into account as a mitigating factor in sentencing. The appeals chamber split 3–2 in upholding the verdict. It wrote that "international law . . . cannot admit duress in cases which involve the slaughter of innocent human beings on a large scale."[88] Judge Antonio Cassese wrote a dissenting opinion in which he argued that duress could be a complete defense under certain conditions: (1) the act charged was committed under an immediate threat of severe and irreparable harm; (2) no adequate means existed to avert the threat; (3) the crime committed was not disproportionate to the evil threatened; and, (4) the person under duress had not voluntarily created the situation.[89] Cassese also argued that

> For offences involving killing, it is true, however, that one of the require-
> ments (discussed at paragraph 42 below)—proportionality—would usually
> not be fulfilled. Nevertheless, in exceptional circumstances this requirement
> might be met, for example, when the killing would be in any case perpetrated
> by persons other than the one acting under duress (since then it is not a ques-
> tion of saving your own life by killing another person, but of simply saving
> your own life when the other person will inevitably die, which may not be
> "disproportionate" as a remedy).[90]

Interestingly, Article 31.1(d) of the ICC Statute reflects the dissent of Cassese,
rather than the view of the majority. It permits duress as a defense when the
duress stems from "a threat of imminent death or of continuing or imminent serious bodily harm to avoid this threat, provided that the person does not intend
to cause a greater harm than the one sought to be avoided." The test is one of
proportionality that is decided as a question of fact in each case.[91]

Mental Incapacity and Diminished Responsibility

While a staple of domestic trials, insanity and mental deficiency have played
only a minor role at the international level. Rudolf Hess utilized such a defense
at Nuremberg without success. To date, no case before the ad hoc tribunals
has relied upon a full defense of mental incapacity or insanity. A few defendants have invoked the "special defense" of "*diminished* mental capacity," but
the courts have not accepted the pleas.[92] Note the distinction between mental
incapacity and diminished mental capacity. Mental incapacity constitutes a full
defense that could lead to acquittal; diminished mental capacity may be invoked
only as a mitigating factor in sentencing.[93] Article 31.1(a) of the ICC Statute
excludes criminal responsibility for persons who suffer "from mental disease or
defect that destroys his or her capacity to appreciate the unlawfulness or nature
of his or her conduct, or capacity to control his or her conduct to conform to
the requirements of law."

The defense flows from the proposition that culpability should not attach if the
accused lacked the ability to control his actions or lacked the ability to make a
reasoned or rational judgment about right and wrong. This could result from insanity or lack of mental capacity. The burden of proof falls upon the accused. The
trial chamber in the *Ĉelibiĉi* case rejected the defense in the case of Esad Landzo,
noting that in "every criminal act there is a presumption of sanity of the person
alleged to have committed the offence. Thus every person charged with an offence
is presumed to be of sound mind and to have been of sound mind at any relevant
time until the contrary is proven."[94] Note the language. The standard is "proof,"
not reasonable doubt.[95]

Some interesting questions remain unanswered here. A full acquittal in most
domestic legal systems does not free the individual; it merely changes the nature of
the detention to one based upon preventive psychiatric care to the extent that the

individual poses a threat to themselves or to the community.[96] The question remains open at the international level. No system of care for the criminally insane exists, nor does appropriate legislation in the Netherlands, Tanzania, or Sierra Leone.[97]

Intoxication

In actual practice, this defense has played a very minor role. Intoxication cannot provide a complete defense, but heavy intoxication from either alcohol or drugs may form an excuse. It can also serve as a defense claiming that, because of intoxication, an accused lacked the *mens rea* for certain crimes. The catch in the defense stems from the caveat that *voluntary* intoxication, to the extent that a person lacks the capacity to control his or her conduct, should not be taken into account as a mitigating factor. The Trial Chamber in *Kvočka* said "the Trial Chamber cannot accept Zigić's contention that an intentionally procured diminished mental state could result in a mitigated sentence."[98]

This seems overly narrow in terms of the provision in the Rome (ICC) Statute (Art. 31.1(b)) that provides for acquittal if an individual has:

> a state of intoxication that destroys that person's capacity to appreciate the unlawfulness or nature of his or her conduct, or capacity to control is or her conduct to conform to the requirements of law, unless the person has become voluntarily intoxicated under such circumstances that the person knew, or disregarded the risk, that, as a result of the intoxication, he or she was likely to engage in conduct constituting a crime within the jurisdiction of the Court.

The question tribunals must address is the extent to which intoxication degraded the "knowledge and intent" element (*mens rea*). The question of diminished capacity, whether voluntary or involuntary, should play a role in determining the degree of culpability.

Self-Defense

While recognized as a legitimate defense in most legal systems, as well as in customary international law, circumstances seldom support a defense on this basis. Before the ad hoc tribunals, no assertion of self-defense has found favor. Article 31.1(c) of the Rome Statute allows pleas of self-defense when an accused "acts reasonably" and in a manner that is "proportionate" to the degree of danger to self or property.

Interestingly, the classic justification of collective self-defense has been invoked. The Bosnian Serb leader Biljana Plavšić, justified the policy of ethnic cleansing as a "matter of survival and self-defense."[99] Similar references appear in cases before the ICTR.[100] These have little salience. Given the definition of self-defense as a response to an imminent unlawful act,[101] such claims appear vacuous on their face. The trial chamber in *Kordić and Čerkez* state that "The Trial Chamber . . . would emphasize that military operations in self-defence do not provide a justification for serious violations of international humanitarian law."[102] As Schabas notes, in this context, the claims are nothing more than an attempt to justify mass atrocities in the name of "just war."[103]

Mistake in Fact or Law

A mistake can be one of fact or of law (Rome Statute, Art. 32). Mistake in either case is a defense only if it negates the mental element required by the crime. An accused who lacks knowledge of an essential fact does not have the *mens rea* (guilty mind) necessary for a conviction. A mistake of fact must be honestly and reasonably made on the basis of the conditions prevailing at the time. The bombing of the embassy of the People's Republic of China during the Kosovo crisis in 1999 serves as a prime example. The pilots were given the wrong coordinates for the target.[104] The panel that reviewed the evidence exonerated both the pilots and the senior command in NATO because they had acted on incorrect information supplied by another agency.

Ignorance of the law is not a defense. Liability attaches regardless of an individual's awareness that a particular conduct has legal consequences. As with a mistake in fact, a mistake in law applies only if the accused can prove that the mistake negated the *mens rea* essential to establish the crime. Conceptualizing a situation where this could apply takes imagination to its limits, though it does dovetail with Article 33 on superior orders (see earlier discussion). In the practice of the ad hoc tribunals, no accused has used this defense.

Tu Quoque (You Also Did It)

The *tu quoque* defense rests upon the assertion that the adversary committed the same or similar illegal acts. As an argument about fairness, it asserts that if the party represented by the prosecution has committed the same or similar crimes, then that party has no valid authority to bring charges again another. At the Nuremberg trials, the rules prohibited this defense, although it did play a role because the sentences of Admiral Erich Raeder and Admiral Karl Dönitz took into account the fact that the United States had pursued a similar strategy in the Pacific.[105] The ICTY has categorically rejected *tu quoque* as a defense. The appeals chamber in *Kunarac* held that

> when there was an attack upon a particular civilian population, it is not relevant that the other side also committed atrocities against its opponent's population. The existence of an attack from one side against the other side's civilian population would neither justify the attack by that other side against the civilian population of its opponent nor displace the conclusion that the other side's forces were in fact targeting a civilian population as such. Each attack against the other's civilian populations would be equally illegitimate.[106]

Note the nature of the venue here. Unlike Nuremberg, it is not one of a victor judging the vanquished. It is one of a presumably impartial third party judging the actions of both sides. The panel essentially said, "Atrocities are atrocities." The fact that one side committed atrocities does not justify or excuse action in kind.

Alibi

An alibi is a claim that the individual was not present at the scene of the crime. This does not erase the possibility that one does not have to be present to be complicit (i.e., aiding and abetting). While the defense must supply evidence to establish the alibi (to raise reasonable doubt), the prosecution still bears the main burden of proof in that it must provide sufficient evidence that the accused committed the crime and was present during its commission. In *Vasilijević,* the trial chamber held that when a defendant raises a defense of alibi, "the accused bears no onus of establishing the alibi. The onus is on the Prosecutor to eliminate any reasonable possibility that the evidence of alibi is true."[107]

Military Necessity

The extent to which military necessity may provide a defense still generates controversy. Kittichaisiree flatly states that military necessity does not constitute a defense because the rule

> governing the conduct of hostilities already take[s] into account the needs of military necessity; . . . if an activity in question fulfils the test of military necessity, it is not a war crime, unless there exists a contrary rule governing the situation in question. If an activity fails the test of military necessity, whenever such a test is applicable, the perpetrator of the activity cannot invoke military necessity in his defence.[108]

This somewhat begs the question. By implication, Article 2(d) of the ICTY Statute mentions "extensive destruction and appropriation of property, not justified by military necessity and carried out unlawfully and wantonly." Article 3(b) refers to "wanton destruction of cities, towns or villages, or devastation not justified by military necessity." This suggests that the Statute anticipated a possible defense based upon military necessity. The real questions revolve around the limits. Two principles apply here: the principle of discrimination and the principle of proportionality. The principle of proportionality requires minimizing "collateral damage" in the sense of civilian lives or property (see Chapter 4). The Appeals Chamber in *Kordić and Čerkez* argued that the principle of distinction "obliges warring parties to distinguish *at all times* between the civilian population and combatants, between civilian objects and military objectives and accordingly to direct military operations only against military objectives."[109] Thus, the deliberate targeting of civilian installations or populations can never be justified through by a claim of military necessity.

A Note on Punishment

Let the punishment fit the crime.[110] Still, the question of what "fit" means generates considerable debate in most domestic legal systems. Often, disagreements flow from assumptions about the purpose of punishment. To keep the discussion focused here, I will use a simple summary of three important views. Is the purpose of punishment retribution, protection of society, or rehabilitation? These are not necessarily mutually exclusive. Sentencing can embody one or more of the rationales. All involve an idea of proportionality, but they have generated an extended debate about what values we should place upon the scales of justice. As we have discussed earlier, in cases of mass atrocities, how is it possible to make the punishment proportional to the seriousness of the crime? Retribution ultimately relies upon the deterrent effect: you do the crime, you do the time; if you do a crime again, you will do the time again or, in the case of serious crimes, you will not have the opportunity to do the crime again (protection of society). Rehabilitation focuses upon the chastening effect of conviction and incarceration as an opportunity for education. While important, deterrence is very difficult to measure. The sentences handed out at the Nuremberg and Tokyo tribunals did not act as deterrents to future perpetrators of mass atrocities. Even, the establishment of the ICTY, with specific jurisdiction over the former Yugoslavia, did not deter the commission of massive crimes well after the tribunal came into existence, most notoriously in the case of the Srebrenica massacres. Yet, as with all of the rationales here, failures stand out; successes may remain hidden. Still, the debate goes on. In considering the nature of the crimes at the international level, is rehabilitation a reasonable expectation?

> The ICTR in the *Kambanda* case saw retribution and deterrence as the appropriate standards: the penalties imposed on accused persons found guilty by the Tribunal must be directed, on the one hand, at retribution of the said accused, who must see their crimes punished, and over and above that, on other hand, at deterrence, namely dissuading for good those who will attempt in future to perpetrate such atrocities by showing them that the international community was not ready to tolerate the serious violations of international humanitarian law and human rights.[111]

Other trial panels have disagreed somewhat on the relative weights to be assigned to the two, but many have emphasized that retribution does not mean vengeance. Still, in light of classic retributive theory, the punishment should embody some idea of proportionality. The idea of rehabilitation has played only a minor role. Indeed, the ICTY appeals chamber has said:

> although both national jurisdictions and certain international and regional human rights instruments provide that rehabilitation should be one of the primary concerns for a court in sentencing, this cannot play a *predominant* role in the decision-making process of a Trial Chamber of the Tribunal.[112]

The Appeals Chamber in *Kordić and Čerkez* argued that "It would violate the principle of proportionality and endanger the pursuit of other sentencing purposes if rehabilitative considerations were given undue prominence in the sentencing process."[113]

With regard to the tribunals, the Statutes prescribe only minimal sentencing guidelines other than that sentences shall be limited to imprisonment only.[114] Article 24.2 of the of the ICTY Statute notes that "in imposing the sentences the Trial Chambers should take into account such factors as the gravity of the offence and the individual circumstances of the convicted person." This means that the critical factors beyond the gravity of the offense are the degree of responsibility of the accused and any exacerbating or mitigating circumstances. Premeditation, adverse impact (psychological or physical effects on the victims), willing participation or support, and, if applicable, the repulsive, bestial, and sadistic nature of the crime serve as aggravating factors.[115]

The exclusion of capital punishment reflects a long-term movement with respect to human rights law at the international level. To illustrate the change in attitude over time, we need only to look at the sentences meted out by the post–World War II tribunals.[116] Of the 19 defendants who received guilty verdicts at Nuremberg, 12 received the death sentence; 16 of the 25 defendants convicted by the IMTFE (Tokyo) received death sentences. The trial chamber in *Stakić* noted, when handing out the first life sentence given by the ICTY, that the Statute "reflects the global policy of the United Nations aiming at the abolition of the death penalty and favours life imprisonment as the maximum sanction to be imposed."[117]

One important criticism has surfaced recently with respect to sentencing. When compared to the sentences meted out by international tribunals at Nuremberg, Tokyo, and Arusha and by domestic courts, sentences handed down at the International Criminal Tribunal for the former Yugoslavia (ICTY) seem inexplicably lenient. Harmon and Gaynor have posed an interesting question: "Why are persons convicted of extraordinary crimes at the ICTY sentenced to such ordinary sentences?"[118] Why do cases of multiple murders, rapes, and other atrocities seemingly carry much lighter sentences than might have been given by domestic courts, where a single murder under aggravated circumstances can merit a life sentence? In his comprehensive study of comparative sentencing across tribunals, Drumbl concludes that current international sentencing schemes do not match up well with the deterrence, retributive, and expressive goals of punishment set forth by sentencing tribunals.[119] The mystery comes from the fact that in none of the ICTY cases has the sentencing chamber appeared to underplay the gravity of the crimes or displayed insensitivity to the suffering of the victims; nor did they ignore aggravating factor. But, in many ICTY cases, the weight given to mitigating circumstances was markedly different from that applied in domestic jurisdictions.

To cite three examples, Momir Nikolić, a Bosnian Serb commander, pled guilty to taking part in the Srebenica massacre, the only incident the ICTY has characterized as genocide. As part of the plea bargain, his original sentence was reduced from 27 to 20 years.[120] Even given his subsequent cooperation, this flies in the face of assertions that these crimes constitute the most shocking offense to the conscience of humanity. Considering this, one must wonder at the reasoning of the chamber concerning the pattern of sentencing:

> With respect to the issue of the excessiveness of a sentence, the Appeals Chamber, as noted by the Trial Chamber in the present case, held in the *Jelisić* case that a sentence should not be capricious or excessive, and that, in principle, it may be thought to be capricious or excessive if it is out of reasonable proportion with a line of sentences passed in similar circumstances for the same offences. Where there is such disparity, the Appeals Chamber may infer that there was disregard of the standard criteria by which sentence should be assessed, as prescribed by the Statute and set out in the Rules.[121]

Similarly, Dragan Nikolić, a Bosnian Serb prison camp commander (at Sušica Camp), received a sentence of 23 years for allowing his troops to rape, torture, and murder Muslim prisoners, often taking part in what the president of the trial court called crimes of "enormous brutality" and "systematic sadism."[122] Given their subsequent discussion, the sentence would seem to rely on a curious definition of "capricious" and "excessive."

Prosecutors originally charged Biljana Plavšić, who succeeded Radovan Karadžić as president of the Republika Sprška, with two counts of committing genocide and complicity to commit genocide and six counts of crimes against humanity against Bosnian Muslims.[123] In return for her guilty plea to one count of persecution (a crime against humanity), thus avoiding a lengthy trial, she received an 11-year sentence with credit for time served.[124] Although acknowledging her guilt, she refused to cooperate further. This included a refusal to testify against Slobodan Milošević. Perhaps the most alarming aspect was the fact that she is serving her sentence in a "posh Swedish prison that reportedly provides prisoners with use of a sauna, solarium, massage room, horse riding paddock, among other amenities."[125] In terms of attitudes, her plea generated accusations of treachery and betrayal, not an examination of conscience.

Scharf suggests that the tribunals have simply followed the wishes of the Security Council. True the panels routinely recite the mantra of rehabilitation and deterrence, but the SC set the principle goals as contributing to the restoration of peace and the rule of law in Yugoslavia and Rwanda. The Council believed that prosecuting the perpetrators would make a major contribution to breaking the cycle of violence in the Balkans.[126] The hope was that this would facilitate the process of reconciliation by permitting new leaders to distance themselves from the past and would prove educational by providing an impartial account of events. At this point, the extent to which the prosecutions have contributed to this goal remain moot. Public opinion seems to demand more in the way of retributive justice.

Plea Bargains The three cases also raise issues concerning the use of plea bargaining at the international level.[127] Widely used in common-law systems, plea bargaining may involve several different types of negotiations: over sentence, over the nature and extent of charges, over stipulating facts, over providing cooperation in another case, or over perhaps forgoing an appeal. At its creation, the ICTY explicitly disavowed the practice on the basis that the crimes within the ambit of the tribunal were too serious to bargain over.[128] Obviously, as caseloads increased, this attitude fell prey to the necessities of time and efficiency. Damaška and Scharf concluded that the need to expedite hearings, procure evidence, and reduce cost has prevailed over attention to the broader goals of international justice. This does not mean that every plea bargain has produced an unacceptable result, but, as we have noted, many have raised serious concerns over the practice.

The extent to which the pragmatism of practice in response to political pressures caused by funding constraints and a desire for efficiency has undermined the legacy of the courts remains an open question. The goal of having full and fair hearings in every case simply proved a goal beyond the willingness of the international community to support, given current procedures and numbers. Moreover, the exercise has taken more than 15 years. What does this say about international justice? These issues will probably not plague the ICC because the issues of large numbers of cases should not be a factor.

Notes

1. Guénaël Mettraux, *International Crimes and the Ad Hoc Tribunals* (Oxford: Oxford University Press, 2005), 270.

2. William A. Schabas, *The UN International Criminal Tribunals: The Former Yugoslavia, Rwanda and Sierra Leone* (Cambridge: Cambridge University Press, 2006), 297.

3. *Prosecutor v. Tadić*, Appeals Chamber, July 15, 1999, para. 189–90.

4. Mettraux, *International Crimes*, 274.

5. Mettraux, *International Crimes*, 275.

6. The concept of "knowledge" is a common-law principle. It does not form part of most civil codes. For a discussion, see Antonio Cassese, *International Criminal Law* (Oxford: Oxford University Press, 2003), 164–67.

7. Mettraux, *International Crimes*, 270–71.

8. See discussions in Chapters 4 and 5. Schabas notes that the Genocide Convention uses "intent," but, in context and in practice, the nature of the evidence needed more accurately reflects motive. Schabas, *The UN International Criminal Tribunals*, 295.

9. Cassese, *International Criminal Law*, 179–80.

10. ICC Statute, Article 25.3(b).

11. ICTY Statute, Article 7.1.

12. *Prosecutor v. Akayesu*, Trial Chamber I, Judgment of September 2, 1998 [ICTR-96–4], paras. 481–82.

13. Mettraux, *International Crimes*, 275–76.

14. An interesting conclusion from this is that a finding that an official or officials bore individual criminal responsibility for acts would not necessarily engage state responsibility.

15. *Prosecutor v. Kunarac, Kovać and Vuković,* Trial Chamber II, Judgment of February 2, 2001 [IT-96–23 & 23–1], para. 494.

16. *Arrest Warrant of 11 April 2000 (Democratic Republic of the Congo v. Belgium) (Merits),* Judgment of February 14, 2002, http://www.icj-cij.org/docket/files/121/8126.pdf.

17. *Prosecutor v. Tadić,* Appeals Chamber, para.188.

18. Rajat Rana, "The Jean Mpambara Case: Outlining 'Culpable Omissions' in International Criminal Law," *Chinese Journal of International Law* 6, no. 2 (2007): 439–43.

19. *Prosecutor v. Kristić,* Trial Chamber I, Judgment of August 2, 2001 [IT-98–33-T], para. 280.

20. Based upon Cassese, *International Criminal Law,* 181.

21. Specifically, *dolus specialis, dolis generalis, dolus directus,* and *dolus eventualis.* The term *dolus* translates as "criminal intent" or "evil intent." For an extended discussion of these, see Jenny S. Martinez, "Understanding *Mens Rea* in Command Responsibility from Yamashita to Blaskić and Beyond," *Journal of International Criminal Justice* 5, no. 3 (2007): 638–64.

22. Schabas, *The UN International Criminal Tribunals,* 293.

23. Schabas, *The UN International Criminal Tribunals,* 295.

24. *Prosecutor v. Blaskić,* Trial Chamber I, Judgment of March 3, 2000 [IT-95–14-T], para. 152.

25. For a quick summary of relevant principles, see http://www.criminal-law-lawyer-source.com/terms/inchoate-crimes.html.

26. See the 2007 film *Fracture,* starring Anthony Hopkins, for a clever use of this distinction.

27. See 18 U.S.C. 371 for the definition of conspiracy in U.S. law. See also http://www.lectlaw.com/def/c103.htm for a brief discussion.

28. Philip R. Piccigallo, *The Japanese on Trial: Allied War Crimes Operations in the Far East, 1945–1951* (Austin: University of Texas Press, 1979), 212. See also the most frequently cited work: Richard Minear, *Victor's Justice* (Princeton: Princeton University Press, 1971).

29. *Prosecutor v. Musema* (ICTR), Trial Chamber I, Judgment of January 27, 2001 [ICTR-96–13-T], para. 189.

30. *Prosecutor v. Musema,* para. 192.

31. *Prosecutor v. Tadić,* Appeals Chamber, paras.195–96 There is a third category, "an extended form," but it does not merit extended discussion here, even though it is the most controversial because it would impose liability for acts that fall outside the common plan if the consequences were "foreseeable." For an extended discussion, see Alison Marston Danner and Jenny S. Martinez, "Guilty Associations: Joint Criminal Enterprise, Command Responsibility and the Development of International Criminal Law," *California Law Review* 93, no. 1 (2005): 103–10.

32. Schabas, *The UN International Criminal Tribunals,* 311.

33. *Prosecutor v. Brdjanin and Talić,* ICTY, Corrected Version of the Fourth Amended Indictment, December 10, 2001 [IT-99–36-PT]; *Prosecutor v. Krasjšnik and Plavšić,* ICTY, Consolidated Amended Indictment, March 7, 2002 [IT-00–39 & 40]; *Prosecutor v. Milošević,* ICTY, Second Amended Indictment (Croatia), October 23, 2002 [IT-02–54-PT].

34. *Prosecutor vs. Charles Ghankay Taylor* (SCSL) Pre-Trial Chamber, Second Amended Indictment of May 29, 2007 [SCSL-03–01-PT]; *Prosecutor vs. Alex Tamba Brima, Brima Bazzy Kamara, and Santigie Borbor Kanu* (SCSL), Pre-Trial Chamber, Further Amended Consolidated Indictment of February 18, 2005 [SCSL-2004–16-PT].

35. *Prosecutor v. Vasilević,* ICTY, Appeals Chamber, para. 101.

36. Mettraux, *International Crimes,* 292.

37. Danner and Martinez, "Guilty Associations," 136–37.

38. See Martinez, "Understanding *Mens Rea* in Command Responsibility from Yamashita to Blaskić and Beyond," 638–64; William H. Parks, "Command Responsibility for War Crimes," *Military Law Review* 62 (1973): 2–4. Some states, such as Canada and Germany, have incorporated the principle with respect to crimes against humanity and genocide.

39. Space does not permit an extensive discussion of the issues. For an account of the trial by one of the General's defense attorneys, see A. Frank Reel, *The Case of General Yamashita* (Chicago: University of Chicago Press, 1949). Associate Supreme Court Justice Wiley B. Rutledge wrote a strong dissenting opinion (as did Associate Justice Frank Murphy). Current Associate Justice John Paul Stevens served as a clerk for Rutledge. See Richard Brust, "Setting Precedent in Two Wars: How Justice Stevens Turned 60-Year-Old Dissents into Major Rulings in the War on Terrorism," *ABA Journal* (September 2007), http://www.abajournal.com/magazine/setting_precedent_in_two_wars/.

40. Article 7(3), ICTY Statute; Article 6(3), ICTR Statute.

41. *Prosecutor v. Delalić et al.* (Čelebići case) (ICTY), Appeals Chamber, Judgment of April 8, 2003 [IT-96–21-A], paras. 196–97.

42. *Prosecutor v. Milošević,* Second Amended Indictment (Croatia), October 23, 2002 [IT-02–54-PT].

43. *Prosecutor v. Kordić and Čerkez,* (ICTY) Trial Chamber I, Judgment of February 26, 2001 [IT-95–14/2], paras. 416–24.

44. *Prosecutor v. Delalić et al.* (Čelebići case) (ICTY), Appeals Chamber, Judgment of February 20, 2001 [IT-96–21-A], para. 197.

45. *Prosecutor v. Delalić et al.* (Čelebići case), Appeals Chamber, Judgment of February 29, 2001, paras. 257–65.

46. *Prosecutor v. Delalić et al.* (Čelebići case) (ICTY), Trial Chamber II, Judgment of November 16, 1998 [IT-96–21-T], para. 395. Note that if that formed the standard for the Yamashita trial, the General would have not been convicted.

47. *Prosecutor v. Strugar,* Trial Chamber II, Judgment of January 31, 2005 [IT-01–42].

48. Schabas, *The UN International Tribunals,* 324.

49. Prosecutor v. *Kordić and Čerkez,* Trial Judgment, para. 386.

50. Mettraux, *International Crimes,* 280.

51. Schabas, *The UN International Criminal Tribunals,* 299. Schabas relies on *Prosecutor v. Musema* (ICTR), Trial Chamber I, Judgment of January 27, 2001 [ICTR-96–13-T], para. 115. For the alternative argument with respect to the ICC, see Robert Cryer et al., *An Introduction to International Criminal Law* (Cambridge: Cambridge University Press, 2007), 336, and Cassese, *International Criminal Law,* 192–93.

52. Cassese, *International Criminal Law,* 193.

53. *Prosecutor v. Kristić* (ICTY), Trial Chamber I, Judgment of August 2, 2001 [IT-98–33-T], para. 601.

54. *Prosecutor v. Kordić and Čerkez,* Trial Judgment, para. 388.

55. Cryer et al., *An Introduction to International Criminal Law,* 313.

56. *Prosecutor v. Blaskić* (ICTY), Trial Chamber I, Judgement of March 3, 2000 [IT-95–14-T], para. 42.

57. Some disagreement exists on this point. Some have suggested that, even if the offense has not been committed, giving the order can still be classified as "attempt." See the discussion in Cryer et al., *An Introduction to International Criminal Law,* 314.

58. *Prosecutor v. Blaskić* (ICTY), Trial Chamber I, Judgment of March 3, 2000 [IT-95–14-T], para. 280.

59. *Prosecutor v. Blaskić*, Trial Judgment, para. 339.

60. *Prosecutor v. Kordić and Čerkez*, (ICTY) Appeals Chamber, Judgment of December 17, 2004 [IT-95–14/2-A], para. 32.

61. *Prosecutor v. Ferdinand Nahimana, Jean-Bosco Barayagwiza and Hassan Ngeze*, ICTR, Trial Chamber I, Judgment and Sentence of December 3, 2003 [ICTR-99–52-T], para. 1012.

62. *Prosecutor v. Akayesu*, ICTR, Trial Judgment, para. 557.

63. *Prosecutor v. Ferdinand Nahimana, Jean-Bosco Barayagwiza & Hassan Ngeze*, para. 1012.

64. *Prosecutor v. Akayesu*, ICTR, Trial Judgment, para. 404.

65. *Prosecutor v. Tadić*, Appeal Judgment, para. 229. *Prosecutor v. Kunarac*, Trial Chamber II, Judgment of February 22, 2002 [IT-96–32-T], para. 391.

66. *Prosecutor v. Kristić*, Tiral Judgment, para. 601; *Prosecutor v. Kunarac*, Trial Judgment, para. 301.

67. *Prosecutor v. Kvoška et al.*, ICTY, Appeals Chamber, Judgment of February 28, 2005 [IT-98–30/1-A], para. 90

68. *Prosecutor v. Akayesu*, ICTR, Trial Judgment, para. 479.

69. Schabas, *The UN International Criminal Tribunals*, 308–9.

70. *Prosecutor v. Kvoćka*, ICTY Appeals Chamber, Judgment of February 28, 2005 [IT-98–30/1-A], para. 98.

71. Albin Eser, quoted in Cryer et al., *An Introduction to International Criminal Law*, 331.

72. *Prosecutor v. Kordić and Čerkez*, Trial Judgment, para. 449.

73. ICTY, Articles 7.2 (head of state), 7.3 and 7.4 (superior orders, command responsibility); ICTR, Articles 6.2–6.4; SCSL, Articles 6.2–6.4.

74. *Convention on the Non-Applicability of Statutory Limitations to War Crimes and Crimes against Humanity* of November 26, 1968; entry into force, November 11, 1970; http://www2.ohchr.org/english/law/warcrimes.htm. The difficulty with this convention is that only 52 states have ratified it. The 52 ratifications do not include any of the permanent members of the Security Council, nor for that matter, any of the *original* members of the European Union. Poland and a number of other Eastern European states, particularly those that seceded from the Soviet Union, have acceded. But, then, see also *European Convention on the Non-Applicability of Statutory Limitation to Crimes against Humanity and War Crimes* of January 25, 1974; http://conventions.coe.int/treaty/EN/Treaties/Html/082.htm. All major European states have ratified this instrument.

75. See, Mark Osiel. *Obeying Orders: Atrocities, Military Discipline and the Law of War* (Brunswick, NJ: Transaction, 1999).

76. Cited in, Howard S. Levie, "The Rise and Fall of an Internationally Codified Denial of the Defense of Superior Orders," *Military Law and Law of War Review* 30 (1991): 186.

77. Lassa Oppenheim, *International Law* (5th ed.), ed. Hersh Lauterpacht (London: Longmans, Green 1940–1947). Oppenheim died in 1919. Lauterpacht later served on the International Court of Justice.

78. Article 6 of the Tokyo Charter contains the same provision.

79. Cited in Cryer et al., *An Introduction to International Criminal Law*, 345.

80. See Mark Osiel, *Mass Atrocity, Ordinary Evil and Hannah Arendt: Criminal Consciousness in Argentina's Dirty War* (New Haven: Yale University Press, 2001).

81. Note that "duress and necessity" as a defense for an individual stands as an issue separable from that of "military necessity," discussed later in this chapter.

82. Sander Janssen, "Mental Condition Defences in Supranational Criminal Law," *International Criminal Law Review* 4, no. 1 (2004): 88.

83. Janssen, "Mental Condition Defences," 88.

84. Janssen, "Mental Condition Defences," 89.

85. Janssen, "Mental Condition Defences," 89.

86. *Prosecutor v. Erdemović* (ICTY), Trial Chamber I, Sentencing Judgment of March 5, 1998 [IT-96–22-S].

87. "(1) The act charged was done to avoid an immediate danger both serious and irreparable; (2) there was no adequate means of escape; and (3) the remedy was not disproportionate to the evil." *Trial of Alfried Felix Alwyn Krupp von Bohlen and Halbach and eleven others,* U.S. Military Tribunal, Nuremberg, November 17, 1947–June 30, 1948, Case No. 58, United Nations War Crimes Commission, Law Reports of Trials of War Criminals (London, 1949), Vol. 10, p. 147.

88. *Prosecutor v. Erdemović,* (ICTY) Appeals Chamber, Judgment of October 7, 1997 [IT-96–22-A], para. 75.

89. *Prosecutor v. Erdemović,* Separate and Dissenting Opinion of Judge Antonio Cassese, para. 16.

90. *Prosecutor v. Erdemović,* Separate and Dissenting Opinion of Judge Antonio Cassese, para. 12.

91. For a discussion of these issues, see Valerie Epps, "The Soldier's Obligation to Die When Ordered to Shoot Civilians or Face Death Himself," *New England Law Review* 37, no. 4 (2003): 987–1014.

92. Schabas, *The UN International Tribunals,* 333–34.

93. *Prosecutor v. Delalić et al.,* Appeals Judgment of February 20, 2001, para. 282.

94. *Prosecutor v. Delalić et al.,* Judgment of November 16, 1998, para. 1157.

95. *Prosecutor v. Delalić et al.,* Appeals Judgment of February 20, 2001, para. 582.

96. See Jeraldine Braff, Thomas Arvanites, and Henry J. Steadman, "Detention Patterns of Successful and Unsuccessful Insanity Defendants," *Criminology* 21, no. 3 (2006): 439–48.

97. Schabas, *The UN International Tribunals,* 334.

98. *Prosecutor v. Kvočka et al.,* Trial Chamber I, Judgment of November 2, 2001 [IT-98-30/1-T], para. 748.

99. *Prosecutor v. Plavšić* (ICTY), Trial Chamber II, Sentencing Judgment of February 27, 2003 [IT-00–39 & 40/1-S], para. 72.

100. For example see *Prosecutor v. Kayishema et al.,* Trial Chamber II, Judgment of June 1, 2001 [ICTR-95-1-A], para. 883.

101. Actually, it must be imminent and overwhelming, leaving no moment for deliberation. See discussion in Gerhard Von Glahn and James Larry Taulbee, *Law among Nations: An Introduction* (8th ed., rev. and ed.) (New York: Pearson-Longman, 2006), Chapter 21.

102. *Prosecutor v. Kordić and Čerkez,* Trial Chamber III, Judgment of February 26, 2001 [IT-95–14/2], para. 452.

103. Schabas, *The UN International Tribunals,* 336.

104. *Final Report to the Prosecutor by the Committee Established to Review the NATO Bombing Campaign against the Federal Republic of Yugoslavia,* June 2000, paras. 80–85; http//www.un.org/icty/pressreal/nato061300.htm.

105. David T. Zabecki, *Doenitz: A Defense* (Bennington, VT: Merriam Press, 1997), 51. Under cross-examination, Admiral Chester W. Nimitz testified that from the first day of the war in the Pacific, the United States practiced unrestricted submarine warfare.

106. *Prosecutor v. Kunarac et al.,* Appeals Chamber, Judgment of June 12, 2002 [IT-96–14/2-A], para. 87.

107. *Prosecutor v. Vasilijević* (ICTY), Trial Chamber I, Judgment of November 29, 2002 [IT-97–32-T], para. 15.

108. Kriangsak Kittichaisaree,. *International Criminal Law* (Oxford: Oxford University Press, 2001), 274–75.

109. *Prosecutor v. Kordić et al.,* Appeals Chamber, Judgment of December 17, 2004 [IT-95–14/2-A], para. 54.

110. See, in general, Mark B. Harmon and Fergal Gaynor, "Ordinary Sentences for Extraordinary Crimes," *Journal of International Criminal Justice* 5 (2007): 683–712; Mark A. Drumbl, *Atrocity, Punishment, and International Law* (Cambridge: Cambridge University Press, 2007), Chapter 1; Olaoluwa Olusanya, *Sentencing War Crimes and Crimes against Humanity Under the International Criminal Tribunal for the Former Yugoslavia* (Groningen: Europa Law, 2005).

111. *Prosecutor v. Kambanda,* Trial Chamber I, Judgment and Sentence of September 4, 1998 [ICTR 97–23-S], para. 28.

112. *Prosecutor v. Delalić et al.* (Čelebići case), Trial Chamber II, Judgment of November 16, 1998 [IT-96–21-T], para. 806. Emphasis in the original.

113. *Prosecutor v. Kordić et al.,* Appeals Chamber, Judgment of December 17, 2004 [IT-95–14/2-A], para. 1079.

114. ICTY Statute, Article 24; ICTR Statute, Article 23; Rome Statute, Article 77.

115. *Prosecutor v. Jelisić,* Trial Chamber I, Judgment of December 14, 1999 [IT-95–10-T], paras. 129–34.

116. For a succinct discussion of the issue with respect to the drafting of the ICTY and ICTR Statutes, see Schabas, *The UN International Tribunals,* 546–49. For a longer treatment of the evolution of country attitudes over time, see William A. Schabas, *The Abolition of the Death Penalty in International Law* (3rd ed.) (Cambridge: Cambridge University Press, 2003).

117. *Prosecutor v. Stakić,* Trial Chamber II, Judgment of July 31, 2003 [IT-97–24-T], para. 890.

118. Harmon and Gaynor, "Ordinary Sentences," 685. Drumbl also poses this as the central question of his book, *Atrocity, Punishment and International Law.*

119. Drumbl, *Atrocity, Punishment and International Law,* Chapter 8.

120. "UN Court Cuts Bosnian Serb's Sentence over Srebrenica Massacre," *Agence France Presse* (March 8, 2006) [Lexis-Nexis]. To the dismay of the trial chamber, the prosecutor had reduced the genocide charge to one of persecution.

121. *Prosecutor v. (Momir) Nikolić,* (ICTY) Appeals Chamber, Judgment of March 8, 2006, [IT-02–60/1-A], para. 39. See also paras. 40–52 concerning comparative sentences.

122. "Barbaric" Bosnian Serb Jailed 23 Years for War Crimes," *Deutsche Presse Agentur* (December 18, 2003) [Lexis-Nexis]. *Prosecutor v. (Dragan) Nikolić ("Sušica Camp"),* (ICTY) Appeals Chamber, Sentencing Judgment of February 4, 2005 [IT-94-2-A].

123. *Prosecutor v. Plavšić* (ICTY) Trial Chamber III, Sentencing Judgment of February 27, 2003 [IT-00–39 & 40/1-S].

124. See Nancy Amoury Combs, "Case Comment: *Prosecutor v. Plavšić,*" *American Journal of International Law* 97 (2003): 929–37. Presumably the court considered her age, but Combs points out that her co-defendant was much younger.

125. Combs, "Case Comment: *Plavšić*," 936.

126. Michael P. Scharf, "Trading Justice for Efficiency: Plea-Bargaining and International Tribunals," *Journal of International Criminal Law* 2 (2004): 1072.

127. Scharf, "Trading Justice for Efficiency: Plea-Bargaining and International Tribunals," 1070–81; Nancy Amoury Combs, *Guilty Pleas in International Criminal Law: Constructing a Restorative Justice Approach* (Palo Alto, CA: Stanford University Press, 2006); Mirjan Damaška, "Negotiated Justice in International Courts," *Journal of International Criminal Justice* 2 (2004): 1018–39; and Henri-D. Bosly, "Admission of Guilt before ICC and in Continental Systems," *Journal of International Criminal Law* 2 (2003): 1040–49.

128. Scharf, "Trading Justice," 1071.

CHAPTER 8

Transnational Crimes: Piracy, Slavery, Terrorism, and Torture

Because, in the case of pirates, say, I should like to know whether that profession of theirs has any peculiar glory about it. It sometimes ends in uncommon elevation, indeed; but only at the gallows.

Herman Melville, *Moby Dick*

To reiterate an earlier point, the crimes discussed in this chapter are enforced as part of *national* legal codes, though the prohibitions may stem from either treaty or custom. International law authorizes each state to take appropriate measures to suppress activities that violate the principles. Over time, as states moved to attach individual criminal liability to certain categories of acts, they left implementation in terms of arrest, prosecution, and punishment to national authorities, rather than constructing new international institutions. While these crimes place liability directly on the individual, no *international* court has the authority to prosecute individuals for violations of the relevant principles. Alleged offenders are tried before national courts. Indeed, the examples given in Chapter 1, as well as the discussion of universal jurisdiction, focused on the activities of national authorities and courts.

Terrorism and torture regularly make contemporary headlines as significant problems. Too often, slavery and piracy are thought of as artifacts of the past. Recent events demonstrate that both slavery and piracy continue as significant problems in the contemporary era.[1] With both piracy and slavery, old stereotypes continue. If one did a "man on the street" interview about the prevalence of either, the answers would presume these do not present a major problem today. Even so, public perceptions differ in one respect. Pirates have always evoked a certain aura of romanticism that belies the reality of the practice; slavery has not. One does not find contemporary adventure or humorous movies, novels, or other presentations about slavery. Pirates seem to evoke an in-your-face, devil-may-care defiance of authority that still finds resonance in modern societies. Outside the states that condone it, slavery evokes revulsion.

Our discussion of these crimes shares some common themes. First, because circumstances have changed, each of these areas of concern needs attention to updating definitions and/or clarifying responsibilities within current regimes. In each case, the issues involve characterizing both substantive acts and the scope of jurisdiction. The "politics of definition" continues to play an important part in developing effective regimes. Second, questions of political will (and cooperation) to enforce existing statutes constitute a vital and continuing concern.

Piracy

Many texts and other sources quote Cicero to support the idea that pirates have always stood outside the law.[2] Yet, in the ancient Greek world, pirates were both feared and admired. Eustathius, in his commentaries, asserted that raiding/robbing was an art or craft (*techné*), not at all "blameworthy or shameful."[3] Consider that Ulysses (Odysseus) made his fortune as a sea raider/pirate. When asked how he acquired his wealth, Odysseus replies: "I had nine times led warriors and swift-faring ships against foreign folk, and great spoil had ever fallen to my hands. Of this I would choose what pleased my mind, and much I afterwards obtained by lot. Thus my house straightway grew rich, and thereafter I became one feared and honored among the Cretans."[4]

Entities without navies regularly made alliances with pirates when they needed ships to counter those of a rival in a conflict. Herodotus reports that Psamettichus recruited Ionian and Carian raiders "who had left home in search of rich pickings" to aid him in his rebellion.[5] Herodotus also spends some time in discussing the exploits of Polycrates of Samos (circa 532–522 B.C.), whose ships cruised the Aegean seizing Greek and foreigner ships alike and extorting payment for safe passage. I should note that Cicero's quote stands almost alone and forms a minuscule part of (indeed, almost an aside in) a moral, not a legal, discourse.

Perhaps the best evidence of the Roman attitude comes from a famous operation against pirates carried out by Pompey the Great. Reacting to an increasing nuisance, in 67 B.C., the Senate gave Pompey proconsular power over the Mediterranean and land up to 50 miles from the coast for three years, along with authority to raise troops and money and to build ships as required. The rapidity with which he carried out the task surprised his contemporaries. In 40 days, he cleared the west; in three months he forced the surrender of the major strongholds in Cilicia itself.[6] The end of the operation demonstrates that the Romans perceived the problem as a political one to be solved by war and treaties, not as an operation against criminals and outlaws. Pompey offered generous treaty terms that required resettlement, but not execution or slavery.

In early modern Europe, Sir Frances Drake and Sir Henry Morgan received their honors in part because of their successful careers as pirates (against Spanish, not English ships, of course). Nonetheless, in modern practice, by the mid-17th century, states had agreed that the pirate had become an outlaw.[7] The United

States fought two wars, in 1803 and in 1815, against the "Barbary pirates" who operated from various North African states.[8]

Over the past several years, a large number of high-profile incidents have occurred off the coast of Somalia.[9] During the first three-quarters of 2008, the International Maritime Bureau (IMB) listed 81 incidents.[10] This represented about a third of the total attacks around the world. The largest vessel taken was a 74,000-ton bulk carrier, fully laden with coal.[11] In late September 2008, Somali pirates hijacked the Ukrainian cargo ship *Faina,* with a crew of 20, carrying a cargo that included 33 battle tanks and assorted heavy weaponry.[12] In early November, a gang of Somali pirates captured a Saudi Arabian oil tanker off the coast of Kenya.[13] The vessel carried two million barrels, more than one-fourth of Saudi Arabia's daily production. In April 2009, Somali pirates attempted to seize an American flagged ship the *Maersk Alabama.*[14] Unexpectedly for the pirates, this ended with three of their number dead and one in the custody of U.S. authorities.

South Asian seas also remain notorious as an area where pirate ships prey on merchant vessels that pass through busy choke points in large numbers. The Strait of Malacca, between Indonesia, Malaysia, and Singapore, the shortest sea route connecting the Indian and Pacific oceans, is the location of most such raids. More than 50,000 vessels a year pass through the strait.[15]

Issues of Jurisdiction

Enforcement of the law at sea generates many more complications than enforcement of land based crimes. To understand the problems here, one must note that the third United Nations Convention on the Law of the Sea (UNCLOSS III) divides the sea into several zones where states may exercise varying degrees of control. These consist of:

1. *Internal waters,* which include ports and rivers where states have absolute control;
2. A *territorial sea* of up to 12 nautical miles, where states exercise jurisdiction with respect to ships, aircraft, and the living and natural resources of the sea, with some limited exceptions such as ships in innocent passage (aircraft have no right of "innocent passage");
3. A *contiguous zone* that may extend to a maximum or 24 nautical miles, in which a state may exercise jurisdiction with respect to customs, environment, and other specified activities;
4. An *exclusive economic zone* (EEZ), where the coastal state has the right to manage (and, presumably, the duty to conserve) the living resources of the sea;
5. The *high (or open) seas,* which are free to all on an equal basis.

There are two other divisions, the *continental shelf* and the *deep seabed,* that also are part of the ocean regime, but these have no bearing on the discussion of piracy.

Another set of problems comes into play here. Ships have nationality, determined by the flag they fly. On the high seas, the jurisdiction of the flag state controls. The flag represents the state of registry. Over the years, because of monetary concerns with regard to issues like the cost of meeting safety and manpower regulations (salary), ship owners have sought out states that have "user-friendly" regulations. Known as "flags of convenience," these states have garnered a large proportion of the registered tonnage. Liberia, Panama, Luxembourg (a land-locked state!), and Vanuatu are among the more interesting contemporary flags of convenience. Aristotle Onassis was often characterized as a Greek ship owner, but in reality this meant that he was a Greek who owned ships that were registered in Liberia and Panama. The criticism of flags of convenience comes from the simple expectation that flag states should have the capacity to police their merchant fleets. The great majority do not; nor do they necessarily have the will to prosecute offenders for fear that this would undercut their business. So enforcement requires answers to two questions: where is the ship, and what flag does it fly? The questions can yield some frustrating answers. Consider the case of the *Maersk Dubai.*[16] In Canada, six Taiwanese officers (including the master) of the container ship *Maersk Dubai,* registered in Taiwan, were accused of throwing three stowaways (of Romanian nationality) overboard on the high seas. The case presented Canadian authorities with an interesting problem. Because the crimes occurred on the high seas, Canada had no basis for jurisdiction. Romanian law permits prosecution on the basis of passive personality, but the extradition treaty with Canada specified territoriality or its equivalent. Canada does not recognize Taiwan as an independent state and has no extradition treaty with it. After the court received assurances from Taipei that the six would be vigorously prosecuted, the judge ordered their deportation to Taiwan to stand trial.

The Problem of Definition

Piracy is a word often used indiscriminately to describe various actions. As with many terms, common usage does not necessarily correspond to the legal definition. For example, we speak of "piracy" with regard to the unauthorized copying and sale of video, tapes, and discs. We do need, however, to focus on the rather narrow specific definition of piracy in international law. Moreover, we need to be aware of an important change in the definition of piracy in contemporary international law. The *traditional* definition of piracy, based upon customary law, is found in Oppenheim:

> Piracy in its original and strict meaning, is every unauthorized act of violence committed by a private vessel on the open sea against another vessel with intent to plunder (*animo furandi*).
>
> If a definition is desired which really covers all such acts as are in practice treated as piratical, piracy must be defined as *every unauthorized act of violence against persons or goods committed on the open sea either by a private vessel against another vessel or by the mutinous crew or passengers against their own vessel.*[17]

Piracy and UNCLOS III UNCLOS III, while mandating that each state pass appropriate national legislation to control piracy (Art. 100), actually narrows the definition in terms of both acts and permissible means of enforcement with respect to the customary law.[18] The Convention deals with piracy in Articles 101 through 107 and 110(a). The most important of these is the definition in Article 101:

> Piracy consists of any of the following acts: (a) any illegal act of violence, detention or any act of depredation, *committed for private ends* by the crew or the passengers of a private ship or a private aircraft, and directed: (I) *on the high seas,* against another ship or aircraft, or against persons or property on board such ship or aircraft; (ii) against a ship, aircraft, persons or property in a place *outside the jurisdiction of any State;* (b) any act of voluntary partici- pation in the operation of a ship or of an aircraft with knowledge of facts making it a pirate ship or aircraft; c) any act of inciting or of intentionally facilitating an act described in subparagraph (a) or subparagraph (b) of this article. (Emphasis added)

UNCLOS III made two important changes to the traditional law governing piracy. First, it added the phrase "for private ends" in Article 101. Second, it specifically prohibited private individuals from undertaking actions against sus- pected pirates (Art. 107). While every state may arrest a pirate (105), it may only do so through the agency of military ships or aircraft or other "clearly marked ves- sels in government service" (Art. 107). The phrase "for private ends" has proven troublesome. No official definition exists either in the Geneva instruments or in their predecessors. In considering the phrase, perhaps we may find a clue if we recall the era that produced the draft treaty. The *travaux préparatoires* of a number of meetings indicate that the phrase was meant to exclude acts of unrecognized rebels who restricted their attacks to the state from which they sought indepen- dence.[19] In an era in which terrorism has become a major concern, the question of "private ends" has become a minefield. Third, the UNCLOS definition has an old- fashioned ring in that it limits piracy to "ship-to-ship" encounters. The two-ship requirement means that one of the most notorious incidents in recent years, the takeover of the Achillle Laura by individuals who had booked as passengers, did not technically meet the definition. After this incident, in 1985, concerned states developed the *Convention on the Suppression of Unlawful Acts against the Safety of Maritime Navigation* to close gaps in the UNCLOS provisions.[20]

But UNCLOS III created another problem, as well. As defined, the characteriza- tion of piracy applies only to acts "on the high seas." The question of what types of jurisdiction states have within the Exclusive Economic Zone (EEZ), which can extend 200 nautical miles from the coast, remains a subject of debate. The EEZ embraces about *a third* of the marine environment. *All* of the important seas and gulfs of the world are composed entirely, or mainly, of waters within 200 miles of some coastal state. While clearly the test of "open" or "high" seas does not apply to the EEZ, questions remains concerning the scope of the jurisdiction a coastal state may exercise. Presumptions here tend to fall on the conservative side, though a distinguished scholar and activist recently noted: "The International Tribunal for the Law of the Sea has been careful in its decisions to keep the competence of the coastal state in the 24-mile contiguous zone confined to that area, and to resist open-ended assertions of similar competence beyond that limit."[21] Logically, this would mean that, with the exception of the specific activities listed in UNCLOS III, the regime of the high seas would apply within the EEZ, except with respect to the management of living resources, to the extent not incompatible with other provisions regarding the zone.[22] Such a definition would permit states to actively pursue and arrest pirates in the EEZ without violating the rights of the coastal state. In practice, other EEZ issues such as fishing rights have taken precedence. Clearly, the issue of whether other states may exercise a right of apprehension involves an interesting tension involving the desire of states to extend jurisdiction on the basis of security concerns, the touchiness of many of these states concerning their sovereign rights, and the desire to create a regime of effective enforcement.

Pirate attacks fall into three categories.[23] The great majority of attacks are simply of the hit-and-run variety. These involve little organization and planning. A second category requires considerable planning, possibly by organized syndicates. A third involves the permanent seizure of a ship, as well as its cargo. They become phantom ships. Burnett asserts that seizure at sea is considerably easier than on land because of the area involved. The ship, with a new paint job and identity, can then be reregistered with little fuss under a friendly flag of convenience and used for years.[24]

Many of the problems in enforcement come from the lack of will or capacity on the part of coastal states. Many lack the resources to mount effective patrols. Many simply lack the will to enforce. Somalia stands as a case in point. In March 2008, the UN Security Council finally persuaded the Transitional Federal Government (TFG) in Somalia to accept a resolution that would permit states, with the express prior agreement of the TFG, to enter the country's territorial waters for a period of six months to use "all necessary means" to repress acts of piracy and armed robbery at sea.[25] The product of two years of international mediation, the TFG is the *14th* attempt to create a functioning government in Somalia since the end of Muhammad Siad Barre's rule, in 1991. Unless renewed, that authority will expire prior to the publication of this book.

Burnett notes that "defining the crime [piracy] has become somewhat of a political football."[26] The International Maritime Organization (IMO) has advocated dividing acts of piracy into the geographical and legal categories of maritime zones (piracy on the high seas, defined as "piracy" in accordance with UNCLOS III) and piracy in ports or national waters (internal waters and territorial seas), which would be defined as "armed robbery against ships." This division has an obvious shortcoming. Piracy and armed robbery are not equivalents. Pirate attacks have become increasingly violent, particularly when the pirates wish to take the ship and its cargo. Two incidents, involving the M/V *Cheung Son* and the *Ten-yu,* sparked international outrage. The pirates systematically murdered the 23-member crew of the *Cheung Son;* the crew of the *Ten-yu* was never found. The *Ten-yu* later turned up in an eastern Chinese port bearing a new name, a paint job in appropriate places, and manned by an Indonesian crew. The Chinese government did prosecute those responsible for the massacre aboard the *Cheung Son* but, pleading lack of jurisdiction and evidence, returned those suspected in the *Ten-yu* to Indonesia.[27]

Many ideas have surfaced on how best to deal with the problem. Some have pushed for having shipping companies retain private military companies as security. This has met resistance for a number of reasons, one suspects primarily because of the expense. Others have pushed for a United Nations task force. Questions concerning time, cost, and ultimate usefulness of the effort beyond another talking point abound. At root, the issue still involves strengthening the political will of states.

Slavery

The movie *Amistad* (1997),[28] based upon a real incident, illustrated many of the political and legal issues of the time. Great Britain abolished slavery within its realm in 1807 and then ordered its navy to stop and search vessels suspected of being engaged in the slave trade. At the Congress of Vienna (1815), the British government proposed the creation of economic boycotts against any country refusing to abolish slavery (Sweden had done away with the institution in 1813 and the Netherlands in 1814). The assembled delegations did not receive the suggestion with enthusiasm. Only the British Navy would have been in a position to enforce such a prohibition. No one at Vienna harbored any desire to strengthen Britain's rule of the oceans. Hence, only a solemn condemnation of "the trade in negroes" was passed, with no enforcement detailed.

The British government then concluded a series of bilateral agreements with several countries, providing in each case for reciprocal rights of visit and search by public ships and private vessels flying the flag of the other party. The United States, because of Article I, section 9, of the Constitution, did not forbid the importation of slaves into its territory until 1808. In that year, Congress did prohibit the further importation of slaves. In 1820, it made trade in slaves an act of piracy.[29]

Bassiouni lists 28 relevant international instruments (1815–2000) directly related to the problem and 47 others that have provisions that relate some way to this category.[30] After 1840, a number of multilateral conventions were developed, culminating in the Convention of St. Germain (1919), which provided for the complete abolition of slavery and any trade in slaves on land or by sea. Another treaty, the *Convention to Suppress the Slave Trade and Slavery* (Geneva, 1926, amended by a Protocol in 1953), entered into force in 1927 (for the United States in 1929).[31] That instrument reaffirmed in much more emphatic terms and for many more countries the contents of the St. Germain agreement. It was updated and enlarged through the *Supplementary Convention on the Abolition of Slavery, the Slave Trade, and Institutions and Practices Similar to Slavery* (Geneva, 1956). The latest is the *Protocol to Prevent, Suppress and Punish Trafficking in Persons, Especially Women and Children*.[32] The *Protocol* adds "trafficking in persons" as an offense to the *United Nations Convention against Transnational Orga-nized Crime*.[33] While not all trafficking in persons is associated with the slave trade and some practices do not involve trafficking, the instrument does extend the authority of states to deal with that aspect of slavery.

The problem is that none of these agreements have realistic international enforcement provisions beyond requiring states to pass appropriate domestic legislation guided by the language of the relevant instruments. Article 3 of the protocol on trafficking serves as an example: "Each State Party shall adopt such legislative and other measures as may be necessary to establish as criminal offences the conduct set forth in article 3 of this Protocol, when committed intention-ally." In addition, it specifies that participation as an accomplice and organizing or directing others should be included. The Convention against Transnational Organized Crime states in Article 4:

1. States Parties shall carry out their obligations under this Convention in a manner con-sistent with the principles of sovereign equality and territorial integrity of States and that of non-intervention in the domestic affairs of other States.
2. Nothing in this Convention entitles a State Party to undertake in the territory of another State the exercise of jurisdiction and performance of functions that are reserved exclu-sively for the authorities of that other State by its domestic law.

Article 6.2(c) also contains a "double criminality" provision in that any activity included in the domestic legislation of one state must also constitute a criminal offense in the other.[34] States have a duty to supply the Conference of Parties to the Convention their plans for implementation, but the Conference of Par-ties has the authority only to review and suggest on the basis of information supplied by the States Parties themselves.

Apart from the political will of states, publicity is the chief enforcement mechanism. The role of NGOs (nongovernmental organizations) here is extremely important, Anti-Slavery International has served as one of the more prominent watchdogs and advocates.[35] Still, despite all efforts, traditional forms still persist in some part of the world. A recent case before the Community Court of the Economic Community of West Africa (ECOWAS) involved the status of a 24-year-old woman, Hadijatou Mani, born into slavery in Niger. The Court found Niger in breach of its own laws and international obligations protecting its citizens from slavery. None-theless, *The Economist* has stated that there are still more than 40,000 "inheritance slaves" in Niger alone.[36] Straightforwardly, the basic problem here, as with piracy, stems from the lack of political will across the board to enforce the prohibitions of existing instruments and, as in Niger, of states to enforce their own internal laws.

Because of the weakness of enforcement, in terms of both legal authority and political will, slavery has not disappeared. The extent of current practice is highly debatable. Not unexpectedly, the governments within whose territories where third parties have established indisputable evidence of the practice of slavery, steadfastly deny that such an institution exists. They may, in some instances, point to solemn governmental prohibitions of the practice. But strong evidence suggests that slavery, in many different forms, does continue to exist in many different areas of the world.[37] The contemporary problem extends considerably beyond traditional forms.

Perspectives on slavery tend to come from the practices in the American South prior to the Civil War. Though this particular form, which involved treating people as personal property that could be bought or sold at the will of the owner, may dominate perceptions, even then the reality was considerably more complex. Bassiouni states that "Slave-related practices have increased, and new forms have developed which lack specific normative instruments and enforcement modalities."[38] The definitions used in these conventions may not cover many contemporary practices. As Bales points out, the problem of precise definition constitutes a problem in two important ways.[39] First, without a definition that specifies type (forms), one cannot either estimate the scope of the problem or develop explicit prohibitions against it. Prosecuting a violation requires a clear statement of what has been forbidden. Needless to say, as with most of the crimes discussed in this section, developing a comprehensive definition takes one into a political minefield. Given our previous discussions, consider the problems of trying to develop general definition of slavery given by Bales, "A person held by violence or the threat of violence for economic exploitation,"[40] into a set of enforceable legal norms.

Under the auspices of the Commission on Human Rights, the United Nations established a Working Commission on Slavery in 1975. Recognizing the changing nature of the issues, this group became the Working Commission on Contemporary Forms of Slavery in 1988.[41] The Commission has identified an extensive list of problems mainly focusing on the exploitation of children. Bales notes that the new slavery, with some few exceptions, avoids ownership and the problems associated with it (e.g., cost of purchase, maintenance). The key factors are low cost, high profits, and, often, a short-term relationship. Because there is a glut of potential workers, slaves can be added or discarded as circumstances dictate.[42] Bales divides the problem into three basic categories: chattel slavery, debt bondage, and contract slavery. Others would add forced labor and would specifically single out sexual slavery, though it may result from the conditions that define the three basic forms.[43]

Chattel slavery is the closest to traditional slavery. A person is born into or sold into permanent servitude. While part of the "new" slavery, chattel slavery has long historical roots. The case of Hadijatou Mani of Niger, discussed earlier, forms a case in point. Of the three forms, chattel slavery is the least prevalent. Debt bondage, or bonded labor, is the most widely practiced form of slavery. Although most prevalent in Southeast Asia, knowledgeable observers estimate that 15 to 20 million people fall into this category. Poverty forces many parents to offer themselves or their own children as collateral against a loan. Though promised they will work only until they repay the debt, once in debt they find that the conditions of work and wages paid are such that they never can realistically expect to repay the loan. Inflated interest rates and fresh debts incurred while being fed and housed mean that the debt increases rather than decreases. In many instances, the debt becomes hereditary. Contract slavery involves a similar practice whereby individuals, usually on promise of a good job, are tricked into working conditions where they receive little or no remuneration for work performed.

In every case, the root is extreme poverty. Yet, calls for complete abolition have to face some interesting moral and pragmatic problems. As Bales argues, liberation is a *process,* not a single event. It involves questions of how individuals may support themselves and their capacity to adapt to a situation where they must make fundamental decisions about their daily lives. It also requires that some responsible agency will ensure that they have the skills to survive in the "free" environment.[44] At the very least, it involves raising awareness of the scope of the problem as the basis for more focused efforts to deal with the problems.

Terrorism

The events of September 11, 2001, caught the attention of the world. Nonetheless, prior to September 11, few terrorist incidents had occurred within the territory of the United States. In contrast, the governments of the United Kingdom, Germany, Italy, Canada, and Spain had faced the problems of dealing with well-organized terrorist movements that carried out numerous attacks on national territory. Given the diverse nature and extent of the U.S. presence outside the country, overseas targets always formed more attractive options for reasons of pragmatism and effect. According to State Department statistics, 652 terrorist attacks occurred worldwide in 1984. About half of these (300) were against U.S. targets. The downing of Pan American flight 103, the hijacking of the *Achille Lauro,* and the TWA hijacking incident captured the attention of the U.S. public for a while, as did the horrific bombing of the U.S. Marine barracks in Lebanon, but the concern over terrorism faded as these events receded from the collective memory and other, even more spectacular events occurred. Terrorism seemed more a problem for others. During the 1990s, the number of attacks worldwide as well as the number against U.S. installations actually declined. Up to September 11, the most devastating attack on U.S. soil, the bombing of the Alfred P. Murrah Federal office building in Oklahoma City, had come from within.

Until the rise of groups driven by apocalyptic religious beliefs or ethnic fervor, terrorists tended to choose targets that produced a lot a publicity, not a lot of people dead. The September 11 attacks reflect the evidence of a disturbing trend confirmed by the bombings in Madrid in March 2004 and in London in July 2005. Drawing attention to their cause and manipulating target governments toward some goal formed the essence of what we might term "traditional" terrorist strategy. Whether of the political right or of the political left, these groups had some appreciation of the idea, no matter how perverse the calculus may seem to us, that violence in service to political aims must be calculated and controlled for effect. A leader of the Irish Republican Army once said, "You just don't bloody well kill people just for the sake of killing them."

Groups motivated primarily by ethnic or religious zeal have no such reservations. While publicity remains an important byproduct of their terrorism, contemporary terrorists have had as much interest in punishment as in publicity. The new breed of terrorists see themselves as representatives of a particular constituency. The appeals and the effects of any action are directed to this narrow constituency, rather than to society at large. Justification comes from the reactions of approval from this constituency. The terrorists may or may not have given any systematic thought to how a specific act may influence target governments on particular issues. Any political calculus clearly forms a secondary motive to retribution for transgressions, real or imagined. As a result, those who see themselves as acting on behalf of these constituencies see little need for restraint.[45] Concerns that if a group such as Al Qaeda were to come into possession of working chemical, bacteriological, or nuclear weapons (weapons of mass destruction, or WMD), they would not hesitate to use them are well founded.[46]

Our focus and concern here is the international linkages that exist between groups and the international legal means available to help states combat the threats. These linkages are not new. Terrorist groups have collaborated on intelligence, training, finances, and operation many times in the past. The case of the Japanese Red Army group in 1972 illustrates the transnational connection among various terrorist groups. The unit, composed of Japanese citizens, was allegedly trained in North Korea, then picked up funds in West Germany, had further training in both Syria and Lebanon, acquired its arms and ammunition in Italy, and attacked the Lod Airport in Israel on behalf of the Popular Front for the Liberation of Palestine.

More recently, in December 2002, Spanish marines acting upon a request from the United States intercepted a North Korean freighter, the *So San,* in the Arabian Sea.[47] The marines found 15 Scud missiles hidden under the bags of cement listed as the official cargo on the manifest. Subsequently, Yemeni officials declared that they had purchased the missiles. Reluctantly, the Spanish and U.S. governments permitted the ship to continue on its way.[48] Nothing in international law prevented North Korea from selling missiles to Yemen.[49] No law permitted seizure of the goods on the high seas no matter the suspicions about their eventual end use.

Definitions

A major problem connected with legal control of "terrorism" is the development of an agreed definition of the term and of the acts to be included as part of the definition.[50] Many scholars have argued that the lack of definition means that no general regime criminalizing terrorism exists.[51] Although a number of treaties prohibit specific acts such as hijacking or murder, there is no international crime of "terrorism" in treaty law or in customary law. Part of the problem stems from the fact that changes in meaning and usage have evolved to reflect the political climate of different eras.[52] In the present era, people use many euphemisms designed to deflect attention from the central reality of terrorist acts. Terrorist groups look to "convoluted semantic obfuscations" to deflect the pejorative connotation associated with "terrorism."[53] Observers often resort to the sentiment that one person's criminal is another person's freedom fighter or hero. Within the context of many conflicts, that statement certainly describes the view of participants and supporters. Additionally, agencies tend to develop definitions specific to their own particular mission. Hence, CIA, the Defense Department, and the State Department have definitions that stress the elements relevant to their concerns. Nonetheless, this only makes the development of a definition difficult, not impossible. It may mean that many will be reluctant to apply the definition because of political calculations and considerations of the moment, not that it cannot be done.[54]

The United Nations and Terrorism

In fact, over the past 15 years, the international community has made some progress in this area by focusing upon specific activities rather than attempting to construct a comprehensive definition.[55] In 1996, the General Assembly established the Ad Hoc Committee on Terrorism, charging it with the task of drafting an international convention for the suppression of terrorist bombings and, subsequently, with drafting an international convention for the suppression of acts of nuclear terrorism to supplement related existing international instruments.[56] To date, the committee has successfully produced texts resulting in the adoption (and entry into force) of two treaties: the *International Convention for the Suppression of Terrorist Bombings* (December 15, 1997)[57] and the *International Convention for the Suppression of the Financing of Terrorism* (December 9, 1999).[58] While the avowed goal of the Committee is to develop a comprehensive definition of terrorism, each instrument has rather specific definitions of prohibited activities. For example, Article 2(1) of the Convention for the Suppression of Terrorist Bombings provides that:

1. Any person commits an offence within the meaning of this Convention if that person unlawfully and intentionally delivers, places, discharges or detonates an explosive or other lethal device in, into or against a place of public use, a State or government facility, a public transportation system or an infrastructure facility:
   a. With the intent to cause death or serious bodily injury; or
   b. With the intent to cause extensive destruction of such a place, facility or system, where such destruction results in or is likely to result in major economic loss.

Sections 2 and 3 deal with accomplices and other contingencies. As with the Suppression of Unlawful Act (SUA) treaties, it also contains an extradite-or-try provision, as well as a prohibition on granting political asylum (Art. 11).[59]

In the wake of the September 11, 2001, attacks on the World Trade Center and the Pentagon, the UN Security Council (SC) condemned global terror as a tactic. The SC also recognized a right of self-defense under Article 51 as a response to these attacks.[60] Perhaps the most important initiative came with the adoption of SC Resolution 1373 (September 28, 2001), which established the Counter-Terrorism Committee (CTC). The resolution declares international terrorism a threat to "international peace and security" and imposes a binding obligation on all member states to support efforts to suppress it.[61] The willingness of the SC to take action marks a new direction because prior discussion had been almost entirely within the General Assembly. Resolution 1373 references SC duties and powers under Chapter VII (threats to the peace, breaches of the peace) but does not seek to define terrorism. Rather, it creates a set of uniform obligations for all members, thus pulling within its reach those states that have not signed or ratified the existing conventions and instruments.

The CTC does not operate as a sanctions committee and has specifically rejected that role. It seeks to work with states to upgrade their legislation and capacities to implement the resolution.[62] It also has engaged in dialogue with other international, regional, and subregional organizations as appropriate mechanisms to discuss and identify appropriate regional policies, as well as potentially providing monitoring capacity.[63] The lack of an agreed definition still inhibits more vigorous action. In part, the success of the CTC has come because it has avoided dealing with questions of precise definition. In the long term, the CTC cannot avoid dealing with the issues. When or if the committee moves beyond its current role of encouraging states to build technical capability to the issues of implementation and monitoring, the definitional questions will become of central rather than peripheral importance for its work.

Two further actions deserve mention. On October 8, 2004, the Security Council unanimously approved Resolution 1566 in response to the deaths of 338 individuals in September from an attack on a school in Beslan, in the Russian Federation, and the suicide bombings that destroyed two Russian airliners.[64] After some debate, the final text eliminated all attempts at definition, relying instead on the restatement of actions considered offenses under current international conventions. More important, the Security Council decided to establish a working group apart from the CTC to consider and submit recommendations to the Council on "practical measures" that could be taken against "individuals, groups or entities involved in or associated with terrorist activities." More recently, SC Resolution 1624 (September 14, 2005) targets the *incitement* of terrorist acts. After restating the duties to cooperate in denying safe havens to terrorists, it condemns all acts of terrorism regardless of their motivation and calls on all states to prohibit by law incitement to commit terrorist acts and to take necessary and appropriate measures to prevent such conduct.

A further complicating factor potentially arises from the proviso in Resolution 1624 that "*Stresses* that States must ensure that any measures taken to implement . . . this resolution comply with all of their obligations under international law, in particular international human rights law, refugee law, and humanitarian law." The UN High Commissioner for Human Rights has voiced concern over the possibility that actions to suppress terrorism (however defined) may be used as a justification for abridging or infringing upon human rights. The CTC has resisted the effort to make this a concern, citing the limitations of its mandate, but publicity from interested advocates will certainly keep the questions in the spotlight.

Regional Treaties

In addition to the multilateral treaties open to all for signature and ratification, there are a number of regional instruments (Table 8.1). Despite the impressive number, not all of these have entered into force. Moreover, with respect to effective enforcement provisions, only the European treaties have any real teeth.

Table 8.1   Regional Conventions on Terrorism

Africa

African Union Convention on the Prevention and Combating of Terrorism (Algiers, July 1999) and the *Protocol to the Convention* (Addis Ababa July 2004)

Europe

Council of Europe

    European Convention on the Suppression of Terrorism (Strasbourg, January 1977) and Protocol (Strasbourg, May 2003)

    Council of Europe Convention on the Prevention of Terrorism (Warsaw, May 2005)

    Council of Europe Convention on Laundering, Search, Seizure and Confiscation of the Proceeds from Crime and on the Financing of Terrorism (Warsaw, May 2005)

European Union

    The EU Framework Decision on Terrorism

Commonwealth of Independent States

    Treaty on Cooperation among State Members of the Commonwealth of Independent States in Combating Terrorism (Minsk, June 1999)

League of Arab States

Arab Convention on the Suppression of Terrorism (Cairo, April 1998)

North and South America

Organization of American States Convention to Prevent and Punish Acts of Terrorism Taking the Form of Crimes against Persons and Related Extortion That Are of International Significance (Washington, DC, February 1971)

Inter-American Convention against Terrorism (Bridgetown, June 2002)

Organization of the Islamic Conference

Convention of the Organization of the Islamic Conference on Combating International Terrorism (Ouagadougou, July 1999)

South Asia

SAARC Regional Convention on Suppression of Terrorism (Kathmandu, November 1987)

Additional Protocol to the Convention (Islamabad, January 2004) (not yet in force)

The ASEAN Convention on Counter Terrorism (Cebu, Philippines, January 13, 2007) (not yet in force)

Retrospect and Prospect

Virtually all commentators on the phenomenon of international terrorism have agreed that no real progress in combating hijacking, hostage taking, and other terrorist activities can be expected until three basic concepts have been incorporated in global conventions and are then implemented without exception. First, the states of the world must agree not to permit their territories to be used as places of asylum by terrorists, regardless of the nationality of the latter. Second, extradition of individuals charged with terrorist offenses must be granted on submission of evidence of presumed guilt. Third, if no extradition is granted, the receiving (or host) state must vigorously prosecute the alleged terrorists. These provisions depend upon a clearly defined characterization of terrorist as criminals. While some progress has occurred, the international community still has far to go in turning these requirements into effective operating principles.

Torture

A strong case can be made that prior to World War II, torture during wartime directed against "protected persons" (see Chapter 6) constituted a war crime. Since World War II, the Geneva Conventions have classified torture during wartime as a "grave breach."[65] Interestingly, in the post–World War II era, as questions concerning human rights became matters of international concern, so seemingly as a contradictory phenomenon did the use of torture by governments against their own citizens. In 1974, Amnesty International listed 61 states in which barbarous tortures occurred on a regular basis.[66] The Pinochet case that opens this book grew out of the practices of his government in the aftermath of the coup that installed him as head of state in Chile. The activities of NGOs such as Amnesty kept the issues front and center. The advocacy eventually produced *The United Nations Convention against Torture and Other Cruel, Inhuman or Degrading Treatment or Punishment.*[67] The United States has ratified the convention, but with several reservations. I shall return to this in the discussion to follow. Two other regional conventions, the *European Convention for the Prevention of Torture and Inhuman or Degrading Treatment or Punishment*[68] and the *Inter-American Convention to Prevent and Punish Torture,*[69] have also entered into force. Many human rights scholars and lawyers have claimed that the ban on torture has become a norm of *jus cogens* and hence is binding on states whether or not they have signed any of the relevant conventions.[70]

Definition

Unlike the terrorism conventions, the UN Torture Convention does have an explicit definition of torture. Article 1.1 defines torture as:

> Any act by which severe pain or suffering, whether physical or mental, is intentionally inflicted on a person for such purposes as obtaining from him

or a third person information or a confession, punishing him for an act he or a third person has committed or is suspected of having committed, or intimidating or coercing him or a third person, or for any reason based on discrimination of any kind, when such pain or suffering is inflicted by or at the instigation of or with the consent or acquiescence of a public official or other person acting in an official capacity. It does not include pain or suffering arising only from, inherent in or incidental to lawful sanctions.

Article 1.2 also provides that states may enact a broader prohibition if they choose to do so. In addition, states have obligations to enact appropriate domestic criminal legislation, to prevent, punish or extradite individuals accused of such activities in territories under their control, and to provide effective remedies for victims of torture.

From the beginning, the definition proved divisive. Some states argued that the concept of torture should be legally distinct from that of "cruel, inhuman or degrading treatment or punishment." They argued that punishment forms part of all criminal justice regimes and that a distinction needed to be made between justifiable forms and those that would fall outside the standard.[71] Additional questions revolved around standards for terms such as "severe" and "mental," the extent to which omissions might engage liability (see Chapter 7), and whether the Convention should specifically list "purposes."[72] The title of the Convention speaks for itself in terms of the outcome of the first of these controversies. Obviously, the broader characterization carried the day. Parameters of the others were left to courts to work out in practice.

The European Court of Human Rights (ECHR) had occasion to visit the issue of appropriate criteria to determine practices that constitute torture in a case brought by Ireland against the United Kingdom. The issues revolved around interrogation methods used by the British in Northern Ireland. These became known as the "five techniques": wall-standing, hooding, subjection to noise, deprivation of sleep, deprivation of food, and deprivation of drink. The court decided that

> Although the five techniques, as applied in combination, undoubtedly amounted to inhuman and degrading treatment, although their object was the extraction of confessions, the naming of others and/or information and although they were used systematically, they did not occasion suffering of the particular intensity and cruelty implied by the word torture as so understood.[73]

Not torture perhaps, but still the court concluded "that recourse to the five techniques amounted to a practice of inhuman and degrading treatment."[74] Similarly, in the debate over the detainees at Guantanamo Bay, administration lawyers have argued that while the Torture Convention bans both torture and "cruel, inhuman, or degrading treatment," the enabling legislating criminalizes only torture.[75]

Enforcement Mechanisms

Actually, the definition is less a problem than the enforcement mechanisms, or lack thereof, set up by the Convention. The Convention follows the model set up for many other human rights instruments. The question, as with other human rights treaties that share similar structures, is the extent to which the mechanisms have any real impact on the conduct of states. The system consists of four elements: reporting, investigation, communication, and individual petitions. The Convention sets up a Committee against Torture to monitor relevant activities. The Committee, elected by States Parties, has 10 members, presumably acting in their individual capacities, who serve four-year terms.[76] In recognition of the proliferation of such committees, Article 17.2 provides that, in nominating members, States Parties should consider nominating individuals who already serve on the Human Rights Committee (HRC).[77]

Every four years, States Parties have to submit a report on their efforts to "give effect to" the convention (Art. 19). If the Committee has an issue with the report, it may designate one or more member to make a confidential inquiry and, with the *consent of the state,* to make a visit to the territory of the state to investigate. If permitted to visit, the investigator(s) make a report that the Committee considers and transmits confidentially to the state for discussion. The only possible public exposure is through inclusion of a summary in the Committee's annual report to the Secretary-General of the United Nations. The emphasis is upon engaging states in a constructive dialogue. Overdue and incomplete or vague reports continue as problems. The Committee has no mechanism other than publicity in the annual report to compel states to submit reports or comply. It cannot, for example, request the Security Council to investigate with the possibility of making a finding that violations constitute a threat to international peace and security. Moreover, States Parties may opt out of the reporting procedure at accession or ratification (Art. 28.1).

Cases may come to the Committee from state-to-state complaints or by individual petition. Under Article 22, individuals may submit petitions to the Committee. Even here, the Committee has no power to make binding decisions or to enforce its findings. In its most recent report, the Committee dealt with 14 periodic reports and 11 individual petitions. It also noted that 227 reports were overdue.[78]

I shall use the report of Norway to illustrate the procedure with respect to examination of state reports.[79] The Committee begins each discussion with a list of what it sees as positive steps since the last report. It then addresses what it sees as problems. In almost every case, Norway included, the first recommendation deals with incorporating the elements of the convention into domestic law in more explicit fashion. In Norway's case, the Committee recommended that:

> The State party should further consider incorporating the Convention into domestic law in order to allow persons to invoke the Convention directly in the courts, to give prominence to the Convention and to raise awareness of the provisions of the Convention among members of the judiciary and the public at large.

The State Party should further consider the possible use of wording similar to that used in the Convention so as to ensure that the definition of torture comprises all types of discrimination as possible motives.[80]

The Committee then expressed concern over reports of excessive use of force by police, the practice of handing over to local authorities all prisoners taken by Norwegian forces in Afghanistan (potential violation of the non-refoulement provision, that is, nonreturn if the individual might be tortured), conditions of pre-trial detention for those accused of immigration violations, and failure to undertake prompt and impartial investigations into allegations of unnecessary use of force, particularly where the allegations involved assertions of discriminatory treatment.[81] A concern with possible discriminatory practices runs through the report.

All but one of the individual petitions concerned cases of non-refoulement (Art. 3). The origins of the petitions are interesting: Sweden (4), Canada (3), Switzerland (2), France (1), and Tunisia (1). The Committee dismissed three of the petitions:

> [T]he Committee declared inadmissible complaints Nos. 264/2005 (A.B.A.O. v. France), 304/2006 (L.Z.B. et al. v. Canada) and 308/2006 (K.A. v. Sweden). The three complaints concerned claims under article 3 of the Convention. The Committee declared them inadmissible, respectively, for incompatibility with the provisions of article 3 of the Convention, for non-exhaustion of domestic remedies and for being manifestly unfounded.[82]

The Tunisian case did not involve the question of return. It concerned a national involved in human rights activities in Tunisia who claimed that the Tunisian police had inflicted severe pain and suffering. The Committee found that the allegations were corroborated by medical certificates and other evidentiary materials. Despite abundant evidence that public officials had perpetrated the acts in question, the State Party had failed to carry out a prompt and impartial investigation. The Committee considered that the acts to which the complainant was subjected amounted to acts of torture within the meaning of Article 1 of the Convention. It also considered that a delay of more than seven years before an investigation was initiated into allegations of torture was unreasonably long and did not meet the requirements of Article 12 of the Convention. It finally concluded that Tunisia had not fulfilled its obligations under Articles 13 and 14 of the Convention.[83]

In other cases, the Committee found Canada in violation of its obligations for deporting a Sikh back to India despite the Committee's request for interim measures while it investigated the claim.[84] In *Iya v. Switzerland,* the Committee found that the complainant's case had not been examined on the merits by the State Party's competent authorities because it had been rejected on procedural grounds.[85] It held that return of Iya to the Democratic Republic of the Congo would constitute a breach of his rights under Article 3 of the Convention. In all of the other cases, the Committee found no basis for the claims.[86]

The Torture Debate

Questions relating to torture have come to the forefront since the 2001 attacks on the World Trade Center in New York City and the Pentagon in Alexandria, Virginia, and the response by the United States. The treatment of prisoners held at Guantanamo Bay and elsewhere has generated an enormous debate over general treatment, methods of interrogation, and justifications. Feelings have run high on both sides of the debate. For human rights advocates, the prohibition against torture stands as an absolute nonderogable duty (one that cannot be suspended or deviated from under any circumstances) and personal right. Others argue that extraordinary circumstances require extraordinary measures. Within the United States, the debate also raises Constitutional issues. Here we should note the difference in response to the incidents at Abu Ghraib, for which individuals were prosecuted, and the response to the status and treatment of prisoners at Guantanamo. The first was universally seen as gratuitous, unnecessary abuse, whereas the other was seen by many as justifiable. Apart from Abu Ghraib, questions still exist with respect to the appropriate standards by which to determine the difference between "harsh" treatment and torture.[87]

Note that, absent a threat to vital interests, it is very easy to be against torture in the abstract.[88] Real life can pose daunting dilemmas. Indeed, often the problem is now presented in the form of "the ticking bomb" dilemma.[89] Suppose the police have detained a terrorist who has planted a deadly device, perhaps a "dirty bomb," someplace in a city.[90] The terrorist has made a number of demands, including a getaway plane, the release of all inmates on death row, and a substantial monetary sum. Does the situation permit the use of extraordinary means in the form of physical torture to obtain information that might avert a tragedy that would cost a great number of innocent lives? Does an exceptional situation justify the use of methods that would ordinarily violate fundamental standards of human decency? Many have pointed out that the "ticking bomb" applies to many different situations. U.S. military and intelligence personnel face such questions on a daily basis in Iraq and Afghanistan, as have Israeli officials for many years.[91] While the space allotted here does not permit more than a cursory examination and summary of the main moral and legal arguments, I shall try to provide a fair summary of the opposing arguments.

Arguments For Keep in mind that the scenario involves extraordinary circumstances where presumably many lives could be at stake. This is not a brief to excuse the actions of dictators and tyrants who routinely resort to torture to intimidate and inhibit political opposition. No one, unless a sadist, makes the case for torture otherwise. I have chosen not to focus on the "Bybee" memo because the arguments there involved questions of technical constitutional interpretation justifying why certain practices were permissible at Guantanamo as a derogation of U.S. obligations as much as arguments related to the permissibility of torture in general.[92] Briefly, then, the rationale for torture rests upon one or more of the following premises:

1. Torture is a question of degree, not defined by an abstract legal principle.
2. Killing is permissible in a justified war. Torture is less harmful to the victim than being killed.[93]
3. Threats to large numbers of innocent lives outweigh legal principles, either those found in the U.S. Constitution or those enshrined in international conventions and practices. Simply, the right of a single individual not to be tortured cannot override the rights of many innocents not to be murdered or maimed.

Arguments Against Arguments for torture rely more on pragmatic dilemmas than universal principles. In contrast, the arguments against torture rest upon the fundamental premises that:

1. Freedom from torture, regardless of circumstance, is an absolute human right. No one, no matter the circumstances, should be subjected to *any* procedure that could be considered torture.
2. In the abstract, numbers matter, but what are the probabilities of producing usable information in an appropriate time frame? Note that the probability argument has another aspect: can you torture anyone that you *think* may have relevant information? Where do you draw the line?
3. Torture degrades and dehumanizes the persons performing the acts.[94]
4. Justifying torture in exceptional circumstances is a "slippery slope." Once admissible in practice, it will expand in scope because of the institutions and practices needed to sustain it.

The Alien Tort Claims Act (United States)

Considering the debate over Guantanamo, the following material should provide an interesting set of counterpoints. The U.S. Congress adopted the Alien Tort Claims Act (ATCA) in 1789 as part of the original Judiciary Act. In its original form, the act made no assertion about legal rights; it simply provided that "[t]he district courts shall have original jurisdiction of *any civil action by an alien for a tort* only, committed in violation of the law of nations or a treaty of the United States."[95] For almost two centuries, the statute remained unnoticed, supporting jurisdiction in only two cases during that time.[96] Then, in 1978, Joel Filartiga, a Paraguayan dissident living in New York City filed suit against Américo Peña-Irala, the inspector general of police in Asunción, alleging that Peña-Irala had abducted and tortured to death Filartiga's son. Filartiga had attempted to commence a criminal action against Peña-Irala in Paraguay but had in turn been arrested. He and his daughter, Dolly, then emigrated to the United States. Peña-Irala entered the United States on a visitor's visa in 1978. When Dolly Filartiga learned of his presence, she informed the Immigration and Naturalization Service. INS agents arrested Peña-Irala and a female companion. During his detention, the Filartigas had Peña-Irala served with a civil complaint alleging his participation in the torture and death. They asked for $10 million in compensatory and punitive damages.

Peña-Irala moved to dismiss the complaint on the ground that the courts lacked subject matter jurisdiction. Peña-Irala's lawyer also asked for dismissal on the ground of *forum non conveniens*,[97] in particular that Paraguayan law provided adequate remedies for the wrong alleged. The Filartigas submitted affidavits by noted legal scholars who unanimously agreed that international law absolutely prohibited the use of torture. On May 15, 1979, the U.S. District Court in New York dismissed the complaint on jurisdictional grounds. Shortly afterward, Peña-Irala and his companion returned to Paraguay. The plaintiffs appealed, and on June 30, 1980, the Circuit Court of Appeals decided in their favor, reversed the decision of the district court, and remanded the case. The Court of Appeals relied heavily on a most interesting and heavily documented Memorandum, filed at the court's request by the U.S. Department of Justice jointly with the Department of State.[98] The Memorandum, asserting that official torture violated international law, centered on the interpretation of the ATCA. The Memorandum pointed out that the view that a state's treatment of its own citizens was beyond the purview of international law was once widely held. However, in consequence of changing standards of behavior in the community of nations, an international law of human rights had begun to develop. This did not mean that all such rights could be judicially enforced. But one thing became clear: the assumption that a state had no obligation to respect the human rights of its citizens was incorrect. Through both treaties and the continuing development of customary law, states had accepted as law a duty to observe basic human rights, and that customary law had been upheld in decisions of the International Court of Justice.[99]

The court argued that among the fundamental human rights protected by every relevant multilateral treaty was freedom from torture and that customary international law condemned torture, as well. Every state accused of torture has denied the accusation, and none has tried to justify torture. Hence, it could be asserted correctly that official torture was a tort "in violation of the law of nations." In January 1984, the same district court (ED N.Y.) awarded the plaintiffs $10 million in compensatory and punitive damages for further proceedings.[100] We should note that the court in *Filartiga* had slightly modified the Act of State Doctrine enunciated in the 1964 *Sabbatino* case. The dicta in *Sabbatino* prohibited U.S. courts from examining the actions of foreign governments upon their own soil. In *Filartiga*, the court had held that the Act of State Doctrine does not extend to justify torture under the color of law.

The success of the suit resulted in a number of other cases. As the result of increasing international concern with human rights issues litigants have begun to seek redress more frequently under the ATCA.[101] *Filartiga v. Peña-Irala* held that deliberate torture perpetrated under the color of official authority violates universally accepted norms of international human rights law *and* that such a violation of international law constituted a violation of the domestic law of the United States. In *Kadić v. Karadžić*,[102] the court held that the ATCA reaches to the conduct of private parties provided that their conduct is undertaken under the aegis of state authority or violates a norm of international law that is recognized as governing the conduct of private parties. Passage of the Torture Victim Protection Act (TVPA), in 1991, specifically permitted suit in U.S. courts against individuals who, acting in an official capacity for any foreign nation, committed torture and/or extrajudicial killing.[103]

Needless to say, the expansion in litigation has caused a great deal of controversy. An interesting recent development has been the effort to use the ATCA to sue transnational corporations for violations of international law in countries outside the United States.[104] Human rights advocates argue that the ATCA could be a valuable and potent tool to increase corporate accountability.[105] Critics maintain that judges have intruded into issues and subject matter that interfere with the management of foreign affairs by the executive and the legislative authority of Congress. What makes the argument interesting is that almost no information exists concerning legislative intent. Why did Congress find it necessary to pass the Alien Tort Statute of 1789? We have no extant legislative findings to illuminate the problems lawmakers sought to address.

Notes

1. John S. Burnett, "Pirates of the 21st Century; Today's Swashbucklers Wield High-Powered Weapons and Demand Millions in Ransom," *Los Angeles Times,* October 4, 2008, A21; "Slavery in West Africa: A Continuing Abomination," *The Economist,* November 1, 2008, 57. David Batstone, *Not for Sale: The Return of the Global Slave Trade—and How We Can Fight It* (New York: Harper One, 2007).

2. For a well-documented journalistic account of recent piracy activity, see John S. Burnett, *Dangerous Waters: Modern Piracy on the High Seas* (New York: Plume, 2002); Cicero, *De Officiis* 3.29. Gregory R. Crane, (ed.) *The Perseus Project,* http://www.per seus.tufts.edu, September 1999. One should not interpret Plutarch's reference to "the common enemies of the world" as any more than hyperbole, much as one should also discount Cicero's single use of *communis hostis omnium* in a discussion of moral duties because neither form any part of the justification for any Roman action against "pirates."

3. Eustathius (Archbishop of Thessalonica) used the word *technê,* an art, craft, or cunning, sometimes meant in a derogatory sense, to characterize the function of raids in early Hellenic culture. Cited in K. S. Pritchett, *The Greek State at War* (5 vols.) (Berkeley and Los Angeles: University of California Press, 1977–1991), 5:316. See also Morris I. Finley, *The World of Odysseus* (2nd rev. ed.) (Baltimore: Pelican Books, 1978), 48–49, 63–64.

4. *Odyssey* 14.230.

5. Herodotus, *The Histories,* trans. R. Waterfield (Oxford: Oxford University Press, 1998), 2.152.4.

6. Plutarch (trans. John Dryden), *Pompey* §28.

7. See Janet Thomson, *Mercenaries, Pirates, and Sovereigns: State-Building and Extraterritorial Violence in Early Modern Europe* (Princeton: Princeton University Press, 1996).

8. Frederick C. Leiner, *The End of Barbary Terror: America's 1815 War against the Pirates of North Africa* (Oxford: Oxford University Press, 2006)—from which the line in the Marine Hymn "to the shores of Tripoli" derives.

9. Andre de Nesnera, "Pirates Step up Attacks on Vessels in Gulf of Aden, off Somalia Coast," newsVOA.com, November 4, 2008, http://www.defenddemocracy.org/index.php?option=com_content&task=view&id=11783580&Itemid=0.

10. The International Maritime Organization, an intergovernmental body unlike the IMB, also keeps totals. See http://www.imo.org/Circulars/mainframe.asp?topic_id=334.

11. De Nesnera, "Pirates Step up Attacks."

12. John S. Burnett, "Pirates of the 21st Century; Today's Swashbucklers Wield High-Powered Weapons and Demand Millions in Ransom," *Los Angeles Times,* October 4, 2008, A21.

13. "Pirates Capture Saudi Oil anker," *BBC News,* November 18, 2008.

14. Mark Mazetti and Sharon Otterman, "U.S. Captain Is Hostage of Pirates; Navy Ship Arrives," *New York Times* (April 8, 2009), http://www.nytimes.com/2009/04/09/world/africa/09pirates.html; Richard D. McFadden and Scott Shane, "In Rescue of Captain, Navy Kills 3 Pirates," *New York Times* (August 13, 2009), http://www.nytimes.com/2009/04/13/world/africa/13pirates.

15. "South Asian Pirates Back on the Rampage"; http://english.chosun.com/w21data/html/news/200503/200503170020.html.

16. Graeme Hamilton; "Death on the High Seas," *Ottawa Citizen,* March 7, 1997, A1; "Taiwan to Hear Case of Romanian Stowaways," *Toronto Star,* March 19, 1997, A13. Compare this incident with the case of the M. C. Ruby; http://www.enm.justice.fr/ihej/comptes_rendus_de_colloques_mcruby.htm.

17. Emphasis in original. Lassa Oppenheim, *International Law: A Treatise* (5th ed.) (2 vols.) (ed. Hersh Lauerpacht) (London and New York: Longmans Green, 1935–1937), 1:607. See Albert P. Rubin, *Piracy, Paramountcy and Protectorates* (Kuala Lumpur: Penerbit Universiti Malaya, 1974) and his *The Law of Piracy* (Boston: Bridge Street Books, 1988), the most comprehensive study available; see also Marjorie M. Whiteman, *Digest of International Law* (11 vols.) (Washington, DC: U.S. Department of State, 1963–1978), 4:648; For historical background, J. E. G. De Montmorency, "The Barbary States in International Law," *Transactions of the Grotius Society* (1919): 87.

18. *Convention of the Law of the Sea* (UNCLOS III), Signed at Montego Bay, Jamaica, December 10, 1982 (entry into force November 16, 1994).

19. Malvina Halberstam, "Terrorism on the High Seas: The Achille Lauro, Piracy and the IMO Convention on Maritime Safety," *American Journal of International Law* 82 (1988): 277.

20. *Convention for the Suppression of Unlawful Acts against the Safety of Maritime Navigation,* of March 10, 1988; entry into force March 1, 1992; Amendments to the *Convention for the Suppression of Unlawful Acts* (SUA) *against the Safety of Maritime Navigation,* 1988, and its related Protocol were adopted by the Diplomatic Conference on the Revision of the SUA Treaties, held October 10–14, 2005. The amendments were adopted in the form of Protocols to the SUA treaties.

21. Bernard H. Oxman, "The Territorial Temptation: A Siren Song at Sea," *American Journal of International Law* 100, no. 4 (2006): 837.

22. Oxman, "The Territorial Temptation," 837.

23. Caroline Liss, "Private Military and Security Companies in the Fight against Piracy in Southeast Asia," in Graham Gerard Ong-Webb (ed.), *Piracy, Maritime Terrorism and Securing the Malacca Straits* (Singapore: Institute of Southeast Asian Studies, 2006), 105–6.

24. Burnett, *Dangerous Waters,* 224.

25. *UN SCOR,* S/RES/1806 (March 20, 2008).

26. Burnett, *Dangerous Waters,* 158.

27. Burnett, *Dangerous Waters,* 225.

28. For an exploration of the issues here, see http://www.law.umkc.edu/faculty/proj ects/ftrials/amistad/AMISTD.HTM; see also Hugh Thomas, *The Slave Trade: The History of the Atlantic Slave Trade, 1140–1870* (New York: Simon and Schuster, 1999); Howard Jones, *Mutiny on the Amistad: The Saga of a Slave Revolt and Its Impact on American Abolition, Law, and Diplomacy* (Oxford: Oxford University Press, 1997).

29. See Ahmed Sheikh, *International Law and National Behavior* (New York: Wiley, 1974), 18.

30. M. Cherif Bassiouni, *Introduction to International Criminal Law* (Ardsley, NY: Transnational, 2003), 145. List of Conventions, 242–45.

31. See Oppenheim, *International Law,* 1:620; Higgins-Colombos, 310

32. UN GAOR, Doc. A/Res/55/25 (November 15, 2000). Entered into force, December 25, 2003; currently 124 States Parties.

33. UN GAOR, Doc. A/Res/55 (November 15, 2000).

34. Article 16.1 on extradition contains a second "double criminality" provision.

35. See Anti-Slavery International, http://www.antislavery.org/.

36. "Slavery in West Africa: A Continuing Abomination," 57.

37. Kevin Bales, *Disposable People: New Slavery in the Global Economy* (rev. ed.) (Berkeley: University of California Press, 2004); E. Benjamin Skinner, *A Crime So Monstrous: Face-to-Face with Modern-Day Slavery* (New York: Free Press, 2008). Batstone, *Not for Sale.*

38. Bassiouni, *An Introduction to International Criminal Law,* 146.

39. For a description of the problem, see Bales, *Disposable People,* 8–9.

40. Bales, *Disposable People,* Chapter 1, 280, n. 4.

41. "Fact Sheet #14: Contemporary Forms of Slavery," Office of the High Commissioner for Human Rights (June 1991); http://www.unhchr.ch/html/menu6/2/fs14.htm.

42. Bales, *Disposable People,* 15–16.

43. iAbolish: American Anti-Slavery Group, "Types of Slavery"; http://www.iabolish. org/slavery_today/primer/types.html.

44. Bales, *Disposable People,* 252–58.

45. See Bruce Hoffman, *Inside Terrorism* (New York: Columbia University Press, 1999), for the best brief introduction to issues and groups. For the list of groups currently considered terrorist organizations by the United States, see U.S. State Department, "Counter-terrorism"; http://www.state.gov/s/ct/. A separate list also includes states identified as supporting terrorism.

46. See Charles D. Ferguson and William C. Potter, *The Four Faces of Nuclear Terrorism* (Monterrey, CA: Center for Non-Proliferation Studies, 2004); Graham T. Allison, *Nuclear Terrorism: The Ultimate Preventable Catastrophe* (New York: Macmillan, 2004); for links and short discussions of chemical and biological weapons, see the Web site of the Federation of American Scientists, http://www.fas.org/main/content.jsp?formAction=325&projectId=4, and the Monterrey Institute of International Studies site, "Chemical and Biological Weapons Resource Page," http://cns.miis.edu/research/cbw/.

47. Thom Shanker, "Threats and Responses: Arms Smuggling; Scud Missiles Found on Ship of North Korea," *New York Times,* December 11, 2002, A1.

48. David E. Sanger and Thom Shanker, "Threats and Responses: War Materiel; Reluctant U.S. Gives Assent for Missiles to Go to Yemen," *New York Times,* December 12, 2002, A1.

49. Neither state was bound by the voluntary guidelines of the Missile Technology Control Regime. For an extended analysis of the issues here, see Michael Byers, "Policing the High Seas: The Proliferation Security Initiative," *American Journal of International Law* 98 (2004): 526.

50. Note that during the negotiations on the Statute of the International Criminal Court, many states supported adding terrorism to the list of crimes over which the court would have jurisdiction. This proposal was not adopted. However, the Statute provides for a review conference to be held seven years after the entry into force of the Statute. The proposed review will consider (among other things) an extension of the court's jurisdiction to include terrorism. For an extended commentary on these issues, see Ben Saul, *Defining Terrorism in International Law* (Oxford: Oxford University Press, 2006).

51. See, for example, Rosalyn Higgins, "The General International Law of Terrorism," in Rosalyn Higgins and Maurice Floury (eds.), *Terrorism and International Law* (London: Routledge, 1997), 14–19; Ben Saul, *Defining Terrorism in International Law* (Oxford: Oxford University Press, 2006); in support of the case for terrorism as an international crime, see Antonio Cassese, "Terrorism as an International Crime," in Andrea Bianchi (ed.), *Enforcing International Law Norms against Terrorism* (Oxford: Hart, 2004), 213–25.

52. Hoffman, *Inside Terrorism*, 28.

53. Hoffman, *Inside Terrorism*, 29.

54. See the interesting discussion by Robert Kolb, "The Exercise of Criminal Jurisdiction over International Terrorists," in Bianchi, *Enforcing International Law Norms*, 227–81.

55. The earliest international effort to create treaty law to combat terrorism was the abortive League of Nations *Convention for the Prevention and Punishment of Terrorism* (1937), drafted in consequence of the assassination of King Alexander of Yugoslavia. That instrument, to date, has received only one ratification. Obviously, it never entered into force.

56. See the 2005 report of the Chair at http://www.unis.unvienna.org/unis/pressrels/2005/13084.html.

57. Entered into force, May 2001; ratified by the United States, September 1999. Text at http://www.unodc.org/unodc/en/terrorism_convention_terrorist_bombing.html. The Senate ratified with a series of Reservations, Understandings and Conditions. First it opted out of Article 20(1), which would refer disputes over the Convention to the ICJ. Second, it narrowed the definition of armed conflict in Article 19(2) to exclude internal disturbances such as riots or other sporadic acts of violence. Third, it equated the phrase "international humanitarian law" with the phrase "law of war." Fourth, it defined coverage to exclude the activities of military forces of the state, those who direct or organize them, and civilians acting in support of, and under the command of, these forces. Fifth, it prohibited extradition to the International Criminal Court. Sixth, it affirmed the supremacy of the U.S. Constitution;. http://www.amicc.org/docs/Terrorbomb ings98.pdf.

58. Entered into force, April 2002. Text at http://untreaty.un.org/English/Terrorism/Conv12.pdf.

59. There are nine current SUA treaties. The Protocol would amend all of them:

1. *Convention for the Suppression of Unlawful Seizure of Aircraft*, done at The Hague on December 16, 1970
2. *Convention for the Suppression of Unlawful Acts against the Safety of Civil Aviation*, done at Montreal on September 23, 1971
3. *Convention on the Prevention and Punishment of Crimes against Internationally Protected Persons, including Diplomatic Agents*, adopted by the General Assembly of the United Nations on December 14, 1973
4. *International Convention against the Taking of Hostages*, adopted by the General Assembly of the United Nations on 17 December 1979

5. *Convention on the Physical Protection of Nuclear Material,* done at Vienna on October 26, 1979
6. *Protocol for the Suppression of Unlawful Acts of Violence at Airports Serving International Civil Aviation,* supplementary to the Convention for the Suppression of Unlawful Acts against the Safety of Civil Aviation, done at Montreal on February 24, 1988
7. *Protocol for the Suppression of Unlawful Acts against the Safety of Fixed Platforms Located on the Continental Shelf,* done at Rome on March 10, 1988
8. *International Convention for the Suppression of Terrorist Bombings,* adopted by the General Assembly of the United Nations on December 15, 1997
9. *International Convention for the Suppression of the Financing of Terrorism,* adopted by the General Assembly of the United Nations on December 9, 1999

60. See Nicholas Rostow, "Before and After: The Changed U.N. Response to Terrorism since September 11th," *Cornell International Law J ournal* 35 (2002): 475–91.

61. For an analysis, see Eric Rosand, "Security Council Resolution 1373: The Counter-Terrorism Committee and the Fight against Terrorism," *American Journal of International Law* 97 (2003): 333–46.

62. Rosand, "Security Council Resolution 1372," 335.

63. See H. E. Permanent Representative of Denmark to the United Nations Ambassador Ellen Margrethe Løj, "Briefing by the Chairman of the Counter-Terrorism Committee to the Security Council," October 26, 2005; http://www.sikkerhedsraadet.um.dk/en/menu/DanishStatements/UNSCBriefingByChairmanOfCTC.htm.

64. See Warren Hoge, "U.N. Council Initiates Effort against Terror," *New York Times,* October 9, 2004, A6.

65. ICRC, "Penal Repression: Punishing War Crimes"; http://www.ehl.icrc.org/images/resources/pdf/penal_repression.pdf. See Liesbeth Zegveld, "Dutch Cases on Torture Committed in Afghanistan," *Journal of International Criminal Law* 4, no. 4 (2006): 878–80. The court convicted two asylum seekers for their roles in torture during the Soviet-Afghan war.

66. See Amnesty International, *Report on Torture* (1975), as well as its *Torture in the Eighties* (1984), which listed abuses in 98 countries.

67. Signed December 10, 1984 (entered into force, June 26, 1987).

68. E.T.S. 126, entered into force, February 1, 1989.

69. Cartagena De Indias, Colombia, of December 9, 1985; OAS, Treaty Series, No. 67 (entered into force, February 28, 1987). The United States has not signed this agreement.

70. See the discussion in Malcolm Shaw, *International Law* (5th ed.) (Cambridge: Cambridge University Press, 2003), 303; Bassiouni, *Introduction to International Criminal Law,* 147.

71. Alicene Boulesbaa, *The UN Convention on Torture and the Prospects for Enforcement* (The Hague: Kluwer Law International, 1999), 6.

72. For a thorough discussion of the drafting process, see Boulesbaa, *The UN Convention on Torture,* Chapter 1, particularly, 16–23.

73. *Ireland v. United Kingdom,* European Court of Human Rights (ECHR), Judgement of January 18, 1978 (No. 91); http://hudoc.echr.coe.int/hudoc/default.asp?Language=en& Advanced=1. para. 167.

74. *Ireland v. United Kingdom,* para. 168.

75. The argument also involves the reach of the Constitution. The Attorney General of the United States, Alberto Gonzalez, argued that the prohibitions applied only to actions

on sovereign U.S. territory. Guantanamo, as leased territory, did not qualify as "U.S. territory." David Luban, "Liberalism, Torture and the Ticking Bomb," *Virginia Law Review* 91, no. 6 (2005): 1458–59.

76. One half are elected every two years. No two may be from the same state.

77. There are seven monitoring "committees." For a summary of their purposes and relationship to the various instrument, see Gerhard von Glahn and James Larry Taulbee, *Law among Nations* (New York: Pearson-Longman, 2006), Chapter 16.

78. Report of the Committee against Torture, UN Doc. A/63/44 (November 2007, April-May 2008).

79. Committee against Torture, CAT/C/81/Add.4. This was Norway's fifth periodic report.

80. Report of the Committee against Torture, 27.

81. Report of the Committee against Torture, 28–29.

82. Report of the Committee against Torture, 103.

83. Complaint No. 269/2005 (*Ali Ben Salem v. Tunisia*), Report of the Committee against Torture, 104.

84. Complaint No. 297/2006 (*Sogi v. Canada*), Report of the Committee against Torture, 104.

85. Complaint No. 299/2006 (*Iya v. Switzerland*), Report of the Committee against Torture, 105.

86. For summaries, see Report of the Committee against Torture, 105–6.

87. *Ireland v. the United Kingdom*, European Court of Human Rights (ECHR), Judgement of January 18, 1978, para 90; http://hudoc.echr.coe.int/hudoc/default.asp?Language=en& Advanced=1. para. 167. See also Florian Jessbrger, "Bad Torture—Good Torture?: What International Criminal Lawyers May Learn from the Recent Trial of Police Officers in Germany," *Journal of International Criminal Justice* 3, no. 5 (2005): 1059–73.

88. See Luban, "Liberalism, Torture and the Ticking Bomb."

89. For two thoughtful responses to this, see Luban, "Liberalism, Torture and the Ticking Bomb," and Sumner B. Twiss, "Torture, Justification and Human Rights: Toward an Absolute Proscription," *Human Rights Quarterly* 29 (2005): 346–67. See also the collection of essays in Sanford Levinson, *Torture: A Collection* (New York: Oxford University Press, 2004), and the documents in Karen J. Greenberg (ed.), *The Torture Debate in America* (Cambridge: Cambridge University Press, 2005).

90. A "dirty bomb" is an ordinary explosive device that disperses radioactive material such as Cesium 137 or Cobalt 60 in addition to the normal heat and blast effects. While not as devastating as an atomic explosion, it still produces horrific side effects.

91. See, for example, Alan Dershowitz, *Why Terrorism Works* (New Haven: Yale University Press, 2002), Chapter 4.

92. Reprinted in Karen J. Greenberg and Joshua L. Dratel (eds.), *The Torture Papers: The Road to Abu Ghraib* (Cambridge: Cambridge University Press, 2005), 172.

93. See Henry Shue, "Torture," *Philosophy and Public Affairs* 7, no. 2 (1978): 125–26, for a discussion of this point.

94. See Phiip Zimbardo, *The Lucifer Effect: Understanding How Good People Turn Evil* (New York: Random House, 2007), for an extended treatment of this point.

95. 28 U.S.C. §1350 (emphasis added).Since *Filartiga*, proponents of the so-called modern position who seek to use §1350 to incorporate international human rights norms have employed the name Alien Tort Claims Act (ATCA), referring to the 1789 version as included in the Judiciary Act. Opponents have referred to the Alien Tort Statute (ATS),

the modified version, emphasizing that the statute merely grants jurisdiction and does not establish a cause of action, that is, the right to make a claim for damages. In *Sosa v. Alvarez-Machain,* 124 S.Ct. 2739 (2004), the Supreme Court chose to use ATS. See Naomi Norberg, "The U.S. Supreme Court Affirms the *Filartiga* Paradigm," *Journal of International Criminal Justice* 4, no. 2 (2006): 387–400.

96. See *Filartiga v. Peña-Irala,* 630 F.2d 876, 887 & n. 21 (2d Cir.1980).

97. *Forum non conveniens,* literally translated, simply means "inconvenient forum." In some instances, a court may have appropriate jurisdiction, but the location would result in great inconvenience for the witnesses or parties. If a party makes an adequate showing of inconvenience, the principle of *forum non conveniens* permits a judge to decline to hear or perhaps to transfer a case even though the court is an appropriate court for the case.

98. See *Memorandum* filed by the United States, 19 *International Legal Materials* 585 (1980); and Jeffrey M. Blum and Ralph G. Steinhard, "Federal Jurisdiction over International Human Rights Claims: The Alien Tort Claim Act after *Filartiga v. Peña-Irala,*" *Harvard International Law Journal* (Winter 1981), 53–114.

99. *Nuclear Tests (Australia v. France),* 1974; *Advisory Opinion on Legal 21 Consequences of Continued Presence of South Africa in Namibia,* 1970.

100. *Filartiga v. Peña-Irala,,* 630 F.2d 876 (2d Cir. 1980), June 30, 1980, on remand, 577 F.Supp. 860 (E.D.N.Y. 1984).See Beth Stephens, "Translating *Filartiga:* A Comparative and International Law Analysis of Domestic Remedies for International Human Rights Violations," *Yale Journal of International Law* 27 (2002): 1–58.

101. See, e.g., *Abebe-Jira v. Negewo,* 72 F.3d 844 (11th Cir. 1996) (alleging torture of Ethiopian prisoners); *Kadić v. Karadžić,* 70 F.3d 232 (2d Cir. 1995) (alleging torture, rape, and other abuses orchestrated by Serbian military leader); *In re Estate of Ferdinand Marcos,* 25 F.3d 1467 (9th Cir. 1994) (alleging torture and other abuses by former President of Philippines); *Tel-Oren v. Libyan Arab Republic,* 726 F.2d 774 (D.C. Cir. 1984)

102. 70 F.3d 232 (2d Cir).

103. Pub. L. 102–256, March 12, 1992, 106 Stat. 73.

104. *Wiwa v. Royal Dutch Petroleum Co.,* 226 F.3d 88 (2d Cir. 14 September 2000), (Cert. Denied) 2001; *Wiwa v. Royal Dutch Petroleum Co.,* 2002 U.S. Dist. LEXIS 3293 (S.D.N.Y. Dist. Ct. 2002); "Wiwa v. Royal Dutch Petroleum/Wiwa v. Anderson: Description and Status,"Center for Constitutional Rights; http://www.ccr-ny.org/v2/legal/corporate_ac countability/corporateArticle.asp?ObjID=sReYTC75tj&Content=46; see also *Doe v. UNO-CAL* (and *Roe v. UNOCAL*). These cases were settled in April 2005. "The US oil company Unocal has agreed to compensate Burmese villagers who sued the firm for complicity in forced labor, rape and murder. The abuses were committed in the mid-1990's by soldiers providing security for Unocal's natural gas pipeline in southern Burma." See "Historic Advance for Universal Human Rights: Unocal to Compensate Burmese Villagers"; http://www. earthrights.org/news/press_unocal_settle.shtml.

105. See Leon Gettler, "Liability Forges a New Morality," August 3, 2005; http://www. globalpolicy.org/intljustice/atca/2005/0803morality.htm; and David Weissbrodt and Muria Kruger, "Norms on the Responsibilities of Transnational Corporations and Other Business Enterprises with Regard to Human Rights," *American Journal of International Law* 97 (2003), 901–922.

Glossary of Latin Terms

actus reus	"guilty acts"—specific definitions of criminal offenses
ad hoc	temporary, for the moment or purpose
ad litem	temporary, for the purpose or function
animo furandi	intent to plunder
de facto	in fact
de jure	in law
forum non conveniens	literally translated, simply means "inconvenient forum." In some instances, a court may have appropriate jurisdiction, but the location would result in great inconvenience for the witnesses or parties
in personam	over the person—a principle of jurisdiction distinct from *in rem,* over the matter
jus ad bellum	law governing the resort to war
jus cogens	a universal norm (i.e., binding on all) of customary law
jus in bello	law governing conduct of war (international humanitarian law)
jus sanguis	through blood—a method of determining citizenship
jus solis	through soil—a method of determining citizenship
mens rea	"guilty mind"—the mental element that accompanies *actus reus*
non (ne) bis in idem	no one can be tried twice for the same thing (double jeopardy)
nullum crimen, nulla poena sine praevia lege poenali	there can be no crime and no penalty without a previously existing law

opinio juris	the psychological element necessary for a customary (habitual) practice to be considered law
pacta sunt servanda	treaties must be observed
proprio motu	on one's own personal initiative—an authority given the prosecutor for the ICC
ratione personae	literally, by means of the person—defines the means by which an international court may assert jurisdiction
status mixtus	literally mixed state—an attempt to define a state of war less than full overt hostilities
tu quoque	you did it also; an argument used in defense

Bibliography and Resources

Articles and Books

Akhavan, Payam. "The Crime of Genocide in the ICTR Jurisprudence." *Journal of International Criminal Justice* 3 (2005): 989–1006.

Allison, Graham T. *Nuclear Terrorism: The Ultimate Preventable Catastrophe*. New York: Macmillan, 2005.

Anderson, Geoffrey. *Crimes against Humanity: The Struggle for Global Justice* (3rd ed.). New York and London: New Press, 2006.

Arend, Anthony, and Robert J. Beck. *International Law and the Use of Force: Beyond the UN Charter Paradigm*. London: Routledge, 1993.

Bales, Kevin. *Disposable People: New Slavery in the Global Economy* (rev. ed.). Berkeley: University of California Press, 2004.

Bass, Gary. *Stay the Hand of Vengeance: The Politics of War Crimes Tribunals*. Princeton: Princeton University Press, 2000.

Bassiouni, M. Cherif. "Combatting Impunity for International Crimes." *Colorado Law Review* 71, no. 2 (2000): 409–19.

Bassiouni, M. Cherif. "Crimes against Humanity," http://www.crimesofwar.org/thebook/crimes-against-humanity.html.

Bassiouni, M. Cherif. *Crimes against Humanity in International Criminal Law* (2nd rev. ed.). The Hague: Martinus Nijhof, 1999.

Bassiouni, M. Cherif. *International Criminal Law Conventions and Their Penal Provisions*. Irvington-on-Hudson, NY: Transnational, 1997.

Bassiouni, M. Cherif. *Introduction to International Criminal Law*. Ardsley, NY: Transnational, 2003.

Batstone, David. *Not for Sale: The Return of the Global Slave Trade—and How We Can Fight It*. New York: Harper One, 2007.

Baxter, R. R. "So-Called 'Unprivileged Belligerency': Spies, Guerrillas and Saboteurs." *Btitish Yearbook of International Law* 28 (1951): 323–45.

Bederman, David J. *The Spirit of International Law*. Athens: University of Georgia Press, 2002.

Beerman, Jack M. *Administrative Law*. New York: Aspen, 2006.

Bell, John, Sophie Boyron, and Simon Whittaker. *Principles of French Law*. New York: Oxford University Press, 1998.

Bell-Fialkoff, Andrew. "A Brief History of Ethnic Cleansing." *Foreign Affairs* 72, no. 3 (Summer 1993): 110–21.

Bertodano, Sylvia de. "What Price Defence? Resourcing the Defence at the ICTY." *Journal of International Criminal Justice* 2 (2004): 503–8.

Bianchi, Andrea (ed.). *Enforcing International Law Norms against Terrorism.* Oxford: Hart, 2004.

Blázquez, Francisco Javier Cabrera. "Plagiarism: An Original Sin?," http://www.obs.coe.int/online_publication/expert/plagiarism.pdf.en.

Boas, Gideon. *The* Milošević *Trial: Lessons for the Conduct of Complex International Criminal Proceedings.* Cambridge: Cambridge University Press, 2007.

Bobbitt, Philip. *The Shield of Achilles: War, Peace and the Course of History.* New York: Knopf, 2002.

Boister, Neil. "Transnational Criminal Law." *European Journal of International Law* 14 (2003): 953–76.

Borchard, Edwin M. (Comment). "The Multilateral Treaty for the Renunciation of War." *American Journal of International Law* 23, no. 1 (1929): 116–20.

Bosly, Henri-D. "Admission of Guilt before ICC and in Continental Systems." *Journal of International Criminal Law* 2 (2003): 1040–49.

Boulesbaa, Ahcene. *The UN Convention on Torture and the: Prospects for Enforcement.* The Hague: Kluwer Law International, 1999.

Bowett, Derek. "Reprisals Involving the Recourse to Armed Force." *American Journal of International Law* 66, no.1 (1972): 1–36.

Braff, Jeraldine, Thomas Arvanites, and Henry J. Steadman. "Detention Patterns of Successful and Unsuccessful Insanity Defendants." *Criminology* 21, no. 3 (2006): 439–48.

Brickhill, Paul. *The Great Escape.* New York: Norton, 1950.

Brierly, James L. *The Law of Nations: An Introduction to the International Law of Peace.* Oxford: Clarendon Press, 1928.

Brooks, Timothy (ed.). *Documents on the Rape of Nanking.* Ann Arbor: University of Michigan Press, 1999.

Brownlie, Ian. *International Law and the Use of Force by States.* Oxford: Clarendon Press, 1963.

Bull, Hedley. *The Anarchical Society.* New York: Columbia University Press, 1977.

Byers, Michael. "Policing the High Seas: The Proliferation Security Initiative." *American Journal of International Law* 98 (2004): 526–45.

Byers, Michael. *War Law: International Law and Armed Conflict.* London: Atlantic, 2005.

Cameron, Iain. *The Protective Principle of International Criminal Jurisdiction.* Aldershot, England: Dartmouth, 1994.

Cassese, Antonio. *International Criminal Law.* Oxford: Oxford University Press, 2003.

Chalk, Frank, and Kurt Jonassohn. *The History and Sociology of Genocide: Analyses and Case Studies.* New Haven: Yale University Press, 1990.

Chang, Maria Hsia, and Robert P. Barker. "Victor's Justice and Japan's Amnesia: The Tokyo War Crimes Trial Reconsidered." *East Asia* 19, no. 4 (2001): 55–84.

Chevigny, Paul. "The Limitations of Universal Jurisdiction." Global Policy Forum, March 2006, http://www.globalpolicy.org/opinion/2006/03universal.htm.

Cicero, *De Officiis* 3.29, in Gregory R. Crane (ed.), *The Perseus Project,* http://www.perseus.tufts.edu, September 1999.

Combs, Nancy. *Guilty Pleas in International Criminal Law: Constructing a Restorative Justice Approach.* Palo Alto, CA: Stanford University Press, 2006.

Combs, Nancy Amoury. "Case Comment: *Prosecutor v.Plavšić*," *American Journal of International Law* 97 (2003): 929–37.

Constable, Pamela, and Arturo Valuenza. *A Nation of Enemies: Chile under Pinochet.* New York: Norton, 1993.

Cowles, William B."Trials of War Criminals (Non-Nuremberg)." *American Journal of International Law* 42, no. 2 (1948): 299–319.

Crocker, David A. "Reckoning with Past Wrongs: A Normative Framework." *Ethics and International Affairs* 13 (1999): 43–64.

Cryer, Robert. *Prosecuting International Crimes: Selectivity and the International Criminal Law Regime.* Cambridge: Cambridge University Press, 2005.

Cryer, Robert, Hakan Friman, Darryl Robinson, and Elizabeth Wilmshurst. *An Introduction to International Criminal Law.* Cambridge: Cambridge University Press, 2007.

Dadrian, Vahakn N. "Genocide as a Problem of National and International Law: The World War I Armenian Case and Its Contemporary Legal Ramifications." *Yale Journal of International Law* 14, no. 2 (1989): 221–328.

Damaška, Mirjan R. *The Faces of Justice and State Authority: A Comparative Approach to the Legal Process.* New Haven: Yale University Press, 1986.

Damaška, Mirjan R. "Negotiated Justice in International Courts." *Journal of International Criminal Justice* 2 (2004): 1018–39.

D'Amato, Anthony."Peace v. Accountability in Bosnia." *American Journal of International Law* 88 (1994): 500.

Danner, Alison Marston, and Jenny S. Martinez, "Guilty Associations: Joint Criminal Enterprise, Command Responsibility and the Development of International Criminal Law." *California Law Review* 93, no. 1 (2005): 77–169.

Davidson, H. Ron. "The International Criminal Tribunal for Rwanda's Decision in *The Prosecutor v .Ferdinand Nahimana et al.*: The Past, Present, and Future of International Incitement Law." *Leiden Journal of International Law* 17 (2004): 505–19.

Dembour, Marie Bénédicte, and Emily Haslam. "Silencing Hearings: Victim-Witnesses at War Crimes Trials." *European Journal of International Law* 15, no. 1 (February 2004): 151–77.

Dershowitz, Alan. *Why Terrorism Works.* New Haven: Yale University Press, 2002.

Dinstein, Yoram. *The Conduct of Hostilities under the Law of International Armed Conflict.* Cambridge: Cambridge University Press, 2004

Dinstein, Yoram. *War, Aggression and Self Defence* (3rd ed.). Cambridge: Cambridge University Press, 2001.

Donner, Ruth. *The Regulation of Nationality in International Law* (2nd ed.). Irvington-on-Hudson, NY: Transnational, 1994.

Dressler, Joshua. *Criminal Law.* Eagan, MN: West, 2005.

Dressler, Joshua. *Understanding Criminal Law* (4th ed.). New York: Lexis, 2006.

Drumbl, Mark A. *Atrocity, Punishment, and International Law.* Cambridge: Cambridge University Press, 2007.

Eagleton, Clyde. "The Attempt to Define War." *International Conciliation,* no. 291 (June 1933).

Emanuel, Steven J. *Criminal Procedure* (4th ed.). New York: Aspen, 2005.

Epps, Valerie. "The Soldier's Obligation to Die When Ordered to Shoot Civilians or Face Death Himself." *New England Law Review* 37, no. 4 (2003): 987–1014.

Eyffinger, Arthur. *The 1899 Hague Peace Conference: The Parliament of Man, the Federation of the World.* The Hague: Martinus Nijhoff, 1999.

Farer, Tom. "Editorial Comment: Beyond the Charter Frame: Unilateralism or Condominium." *American Journal of International Law* 96 (2002): 359–64.

Farer, Tom. *The Laws of War 25 Years after Nuremberg. International Conciliation* no. 538 (1971).

Fay, Stephen, Lewis Chester, and Magnus Linklater. *Hoax: The Inside Story of the Howard Hughes-Clifford Irving Affair.* New York: Viking, 1972.

Fenrick, W. J. "Targeting and Proportionality during the NATO Bombing Campaign against Yugoslavia." *European Journal of International Law* 12, no. 3 (2001): 489–502.

Ferguson, Charles D., and William C. Potter. *The Four Faces of Nuclear Terrorism.* Center for Non-Proliferation Studies. Monterrey, CA: Monterey Institute, 2004.

Fisher, Louis. *Military Tribunals and Presidential Power: American Revolution to the War on Terrorism.* Lawrence: University of Kansas Press, 2005.

Fleck, Dieter (ed.). *The Handbook of Humanitarian Law in Armed Conflicts.* Oxford: Oxford University Press, 1999.

Forsythe, David P. "Legal Management of Internal War: The 1977 Protocol on Noninternational Armed Conflicts." *American Journal of International Law* 72 (1978): 272–95.

Franck, Thomas M. *Recourse to Force: State Action against Threats and Armed Attacks.* Cambridge: Cambridge University Press, 2002.

Gberie, Lansana. *A Dirty War in West Africa: The RUF And the Destruction of Sierra Leone.* Bloomington: Indiana University Press, 2005.

Glenny, Misha. *The Balkans: Nationalism, War and the Great Powers, 1804–1999.* New York: Viking, 2000.

Goldsworthy, Adrian. *The Punic Wars.* London: Cassell, 2000.

Gordley, James, and Arthur Taylor von Mehren. *An Introduction to the Comparative Study of Private Law: Readings, Cases, Materials.* Cambridge: Cambridge University Press, 2006.

Greenberg, Karen J. Greenberg (ed.). *The Torture Debate in America.* Cambridge: Cambridge University Press, 2005.

Greenberg, Karen J., and Joshua L. Dratel (eds.). *The Torture Papers: The Road to Abu Ghraib.* Cambridge: Cambridge University Press, 2005

Grotius. *The Law of War and Peace = De jure belli ac pacis* (trans. L. R. Loomis). Roslyn, NY: W. J. Black, 1949.

Grotius, Hugo. *The Rights of War and Peace* (3 vols.). Ed. Richard Tuck. Indianapolis, IN: The Liberty Fund, 2005.

Gutman, Roy, and David Rieff (eds.). *Crimes of War: What the Public Should Know.* New York: Norton, 1999.

Guy, George F. "The Defense of Yamashita." *Wyoming Law Journal* 4, no. 3 (1950): 153–80.

Halberstam, Malvina. "Terrorism on the High Seas: The Achille Lauro, Piracy and the IMO Convention on Maritime Safety." *American Journal of International Law* 82 (1988): 269–310.

Hansen, Randall. *Dual Nationality, Social Rights and Federal Citizenship in the U.S. and Europe: The Reinvention of Citizenship.* New York: Berghahn Books, 2002.

Harmon, Mark B., and Fergal Gaynor. "Ordinary Sentences for Extraordinary Crimes." *Journal of International Criminal Justice* 5 (2007): 683–712.

Haverman, Roelof, Olga Kavran, and Julian Nicholls (eds.). *Supranational Criminal Law: A System Sui Gneris.* Antwerp: Intersentia, 2003.

Haverman, Roelof, and Olaluwa Olusanya (eds.). *Sentencing and Sanctioning in Supranational Criminal Law.* Antwerp: Intersentia, 2006.

Hayner, Priscilla B. *Unspeakable Truths: Facing the Challenge of Truth Commissions*. New York: Routledge, 2002.

Hayward, Ruth. *Conflict of Laws* (4th ed.). London: Cavendish, 2006.

Hencakerts, Jean-Marie, and Louise Doswald-Beck. *Customary International Humanitarian Law*. Cambridge: Cambridge University Press, 2005.

Herodotus, *The Histories*. Trans. R. Waterfield. Oxford: Oxford University Press, 1998.

Hertz, Randy, and James S. Liebman. *Federal Habeas Corpus Practice and Procedure* (5th ed.) (2 vols.). New York: Michie, 2005.

Higgins, Rosalyn, and Maurice Floury (eds.). *Terrorism and International Law*. London: Routledge, 1997.

Hirst, Michael. *Jurisdiction and the Ambit of the Criminal Law*. New York: Oxford University Press, 2003.

Hoffman, Bruce. *Inside Terrorism*. New York: Columbia University Press, 1999.

Howard, J. Woodford. *Mr. Justice Murphy: A Political Biography*. Princeton: Princeton University Press, 1968.

Hudson, Manley O. "The Proposed International Criminal Court." *American Journal of International Law* 32 (1938): 549–54.

Human Rights Watch. *Genocide in Iraq: The Anfal Campaign against the Kurds*. New York: Human Rights Watch, 1993, http://www.hrw.org/reports/1993/iraqanfal/.

International Committee of the Red Cross. "The Geneva Conventions: The Core of International Humanitarian Law," http://www.icrc.org/Web/Eng/siteeng0.nsf/htmlall/genevaconventions.

International Crisis Group. *Balkans Briefing. Milosevic in the Hague:What It Means for Yugoslavia and the Region*. Belgrade/Brussels, July 6, 2001. http://www.crisisgroup.org/home/index.cfm?id=1791&l=1.

International Crisis Group. *War Criminals in Bosnia's Republika Srpška: Who Are the People in Your Neighbourhood*. Balkans Report No. 103, November 2000. http://www.crisisgroup.org/home/index.cfm?id=1518&l=1.

Janssen, Sander. "Mental Condition Defences in Supranational Criminal Law." *International Criminal Law Review* 4, no. 1 (2004): 83–98.

Jennings, R. Y. "The Judiciary, International, and National and the Development of International Law." *International and Comparative Law Quarterly* 45 (1996), 1–12.

Jessberger, Florian. "Bad Torture—Good Torture?: What International Criminal Lawyers May Learn from the Recent Trial of Police Officers in Germany." *Journal of International Criminal Justice* 3, no. 5 (2005): 1059–73.

Jessup, Philip C. "Should International Law Recognize an Intermediate Status between Peace and War?" *American Journal of International Law* 48, no. 1 (1954): 98–103.

Jinks, Derek. "The Declining Status of POW Status." *Harvard International Law Journal* 45 (2004): 367–442.

Jones, Adam. *Genocide: Comprehensive Introduction*. London: Routledge/Taylor and Francis, 2006.

Jones, Howard. *Mutiny on the Amistad: The Saga of a Slave Revolt and Its Impact on American Abolition, Law, and Diplomacy*. Oxford: Oxford University Press, 1997.

Kapstein, Ethan B. "The New Global Slave Trade." *Foreign Affairs* 85, no. 6 (November-December 2006): 103–15.

Keen, Maurice Hugh. *The Laws of War in the Late Middle Ages*. London: Routledge and Kegan Paul, 1965.

Kennedy, John F. *Profiles in Courage*. New York: Harper and Row, 1964.

Khadduri, Majid. *War and Peace in the Law of Islam.* Baltimore: Johns Hopkins University Press, 1955.

Kiernan, Ben. *Blood and Soil: A World History of Genocide and Extermination from Sparta to Darfur.* New Haven: Yale University Press, 2007.

Kim, Julie. *Balkan Cooperation on War Crimes Issues: 2005 Update.* CRS Report for Congress No. RS22097 (March 28, 2005).

King, Faiza Patel, and Anne-Marie LaRosa, "The Jurisprudence of the Yugoslavia Tribunal: 1994–1996." *European Journal of International Law* 8, no. 1 (1997): 123–80.

Kissinger, Henry A. "The Pitfalls of Universal Jurisdiction." *Foreign Affairs* 80, no. 4 (July-August 2001): 86–96.

Kittichaisaree, Kriangsak. *International Criminal Law.* Oxford: Oxford University Press, 2001.

Koessler, Maximillian. "American War Crimes Trials in Europe." *Georgetown Law Journal* 39, no. 1 (1950): 18–112.

Kunz, Josef L. "The United Nations Convention on Genocide." *American Journal of International Law* 43, no. 4 (1949): 738–46.

Lael, Richard L. *The Yamashita Precedent: War Crimes and Command Responsibility.* Wilmington, DE: Scholarly Resources, 1982.

LaFave, Wayne R., Jerold H. Israel, and Nancy J. King. *Criminal Procedure* (3rd ed.). St. Paul, MN: West, 2000.

Leblanc, Lawrence J. *The United States and the Genocide Convention.* Durham, NC: Duke University Press, 1991.

Lee, Roy S. (ed.). *The International Criminal Court: The Making of the Rome Statute.* The Hague: Kluwer Law, 1999,

Leiner, Frederick C. *The End of Barbary Terror: America's 1815 War against the Pirates of North Africa.* Oxford: Oxford University Press, 2006.

Lemkin, Raphael. *Axis Rule in Occupied Europe.* New York: Carnegie Endowment for International Peace, 1944.

Lemkin, Raphael, "Genocide As a Crime under International Law." *American Journal of International Law* 41, no. 1 (1947), 145–51.

Levie, Howard S. "Legal Aspects of the Continued Detention of the Pakistani Prisoners of War by India." *American Journal of International Law* 67, no. 4 (1973): 512–16.

Levinson, Sanford (ed.). *Torture: A Collection.* New York: Oxford University Press, 2004.

Luban, David. "Liberalism, Torture and the Ticking Bomb." *Virginia Law Review* 91, no. 6 (2005): 1425–61.

Macedo, Stephen (ed.). *Universal Jurisdiction: National Courts and the Prosecution of Serious Crimes under International Law.* Philadelphia: University of Pennsylvania Press, 2004.

Magnarella, Paul J. "The Background and Causes of the Genocide in Rwanda." *Journal of International Criminal Justice* 3, no. 4 (2005): 801–22.

Manner, George. "The Legal Nature and Punishment of Criminal Acts of Violence Contrary to the Laws of War." *American Journal of International Law* 37, no. 3 (1943): 407–35.

Martinez, Jenny S. "Understanding *Mens Rea* in Command Responsibility from Yamashita to Blaskić and Beyond." *Journal of International Criminal Justice* 5, no. 3 (2007): 638–64.

May, Larry. *Crimes against Humanity: A Normative Account.* Cambridge: Cambridge University Press, 2005.

McDougal, Myres, and Florentine Feliciano. "The Initiation of Coercion: A Multi-Temporal Analysis." *American Journal of International Law* 52, no. 2 (1958): 241–59.

Melvern, Linda. *Conspiracy to Murder: The Rwandan Genocide* (rev. ed.). New York: Verso, 2006.

Melvern, Linda. "The Security Council in the Face of Genocide." *Journal of International Criminal Justice* 3, no. 4 (2005): 847–60.

Melville, Herman. *Moby Dick.* New York: Dodd and Mead, 1942.

Meron, Theodor. "The Case for War Crimes Trials in Yugoslavia." *Foreign Affairs* 72, no. 3 (1993) 122–35.

Meron, Theodor. *Henry's Wars and Shakespeare's Laws: Perspectives on the Law of War in the Later Middle Ages.* Oxford: Clarendon Press, 1993.

Meron, Theodor. *Human Rights and Humanitarian Norms as Customary Law.* Oxford: Oxford University Press, 1999.

Meron, Theodor. "Revival of Customary Humanitarian Law." *American Journal of International Law* 99, no. 4 (2005): 817–34.

Meron, Theodor, "War Crimes in Yugoslavia and the Development of International Law." *American Journal of International Law* 88 (1994): 78–88.

Mettraux, Guénaël. "Crimes against Humanity in the Jurisprudence of the International Criminal Tribunals for the Former Yugoslavia and for Rwanda." *Harvard International Law Journal* 43, no. 1 (2002): 237–316.

Mettraux, Guénaël (ed.). *Perspectives on the Nuremberg Trial.* Oxford: Oxford University Press, 2008.

Mettraux, Guénaël. *International Crimes and the Ad Hoc Tribunals.* Oxford: Oxford University Press, 2005.

Minear, Richard. *Victor's Justice.* Princeton: Princeton University Press, 1971.

Minow, Martha. *Between Vengeance and Forgiveness: Facing History after Genocide and Mass Violence.* Boston: Beacon Press, 1998.

Monshipouri, Mahmood, and Claude Emerson Welch. "The Search for International Human Rights and Justice: Coming to Terms with the New Global Realities." *Human Rights Quarterly* 23, no. 2 (May 2001): 370–401.

Møse, Erik. "Main Achievements of the ICTR." *Journal of International Criminal Justice* 3, no. 4 (2005): 920–43.

Mukimbiri, Jean. "The Seven Stages of the Rwandan Genocide." *Journal of International Criminal Justice* 3, no. 4 (2005): 823–36.

Nijman, Janne Elisabeth. *The Concept of International Legal Personality: An Inquiry into the History and Theory of International Law.* Cambridge: Cambridge University Press, 2004.

Norberg, Naomi. "The U.S. Supreme Court Affirms the *Filartiga* Paradigm." *Journal of International Criminal Justice* 4, no. 2 (2006): 387–400.

O'Brien, James C. "The International Tribunal for Violations of International Humanitarian Law in the Former Yugoslavia." *American Journal of International Law* 87, no. 4 (1993): 639–58.

O'Connell, Mary Ellen. *International Law and the Use of Force: Cases and Materials.* New York: Foundation Press, 2005.

Olusanya, Olaoluwa. *Sentencing War Crimes and Crimes against Humanity ander the International Criminal Tribunal for the Former Yugoslavia.* Groningen: Europa Law, 2005.

O'Neill, Kerry Creque."A New Customary Law of Head of State Immunity: Hirohito and Pinochet." *Stanford Journal of International Law* 38 (2002): 289–317.

Oppenheim, Lassa. *International Law: A Treatise* (5th ed.) (2 vols.). Ed. Hersh Lauterpacht. London and New York: Longmans Green, 1935–1937.

Orentlicher, Diane F. "Genocide." In Roy Gutman and David Rieff (eds.), *Crimes of War: What the Public Should Know.* New York: Norton, 1999, 153.

Orentlicher, Diane F. "Symposium: International Criminal Tribunals in the 21st Century: Criminalizing Hate Speech in the Crucible of Trial: *Prosecutor v. Nahimana.*" *American Unviversity International Law Review* 21 (2006): 557–96.

Osiel, Mark. *Mass Atrocity, Ordinary Evil and Hannah Arendt: Criminal Consciousness in Argentina's Dirty War.* New Haven: Yale University Press, 2001.

Osiel, Mark. *Obeying Orders: Atrocities, Military Discipline and the Law of War.* Brunswick, NJ: Transaction, 1999.

Osiel, Mark. "Why Prosecute? Critics of Punishment for Mass Atrocity." *Human Rights Quarterly* 22, no. 1 (February 2000): 118–47.

Oxman, Bernard H. "The Territorial Temptation A Siren Song at Sea." *American Journal of International Law* 100, no. 4 (2006): 830–51.

Parks, William H. "Command Responsibility for War Crimes." *Military Law Review* 62 (1973): 1–104.

Piccigallo, Philip R. *The Japanese on Trial: Allied War Crimes Operations in the Far East, 1945–1951.* Austin: University of Texas Press, 1979.

Plutarch. *Lives of the Noble Romans.* Trans. John Dryden. New York: Modern Library, n.d.

Polybius. *The Histories.* Trans. Evelyn S. Schuckburgh. Bloomington: Indiana University Press, 1962.

Potter, Pittman B. "Repatriation of Korean Prisoners of War." *American Journal of International Law* 47, no. 4 (1953), 661–62.

Power, Samantha. "A Problem from Hell": America and the Age of Genocide. New York: Basic Books, 2002.

Power, Samantha. "Bystanders to Genocide," The Atlantic.Com, http://www.theatlantic.com/doc/200109/power-genocide/2.

Pritchett, K. S. *The Greek State at War* (5 vols.). Berkeley and Los Angeles: University of California Press, 1977–1991.

Prunier, Gerard. *Darfur: The Ambiguous Genocide* (3rd ed.). Ithaca, NY: Cornell University Press, 2008.

Prunier, Gerard. *The Rwanda Crisis.* New York: Columbia University Press, 1997.

Prygoski, Philip J. *Constitutional Law* (12th ed.). St. Paul, MN: Thomson West, 2007.

Quirk, Joel. "The Anti-Slavery Project: Linking the Historical and Contemporary." *Human Rights Quarterly* 28 (2006): 565–98.

Rana, Rajat. "The Jean Mpambara Case: Outlining 'Culpable Omissions' in International Criminal Law." *Chinese Journal of International Law* 6, no. 2 (2007): 439–43.

Reel, A. Frank. *The Case of General Yamashita.* Chicago: University of Chicago Press, 1949.

Roberts, Adam, and Richard Guelff (eds.). *Documents on the Laws of War* (2nd ed.). Oxford: Clarendon Press, 1989.

Robertson, Geoffrey. *Crimes against Humanity: The Struggle for Global Justice* (3rd ed.). New York: New Press, 2006.

Rosand, Eric. "Security Council Resolution 1373: The Counter-Terrorism Committee and the Fight against Terrorism." *American Journal of International Law* 97 (2003): 333–46.

Rosenthal, John. "A Lawless Global Court: How the International Criminal Court Undermines the UN System." *Policy Review* 123 (February-March 2004), http://www.hoover.org/publications/policyreview/3439981.html.

Rostow, Nicholas."Before and After: The Changed U.N. Response to Terrorism since September 11th." *Cornell International Law Journal* 35 (2002): 475–91.

Roth, Kenneth. "The Case for Universal Jurisdiction." *Foreign Affairs* 80, no. 5 (September-October 2001): 150–54.

Rubin, Alfred P. *The Law of Piracy.* Boston: Bridge Street Books, 1988.

Rubin, Alfred P. *Piracy, Paramountcy and Protectorates.* Kuala Lumpur: Penerbit University Malaya, 1974.

Saul, Ben. *Defining Terrorism in International Law.* Oxford: Oxford University Press, 2006.

Schabas, William A. *The Abolition of the Death Penalty in International Law* (3rd ed.). Cambridge: Cambridge University Press, 2003.

Schabas, William A. "Darfur and the 'Odious Scourge': The Commission of Inquiry's Findings on Genocide." *Leiden Journal of International Law* 18, no. 4 (2005): 871–85.

Schabas, William A. *Genocide in International Law: The Crime of Crimes.* Cambridge: Cambridge University Press, 2000.

Schabas, William A. *An Introduction to the International Criminal Court* (3rd ed.). Cambridge: Cambridge University Press, 2007.

Schabas, William A. "The *Jelisić* Case and the *Mens Rea* of the Crime of Genocide." *Leiden Journal of International Law* 14 (2001): 125–39.

Schabas, William A. *The UN International Criminal Tribunals: The Former Yugoslavia, Rwanda and Sierra Leone.* Cambridge: Cambridge University Press, 2006.

Schabas, William A., and Shane Darcy (eds.). *Truth Commissions and Courts: The Tension between Criminal Justice and the Search for Truth.* Dordrecht, Netherlands: Kluwer, 2004.

Scharf, Michael P. *Balkan Justice: The Story behind the First International War Crimes Trial since Nuremberg.* Durham, NC: Carolina Academic Press, 1997.

Scharf, Michael P. "Trading Justice for Efficiency: Plea-Bargaining and International Tribunals." *Journal of International Criminal Law* 2 (2004): 1070–81.

Scharf, Michael P., and Melanie K. Corrin. "On Dangerous Ground: Passive Personality Jurisdiction and the Prohibition of Internet Gambling." *New England Journal of International and Comparative Law* 8, no. 1 (2001): 19–36.

Schlesinger, Rudolph B. "Research on the General Principles of Law Recognized by Civilized Nations." *American Journal of International Law* 51 (1957): 734.

Schwelb, Egon. "Crimes Against Humanity." *British Yearbook of International Law* 23 (1946): 178–226.

Scott, James Brown. "The Sixth Pan American Conference." *American Journal of International Law* 22, no. 2 (April, 1928): 351–62.

Shaw, Malcolm. *International Law* (5th ed.). Cambridge: Cambridge University Press, 2003.

Shawcross, William. *Deliver Us from Evil: Peacekeepers, Warlords and a World of Endless Conflict.* New York: Simon and Schuster, 2000.

Sheikh, Ahmed. *International Law and National Behavior.* New York, Wiley, 1973.

Shraga, Daphana, and Ralph Zacklin. "The International Criminal Court for the Former Yugoslavia." *European Journal of International Law* 5, no. 1 (1994): 1–22.

Shraga, Daphana, and Ralph Zacklin. "The International Criminal Court for Rwanda." *European Journal of International Law* 7, no. 4 (1996): 501–18.

Shue, Henry. "Torture." *Philosophy and Public Affairs* 7, no. 2 (1978): 124–43.

Silber, Laura, and Allan Little. *Yugoslavia: Death of a Nation.* New York: Penguin, 1997.

Skinner, E. Benjamin. *A Crime So Monstrous: Face-to-Face with Modern-Day Slavery.* New York: Free Press, 2008.

Stephens, Beth. "Translating *Filartiga*: A Comparative and International Law Analysis of Domestic Remedies for International Human Rights Violations." *Yale Journal of International Law* 27, no. 1 (2002): 1–58.

Stone, Julius, *Aggression and World Order.* (Berkeley: University of California Press, 1958.

Straus, Scott. *The Order of Genocide: Race, Power, and War in Rwanda.* Ithaca, NY: Cornell University Press, 2008.

Suter, Keith. *An International Law of Guerrilla Warfare: The Global Politics of Lawmaking.* London: Francis Pinter, 1984.

Taulbee, James L. "A Call to Arms Declined: The United States and the International Criminal Court." *Emory International Law Review* 14 (Spring 2000): 105–56.

Taulbee, James L. "Governing the Use of Force: Does the Charter Matter Anymore?" *Civil Wars* 4, no. 2 (2001): 1–58.

Taulbee, James Larry. "Mercenaries, Private Armies and Contemporary Policy Options." *International Politics* 37, no. 4 (December 2000): 433–55.

Taulbee, James Larry. "The Privatization of Security: Modern Conflict, Globalization and Weak States." *Civil Wars* 5, no. 2 (September 2002): 1–24.

Taulbee, James L., and John Anderson. "Reprisal *Redux.*" *Case Western Reserve Journal of International Law* 16 (1984): 309–37.

Taylor, Telford. *The Anatomy of the Nuremberg Trials.* Boston: Little, Brown, 1992.

Taylor, Telford. *Nuremberg and Vietnam: An American Tragedy.* Chicago: Quadrangle Books, 1970.

Thomas, Hugh. *The Slave Trade: The History of the Atlantic Slave Trade, 1140–1870.* New York: Simon and Schuster, 1999.

Thomson, Janice, *Mercenaries, Pirates, and Sovereigns: State-Building and Extraterritorial Violence in Early Modern Europe.* Princeton: Princeton University Press, 1996.

Tucker, Robert W. (Comment). "Reprisals and Self-Defense: The Customary Law." *American Journal of International Law* 66, no. 3 (1972): 586–96.

Twiss, Sumner B. "Torture, Justification and Human Rights: Toward an Absolute Proscription." *Human Rights Quarterly* 29 (2005): 346–67.

U.S. Supreme Court. *Federal Rules of Civil Procedure 3d.* Eagan, MN: Thomson West, 2007.

U.S. Supreme Court. *Federal Rules of Criminal Procedure: Rules of Criminal Procedure for the United States District Courts.* Eagan, MM: Thomson West, 2002.

Van Schaack, Beth. "The Crime of Political Genocide: Repairing the Genocide Convention's Blind Spot,. *Yale Law Journal* 106 (1996–1997): 2259–92.

Van Schaack, Beth. "The Definition of Crimes against Humanity: Resolving the Incoherence." *Columbia Journal of Transnational Law* 37 (1999): 787–850.

Verzijl, J. H. W. *International Law in Historical Perspective* (11 vols.). Leiden: A. W. Sijthof, 1968–.

von Glahn, Gerhard, and James Larry Taulbee. *Law among Nations: An Introduction* (8th ed., rev. and ed.). New York: Pearson-Longman, 2006.

Watkin, Keneth. "Warriors without Rights? Combatants, Unprivileged Belligerents, and the Struggle over Legitimacy." Program on Humanitarian Policy and Conflict Research, Harvard University Occasional Paper Series, No. 2 (Winter 2005), http://www.hpcr.org/pdfs/OccasionalPaper2.pdf.

Watkins, Jr., John C., and John Paul Weber (eds.), *War Crimes and War Crime Trials: From Leipzig to the ICC and Beyond: Cases, Materials and Comments.* Durham, NC: Carolina Academic Press, 2005.

Werle, Gerhard. *Principles of International Criminal Law.* The Hague: T.M.C. Asser Press, 2005.

Whiteman, Marjorie M. *Digest of International Law* (11 vols.). Washington, DC: U.S. Department of State, 1963–1978.

Wright, Quincy. "The Meaning of the Pact of Paris." *American Journal of International Law* 27, no. 1 (1933): 39–61.

Yacker, Marc D. *Private Bills and Federal Charters.* Washington, DC: Library of Congress, Congressional Research Service, 1979.

Yoran, Amit. "Developing Liability Standards for Electronic Commerce." Riptech Security Consulting Group, http://www.isoc.org/inet99/proceedings/1h/1h_2.htm.

Zabecki, David T. *Doenitz: A Defense.* Bennington, VT: Merriam, 1997.

Zahar, Alexander, and Göran Sluiter. *International Criminal Law: A Critical Introduction.* Oxford: Oxford University Press, 2008.

Zappalà, Salvatore. *Human Rights in International Criminal Proceedings.* Oxford: Oxford University Press, 2003.

Zegveld, Liesbeth. "Dutch Cases on Torture Committed in Afghanistan." *Journal of International Criminal Law* 4, no. 4 (2006): 878–80.

Zimbardo, Philip. *The Lucifer Effect: Understanding How Good People Turn Evil.* New York: Random House, 2007.

Selected Resources

American Society of International Law, Electronic Information System for International Law (EISIL), http://www.eisil.org/index.php?sid=142010672&t=index.

ICTY at a Glance, http://www.un.org/icty/glance-e/index.htm.

Raisch, Marilyn J., and Gail Partin, "International Criminal Law: A Selective Resource Guide," http://www.llrx.com/features/int_crim.htm.

Cases

American Military Court (CCL10)

Trial of Alfried Felix Alwyn Krupp von Bohlen and Halbach and eleven others, U.S. Military Tribunal, Nuremberg, November 17, 1947–June 30, 1948, Case No. 58, UN War Crimes Commission, Law Reports of Trials of War Criminals (hereinafter L.R.T.W.C.), Vol. 10, (London, 1949), 147.

The United States of America vs. Wilhelm von Leeb, et al. (Case No. 12); http://www.archives.gov/research/captured-german-records/microfilm/m898.pdf.

British Military Court (CCL 10)

The Belsen Trial (Trial of Josef Kramer and 44 Others),Case No. 10, British Military Court, Luneburg, September 17–November 17, 1945; http://www.ess.uwe.ac.uk/WCC/belsen1.htm.

Canada

Mugesera v. Canada (Minister of Citizenship and Immigration), [2005] 2 S.C.R. 100, 2005 SCC 40.

Rex v. Brosig, Ontario Court of Appeal, March 1, 1945, 2 D. L. R. 232.

European Court of Human Rights

Ireland v. United Kingdom. European Court of Human Rights (ECHR), Judgement of January 18, 1978 (N° 91).

International Court of Justice (http://www.icj-cij.org/)

Application of the Convention on the Prevention and Punishment of the Crime of Genocide (Bosnia and Herzegovina v. Serbia and Montenegro) (1993); Judgment of July 11, 1996.

Application for Revision of the Judgment of 11 July 1996 in the Case concerning Application of the Convention on the Prevention and Punishment of the Crime of Genocide (Bosnia and Herzegovina v. Yugoslavia), Judgment of February 26, 2007.

Application of the Convention on the Prevention and Punishment of the Crime of Genocide (Croatia v. Serbia).

Arrest Warrant of 11 April 2000 (Democratic Republic of the Congo v. Belgium) (Merits), Judgment of February 14, 2002.

Barcelona Traction, Light, and Power Co. (Belgium v. Spain), *ICJ Reports* (1970).

Case Concerning Avena and Other Mexican Nationals, ICJ Reports 128, 43 ILM 581 (2004).

Case Converring Military and Paramilitary Activities in and against Nicaragua (Nicaragua v. United States (Merits), ICJ Reports (1986).

The Corfu Channel Case (Great Britain v. Albania), *ICJ Reports* (1949).

Effects of Awards of Compensation Made by the United Nations Administrative Tribunals, ICJ Reports (1954).

Legal Consequences of Continued Presence of South Africa in Namibia (Advisory Opinion on) (1970).

Legality of the Threat of Use of Nuclear Weapons (Advisory Opinion) (1996), *ICJ Reports* 226.

Nuclear Tests (Australia v. France) (1974).

Reservations to the Convention on the Preservation and Punishment of the Crime of Genocide, Advisory Opinion, *ICJ Reports* May 28, 1951.

International Criminal Tribunal for Rwanda (http://69.94.11.53/default.htm)

Prosecutor v. Akayesu, Trial Chamber I, Judgment of September 2, 1998 [ICTR-96–4].

Prosecutor v. Kambanda, Trial Chamber I, Judgment and Sentence of September 4, 1998 [ICTR 97–23-S].

Prosecutor v. Kayishema et al., Trial Chamber II, Judgment of June 1, 2001 [ICTR-95–1-A].

Prosecutor v. Ferdinand Nahimana, Jean-Bosco Barayagwiza and Hassan Ngeze, Trial Chamber I, Judgment and Sentence of December 3, 2003 [ICTR-99–52-T].

Prosecutor v. Nahimana et al., Appeals Chamber, Judgment of November 28, 2007 [ICTR 99–52-A].

Prosecutor v. Musema, Trial Chamber I, Judgment of January 27, 2001 [ICTR-96–13-T].

International Criminal Tribunal for the Former Yugoslavia (http://www.un.org/icty/)

Prosecutor v. Blaskić, Trial Chamber I, Judgment of March 3, 2000 [IT-95–14-T].

Prosecutor v. Blaskić, Appeals Chamber, July 29, 2004 [IT-95–14-A].

Prosecutor v. Brdjanin and Talić, Corrected Version of the Fourth Amended Indictment, December 10, 2001 [IT-99–36-PT].

Prosecutor v. Delalić et al. (Čelebići case), Trial Chamber II, Judgment of November 16, 1998 [IT-96–21-T].

Prosecutor v. Delalić, et al., Appeals Judgment of February 20, 2001 [IT96–21-A].

Prosecutor v. Delalć et al. (Čelebići case), Appeals Chamber, Judgment of April 8, 2003 [IT-96–21-A].

Prosecutor v. Erdemović Trial Chamber I, Sentencing Judgment of March 5, 1998 [IT-96–22-S].

Prosecutor v. Erdemović, Appeals Chamber, Judgment of October 7, 1997 [IT-96–22-A].

Prosecutor v. Furundžija, Trial Chamber II, Judgment of December 10, 1998 [IT-95–17/1-T].

Prosecutor v. Jelisić, Trial Chamber I, Judgment of December 14, 1999 [IT-95–10-T].

Prosecutor v. Karadžić and Mladić, Transcript of Hearing [IT-95–5 and IT 95–18].

Prosecutor v. Kordić and Čerkez, Trial Chamber III, Judgment of February 26, 2001 [IT-95–14/2].

Prosecutor v. Kordić and Čerkez, Appeals Chamber, Judgment of December 17, 2004 [[IT-95–14/2-A].

Prosecutor v. Krasjśnik and Plavšić, Consolidated Amended Indictment, March 7, 2002 [IT-00–39 & 40].

Prosecutor v. Kristić, Trial Chamber I, Judgment of August 2, 2001 [IT-98–33-T].

Prosecutor v. Krstić, Appeals Chamber, Judgment of April 19, 2004 [IT-98–33-A].

Prosecutor v. Kunarac et al., Trial Chamber II, Judgment of February 22, 2002 [IT-96–32-T].

Prosecutor v. Kunarac et al., Appeals Chamber, Judgment of June 12, 2002 [IT-96–14/2-A].

Prosecutor v. Kupreškić et al., Trial Chamber II, Judgment of January 14, 2000) [IT-95–16-T].

Prosecutor v. Kvočka et al., Trial Chamber I [IT-98–30/1-T].

Prosecutor v. Kvočka et al., Appeals Chamber, Judgment of Februrary 28, 2005 [IT-98–30/1-A].

Prosecutor v. Milošević, Reasons for Decision on Assignment of Defense Counsel, September 22, 2004 [IT-02–54-T].

Prosecutor v. Milošević, Second Amended Indictment (Croatia), October 23, 2002 [IT-02–54-PT].

Prosecutor v. (Dragan) Nikolić ("Sušica Camp"), Trial Chamber II, Sentencing Judgment of December 18, 2003 [IT-94-2-T].

Prosecutor v. (Dragan) Nikolić ("Sušica Camp"), Appeals Chamber, Sentencing Judgment of February 4, 2005 [IT-94-2-A].

Prosecutor v. (Momir) Nikolić, Appeals Chamber, Judgment of March 8, 2006, [IT-02–60/1-A].

Prosecutor v. Plavšić, Trial Chamber III, Sentencing Judgment of February 27, 2003 [IT-00–39 & 40/1-S].

Prosecutor v. Stakić, Trial Chamber II, Judgment of July 31, 2003 [IT-97–24-T].

Prosecutor v. Strugar, Trial Chamber II, Judgment of January 31, 2005 [IT-01–42].

Prosecutor v. Tadić, Trial Chamber II, Judgment of May 7, 1997 [IT-94–1].

Prosecutor v. Tadić, Decision on the Defense Motion for Interlocutory Appeal on Jurisdiction, October 2, 1995 [IT-95–16-AR72].

Prosecutor v. Tadić, Appeals Chamber, Judgment of August 15, 1999 [IT-94–1-A].

Prosecutor v. Vasiljević, Trial Chamber I, Judgment of November 29, 2002 [IT-97–32-T].

Prosecutor v. Vasilević, Appeals Chamber [IT-97–32-A].

Internaational Military Tribunal (Nuremberg)

The Avalon Project at Yale Law School, *Trial of the Major War Criminals before the International Military Tribunal: Proceedings* (8 Volumes) (The Red Set), Vol. 1, http://www.yale.edu/lawweb/avalon/imt/proc/11-21-45.htm.

Trial of the Major War Criminals before the International Tribunal, Nuremberg, 14 November 1945–1 October 1946, 1 (1947): (The Blue Series), Library of Congress, Military Legal Resources, (42 volumes); http://www.loc.gov/rr/frd/Military_Law/NT_major-war-criminals.html.

Special Court for Sierra Leone (http://www.sc-sl.org/)

Prosecutor vs. Charles Ghankay Taylor, Pre-Trial Chamber, Second Amended Indictment of May 29, 2007 [SCSL-03–01-PT].

Prosecutor vs. Alex Tamba Brima, Brima Bazzy Kamara, and Santigie Borbor Kanu, Pre-Trial Chamber, Further Amended Consolidated Indictment of February 18, 2005 [SCSL-2004–16-PT].

U.S. District Courts

Abebe-Jira v. Negewo, 72 F.3d 844 (11th Cir. 1996).

Filartiga v. Pena-Irala, 630 F.2d 876, 887 & n. 21 (2d Cir. 1980).

Kadić v. Karadžić, 70 F.3d 232 (2d Cir. 1995).

Tel-Oren v. Libyan Arab Republic, 726 F.2d 774 (D.C. Cir. 1984).

Wiwa v. Royal Dutch Petroleum Co., 226 F.3d 88 (2d Cir. 14 September 2000) (Cert. Denied).

U.S. Supreme Court

Brown v. Board of Education of Topeka, 347 U.S. 483 (1954).

Hamdi v. Rumsfeld, 124 S. Ct. 2633 (2004).

In Re Yamashita 327 U.S. 1 (1946).

Miranda v. Arizona, 384 U.S. 436 (1966).

Rasul v. Bush, 124 S. Ct. 2686 (2004).

Roe v. Wade, 410 U.S. 113 (1973).

Sapphire, The, 11 Wallace 164 (1871).

Sosa v. Alvarez-Machain, 124 S.Ct. 2739 (2004).

Treaties and Conventions

Charter of the International Military Tribunal at Nuremberg. Annex to the London Agreement of August 8, 1945. 82 U.N.T.S. 279.

Charter of the International Military Tribunal for the Far East (IMTFE), www.icwc.de/file admin/media/IMTFEC.pdf.

Charter of the United Nations, http://www.un.org/aboutun/charter/.

Convention between the United States of America and Other Powers, Relating to Prisoners of War, July 27, 1929 (Geneva Convention).

Convention for the Creation of an International Criminal Court; Convention for the Prevention and Punishment of Terrorism, League of Nations Document, C.547(I).M.384(I).1937.V., reprinted vol. 7, Hudson, International Legislation, No. 500, 878.

Convention on the Prevention and Punishment of the Crime of Genocide, December 9, 1948; text at http://www.unhchr.ch/html/menu3/b/p_genoci.htm.

Convention for the Suppression of Unlawful Acts against the Safety of Maritime Navigation, of March 10, 1988; Entry into force, March 1, 1992, http://www.imo.org/Conventions/mainframe.asp?topic_id=259&doc_id=686.

Convention on the Prohibition of the Development, Production and Stockpiling of Bacteriological and Toxic Weapons of April 10, 1972, http://disarmament.un.org/TreatyStatus.nsf/44E6EEABC9436B78852568770078D9C0/FFA7842E7FD1D0078525688F0070B82D?OpenDocument.

Convention on the Non-Applicability of Statutory Limitations to War Crimes and Crimes against Humanity of 26 November 1968; entry into force, November 11, 1970, http://www2.ohchr.org/english/law/warcrimes.htm.

Convention to Suppress the Slave Trade and Slavery (Geneva 1926) entered into force in 1927, amended by Protocol in 1953.

Draft Convention against Transnational Organized Crime of December 12 2000; text at http://www.uncjin.org/Documents/Conventions/dcatoc/final_documents_2/index.htm.

Draft Treaty of Mutual Assistance. Journal of the British Institute of International Affairs 3, no. 2 (March 1924): 45–82.

European Convention on the Non-Applicability of Statutory Limitation to Crimes against Humanity and War Crimes of January 25, 1974; http://conventions.coe.int/treaty/EN/Treaties/Html/082.htm.

European Convention for the Prevention of Torture and Inhuman or Degrading Treatment or Punishment, E.T.S. 126, entered into force, February 1, 1989, http://conventions. coe.int/Treaty/en/Treaties/Html/126.htm.

General Treaty for the Renunciation of War (Pact of Paris, 1928); text at http://www.yale.edu/ lawweb/avalon/imt/kbpact.htm.

Geneva Convention (1929) relative to the Treatment of Prisoners of War. Geneva, July 27, 1929; text at http://www.icrc.org/ihl.nsf/FULL/305?OpenDocument.

Hague Convention (IV) respecting the Laws and Customs of War on Land and its annex, *Regulations concerning the Laws and Customs of War on Land.* The Hague, October 18, 1907; text at http://www.icrc.org/ihl.nsf/FULL/195.

Inter-American Convention on Forced Disappearance, Belem Do Para, Brazil, September 6, 1994; entry into force, March 28, 1996; text at http://www.oas.org/juridico/English/ sigs/a-60.html.

Inter-American Convention to Prevent and Punish Torture, Cartagena De Indias, Colombia, December 9, 1985; OAS, Treaty Series, No. 67 (entered into force, February 28 1987).

International Convention on the Suppression and Punishment of Apartheid, General Assembly resolution 3068 (XXVIII) of November 30, 1973. Entry into force, July 18, 1976; 1015 UNTS 243; text at http://www.unhchr.ch/html/menu3/b/11.htm.

International Criminal Court, *Elements of Crimes,* http://www.icc-cpi.int/library/about/of ficialjournal/Element_of_Crimes_English.pdf.

Lieber Code of 1863, Correspondence, Orders, Reports, and Returns of the Union Authorities from January 1 to December 31, 1863.—#7 O.r.–Series III—volume III [S# 124] General Orders No. 100; text at http://www.civilwarhome.com/liebercode.htm.

London Agreement for the Prosecution and Punishment of the Major War Criminals of the European Axis, August 8, 1945. *American Journal of International Law* 39, no. 257 (1945 Supp.).

Optional Protocol to the Convention on the Rights of the Child on the involvement of children in armed conflicts, http://www.unhchr.ch/html/menu2/6/protocolchild.htm.

Protocol Additional to the Geneva Conventions of 12 August 1949, and Relating to the Protection of Victims of International Armed Conflicts (PA-I); text at http://www.unhchr.ch/html/ menu3/b/93.htm.

Protocol Additional to the Geneva Conventions of 12 August 1949, and Relating to the Protection of Victims of Non-International Conflicts (PA-II); text at http://www.icrc.org/ihl.nsf/ FULL/475?OpenDocument.

Protocol for the Prohibition of the Use in War of Asphyxiating, Poisonous or Other Gases, and of Bacteriological Methods of Warfare, June 17, 1925; text at http://fas-www.harvard. edu/~hsp/1925.html.

Protocol to Prevent, Suppress and Punish Trafficking in Persons, Especially Women and Children, Supplementing the United Nations Convention against Transnational Organized Crime, UN GAOR, Doc. A/Res/55/25 (November 15, 2000).

Report of the Committee against Torture, UN Doc. A/63/44 (November 2007, April-May 2008).

Report of the International Tribunal for the Prosecution of Persons Responsible for Serious Violations of International Humanitarian Law Committed in the Territory of the Former Yugoslavia since 1991, UN GAOR-SCOR, Doc. A/62/172–S/2007/469 (August 1, 2007).

Report of the International Criminal Tribunal for the Prosecution of Persons Responsible for Genocide and Other Serious Violations of International Humanitarian Law Committed in the Territory of Rwanda and Rwandan Citizens Responsible for Genocide and Other Such

Violations Committed in the Territory of Neighbouring States between 1 January and 31 December 1994, UN GAOR/SCOR, Doc. A/62/284–S/2007/502 (August 21, 2007).

Report of the Secretary-General on the Activities of the Office of Internal Oversight Services, *Follow-up Investigation into Possible Fee-splitting Arrangements between Defence Counsel and Indigent Detainees at the International Tribunal for Rwanda and the International Tribunal for the Former Yugoslavia,* UN GAOR, Doc. A//56/836 (February 26, 2002).

Rome Statute of the International Criminal Court, July 17, 1998, U.N. Doc. A/CONF.183/9; text at http://www.un.org/law/icc/statute/romefra.htm.

Slavery Convention (Geneva), September 25, 1926; text at http://www.ohchr.org/english/law/slavery.htm.

Statute of the International Criminal Tribunal for Rwanda, S/RES/955 (1994), November 8, 1994; http://69.94.11.53/ENGLISH/basicdocs/statute/2007.pdf.

Statute of the International Tribunal for the Former Yugoslavia, adopted May 25, 1993, by UN General Assembly Resolution 827; as amended May 13, 1998, by UN General Assembly Resolution 1166; as amended November 30, 2000, by UN General Assembly Resolution 1329; http://www.icls.de/dokumente/icty_statut.pdf.

Suppression of Unlawful Acts (SUA) Treaties

1. *Convention for the Suppression of Unlawful Seizure of Aircraft,* done at The Hague on December 16, 1970.
2. *Convention for the Suppression of Unlawful Acts against the Safety of Civil Aviation,* done at Montreal on September 23, 1971.
3. *Convention on the Prevention and Punishment of Crimes against Internationally Protected Persons, including Diplomatic Agents,* adopted by the General Assembly of the United Nations on December 14, 1973.
4. *International Convention against the Taking of Hostages,* adopted by the General Assembly of the United Nations on December 17, 1979.
5. *Convention on the Physical Protection of Nuclear Material,* done at Vienna on October 26, 1979.
6. *Protocol for the Suppression of Unlawful Acts of Violence at Airports Serving International Civil Aviation,* supplementary to the Convention for the Suppression of Unlawful Acts against the Safety of Civil Aviation, done at Montreal on February 24, 1988.
7. *Protocol for the Suppression of Unlawful Acts against the Safety of Fixed Platforms Located on the Continental Shelf,* done at Rome on March 10, 1988.
8. *International Convention for the Suppression of Terrorist Bombings,* adopted by the General Assembly of the United Nations on December 15, 1997.
9. *International Convention for the Suppression of the Financing of Terrorism,* adopted by the General Assembly of the United Nations on December 9, 1999.

The Stockholm Declaration on Genocide Prevention (January 28, 2004); http://www.preventgenocide.org/prevent/conferences/StockholmDeclaration28Jan2004.htm.

Supplementary Convention on the Abolition of Slavery, the Slave Trade, and Institutions and Practices Similar to Slavery (Geneva 1956), entry into force April 30, 1957.

UN Convention against Illicit Traffic in Narcotic Drugs and Psychotropic Substances (of December 12, 1988); text at http://www.unodc.org/pdf/convention_1988_en.pdf.

UN Convention of the Law of the Sea (UNCLOS III), signed at Montego Bay, Jamaica, December 10, 1982, entry into force, November 16, 1994.

UN Convention against Torture and Other Cruel, Inhuman or Degrading Treatment or Punishment of December 10, 1984; text at http://www.hrweb.org/legal/cat.html.

Universal Declaration of Human Rights, General Assembly Resolution 217 A (III) of December 10, 1948; text at http://www.un.org/Overview/rights.html.

Vienna Convention on Diplomatic Relations (April 18, 1961); text at http://www.state.gov/s/l/treaty/treaties/2007/index.htm.

Index